Acclaim for Laurence Bergreen's

Marco Polo

"Engrossing. . . . [Bergreen's] narrative moves fluidly without getting bogged down in excessive detail."
—*Los Angeles Times*

"Fascinating. . . . [Bergreen] is the most satisfying of writers, with an unerring sense of what a reader wants to learn."
—*The Plain Dealer*

"Mesmerizing. . . . This is lively history that is richly detailed and destined to be the definitive account of Marco Polo and his adventures for decades to come." —*Tucson Citizen*

"Illuminating. . . . A window into the most exotic of places and times." —*St. Petersburg Times*

"At last! Marco Polo comes to life. Laurence Bergreen, perhaps America's liveliest biographer, has created a triumph of fascinations, a classic portrait that now surely can never be bettered." —Simon Winchester, author of *The Map That Changed the World*

"This is an enthusiastic retelling of Marco Polo's timeless story. Laurence Bergreen draws from a broad range of the surviving Polo manuscripts to create a convincing portrait of how Marco was able to get to thirteenth-century China, and of what he saw, felt, and did when he got there. Readers unfamiliar with Polo's adventures will find much pleasure here." —Jonathan Spence, author of *Emperor of China*

Laurence Bergreen
Marco Polo

Laurence Bergreen is the prizewinning author of *Over the Edge of the World: Magellan's Terrifying Circumnavigation of the Globe*; as well as *James Agee: A Life*; *Louis Armstrong: An Extravagant Life*; *Capone: The Man and the Era*; and *As Thousands Cheer: The Life of Irving Berlin*, each considered the definitive work on the subject. A graduate of Harvard University, he lives in New York City.

Laurence Bergreen is available for select readings and lectures. To inquire about a possible appearance, please visit www.knopfspeakersbureau.com or call 212-572-2013.

www.laurencebergreen.com

Marco Polo

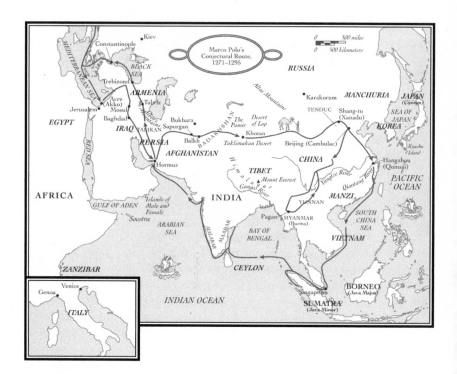

Marco Polo's
Conjectural Route,
1271–1295

0   500 miles
0   500 kilometers

RUSSIA

Kiev

Constantinople

BLACK
SEA

Trebizond

ARMENIA

Tabriz

MEDITERRANEAN SEA

Acre
(Akko)

Jerusalem

Mosul

EGYPT

Baghdad

IRAQ

PERSIA

Zagros Mountains

TAIIKAN

Bukhara

Sapurgan

Balkh

AFGHANISTAN

BADAKHSHAN

The
Pamir

Desert
of Lop

Altai Mountains

Karakorum

MANCHURIA

JAPAN
(Cipingu)

TENDUC

Shang-tu
(Xanadu)

KOREA

SEA OF
JAPAN

Kyushu
Island

Khotan

Taklimakan Desert

Beijing (Cambulac)

CHINA

Hangzhou
(Quinsai)

PACIFIC
OCEAN

Hormuz

Himalayas

TIBET

▲ *Mount Everest*

Ganges River

Yangtze River

YUNNAN

MANZI

Qiantang River

AFRICA

GULF OF ADEN

Islands of
Male and
Female

Socotra

ARABIAN
SEA

INDIA

MALABAR

Pagan

MYANMAR
(Burma)

BAY OF
BENGAL

VIETNAM

SOUTH
CHINA
SEA

ZANZIBAR

CEYLON

BORNEO
(Java Major)

Singapore

SUMATRA
(Java Minor)

INDIAN OCEAN

Genoa

Venice

ITALY

Marco Polo

From Venice to Xanadu

Laurence Bergreen

VINTAGE BOOKS
A DIVISION OF RANDOM HOUSE, INC.
NEW YORK

FIRST VINTAGE BOOKS EDITION, OCTOBER 2008

Copyright © 2007 by Laurence Bergreen

All rights reserved. Published in the United States by Vintage Books,
a division of Random House, Inc., New York, and in Canada by
Random House of Canada Limited, Toronto. Originally published
in hardcover in the United States by Alfred A. Knopf, a division of
Random House, Inc., New York, in 2007.

Vintage and colophon are registered trademarks of Random House, Inc.

The Library of Congress has cataloged the Knopf edition as follows:
Bergreen, Laurence.
Marco Polo : from Venice to Xanadu / by Laurence Bergreen.—1st ed.
p. cm.
Includes bibliographical references and index.
1. Polo, Marco, 1254–1323?—Travel.   2. Explorers—Italy—
Biography.   3. Voyages and travels.   4. Asia—Description and travel.
5. Travel, Medieval.   I. Title.
G370.P9B37 2007
910.4—dc22 [B] 2007021860

Vintage ISBN: 978-1-4000-7880-6

Map on page ii by Mapping Specialists, Madison, Wisconsin

www.vintagebooks.com

Printed in the United States of America
10 9

To my mother,
Adele Gabel Bergreen

Kublai asks Marco, "When you return to the West, will you repeat to your people the same tales you tell me?"

"I speak and speak," Marco says, "but the listener retains only the words he is expecting. The description of the world to which you lend a benevolent ear is one thing; the description that will go the rounds of the groups of stevedores and gondoliers on the street outside my house the day of my return is another; and yet another, that which I might dictate late in life, if I were taken prisoner by Genoese pirates and put in irons in the same cell with a writer of adventure stories. It is not the voice that commands the story: it is the ear."

". . . And I hear, from your voice, the invisible reasons which make cities live, through which perhaps, once dead, they will come to life again."

—Italo Calvino, *Invisible Cities*

CONTENTS

DRAMATIS PERSONAE

WEST

Marco Polo, Venetian merchant

Niccolò Polo, Marco's father

Maffeo Polo, Marco's uncle

Teobaldo of Piacenza, papal legate; later Pope Gregory X

Rustichello of Pisa, Marco's cell mate in Genoa and coauthor

EAST

Genghis (or Chinggis) Khan, founder of the Mongol Empire

Ögödei Khan, Genghis's son and successor

Kublai Khan, one of Genghis's grandsons; the Great Khan of the
Mongols

Möngke Khan, one of Genghis's grandsons

Sorghaghtani Beki, mother of Möngke, Hülegü, and Kublai

Chabi, Kublai's principal wife, a Buddhist

Ahmad, Kublai's Muslim minister of finance

Nayan, Kublai's Christian rival

Arigh Bökh, younger brother of Kublai Khan

Kaidu, one of Kublai's cousins

'Phags-pa, Tibetan Buddhist monk who devised a uniform Mongol
script

Bayan Hundred Eyes, Kublai Khan's trusted general

Marco Polo

The Commander

I N T H E S U M M E R O F 1 2 9 8, Genoa's navy, one of the most powerful in Europe, gathered forces for an assault on the fleet of the Most Serene Republic of Venice. Despite formal truces, these two adversaries had been doing battle for decades, vying for lucrative trade routes to the East.

Crafty and bold, Genoa usually enjoyed the upper hand in their bloody contests. In 1294, the Genoese had won a naval action by lashing their vessels together in an enormous square. When the Venetians attacked, the floating fortress shattered the would-be invaders and put them to flight. The following year, the Genoese again demonstrated dominance of the high seas by sinking the principal Venetian trading fleet, and when they ran out of targets on the water, they pursued the Venetians on land. In 1296, in Constantinople, the Genoese massacred their rivals, acquiring a reputation for cruelty and rapacity.

Venice gradually rallied. Under the leadership of daring naval commanders, sleek Venetian galleys pursued the Genoese wherever they went, setting the stage for the Battle of Curzola, named for an island along the craggy Dalmatian coast, claimed by both of these arrogant city-states in their incessant maritime trade wars.

T H E I M M E N S E Genoese fleet, eighty-eight ships in all, sailed under the confident command of newly appointed admiral Lamba Doria, who pursued a wait-and-see strategy, hiding behind islands, then sailing into warmer waters close to Tunisia, hoping to lure the impatient Venetians into his grasp. The Venetians refused the bait, and the forces of Genoa had to content themselves with random local skirmishes. Finally,

Admiral Doria could wait no more, and he ordered his fleet north, into the Gulf of Venice. The ships met with no significant resistance as they sailed past cities and castles under nominal Venetian control. In the absence of the enemy, they dropped anchor off the coast of Curzola, four hundred miles southeast of Venice. At that moment, a violent storm claimed six of the fleet's eighty-eight vessels, and when it cleared, the survivors proceeded to loot and destroy the island, offering what they assumed would be an irresistible taunt to the invisible Venetians.

On the morning of September 6, 1298, amid gathering heat and humidity, the Venetian fleet suddenly appeared out of the mist: ninety-six galleys under the command of Andrea Dandolo, the scion of a prominent dynasty. The Venetian galleys, renowned for their speed, were slender, elegant affairs resembling giant gondolas, powered by pairs of straining oarsmen. The galleys could plunge into oncoming waves and, with equal confidence, turn to drive a spur projecting from the bow into an opposing ship. The moment this device was in place, Venetian forces rushed across to storm the enemy.

Because oars work most efficiently when they enter the water at a shallow angle, the ships exposed less than three feet of freeboard. (Galleys could also travel under sail, although they were poorly equipped for this technology.) Existence aboard a Venetian galley was misery. Crews of about a hundred men were crowded into narrow spaces; food and water were in short supply. Galleys carried only a week's worth of supplies; short rations for the exhausted rowers were the norm rather than the exception. To cope with these severe limitations, Venetian galleys put in at night, and kept their missions brief—three or four days, at most. With their shallow drafts, they hugged the shore— deadly but surprisingly vulnerable craft lying in wait to strike.

ONE OF THESE ships was commanded by Marco Polo, a merchant who had returned from China three years earlier. At forty-four, he was among the oldest participants in the battle, and by far the best traveled. Marco headed into battle bearing the title of "noble" of Venice, financing his own ship and relying on experienced pilots to do the actual sailing. A global traveler since the age of seventeen, he felt most at home when abroad. Under siege, Marco Polo was in his element, confident and composed. Fighting in the Battle of Curzola was a way to surround himself with glory in the eyes of his fellow Venetians, who regarded his tales of China with skepticism.

Andrea Dandolo led Marco and the other Venetians to the opposite side of Curzola, where his men disembarked—and promptly went into hiding. During the interlude, Lamba Doria had taken the measure of the enemy fleet, and had reached the erroneous conclusion that the Venetians were simply delaying engagement in battle out of fear. But the next morning—Sunday, September 8—the Venetians charged across Curzola toward the Genoese encampment.

Eager to confront the Venetians at last, Doria led his men into an amphibious battle. On land, arrows darkened the skies; at sea, galleys rammed and set fire to one another.

As Doria surveyed the scene at the height of battle alongside his son Ottavio, a Venetian arrow struck the young man in the chest. Ottavio fell at his father's feet, suddenly lifeless. Others aboard the ship attempted to commiserate with Doria, but he refused their pity. "Throw my son overboard into the deep sea," he ordered. "What better resting place can we give him than this spot?"

With the wind at their backs, the Venetians, under Dandolo's leadership, seized the initiative and captured ten Genoese galleys, but in their enthusiasm they ran their ships aground. After nine hours of combat, the exhausted Venetians found themselves overwhelmed. The Genoese captured eighty-four Venetian galleys, sinking some and burning others to the waterline. Only a handful of the once-proud vessels escaped. The human toll proved even greater. In all, the Genoese forces captured 8,000 men—a breathtaking number at a time when the total population of Venice was scarcely 100,000. The defeat amounted to the worst setback that Venice had suffered during a decade of battles with Genoa.

In disgrace, Andrea Dandolo lashed himself to his flagship's mast and beat his head against it until he died of a fractured skull, thus depriving the Genoese of the satisfaction of executing him.

THE SCALE OF the victory astounded the Genoese forces, who marveled at their good fortune as they led the captured Venetian galleys to a grim reckoning in Genoa.

Among the thousands of wretched captives was Marco Polo, nobleman of Venice.

· · ·

FOR THE NEXT four weeks, the Genoese fleet with its captive vessels proceeded on a generally southerly course, and then turned west, under the heel of Italy, and finally north toward Genoa, where the vessels arrived on October 6, 1298. Marco Polo's galley was towed into the harbor stern first, her sail luffing in the breeze, her banners askew, and her commander in shackles.

Further disgrace awaited Marco Polo on land, where, according to some accounts, he was immediately confined to the Palazzo di San Giorgio. Despite its grand name, the structure had grim associations for Venetians because it was built (in 1260) from stones the Genoese had shamelessly stolen from the Venetian consulate in Constantinople. The result was a vulgar monument to Genoese military superiority, complete with ornamental stone lions taken from the original, the lion being the symbol of Venetian power, now tamed by her chief rival.

Stung by the indignity, Venetians claimed that prisoners starved here, while the Genoese maintained that they were well fed and well cared for. The truth probably lay somewhere between the two. Prisoners wandered around the palazzo at will, and even sent for luxuries from home. Prominent detainees, such as Marco Polo, occupied apartments in which their beds were surrounded with curtains made of rich fabrics; it is possible that servants ran errands for them. Life in captivity consisted of tedium rather than cruelty, but it stretched on for years.

Even in these degrading circumstances, Marco Polo kept his wits about him. As a Venetian commander, he was treated with deference. He made himself known throughout the prison, and then Genoa, as a teller of sensational tales of his travels in Asia, just as he had in Venice prior to his capture. He was able to attract attention and elevate his circumstances until he became regarded as a phenomenon. Displaying the same ability he had deployed to survive in the Mongol Empire and in India, he charmed and ingratiated himself with strangers. Eventually, the Genoese, his natural enemies, came to hold the distinguished and entertaining Venetian in high regard. "The whole city gathered to see him and to talk to him, not treating him as a prisoner, but as a very dear friend and greatly honored gentleman, and showed him so much honor and affection that there was never an hour of the day that he was not visited by the most noble gentlemen of that city, and presented with everything necessary for his daily living," wrote Giambattista Ramusio, a Renaissance scholar who composed one of the earliest accounts of Marco Polo's career.

Freed from the constraints of his mundane commercial responsibilities, Marco did not merely survive in jail, he thrived, metamorphosing into a middle-aged male Scheherazade who earned his keep with tales of his adventures, and especially of the Mongol ruler Kublai Khan. The Venetian claimed to have seen him with his own eyes. "Messer Marco," Ramusio wrote, "beholding the great desire that everyone had to hear of the things of the country of Cathay and of the Great Khan, and being forced with great weariness to begin his story all over again each day, was advised that he ought to put it in writing."

As HE LANGUISHED in the Palazzo di San Giorgio, Marco encountered a prolific writer of Arthurian romances named Rustichello of Pisa, a favorite of King Edward I of England. The Genoese had captured the writer years earlier, on August 6, 1284, in the Battle of Meloria, while dealing a decisive blow to rival Pisa. Like the other detainees in the palazzo, Rustichello was looking for a means to cope with the enforced idleness, and Marco provided the necessary distraction. Eloquent and excitable on the subject of his travels, the Venetian talked volubly about his sojourn in the court of the most powerful ruler in the world, Kublai Khan.

Kublai Khan was, at the time, a half-real, half-legendary figure to most Europeans, who considered the Mongol Empire the most savage and dangerous realm on earth. Yet here, in Rustichello's presence, was a man who had not only seen Kublai Khan but appeared to know him well, and who in his service had traveled from one end of Asia to the other, and beyond.

In Rustichello's words, "Marco stayed with the Great Khan fully seventeen years; and in this time he never ceased to travel on special missions. For the Great Khan, seeing that Marco brought him such news from every country and conducted so successfully all the business on which he was sent, used to entrust him with the most interesting and distant missions." Impressed, Rustichello continued, "The Great Khan was so well satisfied with his conduct of affairs that he held him in high esteem and showed him such favor and kept him so near his own person that the other lords were moved to envy. This is how it came to be that Marco observed more of this part of the world than any other man, because he traveled more widely in these outlandish regions than any man who was ever born, and also because he gave his mind more intently to observing them."

The palazzo's better-educated inmates composed poetry or spun elaborate tales of chivalry as a means of diversion. At times the prison resembled a particularly well-guarded literary colony populated with aristocratic writers and would-be writers. In their midst was Rustichello, a quick-witted scribe with a talent for flattery, constantly on the lookout for a story—an adventure, a romance, a battle—to beguile his aristocratic audience.

Hearing Marco Polo's wondrous tales of the East, Rustichello realized he had come across the story of a lifetime, one of the most remarkable true tales ever told. Inevitably, the romance writer suggested to the world traveler that they collaborate on a popular account of Marco's travels. Trying to inject a note of nonchalance into the grim circumstances that had led to the creation of their masterpiece, Rustichello explains, "When he was staying in the prison of Genoa because of the war, not wishing to be idle, he thought he ought to compile this book for the enjoyment of readers."

Marco knew well the uses of adversity, and had been turning them to his advantage during the whole of his extraordinary life. Here was his chance to memorialize his adventures. To refresh his memory, he sent for the records of his journey, and the collaborators set to work on a "Description of the World" as experienced by Marco Polo. It would come to be known simply as his *Travels*.

BOOK ONE

Europa

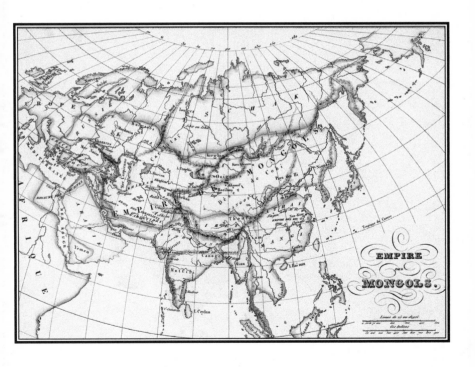

CHAPTER ONE

The Merchants of Venice

Then all the charm
Is broken—all that phantom-world so fair
Vanishes, and a thousand circlets spread. . . .

S HE HID from her enemies amid a seductive array of islands, 118 in all. Damp, dark, cloistered, and crowded, she perched on rocks and silt. Fortifications and spectacular residences rose on foundations of pinewood piles and Istrian stone. In Marco Polo's Venice, few edifices—with the exception of one huge Byzantine basilica and other large churches—stood entirely straight; most structures seemed to rise uncertainly from the water.

Marco Polo came of age in a city of night edging toward dawn; it was opaque, secretive, and rife with transgressions and superstitions. Even those who had lived their entire lives in Venice became disoriented as they wandered down blind alleys that turned without warning from familiar to sinister. The whispers of conspiracy and the laughter of intimacy echoed through narrow passageways from invisible sources; behind dim windows, candles and torches flickered discreetly. In the evening, cobwebs of mist arose from the canals, imposing silence and isolation, obscuring the lanterns in the streets or in windows overlooking the gently heaving canals. Rats were everywhere—emerging from the canals, scurrying along the wharves and streets, gnawing at the city's fragile infrastructure, bringing the plague with them.

The narrow streets and passageways, some barely shoulder-width, took bewildering twists and turns until, without warning, they opened to the broad expanse of the Grand Canal, which divided one-half of the city from the other before running into the lagoon and, beyond that, the expanses of the Adriatic Sea.

In winter, the city hosted Carnival (literally, the playful "bidding farewell to meat" before Lent). Carnival became the occasion for orgies taking place just out of sight behind high courtyard walls and opaque curtains. Rumors of foul play ran rife amid the gaiety and sensuality of the Republic. Venetians bent on evil preferred quiet means of imposing death, such as poisoning or strangulation, and they usually got away with it.

In an uncertain world, thirteenth-century Venetians could feel certain of a few things. Two hundred years before Copernicus and three hundred before Galileo, it was an article of faith that the Sun revolved around the Earth, that the heavenly spheres were perfectly smooth, and that Creation occurred exactly 4,484 years before Rome was founded. Jerusalem was considered "the navel of the world." Entrances to Heaven and Hell existed, somewhere.

The day, for most people, was subdivided into times for prayer: matins at midnight, lauds three hours later, prime at daybreak, terce at midmorning, sext at noon, none at midafternoon, vespers at sunset, and, at bedtime, compline. In the Age of Faith, science consisted largely but not entirely of spurious pursuits such as alchemy—the effort to transmute so-called base metals into gold—and astrology, which went hand in hand with astronomy.

People depended on wind, water, and animals for power. In Western Europe, coal had yet to be exploited as an energy source; paper money and the printing press also lay two hundred years in the future. The most advanced technology consisted of ships—considered a marvel of transport, though very dangerous.

Throughout Europe, travel was exceedingly slow and hazardous. Crossing the English Channel was a dreaded undertaking; those who completed the ordeal would claim that the effort had impaired their health. Over land, people moved no faster than a horse could take them; the average land journey covered eight to ten miles a day, or under special circumstances, for brief durations, fifteen to twenty miles. Superstition led those who undertook such journeys to seek shelter at nightfall in primitive inns, infested with vermin, where two or three sojourners shared a single bed. It took five harrowing weeks to ride by cart from Paris to Venice.

But in Venice, conditions were very different. Tiny in size, yet global in outlook, Venice was entering the Late Middle Ages, a period of economic expansion, cultural achievement, and the lowering of barriers to commercial activity. Travel was not the exception, it was the norm. Everyone in Venice, it seemed, was a traveler and a merchant, or aspired to be. Across Europe, political power, formerly scattered among disorganized and crumbling empires reaching back to Roman times, had coalesced in well-armed and well-organized city-states, such as Venice. The growth in commerce among European city-states contributed to rapid advances in art, technology, exploration, and finance. The compass and clock, windmill and watermill—all vital to the smooth functioning of European economies—came into being, and great universities that survive to this day were being founded. As a result of all these advances, Venice—indeed, all of Europe as we know it—began to emerge.

VENICE—SEDUCTIVE, Byzantine, and water-bound—was among the most important centers of commerce and culture in thirteenth-century Europe, a flourishing city-state that lived by trade. Her economy thrived thanks to her aggressive navy, which vigorously defended the city from repeated onslaughts by rapacious Genoese rivals and Arab marauders. Unlike other medieval cities, Venice had no walls or gates. They were not necessary. The lagoon and swamps protected Venice from invaders by land or by sea.

As the gateway to the riches of the East, Venice gave rise to a sophisticated merchant aristocracy, including the Polo family, known for frequent journeys to the East, especially Constantinople, in search of jewels, silks, and spices. Venice was highly structured, fiercely independent and commercial, and based on a unique combination of feudal obligation and global outlook.

Because Venice was compact, hemmed in by the lagoon and by its enemies, the sense of common cause among its inhabitants was strong. "By virtually confining the Venetians to so restricted a space," says the historian John Julius Norwich, "it had created in them a unique spirit of cohesion and cooperation . . . not only at times of national crisis but also, and still more impressively, in the day-to-day handling of their affairs. Among Venice's rich merchant aristocracy everyone knew everyone else, and close acquaintance led to mutual trust of a kind that in other cities seldom extended far outside the family circle."

As a result, Venetians developed a reputation for efficient and thorough business administration—the most advanced in Europe. "A trading venture," Norwich says, "even one that involved immense initial outlay, several years' duration, and considerable risk, could be arranged on the Rialto in a matter of hours. It might take the form of a simple partnership between two merchants, or that of a large corporation of the kind needed to finance a full-sized fleet or trans-Asiatic caravan." Either way, Norwich concludes, "it would be founded on trust, and it would be inviolable."

JUST ABOUT EVERYONE in Venice engaged in commerce. Widows invested in merchant activity, and any young man without means could describe himself as a "merchant" simply by launching himself in business. Although the risks were great, riches beyond imagining lured the adventurous, the willing, and the foolish. Fortunes were made and lost overnight, and Venetian family fortunes were built on the success of a single trade expedition to Constantinople.

Venetian merchants had developed all sorts of strategies for dealing with the vagaries of their livelihood, global trade. In the absence of standard exchange rates, the many types of coins in use created a nightmare of conversion. The Byzantine Empire had its bezants, Arabic lands their drachmas, Florence its florins. Venice, relying on the ratio of gold to silver in a given coin to determine its true value, tried to accommodate them all. Merchants such as the Polos sought to circumvent the vexed system of coins, with its inevitable confusion and debasement, by trading in gems such as rubies and sapphires and in pearls.

To meet these sophisticated and exotic financial needs, Venice developed the most advanced banking system in Western Europe. Banks of deposit on the Continent originated there. In 1156, the Republic of Venice became the first state since antiquity to raise a public loan. It also passed the first banking laws in Europe to regulate the nascent banking industry. As a result of these innovations, Venice offered the most advanced business practices in Europe.

Venice adapted Roman contracts to the needs of merchants trading with the East. Sophisticated sea-loan and sea-exchange contracts spelled out obligations between shipowners and merchants, and even offered insurance—mandatory in Venice beginning in 1253. The most widespread type of agreement among merchants was the *commenda,* or, in Venetian dialect, the *collegantia,* a contract based on ancient models. Loosely translated, the term meant "business venture," and it reflected prevailing customs of the trade rather than a set of consistent legal principles. Although these twelfth- and thirteenth-century contracts seem antiquated, they are startlingly modern in their calls for precise accounting. Contracts like these reflected and sustained a rudimentary form of capitalism long before the concept came into existence.

For Venetians, the world was startlingly modern in another way: it was "flat," that is to say, globally connected across boundaries and borders, both natural and artificial. They saw the world as a network of endlessly changing trade routes and opportunities extending over land and sea. By ship or caravan, Venetian merchants traveled to the four corners of the world in search of valuable spices, gems, and fabrics. Through their enterprise, minerals, salt, wax, drugs, camphor, gum arabic, myrrh, sandalwood, cinnamon, nutmeg, grapes, figs, pomegranates, fabrics (especially silk), hides, weapons, ivory, wool, ostrich and parrot feathers, pearls, iron, copper, gold dust, gold bars, silver bars, and Asian slaves all poured into Venice via complex trade routes from Africa, the Middle East, and Western Europe.

Even more exotic items flowed into the city aboard foreign galleys. Huge marble columns, pedestals, panels, and blocks piled up on the docks, having been taken from some ruined temple or civic edifice in Constantinople, or another Greek or Egyptian city. These remnants of antiquity, the very headstones of dead or moribund civilizations, would wind up in an obscure corner of the Piazza San Marco, or on the façade of some ostentatious palazzo inhabited by a duke or a wealthy merchant of Venice.

The variety of goods moved Shakespeare to observe, through the character Antonio in *The Merchant of Venice,* that "the trade and profit of the city / Consisteth of all nations." Venetian trade was synonymous with globalization—another embryonic concept of the era. To extend their reach, Venetians formed partnerships with distant governments and merchants that cut across racial and religious divisions. Arabs, Jews, Turks, Greeks, and eventually the Mongols became trading partners with Venice even when they seemed to be political enemies. The Polos were not the first merchants to travel from Venice to Asia, but thanks to Marco Polo's exploits, they became the most celebrated.

· · ·

WHEREVER VENETIANS WENT, they announced themselves with their distinctive accent and dialect, *veneto*. This tongue, like other Romance languages, was based on Latin, and it incorporated vocabulary, syntax, and pronunciation from other languages—some German and Spanish (in the form of the Castilian *s*, pronounced "th"), and some Croatian. There was even a little French thrown into the mix. There are lots of *x*'s and *z*'s in *veneto*, but almost no *l*'s. Lord Byron, who claimed to have enjoyed two hundred women in Venice in as many consecutive evenings, called *veneto* a "sweet bastard Latin." To further complicate matters, *veneto* had numerous variants. The Polos of Venice would have strained to understand the dialect spoken elsewhere in the area by the inhabitants of Padua, Treviso, or Verona.

Some distinctive words in Marco Polo's world have leapt from *veneto* to English. Venetians of Polo's day bade one another *ciao*—or, to be more precise, *sciavo* or *sciao vostro*—which means, literally, "I am your slave." (The word came into the Venetian language from Croatian.) *Gondola* is another Venetian word, although it is not clear when the long, elegant, black vessel itself came into use. It is likely that in Marco Polo's day, a wide variety of small craft, including sailboats, rowboats, and galleys, jostled one another in the city's winding canals.

And *arsenal*, or a place where weapons are manufactured and stored, entered the Venetian language by way of the Arabic term *dar al sina'ah*, meaning "workshop." When Europeans of Marco Polo's era employed this word, they meant the Arsenal in Venice, renowned as a center of shipbuilding. Here shipwrights operated an early assembly line devoted to turning out galleys at a furious rate from standardized, prefabricated components such as keels and masts. A Spanish visitor named Pero Tafur described the precisely choreographed activity devoted to launching the galleys: "Out came a galley towed by a boat, and from the windows they came out to them, from one the cordage, from another the bread, from another the arms, and from another the ballistas and mortars, and so from all sides everything that was required. And when the galley had reached the end of the street all the men required were on board, together with the complement of oars, and she was equipped from end to end."

Tafur counted the launching of ten "fully-armed" galleys within a six-hour span: one new warship every thirty-six minutes. No wonder that the speed with which the Arsenal of Venice could turn a bare keel into a fully rigged craft was admired throughout Europe. And commanders could have their galleys in any color they wanted—as long as it was black.

VENICE'S SUCCESS DERIVED, in part, from its single-minded sense of civic and spiritual destiny. Venetian mythology was potent and telling. Marco's namesake, Saint Mark, was the city's patron saint. In 828, a group of Venetian merchants conspired to snatch Mark's body from its resting place in Alexandria and deliver it in triumph to the doge of Venice.

To justify their deed, the merchants devised a theory that they were preserving the body from the evil designs of Muslims, and they concocted a beguiling but apocryphal story that Mark, while sailing the waters of the Adriatic, encountered a storm that blew his craft into the lagoon on which Venice would later rise, and the boat remained overnight at just the spot on which the Doge's Palace would be built. To top off the story, an angel supposedly appeared to Mark in a dream, uttering the comforting words "Be at rest here." Over time, those words came to mean both that Mark would be safe from the storm in the lagoon and that he belonged—where else?—in Venice. The transfer of Mark's body to Venice became perhaps the most prominent theft of a relic in all Christian history.

Mark's body remained in Venice up to Marco Polo's day and beyond, sheltered in the private chapel of the doge. The doge's residence was the only building in Venice known as a palace; every other dwelling, no matter how large or prominently situated, even those along the Grand Canal, was known as a *casa*—that is, a home—usually abbreviated as "Ca'." Thus, the Polos' home was known as the Ca' Polo, and is to this day.

Venice was an oligarchy ruled by 150 families comprising the city's merchant aristocracy. Less than 1 percent of the population controlled the destiny of the other 99 percent. Occasionally, a family managed to break into this tightly knit fraternity to become new aristocrats, but the practice was ended in 1297. The Council of Venice did permit the city's middle class to form guilds to further commerce. These associations and schools trained workers and craftsmen and helped the poor, and even paid for hospitals. It is possible that the Polos belonged to one or more guilds to further their commercial interests. They were recognized as prosperous merchants, but not civic leaders. It seems unlikely they would have been remembered at all, were it not for Marco Polo's fantastic exploits and his zeal for self-promotion.

DOGE IS A Venetian word, as well as a Venetian concept. It comes from the Latin *dux*, or leader. The first doges were military commanders appointed by the Byzantine emperor. Once Venice started to emerge from obscurity, the city needed its own leader, and the concept of the doge became localized and self-perpetuating.

The secular doge retained a close connection with the imported saint, and was required to defend the holy relic in his charge. In exchange, Saint Mark was believed to offer Venice his blessing and protection. The peculiar nature of the agreement ensured that Venice would retain a Western, and Christian, ethos rather than align with Eastern sects, whose saints yielded to Mark in the Venetian pantheon. Henceforth, Saint Mark and the doge shared control of Venetian destiny.

The combination of the doge's secular power and Mark's spiritual authority imparted a sense of political destiny to the Republic—a secular destiny, despite everything.

THE DOGE was a mystical figure, rarely glimpsed by the public, who presided over Venice's longstanding, mystical relationship with the sea, often portrayed as a marriage. Venetians took this concept to such an extreme that every spring, the doge tossed a gold ring into the Adriatic in a ceremony designed to renew the partnership, much as he signed his mutual-protection contract with Mark.

The cult of the doge received affirmation each year on Ascension Day, the most important holiday in the Venetian calendar. The date marked the Venetian occupation of Dalmatia in AD 1000 under the leadership of Doge Pietro Orseolo II. Henceforth, all Venice—doge, citizens, and clergy—would remember the event by blessing the Adriatic Sea. Venetians were addicted to displays of color and spectacle, and none surpassed the rites of Ascension Day.

The ceremony began when officials carrying water, salt, and olive branches—all blessed for the occasion—boarded a convoy of galleys known as a *mude*. Along the way, the doge, atop an ornate barge, joined them. As they made their way to the Lido, the clergy chanted as a bishop prayed to God "to grant unto us this sea."

Evolving into a symbolic marriage between the doge and the Adriatic, the Sposalizio del Mare, the ceremony became even more elaborate and revealing of the Venetian psyche. In 1177, Pope Alexander III went so far as to present a ring to the doge, declaring, "Receive this as a pledge of the sovereignty that you and your successors shall have in perpetuity over the sea." Rising from his throne with a flourish, the doge hurled the consecrated ring into the Adriatic, intoning, "We wed thee, O Sea, in token of the true and perpetual dominion of the Most Serene Venetian Republic."

After attending Mass, the doge hosted an elaborate banquet for the clergy and dignitaries. The Piazza San Marco became the scene of eight days of nonstop feasting and drinking that culminated in a trade fair famous throughout Europe for offering goods carried to Venice from the ends of the earth. Even the Church entered the festivities, offering indulgences to everyone in attendance.

IN 1268, when Marco was fourteen, the celebration surrounding the installation of the new doge, Lorenzo Tiepolo, outdid even the annual rite of marriage to the sea.

The ceremony began on a gracious note, as the doge formally met with all his political and personal enemies to establish a new tone of goodwill and trust.

With the conclusion of this private ceremony, the captain of the Republic's fleet led the ships past the Doge's Palace as he recited prayers for the doge and for Venice, ending with the words "May Saint Mark aid you!" The galleys dispersed through the canals of the city, and waterborne craft of every description from the surrounding islands followed.

Later the spectacle moved to land, where guild members marched through the narrow streets of Venice two by two, resplendent in the costumes representative of their various trades, all of them passing before the new doge and his wife, the dogaressa. There were sailors clad in white accented with red stars; furriers distinguished by their ermine-trimmed capes; textile workers bearing olive branches and wearing olive wreaths; master craftsmen attired in clothing of gold and purple; even quilt makers, their cloaks adorned with fleurs-de-lis, and garlands of beads wrapped around their heads; shoemakers; barbers; glassblowers in scarlet cloaks trimmed with fur—the wealth and finery of Venice on display.

Beneath the celebrations, life in Venice could be cruel. Women, considered second-class citizens, were treated as chattel. Slavery was common, especially the ownership (and abuse) of female slaves by masters, who, married or not, used them for sexual services. Ingrained social customs reinforced the inferior status of women. A popular piece of advice to prospective Venetian husbands about their wives-to-be urged, "The husband should not be guided by the advice of his wife, who has not sound judgment, because she has neither a sound nor a strong constitution, but one poor and weak."

Yet, in the midst of this gloomy social environment, the Polo home, with its complement of illegitimate children and slaves, was stable and secure, and in a scandalous city, it remained relatively scandal free.

LESS THAN two hundred years after the arrival of Saint Mark's body consecrated Venice, the Republic was well on its way to conquering the Adriatic and surrounding regions.

Venetian fleets became adept at engaging would-be invaders, such as the Normans, led by Robert Guiscard, whose armada threatened to obstruct Venetian access to the Mediterranean. In a fierce engagement with Guiscard's vessels in the Adriatic, off the west Albanian city of Durazzo, Venetian ships, prevented from entering the harbor, were grappled together to form a floating island blocking the entrance. When enemy craft approached, the Venetian sailors, poised in boats suspended from their floating "island," thrust primitive torpedoes in the form of logs at the oncoming ships, sinking or badly damaging them. Nevertheless, the Normans eventually claimed Durazzo, even as Venetian merchants and battleships roamed the Mediterranean in search of profit. In perhaps no other city-state did the exercise of commerce approach the practice of war as it did in Venice, where the two became virtually synonymous. The Republic existed amid an almost continual state of warfare, sometimes in the form of a distant guerrilla struggle, sometimes in a cold war designed to rebuff rivals, and sometimes in furious battles against determined enemies. Venice did not always win, but the city's soldiers and sailors were expected to fight for their commercial enterprises.

No other city-state equaled Venice's skill and daring on the sea. If the Republic was celebrated for its merchants, it was equally feared for its ruthless naval warriors. In time, Marco Polo would have a chance to play both roles, a trader in peacetime and as a commander in battle.

IN 1204, Venice celebrated a major victory: the capture of Constantinople, by combined European forces, at the height of the Fourth Crusade.

The triumph of Christianity was not a sure thing in Marco Polo's day. The Church of Rome was fighting for its place in the world against an array of enemies—Islam, the Mongols, the Greek Orthodox Church, even itself. The Age of Faith was also an age of peril, turmoil, and war.

The Crusades began with a simple goal: to permit Christians to continue to make pilgrimages to the Holy Sepulcher, the tomb in Jerusalem in which the body of the crucified Jesus was believed to be laid to rest. Pilgrims had been visiting this holiest of Christian shrines since at least the eighth century AD. Matters changed dramatically in 1009 when Hakim, the Fatimid caliph—that is, Muslim ruler—of Cairo, called for the Holy Sepulcher's destruction. Afterward, unlucky Christians and Jews who found themselves in Jerusalem were likely to be persecuted, and the city's Christian quarter was surrounded by a forbidding wall that controlled access. Within five years, thousands of churches had been burned or ransacked.

The violence only increased the desire of Christians to make the pilgrimage to Jerusalem, and the Church undertook a series of Crusades, eventually eight in all, with the avowed goal of delivering places sacred to Christians from the Muslim oppressors. Conceived as religious wars against a suddenly ascendant Islam, the Crusades quickly deteriorated into a series of battles for political and military spoils. By the time of the brief Fourth Crusade (1202–1204), the Papacy was losing its grip on the endeavor, as secular leaders across Europe acquired ever more power and influence. Eventually, individual monarchs launched their own Crusades.

The original plan for the Fourth Crusade was simple enough: Pope Innocent III and the preacher Foulques of Neuilly-sur-Marne pro-

posed to conquer the Muslim warriors. The Crusaders planned ultimately to take Jerusalem by way of Egypt, and they wanted the support
of Venice.

VENETIANS, true to their commercial agenda, had maintained an
arm's-length relationship with the Crusades. But in this case, Venetian
authorities realized there might be some money to be made out of a
religious war. From their point of view, it was actually a military campaign with a political and financial agenda, and that was something
Venetians could understand and endorse. After a careful negotiation
lasting eight days, the Republic agreed to furnish 35,000 knights,
squires, and foot soldiers; 4,500 horses; ships specially built for the
occasion; and supplies—all for a steep price. The idea of harnessing
Venetian naval prowess to their cause proved irresistible to the French
leaders of the Crusade, no matter what the cost, but they proved slow
to pay, and as a result, thousands of would-be Crusaders congregated
on the outskirts of Venice, on what is now the Lido, awaiting orders
and diverting themselves with gambling and whoring.

Realizing that France would not be able to honor its obligation,
Venetian representatives proposed a new deal; they would forgive the
debt if the unemployed Crusaders would assist them in achieving a
slightly different goal: subduing Zara, a rebellious city across the Adriatic Sea. The French agreed. Zara fell, and the two sides shared the
plunder equally. The arrangement completed the transformation of
the Crusade from a religious campaign into a commercial enterprise.

The emboldened Crusaders then sailed to Constantinople, the
capital of the Byzantine Empire, which was the successor to the Eastern portion of the Roman Empire. Named after the Roman emperor
Constantine the Great, who ruled in the fourth century AD, Constantinople was a city of many faiths, but Orthodox Christianity predominated. In the mental calculus of the Crusaders, the Orthodox
Church had come to seem almost as nefarious as Islam, and therefore
deserving of vengeance. Any justification, no matter how far-fetched,
would do, because Constantinople was an extremely rich and vulnerable prize.

Constantinople boasted not of its military prowess but of its
libraries, works of art, and public monuments on a scale far greater
than those in Western Europe. The architectural style of much of the

city drew on Roman principles; Roman arches, columns, and adornments—along with Eastern elements—became the basis of Byzantine architecture. The population was immense, as many as a million people, more than ten times greater than that of Venice. And the city was ripe for conquest.

The sack of Constantinople in April 1204 lasted for three days of destruction and death. Laymen and clergymen, women, children—everyone fell beneath the Crusaders' swords. When the worst of the violence was over, mobs rushed into churches, broke up altars, and carried off sacred vessels. Drunken soldiers snatched priestly vestments, which they used to cover their horses. A drunken prostitute danced on the patriarch's throne as she sang out obscene ditties. Tombs and statuary dating back to antiquity were shattered—or carried off. Afterward, many of the city's artworks, manuscripts, and religious items were spirited away to relative safety in outlying villages, towns, and monasteries. Even after the Crusaders left, the looting continued for years.

Venetians excelled in plundering; they knew all the best religious artifacts, the most precious gems, the most important statuary to carry away. As a visible symbol of conquest, four bronze horses were taken out of Constantinople to adorn the façade of the Basilica di San Marco; they represented the choicest booty of empire, another stolen treasure that came to reside in Venice.

The best craftsmen from Constantinople also found their way to Venice. Legions of glassblowers, silversmiths and goldsmiths, iconographers, artists, and sculptors were brought to Venice, where they practiced trades that in time came to seem synonymous with their adoptive city rather than their homeland.

POPE INNOCENT III professed himself horrified when news of the sack of Constantinople and the atrocities undertaken in the name of Christendom reached his ears. He excommunicated multitudes of Crusaders before realizing that they had been absolved of their crimes in advance, and that his stance might weaken the Papacy in the face of determined adversaries. At that, he fell silent, and stood by as the wealth of Constantinople found its way into Roman churches and cathedrals.

The Orthodox Church never forgave Venice for its role in the sack, and Constantinople never fully recovered its former glory. The conquest reversed the balance of power and brought major parts of the empire under Venetian control. Constantinople eventually resumed its role as an important commercial center, a gateway to the East for Marco Polo and other merchants, but it had lost its coherence and luster, and, with a population consisting of Greeks, Venetians, Egyptians, and Turks, among others, was more notable for disarray than for splendor.

VENICE, BY COMPARISON, presented a unified front to the world, a society dominated by a handful of powerful families. Marco Polo's ancestors, although reasonably prominent, were hardly the wealthiest or grandest clan in Venice. That honor resided with the Zenos, Querinis, and Dandolos, who all produced doges to rule the city-state and admirals to defend it. In this highly stratified society, the Polos came in several notches below those civic leaders. They were a respected family of substance, but beholden to Venice's rulers for their continued prosperity.

Although complete agreement on the origins of the family is lacking, one tradition suggests that the Polos migrated from the Dalmatian town of Sebenico to the Venetian lagoon in 1033. At various times, Sebenico was ruled by Hungarians and Croatians, and it would later join the Venetian empire. Another tradition holds that Marco Polo was born on Curzola, the island where he would later be captured by the Genoese, while a third asserts that Polos had been entrenched in the Venetian lagoon prior to all these events. No matter what his origins, Marco had a foot in both the fading civilizations of antiquity and the bold Renaissance that was beginning to appear throughout Europe.

The name Polo—Venetian vernacular derived from the Latin Paulus—appears with frequency in civic records beginning in 971, when a Venetian named Domenico Polo signed a petition forbidding commerce with Arabs, and later entries show that various Polos owned land and salt mines, and served as judges throughout the realm. This activity suggests that Marco Polo's ancestors shuttled between Venice and her embattled satellite, Dalmatia.

The Polo family's trading ambitions took one branch to Constantinople. In 1168, with the Byzantine Empire still at its height, records show Marco Polo's great-uncle, bearing the same name, borrowing money and commanding a ship in Constantinople, much as the younger Marco would later do in the Battle of Curzola.

Other members of the Polo family continued the pursuit of wealth and honors in Venice. Marco Polo's grandfather, Andrea Polo of the parish of San Felice, had three sons, Maffeo, yet another Marco, and Niccolò, the traveler's father, and they likely were counted among the nobility of Venice, even if they did not belong to the upper echelons. Venetian archival records refer to young Marco as a *nobilis vir*, or nobleman. The title mattered greatly to Marco Polo, who thought of himself as nobility, the holder of a rank that gave him status wherever he went. In his mind, the title of Venetian nobleman constituted his passport to the world. He always acted on the assumption that being of noble birth would protect him from the depredations of thieves and scoundrels who preyed on lesser mortals. No matter how far he ventured from home, he made sure that his hosts, no matter how strange or august, understood that he was a Venetian nobleman and expected to be treated accordingly.

MARCO POLO'S FATHER, Niccolò, and uncle Maffeo operated a prosperous, tightly knit family trading business in Venice. In 1253, the two brothers left home for an extended trading journey to the East. Niccolò may not have known that the wife he left behind was pregnant; the following year, 1254, Marco Polo was born.

By that time, the infant's father and uncle were in Constantinople, long past its glorious prime, but still under Venetian control imposed after the sack of 1204. Their apparently routine excursion from one trading center to another was, by the standard of the day, exceedingly adventurous. Ships were outfitted and operated by the Republic of Venice. Passengers brought their own trunks, bedding, water, and biscuits. And they had to be prepared to endure the rigors of combat. The ships were capable of doing battle against any enemy that might attack them, and passengers were expected to join in the conflict.

Even a peaceful voyage was remarkably distasteful, uncomfortable, and dangerous. The dank, crowded ships stank of rotting food and human waste. Vermin ran riot, and passengers like the Polos had to coexist with cockroaches, lice, and rats. After a month or more of enduring all these conditions, with sleeplessness and seasickness thrown in to complete their misery, the two Polo brothers arrived safely in Constantinople. In no hurry to risk another grueling voyage, they remained for six years, managing an outpost of their little empire, and trading with merchants from across the globe, especially those from the East.

During their stay, Constantinople sank ever deeper into debt. Baldwin II, the last in a line of Latin emperors, was forced to sell off priceless relics to Venice to liquidate debts and retain his slender grasp on power. Matters became so dire that he pledged a relic supposed to be Jesus's crown of thorns to Venetian bankers willing to accept it as collateral for their loans. He even pawned his son to the Venetians. Eventually Louis IX of France came to Baldwin's aid, while a rival, Michael VIII Paleologus, descended from the city's former Greek emperor, entered into a pact with Genoa to rip Constantinople from the arms of Venice. The unsettled political climate led to rioting in the streets among the Venetians, Genoese, Greeks, and other groups who had coexisted uneasily there after the city's fall.

NICCOLÒ AND MAFFEO POLO decided to flee the unstable city for Soldaia (now known as Sudak), where the Polo family also maintained an outpost. This was a rugged fortress of a town on the Crimean Peninsula with a spectacular view of the Black Sea. (The name Black Sea, by the way, was something new in the Polos' era. Before then, this immense inland waterway was known to all who plied its waters simply as "the Sea.") What little is known of the Polo brothers' time in Soldaia suggests that they did not prosper.

Early accounts show that the brothers wanted nothing more than to return home to Venice, but travel was too unsafe to permit the journey. On land, murderous thieves patrolled the paths; on water, pirates laid waste to any ship they spied. Given these forbidding conditions, the brothers Polo would not soon be returning to Venice.

TRAVEL AND TRADING conditions to the east were better, thanks to the most unlikely of causes: the Mongols, who had violently conquered most of Asia and a significant part of Europe, all the way to the eastern shore of the Danube. (Mongols were sometimes called "Tartars," but the Tartars were, in reality, just one of the tribes belonging to the Mongol Empire. Russians originally used the name to describe Mongols, as well as other invaders from the east, and Europeans followed suit.)

By any name, the Mongols were considered Satan's spawn, among the most lawless, violent, and sinful people on the face of the earth. In 1260, Pope Alexander IV issued a papal bull, *Clamat in auribus* (the Latin title taken from the opening words), to warn Christendom of the Mongol threat: "There rings in the ears of all, and rouses to a vigilant alertness those who are not befuddled by mental torpor, a terrible trumpet of dire forewarning, which, corroborated by the evidence of events, proclaims with unmistakable sound the wars of universal destruction wherewith the scourge of Heaven's wrath in the hands of the inhuman Tartars, erupting as it were from the secret confines of Hell, oppresses and crushes the earth." The pope went on to condemn the Mongol Empire as a "peril impending and palpably approaching."

While the pope was busy denouncing the Mongol threat, the object of his fury had been transformed. Genghis Khan's quest for an endlessly expanding Mongol Empire had given way to a relatively stable regime under his enlightened grandson Kublai Khan. "Kublai was not a barbarian," Venetian historian Alvise Zorzi observes. Rather, he was "a monarch pursuing high standards of governance, dedicated to learning and implementing the most efficient means to that end," which meant that "he was constantly seeking better ways to govern and apply spiritual pressure points that would serve his aim of authority better than force."

Kublai's most potent weapon was not the sword or spear, fire or poison, but commerce with the world beyond the borders of his empire. Indeed, the Mongols needed European, Persian, and Arab goods and technology to survive in the new world order they had created. To this end, they reopened a series of trade routes that much later—in the nineteenth century—came to be known as the Silk Road. The routes carried all manner of goods—gems, fabrics, spices, precious metals, weapons—as well as ideas and religions. Buddhist monks and Christian missionaries made use of it, as did Venetian, Genoese, Arab, and Jewish merchants.

To make this exchange of ideas and commerce possible, Kublai Khan imposed on his unruly realm a Pax Mongolica, achieved at the cost of harsh oppression. To Zorzi, the Pax Mongolica was a "peace of smoking ruins." Yet, as a direct consequence of Mongol tyranny, the Silk Road became safe for commerce, so safe that one traveler claimed "a young woman would have been able to travel with a golden tray on her head with no fear." And it was safe enough for merchants like the Polos to travel its great length into the heart of Asia and the Mongol Empire.

The Mongols and Venetians had both made the world "flat," the Venetians traveling over water with their ships, and the Mongols over land by reviving the Silk Road. And in a flat, interactive world, goods and ideas mingled in surprising ways, and empires flourished.

NICCOLÒ AND MAFFEO POLO traveled east along a northern branch of the Silk Road, venturing ever deeper into the Mongol Empire. In his book, Marco offers only scant details of the trek his father and uncle took, but it is likely that they traveled on horseback and by cart.

While traversing what is now Iraq, Marco relates, his father and uncle entered the realm of Barka Khan—another of Genghis's many grandsons—"who had the reputation of being one of the most liberal and civilized princes among the tribes of the Mongol Empire." Sometimes known as the Western Khan, Barka received them with "great honor," which was reciprocated. "The two brothers gave him freely, seeing that they pleased him, all the jewels which they had brought with them from Constantinople," Marco says. Not wanting to be outdone by his visitors' generosity, Barka "directed double the value of the jewels to be paid to them," along with "generous presents." The merchants of Venice had found a safe haven in the Mongol Empire.

In Barka's realm, the brothers probably pursued their primary interest: drawing on their store of jewels and coins and fabrics to enrich themselves in dealings with other merchants. They might be compared to a traveling emporium, ready to deal in anything that would bring a profit. Marco frequently notes different types of fabrics being traded—muslin, damask, and of course silk—and it is reasonable to assume that his father and uncle did a brisk business in those items with other traders, the Muslims, Jews, and other Europeans, especially those from Genoa, who were better represented in Asia than Venetians. They may have traded in slaves on a very limited scale and returned to Venice with an Arab indentured servant.

After a year, the brothers had had enough of Mongol hospitality and wished to return home, but by then Barka had become enmeshed in a civil war with another grandson of Genghis Khan, Hülegü, who ruled over eastern territories. "In a fierce and bloody battle," says Marco, "Hülegü was victorious, in consequence of which, the roads being rendered unsafe, the brothers could not return by the way they came." They were told that the best way to reach Constantinople in wartime was to "skirt the limits of Barka's territories," and in following this advice, they incurred considerable hardship. They reached a desert, "the extent of which was seventeen days' journey, wherein they found neither town, castle, nor any substantial building, but only Mongols with their herds, dwelling in tents on the plain."

During the trek, they became familiar with the circular *ger*s, felt tents, in which the Mongols lived, and with koumiss, the fermented mare's milk they drank. Koumiss has a strong, sour taste, and the brothers resisted it at first. (When they did consent to drink, the Mongol who had offered it violently pulled their ears to make sure that they imbibed deeply.) In the same spirit of accommodation, the brothers learned to adapt to the Mongols' aversion to bathing. True, Venetians of that era rarely bathed, but the Mongols' abhorrence of water, combined with their proximity to animals, rendered them and their odors profoundly repugnant to Westerners who wandered into their midst. In time, the Polos mastered their revulsion and began to feel at home with their rough-hewn hosts. Even more important, they learned to converse with the Mongols, and that, more than any amount of koumiss they drank, established a bond between the merchants and their hosts.

THE BROTHERS POLO made their way to Bukhara, located in today's Uzbekistan and the capital of several empires from the ninth to the thirteenth century. The Polo company found Bukhara and its varied population hospitable; the city had long been a crossroads for traders from the East and the West trading in silk, porcelain, spices, ivory, and rugs. But beyond Bukhara's ramparts, chaos ruled. Strife between various tribes rendered the local branches of the Silk Road impassable, and the Polos found to their dismay that they could not reach home anytime soon. Marco tersely comments, "Unable to proceed further, they remained here three years." The delay made all the difference in their fortunes.

During their extended stay in Bukhara, Niccolò and Maffeo encountered "a person of consequence and gifted with great talents." He was, as it happened, an ambassador from Hülegü on his way east to visit Kublai Khan, "the supreme chief of all the Mongols, who lived at the far edge of the continent." If the Polo brothers were skillful in their negotiations, the ambassador could open the way to the entire Mongol Empire for them.

CHAPTER TWO

The Golden Passport

And soon the fragments dim of lovely forms
Come trembling back, unite, and now once more
The pool becomes a mirror.

NICCOLÒ AND MAFFEO POLO spent days immersed in conversation with the Mongol ambassador, earning his confidence and respect. "Never having had an opportunity of seeing any natives of Italy," Marco comments, "he was highly gratified at meeting and conversing with these brothers, who had become proficient in the Mongol language." Those difficult days on the Silk Road, during which they had troubled to learn Mongolian dialects, greatly benefited the Venetians. The ambassador—never named—offered to introduce them to the Great Khan, exactly as they had hoped. To make the prospect still more attractive, the ambassador "added assurances that they would be honorably received and rewarded with many gifts."

Niccolò and Maffeo believed they had no other choice, because the return to Venice "would expose them to the gravest risks." In contrast, the ambassador offered his assurance that they would be safe—if he accompanied them. So it was that they agreed to venture farther east than they had ever expected, to meet the leader who was hated and feared throughout Europe, and, in particular, by the pope.

The journey to the court of Kublai Khan occupied a full year. Although the location of their meeting is not specified, it was likely the Mongol capital of Cambulac, to which travelers from afar gravitated. Eager to trade with foreigners, and to learn from them, the Mongols had devoted a portion of their capital to sheltering government officials and private merchants who ventured to the heart of the Mongol Empire to trade, to exchange ideas, or to establish diplomatic relations.

Outnumbered by their subjects, the Mongols had become heavily dependent on foreigners to administer sensitive aspects of running the empire, especially tax collection. The foreigners came from across Asia and Europe, and among their number were Genoese and Venetians, Jews and Muslims, Uighurs, Russians, and Persians. To lessen corruption, and to preserve their identity amid the overwhelming number of Chinese, the Mongols enforced segregation. The Chinese whom they ruled were not permitted to learn the Mongol tongue; nor could they bear arms or marry Mongols.

NATURAL HARDSHIPS made travel along the Silk Road an ordeal. Marco mentions snows and swollen rivers and floods impeding the expedition's progress. But the Polo brothers recovered their poise and sense of purpose when they met the leader of the Mongols.

Everything about Kublai Khan took them by surprise: his elaborate courteousness, so unlike the savagery for which the Mongols were notorious; his curiosity concerning Italy and Christianity; and his receptiveness to doing business. And Kublai Khan, for his part, was pleased that these two representatives of a different culture were able to converse in his own language.

Marco insists that his father and uncle were the "first Latins"—that is, Christians—"to visit that country," and as such "were entertained with feasts and other marks of distinction," but this assertion has long been open to question. A handful of European travelers, including missionaries and knights, had preceded them to the Mongol court, and some left detailed records of their travels. The Polo brothers, cut off from the mainstream of commerce for years on end, were likely unaware of those who had come before, and believed they were, in fact, the first Europeans to meet the most powerful ruler alive.

During their feasts, Kublai Khan probed his exotic visitors for intelligence about the "western parts of the world, the Emperor of the Romans, and other Christian kings and princes." In particular, the Mongol leader wished to be informed of those rulers' "relative importance, their possessions, the manner in which justice was administered in their kingdoms, and how they conducted themselves in warfare. Above all, he questioned them about the pope, the affairs of the

Church, and the religious worship and doctrine of the Christians."
The merchant brothers were hardly experts on such complex subjects,
but according to Marco, they supplied "appropriate answers on all
these points in the Mongol language, with which they were perfectly
acquainted." Kublai Khan was so gratified that he summoned them
repeatedly for conferences on the state of Christendom.

Once he had debriefed Niccolò and Maffeo, and developed a close
rapport with them, Kublai Khan decided to deploy them as double
agents; henceforth, they would serve him as ambassadors to the West,
and, in particular, to the pope. Skillful at diplomacy, the Great Khan
couched his plan in flattery, or, as Marco puts it, "many kind entreaties
that they should accompany one of his barons"—as the khans called
their loyal vassals—"named Kogatal on a mission to the Pope."

The brothers hesitated before accepting the overwhelming assignment. "It is a great while since we left those parts," they reminded the
Great Khan, "and we do not know what may have happened or been
done, because conditions of those lands are changed, and we are much
afraid that we cannot fulfill thy commandment." Nevertheless, they
agreed—or were made to do so.

In an official communiqué to the pope, Kublai Khan demanded the
presence of "as many as a hundred wise men of learning in the Christian religion and doctrine, and who should know also the seven arts
and be fitted to teach his people and who know well how to argue."
They should also be prepared to proselytize among the Mongols, that
is, "to show plainly to him and to the idolaters and to the other classes
of people submitted to his rule that all their religion was erroneous and
all the idols that they keep in their houses are devilish things." The
pope's emissaries "should know well how to show clearly by reason that
the Christian faith and religion is better than theirs and more true than
all the other religions." To a pope convinced that the khan was the
spawn of the devil, this would have been an astounding request, yet it
was in keeping with Kublai's inquiring nature. If the pope or his emissaries made their case, "he and all his potentates would become men of
the Church." But that did not mean they would renounce their adher-
ence to other religions.

The Great Khan had one other request: "some of the oil of the
lamp that burns above the sepulcher of Jesus Christ our Lord in
Jerusalem, in whom he had the greatest devotion, for he believed
Christ to be in the number of blessed Gods." Kublai Khan was not

offering to replace other deities with Jesus, as the pope might have been led to expect when dealing with conventional infidels, but rather to add this figure to the Mongol pantheon. The nature of the request would never register with Rome, of course, but the Polo brothers were too preoccupied with their personal fate to argue theology with the Mongol leader. Instead, they vowed to return to Kublai Khan one day with one hundred wise men, oil from the Holy Sepulcher, and whatever else he required, in exchange for safe passage back to Venice. There is no indication that Niccolò and Maffeo seriously considered fulfilling every component of their vow; to bring one hundred wise men with them on a second journey was fantasy. Oil from the Holy Sepulcher, believed to have great healing powers for the body and mind, was another matter. At the time, the Armenian clergy did a brisk trade in it. The Polo brothers would have found it entirely possible to obtain the oil, at a steep price.

KUBLAI KHAN'S guarantee of safe passage for his Venetian visitors came in the form of a magnificent "tablet of gold engraved with the royal seal and signed according to the custom of his estate." This was the celebrated *paiza*, the royal Mongol passport that seemed to confer magical powers of protection. (The name was actually derived from Chinese; the Mongols called it a *gerega*.) The precious object certified that Niccolò, Maffeo, and the Mongol baron Kogatal were emissaries of Kublai Khan himself, and that local rulers in the Mongol Empire must provide lodging, horses, and escorts, just as they would for the emperor, "on pain of their disgrace" if they failed to follow this edict.

JUST TWENTY DAYS after the Polo brothers' departure, their Mongol traveling companion, Kogatal, became seriously ill and was obliged to stay behind. Even without the benefit of his presence, the *paiza* assured the brothers of safe passage and respect wherever they went.

The brothers arrived unscathed at the small port city of Layas, in what was then known as Lesser or Little Armenia, a territory lying west of the Euphrates. Here they boarded a ship to begin the most hazardous segment of their journey. On land, they had only enemies to fear, but journeys over water were occasions for dread; only the most intrepid, desperate, or foolish of travelers entrusted their lives to the vagaries of wind and water.

This time, fortune favored the Polo brothers. In 1269 they arrived safely at their destination, Acre (or Akko), an ancient seaport on what is now the northern coast of Israel, just south of Lebanon.

AMONG THE MOST ancient settlements in the world, Acre had changed hands many times during the course of its history. In 1191, Philip II of France and Richard the Lion-Hearted of England wrested it away from the Muslim sultan Saladin, and it served as the capital of the Kingdom of Jerusalem, and, for the moment, a stronghold of Crusaders.

In 1350, the German cleric Ludolph von Suchem described "this glorious city of Acre." It was "built of square hewn stones," he noted, "with lofty and exceedingly strong towers." Within, the streets were "exceeding neat, all the walls of the houses being of the same height and all alike built of hewn stone, wondrously adorned with glass windows and painting. . . . The streets of the city were covered with silken clothes, or other fair awnings, to keep out the sun's rays."

Acre served as a natural point of departure for travelers to the East such as the Polos, who mingled with the population of about fifty thousand, including Christian Crusaders, Muslim warriors, and Jewish merchants. To his astonishment, Ludolph found that nobles visiting the city "walked about the streets in royal state, with golden coronets on their heads, each of them like a king, with his knights, his followers, his mercenaries and his retainers, his clothing and his warhorse wondrously bedecked with gold and silver, all vying one with another in beauty and novelty of device, each man appareling himself with the utmost care."

The Polo brothers found themselves outclassed by the other merchants in Acre, "the richest under Heaven," according to Ludolph. "Everything that can be found in the world that is wondrous or strange used to be brought thither because of the nobles and princes who dwelt there."

THE BROTHERS' PLANS once again fell apart when they learned, a few months after the fact, that Pope Clement IV had died on November 23, 1268, at Viterbo. It seemed as if turmoil would trap the Polo company indefinitely. In desperation, notes Marco, they went to "a learned clerk who was the legate"—that is, the official emissary—"of the Pope for the Church of Rome in all the realm of Egypt. He was a man of great authority and was named Teobaldo of Piacenza." On bended knee, the Polo brothers told the legate their entire fantastic tale concerning their goodwill mission to the pope commissioned by the Great Khan.

The legate expressed "great wonder at it." To his credit, he believed that "great good and great honor" for all Christendom could come from the proposal. He counseled the anxious Venetians to linger. "And when there shall be a Pope, you will be able to fulfill your mission," he assured them. The wait for the election dragged on, with no end in sight. Restless, Niccolò and Maffeo decided to slip back to Venice and then to return to Acre in time to complete their task in conjunction with Clement IV's successor. Moving nimbly for once, they left Acre for the island of Negrepont (now Euboea), boarded a ship, and reached Venice at last.

MORE THAN sixteen years had passed since Niccolò and Maffeo Polo had last seen their home, sixteen years spent traversing the largest continent not once but twice, sixteen years during which they had lived by their wits, and come to enjoy the patronage of the most feared and powerful ruler on earth. Their journey had contained enough adventure for a lifetime, but for all its daring and accomplishment, it merely laid the groundwork for the celebrated expedition they would eventually take with young Marco.

Stunning developments awaited them. Niccolò learned that his wife was dead. Perhaps even more startling, she had left him a "small son of fifteen years who had the name Marco." This was Marco Polo, a boy who had spent his entire life in Venice, had never known his father, and until Niccolò's return had had every reason to believe that he was an orphan.

For two years, Niccolò and Maffeo languished in Venice, awaiting news of the next pope's identity. It would be satisfying to assume that Niccolò, now a widower, spent time becoming acquainted with the "small son" he had never known to exist, but the record states otherwise. In short order, Niccolò remarried, and his new wife became pregnant.

. . .

ALTHOUGH MARCO had known nothing of his father or uncle, their adventures became deeply imprinted on his psyche and determined his entire future. He heard their tales of the Silk Road and of the Mongols, with their *gers* and koumiss. Most of all, he heard their accounts of meeting the extraordinary figure Kublai Khan, beside whom even the doge seemed puny. Like his older relatives, Marco would be a traveler, a wanderer through the East.

At last, Niccolò and Maffeo decided that the moment had come to return to Acre to await the election of the next pope. This time, they would take the seventeen-year-old Marco with them. And once the new pope was elected, they would arrange to bring documents from him to Kublai Khan. No mention was made of the one hundred wise men they had promised, or of the oil from the Holy Sepulcher. They had only young Marco to offer to Kublai Khan.

If the first journey into the Mongol Empire had come about through a series of mishaps, as chance carried Niccolò and Maffeo Polo from one trading center to the next, the second, undertaken in fulfillment of a vow, promised to be far more purposeful. They would go not as emissaries of the Republic of Venice, or of the pope, but of the Mongol Empire, and this time they would be far surer of themselves. They had their *paiza* to guarantee them safe passage across the hazardous stretches of Asia, and they had their knowledge of the Mongol tongue.

MARCO LEFT VENICE in the spring of 1271 with Niccolò and Maffeo to begin the long and uncertain pilgrimage to a distant capital to meet an unimaginably powerful leader in the company of his father and uncle, whom he had met for the first time only two years before.

The Polos joined a flotilla of Venetian ships known as a *muda*, which slowly made its way along the eastern coast of the Adriatic, hugging the shore, stopping at familiar ports to take on supplies. As it proceeded in a generally southeasterly course, the *muda* split into five convoys, each bound for a different destination.

The convoy bearing the Polo company headed for Acre. The passengers consisted primarily of pilgrims on their way to the Holy Land and Jerusalem, along with the Polo company, two seasoned travelers on a mission to fulfill a vow and an impressionable lad coming of age far from home.

· · ·

THE FORTRESS known as Acre stood as a poignant reminder of
the former Kingdom of Jerusalem, held in the thirteenth century by
Muslims and other groups. Acre itself was subdivided into quarters,
each housing representatives of rival states such as Venice and Genoa.
The tiny port was so crowded that many ships were forced to anchor
far offshore. Christian pilgrims streamed through on their way to
Jerusalem.

Despite its cramped dimensions, Acre claimed two important per-
sonages at the time. Accompanied by a retinue of English knights,
Prince Edward of England could be found there, allied with the Mongols in his own private crusade against Muslims. The other notable
was the papal legate Teobaldo of Piacenza. In the small world of Acre,
Edward and Teobaldo were acquainted, and it is possible that Edward
also knew of the Polos.

On returning to Acre, the Polos made straight for their old friend
to renew their acquaintance after a two-year lapse. When they met, the
elder Polos expressed their wish to obtain oil from the Holy Sepulcher
to fulfill their vow to Kublai Khan. Teobaldo gave them permission to
proceed to Jerusalem to negotiate for the valuable substance.

It was here that King Solomon had caused the Temple to be built,
and here that Jesus was crucified. And it was from here that the
prophet Muhammad ascended to Heaven. (Muslims refer to Jerusalem
as al-Quds, "The Holy.") By the time the Polo company arrived, the
city had been under siege for two thousand years, as one conquering
army succeeded another, from Romans to Muslims. Each faith—and
each army—claimed the city as its own. In Jerusalem, strife and prayer
were constants; uncertainty was a way of life.

All the while, pilgrims led by guides swarmed from one holy shrine
to another, as Muslims and Christians competed for ownership of and
access to sacred locations and relics. The Polos were only three more
pilgrims amid the crowd, but they were on a most unusual mission. To
obtain the oil they had promised Kublai Khan, they went to the Holy
Sepulcher at the base of the Mount of Olives.

Despite the misgivings of biblical scholars who say that the Holy
Sepulcher may not be the actual site of Jesus's burial, it continues to be
venerated as such, and the Polos had no cause to doubt its authenticity
as they pursued the necessary oil.

The setting (in what is now Old Jerusalem) was described by Ludolph von Suchem: "There dwell in the Church of the Holy Sepulchre ancient Georgians who have the key of the Chapel of the Holy Sepulchre, and food, alms, candles, and oil for lamps to burn round about the Holy Sepulchre are given them by pilgrims through a little window in the south door of the church." Along with other pilgrims to this holiest of shrines, the Polos received their oil, for which they probably made a generous contribution. Then they returned to Acre as swiftly as they could.

LITTLE HAD CHANGED in the Polos' absence. Teobaldo informed them that the cardinals had failed to elect a new pope, despite more than two years of deliberations. Feeling impatient and emboldened now that they had their consecrated oil, the travelers decided to leave immediately for the court of Kublai Khan rather than wait indefinitely for the election of the next pope.

They implored Teobaldo, who was, after all, the papal legate, to supply them with official documents that would satisfy the Mongol leader and explain that Pope Clement's death and the lack of a successor had prevented them from carrying out their mission. "Sir," they said to Teobaldo, as Marco recalls, "since we see that there is no Apostle, we wish to go back to the great lord"—the Venetians' reverential expression for the Mongol leader—"because we know that against our will we have stayed too long and waited enough. And so with your good will we have presumed to go back. But one thing we wish to ask of you, may it please you to make privileges and letters certifying that we came to do the embassy to the Pope and found him dead, and have waited if there should be made another, and seeing that after so long a time none has been chosen, you as legate certify all that you have seen."

As this speech reveals, the Polos knew how to negotiate with powerful officials, and they received the desired reply: "Since you wish to go back to the great lord it pleases me well." Although it is doubtful that Teobaldo referred to Kublai Khan as "the great lord," the legate was eager to use the Polos to establish diplomatic relations with the leader of the Mongols. Even better, Teobaldo promised to inform Kublai Khan as soon as the next pope was elected.

The Polos believed they had finally assembled everything required of them to return in safety to the Mongol leader, and they proceeded to the point of departure, the Armenian port of Layas, through which they had passed three years earlier on the way home. Despite its diminutive size, Marco reports, Layas bustled with "merchants from Venice, from Pisa, and from Genoa, and from all inland parts [who] come there [to] buy and sell their own things, and keep their warehouses in that city."

JUST WHEN conditions approached the ideal, a rebellion broke out, as Marco explains: "A grandson of the Great Khan . . . went destroying all the roads of the desert, making many great trenches and pits; and this he did so that the armies should not be able to follow him."

The uprising stranded the Polos in Layas. As they waited helplessly for the rebellion to subside, they were approached by a courier who brought astonishing news: on September 1, 1271, after thirty-four months of deliberation (the longest in the history of the Papacy), the cardinals had finally elected a new pope, and he was none other than their trusted friend and mentor Teobaldo of Piacenza—or Teobaldo Visconti. "The brothers had great joy at this," Marco notes.

Yet the election led to another delay because the courier brought a summons from the newly elected pope. Once again, the Polo brothers returned to Acre, this time under armed escort. The trip was very much worth the trouble. Teobaldo, now the leading figure in Christendom, greeted them effusively and honored them with blessings and feasts. In the interim, the pontiff-elect had considered their proposed mission to Kublai Khan and concluded that it would provide the ideal opportunity to spread Christianity throughout the Mongol Empire and especially China. In this spirit, he offered the services of two friars "who were really the most learned and worthy that were in all that province," according to Marco. "The one had the name Brother Nicolau de Vicense, the other had the name Brother Guilielme de Tripule." They came armed with extraordinary powers, both ecclesiastical and material: "privileges, charters, and letters with full authority that they might be able to do everything freely in those parts that the Pope himself can do, that they might be able to make bishops and priests and to absolve and bind as he himself, and he gave them many jewels of crystal and other gifts to give to the Great Khan and his embassy." In all, the elevation of their friend and protector to the papacy appeared to be a piece of wonderful fortune for the Polos, who headed east with excellent prospects.

The favorable conditions soon vanished. While traversing Armenia, the Polos incurred the wrath of a local potentate, the sultan Bibara, who threatened to imprison them, or worse. Afraid for their lives, the two learned friars refused to proceed. But the Polo company had not come this far, and waited this long, to turn back when confronted with an obstacle. Confident that they could negotiate with the local tribes they encountered, most likely by bribing them with gems, Niccolò, Maffeo, and Marco stubbornly continued without their papal escort.

ON MARCH 27, 1272, Teobaldo of Piacenza was consecrated in Rome as Pope Gregory X. By then, his Venetian protégés were launched on an adventure of tremendous length, complexity, and implications for the Church, for the Mongol Empire, and for the delicate and volatile relationship between East and West.

The Polos' decision to press on despite all obstacles meant that they were embarking on what many in Christendom would have considered a journey to certain destruction and damnation. To rational minds, it seemed impossible that they would succeed in their quest, a miracle if they even survived the ordeal.

Yet the Polos looked at matters quite differently. They were inclined to believe that trading opportunities abounded in the East, and that those who were skillful could reap great profits. They did not regard themselves as defenders of the Christian faith, or as diplomats, but as merchants. To their way of thinking, commerce was bound to prevail over the impending clash of civilizations. Now their theory would be put to the test. If correct, they could return to Venice someday as very wealthy men. If false, they might never be heard from again.

CHAPTER THREE

The Apprentice

And here were forests ancient as the hills,
Enfolding sunny spots of greenery.

T HERE WOULD BE no turning back. Leaving behind the frustrating delays endured in Venice, Acre, and Jerusalem, the Polo company reached Armenia, where, to Marco's way of thinking, their journey to the heart of the Mongol Empire began in earnest. Contrary to expectations, they found it easier to travel without a conspicuous papal escort attracting notice and entangling them in officialdom.

They were soon engulfed by doubt. At this early stage, Niccolò and Maffeo were more adept at negotiation and diplomacy than at long-distance travel. The tangle of roads and trails extending before them occasioned confusion. Even in an age of faith, a successful expedition depended on preparation and knowledge leavened with luck, which found expression in timing. In the months ahead, the Polo company would come up short.

They had planned to make their way south from Armenia by camel or ox, or, if necessary, on foot across hundreds of miles of dangerous mountain trails until they reached the strategically located port city of Hormuz, on the Persian Gulf. From there, they would arrange for passage on a sailboat and navigate the Strait of Hormuz into the Indian Ocean. If they had a particular landfall in mind, Marco does not reveal it; perhaps they intended to decide once they reached Hormuz and took stock of conditions there. Among merchants plying the Indian Ocean, major port cities scattered along India's western coast were favored destinations. From there, the Polo company could trek overland to the Mongol capital.

The vague plan placed them in harm's way. Marco quickly realized that Armenia was among the most bitterly contested regions they planned to traverse. If only things were as they had been in the days of Alexander the Great—or so Marco implies in his frequent and admiring references to that youthful military figure, who cast a giant shadow across the landscape. In 330 BC, Armenia had been Alexander's base of operations, and his countless descendants were everywhere, or so Marco believed. Alexander was the one figure in antiquity with whom Marco appears to have been familiar, mostly through exposure to Alexander romances, those spurious but entertaining accounts of the heroic conqueror's deeds; such stories were common in this part of the world, where the Mongols had their own Alexander legends as well.

Alexander's armies were succeeded by waves of Muslims, Byzantine subjects, Turks, Egyptian Mamluks, and eventually European Crusaders, all of whom staked claims to Armenia in bloody succession. By the time the Polos reached Armenia, they found it "subject to the lord Great Khan"—that is, Kublai Khan—but with a twist. "Though the inhabitants are Christians," Marco writes, "they are not rightly of the true faith as the Romans are"—in other words, they were heretics— "and this is for want of teachers, for they were formerly good Christians." They were devoted to amusing themselves in this "land of great enjoyment." In days long past, the Armenians had been renowned as valiant warriors, and well-mannered, "but now they are all become very slavish and mean and have no goodness, except that they are very good gluttons"—or so they appeared to the anxious tenderfoot from Venice. Perhaps that situation was for the best, and the vulnerable Polo company survived the time spent traveling through Armenia without incident.

THE CAUTION young Marco experienced in Armenia turned to revulsion when he encountered "the province of Turkoman," today's Turkey. For one thing, he says, the inhabitants "worship Mohammed and hold his religion," which was off-putting for him. More than that, they "have a brutish law and live like beasts in all things; and they are ignorant people and have a barbarous language." This was another way of saying that the people of the region were so different from any he had encountered, and so incomprehensible, that he regarded them with conventional European disdain. He did overcome his distaste long enough to remark on their nomadic ways: "Sometimes they stay on mountains, and sometimes on moors according to where they know there is good pasture for their flocks, because they do not plough the land but make their living from flocks alone. And these Turkomans rarely dwell except in the fields with their flocks, and they have garments of skins and houses of felt or skins."

Their carpets, on the other hand, attracted his merchant's eye, already attuned to fine craftsmanship. "The sovereign carpets of the world," he notes, as if delivering a sales pitch, "and of the most beautiful colors." He appraises "cloth of crimson silk and of other colors and of gold, very beautiful and rich, in very great quantity." His keen appreciation suggests that he traded enthusiastically in them, and that their "beautiful and rich" colors helped the Polo company profit from the transactions. The Polos were as happy to trade as to travel.

TRYING TO ADJUST to life on the road, Marco found the mingling of cultural and spiritual traditions—to say nothing of language, diet, and dress—unnerving. "These Mongols do not care what God is worshipped in their lands," he exclaims. "If only all are faithful to the lord Khan and quite obedient and give therefore the appointed tribute, and justice is well kept, thou mayest do what pleaseth thee with the soul." Those living under Mongol rule could do whatever they wished, whether they were "Jew or Pagan or Saracen"—that is, Muslim—"or Christian."

This religious freedom was a source of amazement to young Marco, but the Mongols' attitude toward Christianity baffled him. "They confess . . . that Christ is Lord, but they say he is a proud Lord because he will not be with other gods but will be God above all others in the world. And so in some places they have a Christ of gold or silver and keep him hidden in some chest, and say that he is the great Lord supreme of the Christians."

Marco would have to adapt; the Silk Road was no place for orthodoxy or single-mindedness.

IN TURKEY, Marco gathered tales of Noah's Ark, said to perch atop Mount Ararat, the tallest peak in the country. Even as he became aware of the multiplicity of religions all around him, he remained eager for this proof of biblical events concerning "the ship of the world." As he recalled, the Book of Genesis states that "on the seventeenth day of the seventh month the ark came to rest on the mountains of Ararat."

In the spirit of innocent belief, Marco searched for the evidence, only to be frustrated. In its unlikely resting place, "this ark is seen from very far because the mountain on which it rests is very high, and there is snow there almost all the year, and in one part there is . . . a large black thing seen from far amidst those snows; but close by nothing of it is seen." The tantalizing feature was likely a frozen lava field glimpsed from afar, alternately revealed and concealed by shifting snows, not a ship.

As Marco related the story of the final resting place of the Ark, he lost his enthusiasm for it. He implicitly acknowledged that there was no Ark on Mount Ararat, at least none that he could see—but how wonderful if there were.

MARCO RETURNED to reality when he reached the thriving commercial center of Mosul, on the Tigris River. Here he had his first taste of a desert empire, with its frenzied bazaars and outpouring of goods. Mosul had been under strict Muslim rule until the Mongols conquered the city in 1182, and by the time the Polo company arrived, it was open to various religions, including Christianity. The tomb of the Old Testament prophet Jonah was to be found here, although Marco was unaware of it. As an aspiring merchant, he more likely became familiar with muslin, the strong, densely woven, unbleached fabric that had long been locally produced.

In Mosul, Marco encountered the followers of Nestorius, a fifth-century patriarch of Constantinople who taught that Jesus was divided into two natures, one human and the other divine, loosely bound together in what Nestorians called *synapheia*, or conjunction. According to the historian Edward Gibbon, Nestorius learned "nicely to discriminate the humanity of his *master* Christ from the divinity of the *Lord* Jesus." But to the Roman Christians of Marco's time, this notion amounted to heresy, although the issue was more subtle than Gibbon's offhand remark would suggest. In Nestorian teaching, Mary could be venerated only as the mother of the human Jesus, not as the Mother of God. Rome, in contrast, insisted on the "hypostatic" or fundamental unity of Jesus' two natures. Intellectuals on all sides of the question debated this subject endlessly, and it is entirely possible that the dis-

pute arose more from varying interpretations of the Greek philosophical terms in which they framed their discussion than from actual differences. Nevertheless, a permanent rift between the Nestorians and
Rome remained in place.

Nestorians established their patriarchate at Baghdad, and their
influence expanded throughout Syria, Asia Minor, Iraq, Persia, and
even China. In 735, they had applied to the emperor of the Tang
dynasty to build a church in the imperial capital, Ch'ang-an (now
Xi'an). They received permission and made the city into a Nestorian
hub, where they taught their adherents both the Old and New Testa-
ments and occasionally converted Chinese and others. They prospered
despite efforts to suppress their church until the end of the Tang
dynasty in 907, when they scattered.

Throughout the Nestorians' struggle to find a safe haven in Asia,
much of Western Europe remained perplexed by these devout "Eastern Christians," as they were sometimes called. Marco frequently took
note of the Nestorians he encountered, but he considered them enigmatic and "inferior"—that is, heretical.

BAGHDAD, still the seat of the Nestorian Church in Marco Polo's day,
lies 220 miles to the southeast of Mosul. Marco discusses Baghdad
with an air of confidence, but it is unlikely that he actually visited the
city. To obscure that omission, he resorts to telling stories, beginning
with a lengthy miracle tale pitting the thirty-seventh caliph, or Muslim ruler, of Baghdad against a humble Christian cobbler, with the
fantastic outcome that the caliph secretly converted to Christianity.
Rustichello's fingerprints can be found all over this elaborate and
somewhat cloying set piece.

In a similar spirit, Marco speaks with gusto about the end of the
caliphate at the hands of the Mongols. In this case, his account follows
what is known about actual events. He sets the scene in 1255—actually,
it was 1258—when Hülegü, one of Genghis Khan's grandsons, vowed
to conquer the ancient caliphate and claim it for the rapidly expanding
Mongol Empire. Since its heyday under Harun ar-Rashid over four
centuries earlier, Baghdad had deteriorated, but it still posed a formidable challenge to would-be invaders. To forestall an assault, envoys of
the caliph called on Hülegü and cautioned, "If the Caliph is killed, the
whole universe will fall into chaos, the sun will hide its face, rain will
no longer fall, and plants will cease to grow."

Undeterred, and perhaps even provoked by the warning, Hülegü "resolved to capture it by a ruse rather than by force. Having about a hundred thousand cavalry, without counting infantry, he wished to give the Caliph and his followers in the city the impression that they were only a few." Hülegü charged the city gates with few warriors, and "the Caliph, seeing this force was a small one, did not take much account of it," whereupon Hülegü made a "pretence of flight and so lured [the caliph] back past the woods and thickets where his troops lay in ambush. Here he trapped his pursuers and crushed them. So the Caliph was captured together with the city." Mongol warriors killed eight thousand inhabitants in the attack; only the lives of Christians were spared, thanks to the intervention of Hülegü's wife, who shared their faith.

Marco describes a grotesque end to the caliph's life: Hülegü confined the Muslim leader to his tower of treasure and let him starve to death amid his wealth. In fact, the caliph's execution was more bizarre.

Despite their brutality, the Mongols abhorred the thought of spilling blood. Their methods of "bloodless" execution included smothering by stuffing the victim's mouth with stones or feces. The caliph was subjected to a more dignified but even harsher ordeal. On February 10, 1258, he was wrapped in a carpet and trodden to death by horses. His family was also said to be executed, with the exception of a daughter, who became a slave in Hülegü's harem.

After the Mongol conquest, Baghdad's population shrank to a tenth of its former size. Nevertheless, the provincial capital still traded on its reputation as a center of commerce and of intellect, storied for its madrassas, libraries, giant moat, and, it was said, 27,000 public baths. Legends of the former glories of Baghdad and the court of Harun ar-Rashid remained potent enough to impress even Marco Polo.

IN HIS ACCOUNT, Marco abruptly turns his attention from Baghdad to Tabriz, the city reputedly built by one of the wives of Harun ar-Rashid, whose luxurious court served as the setting for the tales known as *The Arabian Nights' Entertainment*. In this instance, the Venetian actually visited, and came away impressed by, the thriving commercial center—"the most splendid city in the province," he calls it, as if compiling a guidebook for travelers. With its "market for merchandise from India and Baghdad, from Mosul and Hormuz, and from many other places," Tabriz is worth a journey, he says, if only to see the "attractive orchards, full of excellent fruit" surrounding the city.

Even as he extols the commercial life of Tabriz, Marco expresses misgivings about the inhabitants, a "mixed lot" who were "good for very little." The variety of people—"Armenians and Nestorians, Jacobites and Georgians and Persians"—competed strenuously against one another, and despite its prosperity, the area seethed with religious violence. "The Saracens of the region are wicked and treacherous," he reports. He deviates from his habit of dismissing Muslims as idolaters, and sets forth his understanding of some disturbing facets of their laws: "Any harm they may do to one who does not accept their law, and any appropriation of his goods, is no sin at all. And if they suffer death or injury at the hands of Christians, they are accounted martyrs." He asserts, "That is why they are converting the Tartars and many other nations to their law, because they are allowed great license to sin."

It came as a relief to Marco to learn that Tabriz harbored a monastery housing a mendicant order of monks. Judging from their clothing, he guessed they were Carmelites, and noted the time they spent "weaving woolen girdles" to lay on the altar during Mass and to distribute to "their friends and to noblemen" in the belief that the girdles relieved pain. These phenomena Marco reports as if they were the most natural things in the world.

Although other Venetians were scarce, merchants from Genoa had long been represented in Tabriz, and were much better known. For them, as for merchants across Asia, Tabriz served as an important pearl market, perhaps the largest of all, supplied by abundant harvests from the Persian Gulf. The Polo company found that bargaining for pearls in the Tabriz market was a serious matter governed by firm rules. A buyer and seller squatted facing each other, their hands swathed in fabric. They haggled over the price not by speaking aloud, lest the terms be overheard by others seeking an advantage, but by squeezing each other's fingers and wrists to describe and dispute the quality of the goods, and to convey the amount of the bid offered, and accepted. This unusual form of negotiation meant that bystanders had no indication of the actual terms of the deal, and the price remained flexible from one transaction to the next.

FROM TABRIZ, Marco entered Savah, in Persia, and then Kerman, known for its Persian rugs. Here Marco's concerns about Islam relaxed a bit, and he found himself enjoying the climate and coveting the turquoise concealed in nearby mountains. He expresses admiration for the locals' skill in fashioning "the equipment of a mounted warrior— bridles, saddles, spurs, swords, bows, quivers, and every sort of armor." Even their artful needlework attracted his eye, as did the spectacle of falconry.

In the brilliant skies overhead, Marco caught his first glimpse of the aristocratic sport that would become a passion for him in his travels throughout Asia. It was one of the few endeavors common to both East and West, and for Marco, as for other gentlemen, it was the embodiment of power and grace. "In the mountains are bred the best falcons in the world, and the swiftest in flight," he reports. "They are red on the breast and under the tail between the thighs. And you may take my word that they fly at such incalculable speed that there is no bird that can escape from them by flight." So young Marco scanned the firmament, studying the swift aerial combat that mirrored human predatory behavior.

In his survey of Persia, Marco never pauses to indicate when, or even whether, he visited all the places that he describes, but occasionally he traces these early travels of his with a precision born of experience. His departure from the Persian kingdom of Kerman, in which he tarried, conveys a sense of the endlessly unfolding vistas before him. "When the traveler leaves the city of Kerman, he rides for seven days across a plateau, finding no lack of towns and villages and homesteads. It is a pleasant and satisfying country to ride through," he notes, "for it is well stocked with game and teems with partridges." After this passage, he writes of coming to a great escarpment, "from which the road leads steadily downhill for two days through a country abounding all the way in fruits of many kinds. There used to be homesteads here; but now there is not one, but nomads live here with their grazing flocks. Between the city of Kerman and this escarpment the cold winter is so intense that it can scarcely be warded off by any number of garments and furs."

In Persia, he beheld evidence of the region's intense geologic activity. Here, active faults and volcanoes had created some of the most calamitous events on the planet. The Polo company sought safer surroundings in the pleasant town of Rudbar, high in the Alborz Mountains in northwest Persia. Rudbar served as a merchants' gathering place and offered lush pasture for livestock. The picturesque grazing herds inspired Marco to exercise the powers of description that would eventually win him fame. "Let me tell you first about the oxen," he writes. "They are of great size and pure white like snow. Their hair is short and smooth because of the heat. Their horns are thick and stumpy and not pointed. Between their shoulders they have a round hump fully two palms in height. They are the loveliest things in the world to look at. When you want to load them, they lie down like camels; then, when they are loaded, they stand up and carry their loads very well, because they are exceedingly strong. There are also sheep as big as asses, with tails so thick and plump that they weigh a good thirty pounds. Fine, fat beasts they are, and good eating."

JUST AS MARCO was beginning to feel at home in the Persian mountains, he stiffened at the mention of the Karaunas, "bands of marauders who infest the country." The Karaunas preyed on the plump, grazing herds. More terrifying still, they were reputed to be adept at performing a diabolic enchantment that turned day into night over a distance as far as a man could ride during the space of seven days. "They know this country very well," Marco says. "When they have brought on the darkness, they ride side by side, sometimes as many as ten thousand of them together, . . . so that they overspread the region they mean to rob. Nothing they find in the open country, neither man nor beast nor goods, can escape capture."

The Polo company fled to the seaport of Hormuz, but not before they had several close encounters with these predators. "I assure you," Marco's account states with emphasis, "that Master Marco himself narrowly evaded capture by these robbers in the darkness they had made. He"—that is, Marco—"escaped to a town called Kamasal; but not before many of his companions were taken captive and sold [as slaves], and some put to death."

Of this dangerous episode, Marco says nothing more. Events at their next stop outweighed all else.

HORMUZ ENJOYED a reputation as a prosperous haven on the Persian Gulf. Here the Polos expected to travel aboard one of the port's many sailing vessels to a destination in India, and then proceed to

China. Marco remarks on the "excellent harbor" and confidently notes that "merchants come here by ship from India, bringing all sorts of spices and precious stones and pearls and cloths of silk and gold and elephants' tusks and many other wares. In this city they sell them to others, who distribute them to various customers through the length and breadth of the world. It is a great center of commerce, with many cities and towns subordinate to it."

For the wandering Polo company, the sight of so much water after months in the desert evoked memories of Venice and the Adriatic Sea, but on closer inspection, Hormuz was not quite the gem it had seemed from afar. For one thing, "If a merchant dies here, the king confiscates all his possessions." The climate also presented a hazard to unwary travelers. Wind from the surrounding desert could turn "so overpoweringly hot that it would be deadly if it did not happen that, as soon as men are aware of its approach, they plunge neck-deep into the water and so escape from the heat."

While in Hormuz, Marco was horrified to learn that the deadly wind had surprised no less than six thousand soldiers (five thousand on foot, the rest on horseback) in the desert and "stifled them all, so that not one survived to carry back the news to their lord." Eventually, the "men of Hormuz" learned of the mass deaths and decided to bury the corpses to prevent infection, but "when they gripped them by the arms to drag them to the graves, they [the corpses] were so parched by the tremendous heat that the arms came loose from the trunk, so that they [the men] had to dig the graves beside the corpses and heave them in."

The sailing vessels, when he finally inspected them, were a disappointment. "Their ships are very bad, and many of them founder, because they are not fastened with iron nails but stitched together with thread made of coconut husks," Marco reports in dismay. Nor did their other features inspire much confidence. "The ships have one mast, one sail, and one rudder, and are not decked; when they have loaded them, they cover the cargo with skins, and on top of these they put the horses that they ship to India for sale." The design was cause for concern; Marco preferred the security of two rudders, two masts, and proper decks. These stripped-down vessels seemed to ask for trouble at the first hint of foul weather. Worse, "They have no iron for nails; so they employ wooden pegs and stitch [them] with thread. This makes it very risky to sail in these ships. And," Marco says, "you can take my word that many of them sink, because the Indian Ocean is very stormy." As if all that were not bad enough, these leaky ships were not even caulked properly with pitch; instead, they were "anointed with a sort of fish oil."

The Polo company had seen enough. They would not sail to India, after all. Earning their livelihood by making calculations, and accustomed to living by their wits, they decided the prospect was too dangerous.

They left Hormuz as quickly as they had come, and returned to Kerman, where they rethought their method for reaching China and the court of Kublai Khan. Rather than trust their lives to precarious water craft, they would move in accordance with the rhythm of the camel's languorous gait along the ancient traders' routes that have come to be known as the Silk Road.

AS THEIR CAMELS and donkeys headed into the wasteland, Marco apprehensively noted "a desert of sixty miles in which water to drink is sometimes not found." The Polos were concerned both for themselves and for the beasts of burden on which their lives and fortunes depended. At one point, they spent three days without sighting water they could use. "What water there is," Marco reports, "is brackish and green as meadow grass and so bitter that no one could bear to drink it." It was not only unpleasant, it was downright dangerous: "Drink one drop of it and you void your bowels ten times over. It is the same with the salt that is made from it. If you eat one little granule, it produces violent diarrhea." Driven mad with thirst, animals that drank the water suffered as terribly.

And so their caravan moved on. For transportation—indeed, for survival itself—the Polo company relied on the Bactrian camel (*Camelus bactrianus*), which had served travelers along the Silk Road since biblical times. Unlike the single-humped dromedary, common in North Africa, the Bactrian camel has two lopsided humps to store fat, a long neck, minimal ears, and massive teeth, some of them pointed. The animals come in as many colors as the desert itself, from dirty white to deep, gritty brown.

Camels are suited to desert crossings. Their broad cloven hoofs resist sinking into loose sand, and their large nostrils are lined with hairs and can close like valves to prevent the inhalation of flying sand. Bactrians are especially sturdy animals, accustomed to sleeping on hard surfaces, with a thick, heavy coat to protect their bodies. They can go for several days without water, and even longer if they find plants on which to feed.

It has long been noted that camels possess a sixth sense for traversing the desert. In the third century AD, the Chinese writer Kuo P'u observed, "The camel is an unusual domestic animal; it carries a saddle of flesh on its back; swiftly it dashes over the shifting sands; it manifests its merit in dangerous places; it has secret understanding of springs and sources; subtle indeed is its knowledge!"

Marco, his father, and his uncle were acutely aware of their beasts of burden; the animals' coarse, vital smell filled the nostrils of their masters. Atop their camels, the Polos did not so much stride as stagger. Yet a sturdy Bactrian camel can carry more than six hundred pounds, and under favorable conditions can cover thirty miles a day. For reliable transport across the desert, no other creature could match these characteristics.

After several days of strenuous travel atop their camels, the exhausted and thirsty travelers reached their first oasis.

SAPURGAN was the name of their salvation, "a town beautiful and great and fertile and of great plenty of all things needful for life." There were stands of trees, perhaps poplars, their leaves bright and vivid in the desert air, and the region's famous melons, tasting so ripe and sweet as to seem "the best in the world." They sustained life year round, thanks to the preservation techniques Marco observed. "When they are dried they cut them in slices like threads or strips of leather," he says, "and they become sweeter than honey."

Still in the Persian mountains, Marco fell under the spell of another town, Tunocain. Entering early manhood, he was becoming acutely aware of women, and he dared to describe them with a robust appreciation and informality at odds with the accounts of pious miracles that Rustichello slipped into the account. The women of Tunocain caught his eye and, for the moment, engaged his heart; he calls them "the most beautiful in the world." They were Muslim women, whose like he had previously dismissed as idolaters, but now he thought of them constantly. Even allowing for his penchant for overstatement, this revelation suggests that Marco's experiences on the road were beginning to influence his assumptions about the world around him.

Near Tunocain, Marco took note of another shrine, the Dry Tree. Although he did not trouble to explain the tree's significance to his audience, many knew that the Dry Tree appeared in Christian legends, and in Alexander romances, as an ancient, even immortal phenomenon possessing magical powers. Reverence for the Dry Tree, a startling apparition in this arid, mountainous area, seems to hark back to a primitive form of tree or nature worship. Marco describes the phenomenon with enough detail to suggest that he had actually seen it: "It is very large and thick, and its leaves are green on one side and white on the other, and it forms burrs like the burrs of chestnuts, but there is nothing inside them. They are not good to eat. Of its wood balsam is made. It is solid and very hard wood." But he may have been relying on hearsay for his information.

As MARCO LOST HIMSELF in a reverie of the region's lore, his company advanced into the territory of the Assassins, who threatened powerful warlords and heads of state. Their notoriety had reached Western Europe as a result of a knife-wielding Assassin's attack on Prince Edward (shortly to become King Edward I) in Jerusalem barely a year after the Polo company departed. Seriously wounded, Edward survived multiple stab wounds and fled home to England, but incidents such as these gave the Assassins a lasting mystique as a secretive fraternity of terrorists capable of striking when least expected. Marco and his collaborator realized that recounting tales of the Assassins would send a frisson of horror through their audience, and they played up the cult's sinister mystique for all it was worth.

Relying on stories passed to him by his father and uncle, Marco explains that these notorious raiders were followers of a mythical-sounding but all-too-real figure known as the Old Man, who ruled from a fastness called Alamut, "Eagle's Nest." The Assassins' name, he says, derived from the Arabic phrase meaning "those who eat hashish"—a ritual they performed to nerve themselves for their missions. He relates how the Old Man drugged and manipulated his followers to do his bidding: "Sometimes the Old Man, when he wished to kill any lord who made war or was his enemy, made them put some of these youths into that Paradise by fours and by tens and by twenties just as he wished, in this way. For he had opium . . . given to them by which they fell asleep immediately . . . and they slept three days and three nights. Then he had them taken and put into that garden, and made them wake." At that moment, they beheld alluring women "singing and playing and making all the caresses and dalliance that they could imagine, giving them food and most delicate wines, so that intoxicated with so many pleasures and with the little streams of milk and wine that they saw," they were made to believe that they were "truly in Paradise." In summoning this vision of evil, Marco may well have exaggerated the role hashish played in the Assassin cult. Use of the drug was widespread in the region, not confined to Assassins, and the effects may have debilitated rather than emboldened its users.

The zealous Assassins inspired dread in surrounding kingdoms. Marco reports: "Many kings and many lords paid tribute to him [the Old Man] and cultivated his friendship for fear that he might bring about their death. This happened because at the time the nations were not united in their allegiance, but torn apart by conflicting loyalties and purposes."

That was the state of affairs until 1256, when Kublai Khan's brother, Hülegü, dislodged the Assassins from their Eagle's Nest. Marco writes of a three-year-long siege that starved out the dangerous band and ended with their deaths. And he confidently reports, "To this moment, there has not been found any such Old Man nor any such assassin." That was not strictly true, for remnants of the Assassins concealed themselves in the mountains in Marco's day, their ability to menace their neighbors greatly reduced, but their notorious reputation still vital.

With his artful description, Marco perpetuated the Assassins' infamy in the Western consciousness, but as he admitted, his account was based on dramatic hearsay rather than personal experience. In reality, the sect, founded by Hasan ibn al-Sabbah in 1090, was more complex than he suggested. Its fanatical members came to be known as Nizaris (so called after their caliph, Nizar ibn al-Sabbah) or as Ismai'ilis (a type of Shiite). They did inhabit a mountain fastness called Alamut, located south of the Caspian Sea. As the sect grew, outposts spread across Persia and Syria, and members were rigidly segregated into classes; potential martyrs and assassins belonged to the highest category. The young Venetian was unaware that Muslims also dreaded and stigmatized the Ismai'ilis, whom they considered dangerously heretical.

MARCO REMAINED uneasy as the Polo company gradually descended from the terrifying castle "through beautiful valleys and through beautiful slopes" to a lush plain "where there is much beautiful grass and much good pasture for cattle and fruit enough and of all things to eat in great abundance."

The Polo company then made its cautious way eastward through what is now Afghanistan, the nexus of Central Asia. Seven hundred years later, the legendary English voyager Nancy Hatch Dupree would describe the road to Balkh in her book of the same name: "Here gnarled branches, blackened with dampness, form abstract patterns against the glistening snows of winter. These stark pictures soften as spring spreads a blanket of soft green; tulips bloom and children fashion delicate pink wands for the passerby. As spring advances, cherry, apricot, pear, and almond burst into bloom, their beauty sharp against brilliant blue skies or rain-laden black clouds. With summer the valley grows lush and fills with busy activity until the cold night air of fall adds riotous shades of yellow, gold and red before winter descends once more." Such was the enchanted landscape that greeted the Polo company.

For six days they rode through these idyllic valleys dotted with peaceful Muslim villages and towns, a passage marking the beginning in earnest of their journey to China.

BALKH, their next stopover, was the most renowned and troubled metropolis in Afghanistan. It was, Marco says, "a noble city and great" and "the largest and most beautiful [city] found in those parts." Or so it had been.

In its ancient prime, Balkh (or Bactria, as it was then known) had been home to the prophet Zarathustra (or Zoroaster), believed to have been born in about 628 BC, who brought a new religion to Persia. Zoroastrianism incorporated fire worship, a belief in the occult, many deities, and, in its later forms, an eternal flame burning at its Temple of Fire. Zarathustra's mystique spread far and wide. Tradition holds that the prophet was murdered by nomads at the age of seventy-seven as he worshiped before his fire altar in Balkh. Much later, Arabs swept in and imposed Islam, designating Balkh as the Mother of Cities. And so it remained until the Mongols overran the region, and, in Marco's words, "ravaged and wickedly damaged it." Marco was referring to the events of 1220, when Genghis Khan led 100,000 cavalry through Balkh, leveling the city for all time.

His methods were exceptionally brutal. The thirteenth-century

Persian historian Juvaini wrote that Genghis Khan "commanded that the population of Balkh, small and great, few and many, both men and women, should be driven out onto the plain and divided up according to the usual custom into hundreds and thousands to be put to the sword." Returning to Balkh, he ordered that "a number of fugitives hidden in nooks and crannies . . . be killed. And whenever a wall was left standing, the Mongols pulled it down and . . . wiped out all traces of culture from the region."

For the Mongols, these atrocities formed a necessary part of empire building. For their victims, the War of Mongol Aggression, as it might be termed, was a calamity without end. "With one stroke," Juvaini continued, "the regions thereof became a desert and the greater part of the living [became] dead and their skin and bones [became] crumbling dust; and the mighty were humbled." A devastated fort in the Islamic city of Bamiyan became known as Sharhr-i-Gholghola, "City of Noise." It was also known as the Silent City, the Screaming City, or even the Cursed City, in memory of the Mongol massacre that exterminated every man, woman, child, and beast. Not even plants survived the Mongol assault. Although it remained a gateway to the Silk Road and the riches of China, Balkh never recovered from the slaughter.

In Balkh, Marco felt the endless pain of conquest. His powers of empathy growing, he could practically hear the screams of the victims as the Mongol invaders destroyed this once-prosperous enclave, and he recoiled at the spectacle of a civilization reduced to ashes by cruel invaders. He preferred boyish reveries of a prior invader, Alexander the Great, and marveled that he was following in the footsteps of Alexander's army. It was said, and Marco believed, that blue-eyed inhabitants of the area were descended from Alexander's soldiers (though the soldiers did not necessarily have blue eyes), and that local sheep and horses had as their ancestors the army's animals. Alexander's horse, Bucephalus, had reputedly sired local horses whose descendants still roamed the hills.

Marco took heart from Alexander's superhuman example: if the young general could survive these treacherous parts, so could he. The Polos, of course, were merchants and traders, not conquerors, but they faced many of the same obstacles in their quest to lay claim to great wealth. Passing through these violent historical currents as if in a slipstream, the Polos were a commercial army in search of great natural riches.

CHAPTER FOUR

The Opium Eater

And there were gardens bright with sinuous rills,
Where blossomed many an incense-bearing tree. . . .

THE POLO COMPANY found the riches they sought in Taican (now the Afghan province of Talikan), where they encountered a precious commodity: salt. Mountains of salt, to be exact, "the best in the world," and so hard that it took a great iron pick to pry it loose. Salt was a form of currency (Roman soldiers had been paid in salt), salt was preservation; salt was an engine of ancient and medieval economies. There was more to attract the Polos' interest, for the region's markets abounded in almonds, pistachios, and corn harvested from the alluring surrounding groves and fields. They were ready to get down to the business of trading.

Marco could not abide the people whom they encountered, "thieves and robbers and murderers" whose misdeeds were fueled by liquor. He reports: "They stay a great deal in taverns," drinking fermented wine. Still, he was fascinated by their hunting prowess, which extended to the bloody chore of capturing porcupines: "When the hunters wish to catch them and set the very fierce large dogs upon them, the porcupines gather themselves all together and . . . shake themselves each with great fury and run and then throw the quills, which are lightly fastened on their backs, . . . at the dogs and men and wound them badly, very often in several places. Then the hunters go upon them and take them."

Before long, Marco and his father and uncle were on their way once more.

.   .   .

No ONE in the Polo company, or anyone else at that time, announced that he was going on the Silk Road; there was no such thing. Dealers trading in gems, spices, and silks and other fabrics traveled along a casual but ancient network of tracks, trails, and mountain passes snaking across Central Asia and China, encountering the occasional monk or missionary. The Silk Road as a distinct entity was not so christened until 1877, when Baron Ferdinand von Richtofen, a German geographer, conceived of the evocative but artificial image *Seidenstrasse*. Although the name suggests romance, luxury, and sensuality, the arduous experience of traveling the route was one of hardship and danger undertaken by those in search of wealth, conquest, or salvation.

Its tributaries extended from Central Asia—precisely where the "Silk Road" began would be impossible to say—to the eastern shore of China. Parts of the route ran south, deep into India. The Polo company entered near the westernmost reaches. Like other merchants, they traveled as part of a large caravan (in Persian, the word *karvan* meant "company") and soon found themselves dependent on an extraordinary network of caravansaries—combination dormitories and stables catering to itinerant merchants. Often located near a stream, an oasis, or a village with a mosque, the caravansary gave an appearance of forbidding and secure massiveness, a sheer wall rising several stories above the ground, relieved by air holes near the bottom and small windows near the top. Travelers seeking entrance had to pass through a massive gate, which admitted them, camels and all, and was secured at night with iron chains. Within, they found a courtyard paved with flagstones on which dozens of exhausted camels and donkeys crouched around a central fountain ringed by a cloister, and beyond that area, storerooms and stables. In one corner of the quadrangular structure, a cooking fire burned, the food giving off pungent, mouthwatering aromas. A steward posted near the entrance supplied food and water, and kept order within. Stairways led to small, austere lodging rooms above the stables. Meanwhile, the travelers' animals were tied up in the *serai*, or stables, below.

In Afghanistan, the caravansaries were known as *robats*—from an ancient term for rope to tie a horse. The Polos encountered *robats* throughout their travels along the Silk Road in Afghanistan; the structures were closely spaced, with a bit less than twenty miles (roughly a day's journey) separating them. The distance was measured locally in *farsakhs*, with five *farsakhs* adding up to a full day's journey. Caravans usually included both camels and donkeys, handled by a trainer known as a *sareban*, or camel rider, who rode atop the first camel. A sure-footed donkey often preceded the camel, whose head was tied to the donkey's tail. With this simple but practical method of travel, merchants trekked thousands of miles across Asia.

MARCO WAS NOT the first to travel what came to be called the Silk Road; he had been preceded by generations of Mongols, Turks, Arabs, mercenaries, and monks. Nor was he the first Westerner to describe his adventures in Asia. Nearly a hundred years earlier, Benjamin of Tudela, a rabbi from Navarre, had much the same idea concerning his journey. Benjamin's travels brought him into contact with local officials, colorful characters, and other merchants. His account described commercial conditions from Barcelona to Constantinople, Baghdad, and points east.

From his vantage point in Baghdad, Benjamin compiled a *Book of Travels*, covering the years 1160 to 1173. Collecting reliable information about Jews in Palestine, Thebes, Antioch, and Tyre and on Mount Parnassus, he took note of Jewish merchants, dyers, shipowners, peasants, and laborers. He remarked on practices of obscure Jewish sects and wrote an account of a Jewish pseudo-Messiah and mystic in Persia, David Alroy, who had burst into prominence shortly before Benjamin's excursion. In all, he included the names of 248 leaders of Jewish communities that he encountered throughout the Diaspora.

His curiosity led him to the cult of the Assassins—the same sect that would later alarm Marco Polo. "They fulfill whatever he commands them, whether it be a matter of life or death," wrote Benjamin of their leader, in words that prefigure the Venetian's account.

Unlike later merchants, Benjamin of Tudela did not penetrate deeply into Asia. After getting as far east as Baghdad, he returned home safely to Spain by way of Sicily. Nevertheless, he had seen much of the world. Despite his accomplishment, Benjamin of Tudela's account, written with a collaborator in Hebrew, remained unknown in Europe, except among a handful of Jews. It was not published until 1543, and not translated into other tongues until the seventeenth century.

EUROPE remained in the thrall of legends of Prester John, the Christian leader who supposedly occupied a wealthy empire somewhere in

Asia or Africa—no one knew exactly where, but theories abounded. The Church longed to make contact with him in order to fight the infidels inhabiting the gulf between East and West. Prester John was an illusion, but a powerful one, inspiring Christian missionaries to undertake pilgrimages to the East. Beginning in 1235, a series of papal bulls conferred upon missionary friars spiritual powers exceeding those of European bishops. They could, all on their own, undertake to combat heretics, convert infidels, reconcile schismatics—in other words, do whatever it took to bring recognizable, uniform Christianity to those who knew little of Rome, or who belonged to ancient sects that had gone their own way for centuries.

The earliest known missionary to travel to China, pioneering the route that the Polo company would follow, was Giovanni da Pian del Carpini, a Franciscan based in Cologne. Like Buddhist monks, Franciscans combined a vow of strict poverty with strong evangelical tendencies, and like Buddhists, they were suited for the rigors of life along the Silk Road. In 1245, carrying documents from Pope Innocent IV, Carpini and another Franciscan known as Benedict of Poland endured severe privation as they journeyed to an outpost on the bank of the Dnieper River, at the western edge of the Mongol Empire. Then, trekking to another Mongol outpost on the Lower Volga, they underwent the indignity of submitting, or being forced to submit, to a Mongol purification rite involving close proximity to crackling fires.

As they waited for the papal letters to be translated from Latin into Russian, Arabic, and Mongol tongues, they nearly perished from starvation, subsisting on a diet of millet gruel made with snow melt. Given the treatment to which they were subjected, the two beleaguered missionaries may not have realized that the Mongols were inclined to be respectful of holy men, no matter what their affiliation. Once their identity was confirmed, the missionaries were free to travel east.

Ahead lay a trek of three thousand miles across the Steppe and arid desert of Mongolia. The travelers covered the distance in fifteen months to reach the Mongol capital of Karakorum as a new khan, Güyük, was about to receive his title. Güyük welcomed the two missionaries from the West, heard their summons to Christianity, and replied that he would oblige only if the pope and all the secular leaders of Europe came to Karakorum to swear allegiance to him. Or, in the words of the new khan, "You must come yourself at the head of all your kings and prove to us your fealty and allegiance. And if you disregard the command of God and disobey Our instructions, we shall look upon you as Our enemy. Who ever recognizes and submits to the Son of God . . . will be wiped out." It was a dispiriting conclusion to their arduous journey.

In November 1246, the two monks made their way back through wind-whipped snowstorms bearing disappointing news for Pope Innocent IV. Although the mission failed to achieve its stated purpose, it had been a remarkable journey of exploration. Carpini is believed to have been the first Westerner since AD 900 to travel east of Baghdad and return safely from the great no-man's-land that was Asia.

CARPINI compiled the first comprehensive description of Mongol life for Western audiences, a work called *Historia Mongalorum* (History of the Mongols), or occasionally *Liber Tartarorum* (Book of the Tartars). No match for the drama animating Marco's account, Carpini's has the benefit of clarity and simplicity. The first eight chapters cover the country, climate, manners, religion, character, history, policies, and military tactics of the Mongols; the ninth is devoted to the other regions Carpini visited along the way. The account helped to explain and humanize the Mongols for Western readers by characterizing them as a remarkable and resourceful people.

Carpini vividly evoked the strange but noble appearance of the people who seemed destined to rule Asia and possibly Europe: "In appearance, the Tartars are quite different from all other men, for they are broader than other people between the eyes and across the cheek-bones. Their cheeks also are rather prominent above their jaws; they have a flat and small nose, their eyes are little, and their eyelids raised up to the eyebrows. For the most part, but with a few exceptions, they are slender about the waist; almost all are of medium height. Hardly any of them grow beards, although some have a little hair on the upper lip and chin and this they do not trim."

He was also alert to the most distinctive feature of Mongol grooming, the tonsure: "On the top of the head they have a tonsure like clerics, and as a general rule all shave from one ear to the other to the breadth of three fingers, and this shaving joins on to the tonsure. Above the forehead also they all likewise shave to two fingers' breadth, but the hair between this shaving and the tonsure they allow to grow until it reaches their eyebrows, and, cutting more from each side of the forehead than in the middle, they make the hair . . . long; the rest of the hair they grow like women, and they make it into two braids which they bind, one behind each ear."

He provided a close-up of Mongol dress: "The married women have a very full tunic, open to the ground in front. On their head, they have a round thing made of twigs or bark . . . and on the top there is a long and slender cane of gold or silver or wood, or even a feather, and it is sewn into a cap which reaches to the shoulders. The cap as well as the object is covered with buckram, velvet, or brocade, and without this headgear they never go into the presence of men and by it they are distinguished from other women."

Despite his observation that some Mongol men kept as many as fifty or even a hundred wives, Carpini complimented the women on their chastity, and the Mongols as a whole on their honesty. He seems less secure but equally intrigued when discussing their fervent shamanism. They appeared to lack a concept of damnation and Hell everlasting, but, to his relief, they did believe in an afterlife, although it bore a strong resemblance to their present circumstances—eating, drinking koumiss, and tending their herds.

He warned of the extreme climate conditions awaiting travelers on the Silk Road: "The weather there is astonishingly irregular, for in the middle of the summer, when other places are normally enjoying very great heat, there is fierce thunder and lightning, which cause the death of many men, and at the same time there are very heavy snowfalls." As if that were not bad enough, "there are also bitterly cold winds, so violent that at times men can ride on horseback only with great effort." Such was the daunting prospect Marco faced as he made his way slowly to Kublai Khan.

CARPINI'S DATA, gleaned from personal observation, circulated across Europe in manuscript form, and became part of a popular medieval encyclopedia, the *Speculum historiale* of Vincent of Beauvais.

In its organization, subject matter, and scope, Carpini's *Historia* anticipated Marco Polo's *Travels*. Although he had not seen Carpini's account before setting out for China, Marco gave every sign of having become familiar with it by the time he wrote his own, far more elaborate work, and he took significant cues from it. Like Carpini, Marco divided his account into sections discussing aspects of Mongol life, and like Carpini, he wished to humanize this tribe of noble savages. But Marco possessed a far more extravagant and excitable temperament than the dutiful, self-effacing Franciscan friar. He did not just humanize the Mongols, he extolled them. He did not simply describe the Mongol way of life, he lived it.

INSPIRED BY Carpini's example, other travelers took to the Silk Road and returned to write of the wondrous and appalling things they had seen.

The missionary William of Rubruck, a Franciscan, set out with another Franciscan friar, Bartholomew of Cremona; a slave purchased in Constantinople; an interpreter; and several oxcarts adapted to crossing the Mongolian desert. His unsparing account of their adventures revealed the strangeness and adversity confronting those who dared to travel east. "When we arrived among those barbarians, it seemed to me," remarked William, "that we were stepping into another world."

He and his companions learned to bear the constant hunger, thirst, and loneliness of empty stretches of the Silk Road, but not, he wrote, "the wretchedness I endured when we came to inhabited places. I cannot find the words to tell you of the misery we suffered when we came to the encampments."

To William, the Mongols seemed more interested in drinking and carousing than in wreaking havoc on Christians. They were—and this came as a revelation to Europeans predisposed to regard them as barbarians—thoroughly human. In passages strongly prefiguring Marco Polo's acute observations, William commented on the makeup worn by the women. "It seemed to me her whole nose had been cut off, so snub-nosed was she," he wrote of a chieftain's wife. "She had greased this part of her face with some black unguent, and also her eyebrows, so that she appeared most hideous to us." He unabashedly conveyed the nature of Mongol domestic arrangements. Men took "as many wives as they would," and kept female slaves who served as concubines. When a maiden reached the age of marriage, her suitor claimed her by force, often with the help of the young woman's father.

Accounts such as these fascinated those few scholars, noblemen, and clergy able to read them. William's descriptions humanized the Mongols. They took care of their own, tolerated strangers, respected other religious beliefs—how different from more "civilized" Europeans they were in that regard—and lived in spiritual harmony with nature, both the seasons and the land. The Mongols, it turned out, were more complicated than even Carpini had reported.

IN SEARCH OF a rumored Christian khan, William of Rubruck endured terrible privations on various branches of the Silk Road. He was reduced, as Carpini had been, to eating cold millet, occasionally supplemented with semifrozen raw meat. William eventually made it to Karakorum, and he described this destination in all-too-realistic terms. It was, he said, a small village, not quite as large as Saint-Denis (the seat of French kings) outside Paris. Rather than a fortress of monolithic Mongol power, Karakorum showcased diversity. "It had two quarters. In that of the Saracens [Muslims] are the markets, and here a great many Tartars gather on account of the court," he noted. "The other is the quarter of the Cathayans [Chinese], all of whom are artisans. . . . There are twelve temples of idols of different nations, two mosques, . . . and one Christian church at the very end of the city." Karakorum was also a busy diplomatic center, receiving not just emissaries from the pope but delegations from emperors, sultans, and kings across Asia and Eastern Europe, all of them braving the intense cold.

Despite the atmosphere of religious variety and tolerance encouraged by the Mongols, William of Rubruck performed only six baptisms. He seems to have lost his theological bearings in this distant land, where religious beliefs did not conform to the strict categories with which he was familiar. He wrote of coming upon a man with a "cross painted in ink upon his hand," whom he took to be a Christian, "for he answered like a Christian to questions which I asked him." Yet the religious symbols that this man and others like him displayed did not strike Friar William as sufficiently orthodox. He concluded that the devotees were Christians who lacked adequate instruction in the practice of their religion.

WANDERING through Karakorum, William of Rubruck chanced on an "idol temple," where the inhabitants, he noted, "do courteously invite and lovingly entertain all messengers, every man according to his ability and station." He had located a Buddhist monastery, whose sacred aura seduced him with its parallel religious reality: "Their temples are built east and west; and upon the north side is a chamber, in [the] manner of a vestry. Sometimes, if it is a square temple, the vestry or choir place is built in the center. Within this chamber they place a chest long and broad like a table, and behind this, facing south, stands their principal idol. . . . They place other idols round about the principal one, all of them finely gilt over with pure gold; and upon the chest, which is in the manner of a table, they set candles and offerings. . . . They also have great bells like we have."

The Buddhist priests beguiled Friar William, as they would later fascinate Marco Polo. "All their priests have their heads and beards shaved quite close and they are clad in orange-coloured garments; and being once shaven, they lead a chaste life, in groups of a hundred or two hundred together in one cloister. On the days when they enter into their temples, they place two long benches inside. Upon these they sit facing the singing men in the choir. They have certain books in their hands, which sometimes they lay down upon the benches, and their heads are bare as long as they remain in the temple," he observed. "They read softly to themselves, hardly uttering any sound at all. Coming in amongst them, at the time of their devotions, and finding them all sitting mute, I attempted to get them to answer me, but could not by any means possible."

The Buddhist manuscripts proved more eloquent: "They begin to write at the top of their paper, drawing their lines right down; and so they read and multiply their lines from the left hand to the right. They do use certain papers and characters in their magical practices, and their temples are full of such short scrolls hung round."

William was sufficiently alert to detect other types of written communication. "The Cathayans write with a brush like painters use, and a single figure comprises several letters [and] signifies a word. The Tibet people write as we do, from left to right, and have characters quite similar to ours. The people of Tangut write from right to left as the Arabs do and multiply the lines going upwards."

Decades before Marco Polo appeared on the scene, William reported on the existence of currency printed on "paper made of cotton the length and breadth of a palm"—a system of commerce so far in advance of anything in the West that it mystified Europeans.

· · ·

WILLIAM ENGAGED the Buddhist monks in spirited theological debate, only to have his expectations confounded. When he inquired "what they believed concerning God," they replied, to the friar's dismay, "We believe there is only one God." That was not the anticipated answer; William expected to hear about idol worship and other heathen practices among these non-Christians.

He tried again: "Do you believe that he is a spirit or some bodily substance?"

"We believe that he is a spirit," came their reply.

Convinced this was an evasion, William demanded to know why, if they believed God to be a spirit, they made so many images to represent him. To this he added: "Since also you believe not that he was made man, why do you make him more like the image of a man than any other creature?"

The monks responded that William was mistaken; the images to which he referred did not represent God; they were tributes to the wealthy dead, whose relatives commissioned each image. "We, in remembrance of the dead, do reverence to it."

Surely this was a corrupt practice. William said scornfully, "You do these things only for the friendship and flattery of men."

"No, only for their memory." With that, the monks turned the tables. "Where is God?" they asked the friar.

"Where is your soul?" William shot back. His hosts replied that their souls resided in their bodies.

William launched into a harangue. "Is it not in every part of your body, ruling and guiding the whole body, and yet it is invisible? Even so God is everywhere and ruleth all things, and yet he is invisible, being understanding and wisdom itself."

Just as William was warming to his theme, his interpreter "became weary," and the debate ended abruptly.

A PALPABLE spiritual thaw lessened the grip of the Karakorum winter as the region's ruler, Möngke Khan, a grandson of Genghis Khan, explained to William that as God had given humans five fingers on each hand, so the Supreme Being had passed on various religious beliefs to different peoples. This vision of religious tolerance, deeply ingrained in the Mongol consciousness, challenged everything that William, as a Christian missionary, believed; yet he could not deny the appeal of the khan's point of view, or the implication that the totality of faith exceeded any single approach.

On the heels of this intriguing dialogue with William, Möngke expressed a guarded wish to establish diplomatic relations, or at least a dialogue, with the Christian West: "If you will obey us, send your ambassadors, that we may know whether you wish for peace or war."

William of Rubruck never delivered this message, but his mission, which had lasted from 1253 to 1255, achieved partial success. Henceforth, the Mongol Empire would take a greater interest in the West, at least in matters of trade, if not religion.

WITH EACH JOURNEY, and each subsequent written account, the world appeared to Europeans to be getting bigger and more chaotic rather than smaller and more manageable. The travelers emphasized the great distances and unavoidable hardships they endured, and the irreconcilable differences that characterized the innumerable countries, cultures, languages, customs, and religions they encountered. The reports of emissaries as varied as Benjamin of Tudela, Giovanni da Pian del Carpini, and William of Rubruck all told of a world beyond Europe that was complex, tumultuous, and menacing, but nonetheless porous.

One way of appreciating the magnitude of Marco Polo's accomplishment is to compare his account to those given by his predecessors. For all their fascination, the early observations were one-dimensional and literal. Marco, in contrast, freely mingled fact and fantasy, personal experience and legend, all of it buttressed by straightforward assessments of the people and places he encountered, and all of it energized by his braggadocio.

AS MARCO VENTURED into Afghanistan, he apparently lost himself in a series of idylls until he reached the remote province of Badakhshan in the northeast. Here, in what had been part of the ancient kingdom of Bactria, his characteristic purposefulness returned, as the trade route to the East began in earnest.

Marco Polo's Afghanistan extended north to Turkistan, northeast to China with its occupying Mongols, south to the Indian subcontinent, and west to Persia. A crossroads of cultures, languages, and reli-

gions, Afghanistan had evolved into a center of trade and transportation, its dry plains, lush valleys, and snowy peaks crisscrossed by foot-
paths, equine trails, and caravan routes suitable for merchants such as
the Polos.

This ancient network of trails had caught the attention of invaders,
who turned Afghanistan into a sprawling battleground over the centuries. In time, it fell to Seleucids, Ephthalites, and eventually Turks,
who ruled from the sixth century until the arrival of the Mongol
armies in the service of Genghis Khan.

No other invaders did as much damage to Afghanistan's delicate
infrastructure as the Mongols. Their numbers were immense; an army
of sixty or seventy thousand Mongol warriors on horseback would suddenly appear and overwhelm the region of their choice. The warriors
could fire as many as six arrows a minute on horseback, facing forward
or backward, at a full gallop. Their arrows darkening the sky, they
chased down their enemies wherever they hid. (During one campaign
in 1220, Genghis Khan himself rode into a mosque, slaughtering those
who had fled there for safety. Later, chests intended to hold the Koran
were filled with grain to feed the invaders' horses.) The Mongols' efficient armies destroyed the region's irrigation system and turned fertile
fields into the arid wastes confronting travelers like the Polos. Despite
their small numbers, the Mongols had made themselves into the masters of this realm through sheer force and superior military ability.
Their rapid and dramatic expansion into distant territories put all
potential enemies on notice that resistance would be met with annihi-
lation. The new Mongol order proved terrifying indeed.

YOUNG MARCO's descriptions of travel along the Silk Road conveyed the vulnerability of his small family. Letters assuring papal
protection for the Polo company were of no use in fending off high-
waymen or religious zealots. If Marco or his traveling companions
bore arms or other means of self-defense besides guile and cunning, he
never mentions them. Nor does he refer to any extraordinary measures
they may have taken to protect themselves against hunger, disease, or
the elements. A drought; a sandstorm; a debilitating disease; a rene-
gade squad of murderous thieves; jealous rivals; predators alerted by
the approaching travelers' scent; poor directions; a poisonous spring;
the lethal bite of a snake, insect, or scorpion; a parasite lurking in food

or underfoot; a sudden snowstorm or bolt of lightning—any of these common occurrences could have brought the expedition to a sudden end. No rescue party would have come looking for them, and few in Venice would have mourned their passing.

Despite these perils, the Polo company enjoyed several advantages. For one thing, the two elder Polos had come this way before. For another, the three Venetians were rarely alone. Wherever they went on the routes later known as the Silk Road, they passed other merchants, as well as holy men ranging from Nestorian Christians to Buddhists. The Silk Road, in reality, carried so much more than silk. And the Polos encountered an assortment of highly organized tradesmen and innkeepers who—for a price—served the needs of travelers before they departed in the predawn darkness and chill for the immense wasteland.

MARCO AND COMPANY spent three days riding their camels through a wasteland with "no dwelling nor food nor drink for the wayfarer except water; but grass enough for horses." Finally, with the greatest relief, they reached Badakhshan, a "large province," Marco writes, populated with Muslims, a "very great and broad realm which for length lasts quite twelve days' marches." The kings of Badakhshan, Marco believed, descended directly from Alexander the Great "and from his wife who was the daughter of Darius the Great who was lord of the great realm of Persia."

The Badakhshan that greeted Marco Polo was, like the Badakhshan of today, a lush oasis in the desert. To come upon it after weeks on dusty, twisting trails was to encounter a haven promising ease and delight for the exhausted wayfarer. As Marco immediately noticed, the city owed its wealth and notoriety more to its rubies than to legends of Alexander. The rubies, he explains, "are produced in the rocks of great mountains, and when they wish to dig them they are gotten with great trouble, for they make great caverns in the mountains with very great expense and trouble to find them, and go far underground as in these parts here they do who dig the veins of gold and silver." The king, according to Marco, dug for the gems himself, kept the most precious specimens, and killed anyone who dared to mine them without permission. "The king," Marco says, "does this for his own honor that the *balasci* [rubies] may be dear and of great value everywhere as they are, for if he let other men dig them and carry them through the world so many of them would be taken away that all the world would be full of them and they would not be so dear nor of so great value, so that the king would make little or no gain." The same principles applied to the sapphires in these mountains, as well as "ultramarine azure" (lapis lazuli), silver, copper, gold, and lead. Although Marco does not say so, it is likely that his father and uncle bargained for the gems with the king's representatives, trading gold or stones that they brought with them for rubies and sapphires, which they concealed by sewing into the folds of their cloaks, keeping them close at all times, day or night. Camels needed water and grass to survive, while merchants such as the Polos needed gems to thrive.

Marco's youthful imagination was caught by the sturdy horses of the area, who cantered over the stones without the protection of horseshoes. "They go in the mountains and on bad roads always, and do not hurt their feet, and the men gallop with them over the mountain slopes where other animals could not gallop," he marvels, "nor would they dare to gallop there." Marco reports with satisfaction a story that long ago in this region all horses were "born with a horn, with a mark, on the forehead like Bucephalus"—Alexander the Great's famous mount—"because mares had conceived from that very horse. But afterwards the whole breed of them was destroyed. And the breed of them was only in the power of an uncle of the king, and when he refused to allow the king to have any of them, he was put to death by him; and the wife out of spite for the death of the husband destroyed the said breed, and so it is lost."

In this region, Marco saw hawks and falcons above, and fields covered with grain underfoot, all dwarfed by steep, rugged mountains concealing towns that resembled fortresses.

AMID THIS spectacular setting, something peculiar befell the young Marco, about which he dropped only the slenderest of hints. "When he was in those parts he remained sick for about a year," he says of himself, "and when he was advised to go up to the mountain"—by whom he does not say—"he was well again." Those few words suggest an ordeal.

It is unlikely that he contracted malaria, as is often assumed, since there are no mosquitoes at that high altitude to carry the parasite. Instead, he may have suffered from the effects of syphilis, or severe

emotional problems. But more likely, he had tuberculosis. The disease
was prevalent in Europe during the years of his childhood. If he had
contracted tuberculosis then, the infection could have lain dormant,
and become active years later in response to stress induced by travel.
He would have developed a fever and a cough, for which opium, or an
opium derivative, was a common treatment, and as he recovered, he
might have become addicted to the remedy.

In Marco's day, Badakhshan was Afghanistan's leading producer of
the opium poppy (*Papaver somniferum*), and Afghanistan was, and
remains, the leading opium producer in the world. The colorful fields
through which he passed produced enormous quantities of poppies,
but he would not have considered them flowers of evil. Their bright
blossoms, gently swaying in the fresh breeze, looked harmless enough
to a lad, as were many of their uses. Tiny black poppy seeds were used
in cooking, imparting their nutty flavor to sweet pastries.

If he became an opium user for medical reasons, or simply to experience the drug's effects, he would have begun by ingesting the poppy,
and perhaps progressed to smoking it, or more precisely, its resin.
(Injection did not exist at the time.) One explanation for the unusual
length of time that he languished in Badakhshan could be that in the
course of trying to recover from a febrile illness, he became dependent
on opium, and had to detoxify—a protracted and agonizing process.
The symptoms of withdrawal that he might have suffered include nau-
sea, sweating, cramps, vomiting, diarrhea, depression, loss of appetite,
anxiety, and rapid changes in mood. He would have become edgier,
moodier, more sensitive to light, and more highly suggestible. Where
his father and uncle saw a road or a bridge or a storm, Marco might
have seen evidence of impersonal cosmic forces at work, sweeping
them toward an inchoate destiny.

Fortunately, the mountains of Afghanistan were supremely benefi-
cial to his health. "On the tops of the mountains the air is so pure and
the sojourn there so health-giving that if, while he lives in the cities
and houses built on the plain and in the valleys near the mountains, a
man catches fevers of any kind, . . . he immediately climbs the mountains and, resting there two or three days, the sickness is driven away,"
Marco marvels.

There is a sound medical basis for his confidence. High altitude and
fresh air have long been known as effective treatments for tuberculosis.
The low-oxygen mountain air inhibits the growth of mycobacteria,

including those that cause tuberculosis. And exposure to sunlight—abundant at high altitudes—increases the body's vitamin D, which in turn destroys pathogens. In all, the mountains of Afghanistan were a mixed blessing, promoting Marco's rapid recovery from tuberculosis (if that was his affliction) even while snaring the young man in the coils of addiction.

No matter what happened to Marco at Badakhshan, he departed a more seasoned traveler, able to cope with the hardships and dangers of life along the Silk Road.

CHAPTER FIVE

High Plains Drifters

But oh! that deep romantic chasm which slanted
Down the green hill athwart a cedarn cover!
A savage place!

THE DELAY at Badakhshan placed the Polo company a full
year behind schedule; it was now 1273, they had been away
for two years, and their journey east had only begun.

Once Marco recovered, they proceeded along the Silk Road to
higher altitudes, surrounded by wild sheep—*Ovis ammon.* "They go
sometimes in one flock four hundred, five hundred, six hundred," he
says. "And many of them are taken, but they never fail." These gentle
creatures later became known as "Marco Polo sheep," and they were
prized by the region's capable if slightly desperate hunters. "They are
very good archers," he writes of the hunters, "and the greater part of
them are dressed in skins of beasts because they have great dearth of
other garments of cloth, for woolen garments are either quite impossible to be had there or are exceedingly dear." For that reason, "the great
ladies of this land and the gentle wear cloth."

Women dressed in this manner caught Marco's attention, if not his
fancy, and he offers a description based on a careful personal inspection: "They wear garments like trousers down to the feet like men such
as I shall tell you, and make them of cotton and of very fine silk, with
musk inside. And they put much cloth into their trousers. There are
some ladies who put quite a hundred ells"—equivalent to three feet,
nine inches—"of very fine stuff made of flax and of cotton cloth,
wrapped about the body like swathing bands, . . . and make them
pleated all round."

The fat-bottomed sheep climbing the mountains may have inspired women in the area to exaggerate their physiques. "They do this to show that they have large hips to become beautiful, because in that region their men delight in fat women, and she who appears more stout below the waist seems to them more beautiful," and not only that, but "more glorious among other women." Marco's exploration of the erotic is making only its second appearance here, as he languishes in the aftermath of his illness. He is still timid compared with all that he will later set down.

MARCO SHIFTED HIS gaze from these oddly appealing women to the arduous trail ahead. There was a twelve-day-long trek upriver, past lively villages populated with Muslims, Nestorian Christians, and Buddhists who had come this way on the Silk Road. Eventually the Polo company, with its camels and donkeys, reached another, and lesser, province that Marco called Vocan, which was "subject to the rule of the lord of Badakhshan." After a brief stopover, the party ascended the steep trail again, "almost always going up through mountains, and one rises so much that the top of those mountains is the highest place, or one of the highest, in the whole world." For once, Marco did not exaggerate. His party was ascending the Terak Pass, through the Pamir, the traditional dividing line between East and West, heading toward the farthest and wildest western border of China.

In Turkic, *pamir* indicates high-altitude rolling grasslands. The Pamir highlands were passable only during cool, dry summers. In season, the Pamir offered pleasant, expansive meadows, unlike anything in Western Europe. Trees were a rarity, as were rivers, but runoff from glaciers provided water. The region's sunlight was harsh and seemingly gray, barely filtered by the thin atmosphere. Simply breathing posed a great hardship for the wayfarers; they were traversing a region that came to be known as "the roof of the world," fourteen thousand feet above sea level, surrounded by the highest mountain peaks on earth— Mount Everest among them. The extreme altitude's thin atmosphere made cooking, or even boiling water, inordinately difficult. Marco could not calculate the altitude of the Pamir, but he noticed that "flying birds there are none because of the high place and intense cold, and because they could have nothing to eat there."

For the Polos' determined little band, the trek through the Pamir required stamina and patience to venture where not even birds would go. They were not the first to test their strength against these ancient mountain passes. Nomads had traversed this harsh landscape for centuries, and along this trail Kublai Khan's grandfather, Genghis Khan, once led his Mongol troops on their murderous conquests.

The trek through the Pamir took the Polo company across some of the most extraordinary geologic formations on the planet. The Pamir forms a quadrangle about 150 miles long on each side, marked by snow-capped peaks. The highest mountain ranges in the world radiate from the Pamir: the Hindu Kush extends to the northwest, the Tian Shan—"Celestial Mountains"—system to the northeast, the Karakorum and Himalaya ranges to the southeast.

The region started to emerge about forty million years ago when the Indian subcontinent collided with Eurasia, a notable instance of plate tectonics—the movement, occasionally violent, of the geologic plates that form Earth's crust, or lithosphere. In the case of the Pamir, the deformation caused by the immense collision spread all the way to the interior of Eurasia, uplifting Tibet, and created a fault near the Mongolian border. (The collision and deformation continue to this day.) For geologists, the Pamir represents an unusual form of horizontal tectonism, in which colliding plates move sideways as well as up and down. In this case, the horizontal movement may have been caused by the plates' cooling and shrinking over millions of years.

Here, on the roof of the world, the Polo company encountered a plateau, an astonishing Shangri-la created by these geologic forces. Marco's appreciative portrait of this changeless scene remains accurate today: "When one is in that high place, then he finds a large plain between two mountains in which is very beautiful pasture and a great lake from which runs a very beautiful river, both good and large." Even more remarkably, "Up there in that plain is the best and fattest pasture of the world that can be found; for a thin horse or ox or any thin beast (let it be as thin as you please) put there to graze grows very fat in ten days." He writes of "multitudes of wild sheep," distinguished by enormous horns, "some quite six palms long," from which shepherds made bowls and other vessels, as well as fencing to pen in other animals. Yet nature was not as peaceful as it seemed in the Pamir. By night, wolves descended from the slopes to "eat up and kill many of those sheep."

For twelve days the travelers rode through this savage paradise, finding neither "dwelling nor inn, but in the course of the road it is desert and nothing is found there to eat." They suffered from the rapidly increasing cold and thinning air. Their campfires, starved for oxygen, were dull and stunted, scarcely sufficient to cook their meals.

At the plain's end, they followed the trail for another forty days through mountain valleys and slopes, their way marked by piles of animal bones left by previous travelers. As before, their isolation was complete: "Not in all these forty days' marches is there dwelling nor inn, nor even food, but the travelers are obliged to carry that which they need with them." There was no caravansary to offer security for the lonely travelers, nor even the evanescent companionship of the road.

WHEN MARCO at last encountered humanity in the form of mountain dwellers, their primitive state only increased his apprehensiveness. "They are idolaters, even more unfathomable than Muslims," he writes, "and very savage, and they live by nothing but the chase of animals." As evidence of their savagery, they wore only animal skins—they were "a mighty cruel and evil people." Despite the cold and the altitude, the little Polo company picked up the pace, and hurried past without incident.

THE WORST hardships of the Pamir abated by the time the Polo company reached the thriving oasis town of Khotan, an important stop on the Silk Road, at the edge of the Taklimakan Desert in western China. The region was forbidding in the extreme. The name Taklimakan was said to mean "Desert of Death" or "Place of No Return," and temperatures varied as much as 68 degrees Fahrenheit in the course of a day. By this point, a bewildered and parched Marco may have thought he was in the middle of nowhere, and in a sense he was correct; Khotan is farther from the ocean than nearly any other place in the world.

Although nominally loyal to Kublai Khan, Khotan had once been a center of Buddhism, and the lingering Buddhist presence here afforded Marco his first serious exposure to the spiritual system and philosophy that at first repelled him, then intrigued him, and finally won his admiration. The ancestors of the inhabitants were Persian or Indic immigrants from the west and Chinese from the east, who had settled in a fertile strip of land along a river flowing north from the

Kunlun Mountains. China conquered Khotan in AD 73; it was succeeded soon after by the Kushana empire from the west, and later on
by Tibetan forces. Under Tibetan influence, Buddhism arrived from
the East via the Silk Road and flourished here, and temples populated
by tens of thousands of Buddhist monks abounded until AD 1000,
when Islam abruptly dislodged the Buddhists from their ancient seat.
Nevertheless, evidence of Buddhism's profound impact on Khotan was
all around, in the form of images of Buddha ("idols," Marco calls
them), and distant monasteries clinging to mountain overhangs.

If Marco had overcome his repugnance to "idolatry" and troubled
to familiarize himself with Buddhism, he would have learned that the
Buddha taught that life is experienced as suffering, brought about by
one's attachment to oneself and to people and objects, all of which are
impermanent, and by the resultant craving, which nothing can satisfy.
He would have heard that the Buddha said that all sentient beings,
including animals and insects, are caught in a cycle of suffering, or
samsara, and the results of their actions, or karma, simply create more
attachment and more suffering. He would have heard that this cycle
continues even after death, since Buddhism held that living creatures
are reborn. He would have been relieved, then, to hear that there was a
way to escape from the cycle of suffering and to achieve enlightenment, known as nirvana. Had he looked up to the monasteries in the
mountains, he would have seen examples of men and women who had
renounced their attachments and become monks and nuns, meditating
and studying Buddhist scriptures night and day. A traveler like Marco
would not have found this so strange, after all, and might have seen
more than a little of himself in the Buddhists' scheme of things; like
them, he had given up his home, comforts, and possessions. Like them,
he lived a life of danger and anxiety, of loneliness, of suffering from
extreme heat and cold, from thirst, and from deprivation. His life was
as empty as the trade route he traveled, his pleasures were fitful and
his prospects unknowable, and his goal was distant and seemingly
unattainable.

After the deprivations endured while traversing the roof of the
world, Marco had learned to appreciate the luxuries that Khotan
offered the traveler. The inhabitants, he says, are "noble"—especially
in comparison to the odd creatures he had passed in the mountains—
and the city itself is "noble," as was the surrounding region. "It is fertile and it has abundance of all things needful for the life of man," he

says. "And there grows cotton enough, and flax and hemp, and oil, wheat, corn, and wine and the rest is as done rightly in our lands." But then he adds smugly that the inhabitants "are not men of arms, but mean enough and very cowardly." This meant that he felt relatively safe in their midst.

Having replenished their supplies in Khotan, Marco and his company, trying to make up for time lost in Badakhshan, set out once again for Kublai Khan's court.

HEADING EAST, the Polo company faced more than four thousand miles of grassy plains interrupted by occasional mountain ranges. This terrain was known by its Russian name, the Steppe, and it was divided into two parts. The western Steppe extended from the Danube River to the Altai mountain range in Siberia; often described as a sea of grass, it was an area through which rivers and streams flowed freely. The open spaces of the western Steppe enabled caravans and horsemen to travel along the trails and roads that ran its length and breadth.

The eastern Steppe, extending into Mongolia, was drier and harsher. Grass for grazing was far more sparse, and free-flowing streams yielded to infrequent oases. Negotiating the rigors of the eastern Steppe required endurance and indifference to the elements from those who dared to venture into its expanse.

FIVE DAYS after leaving Khotan, the Polo company arrived in the province of Pem, inhabited by Muslims and enriched by a river "running through it where precious stones are found that one calls jasper and chalcedony"—all very interesting to note, but the inviting women of Pem made a much stronger impression on the young traveler: "When a woman has a husband, and it happens that he leaves her to go on a journey, and provided that he must stay away from twenty or thirty days upwards, the woman who stays home, as soon as her husband is set from home to go on a journey, takes another husband till his return." And the men, on their journeys, took other wives. It was only a matter of time until Marco succumbed to the lure of the lonely women of the open spaces.

.   .   .

WHEREVER HE RAMBLED, people were on the move. In Ciarcian, the Mongols were plundering the region as they had since the days of Genghis Khan. "When it happens that an army of Tartars, as well friends and enemies, passes through the country of Ciarcian, if they are enemies they carry off all their goods, and if they are friends they kill and eat their cattle." Those men who considered themselves enemies of the Mongols adapted to the onslaught by fleeing with their wives, children, animals, and possessions across the desert sands for two or three days "into other places where they knew that there was pasture to be found and good water." There they could wait until the army passed. Marco's description reveals some compassion for the uprooted villagers, but at the same time, their stratagems for survival struck him as pathetic and cowardly. Yet he had not come face to face with the Mongols himself, and could only guess at the terror their ruthlessness inspired.

The Polo company pushed on through five more days of desert, occasionally stopping at oases—some sweet, others "very bad"—until they reached Lop, a name synonymous with the edge of the unknown. An immense, dry, salt-encrusted lake bed covering extreme northwestern China, the wasteland was notorious for its special hazards, which seduced and misled even the most wary travelers.

"LOP IS A great city at the end of the desert, from which one enters into the very great desert which is called the Desert of Lop," Marco records, noting that Kublai Khan's rule extended even here. "All things needful for travelers who wish to cross the desert are made ready in this city," he warns. "I tell you that those who wish to cross the great desert must rest in this town at the least a week to refresh themselves and their beasts. At the end of a week they must take food for a month for themselves and for their beasts, because they take so long to pass across that desert."

The scale of the desert defied the imagination, but Marco tried to make his European audience, accustomed to a dense, compact landscape, comprehend something of its emptiness, reporting that crossing even the narrowest portion would require a month's hard riding. Traversing its length was simply beyond human endurance and ingenuity: "Lengthwise it cannot be passed because of the great length of it, for it would be impossible to carry enough food. . . . One travels for a month of marches without finding any dwelling. It is all barren mountains and plains of sand and valleys, and nothing to eat is found there." There was sweet water, it was true, "but no water that a sufficiently large company could take, but as much as is needed for quite fifty or a hundred men, but not yet with their beasts." Fifty struck him as the largest number that could form a caravan, fifty hostages to heat and sandstorms and elusive water supplies. "You must always go a day and a night finding nothing before you find water to drink in this way. Moreover, I tell you that in three places in four one finds bitter and salt and evil water." No livestock, he reports, nor birds, "because they would find nothing to eat here."

Marco's stark characterization of the Desert of Lop was entirely accurate. The region, at an altitude of slightly under three thousand feet, is nearly flat across its length and breadth. Underfoot, a mixture of fine yellow or yellow-gray gravel and clayey sand extends to the horizon in every direction. At times the windstorms the Polos encountered became so powerful that they swept the desert bare of sand, with the wind-borne granules blasting rocks below, and carving furrows as deep as twenty feet, creating a series of undulating dunes hypnotic to the traveler. Marco does not indicate the time of year they made their crossing, but if he and his party ventured into the desert in spring, the desert would have been, in the words of another visitor, "so heavily charged with dust as to be a veritable pall of desolation." In this moonscape, daily temperatures fluctuated wildly. Marco endured highs of over 100 degrees Fahrenheit by day and subfreezing temperatures at night.

Amid the desolation of the Desert of Lop, Marco found remarkable beauty and a palpable sense of the supernatural. Like a saint of ancient times, he went into the desert and he beheld visions, especially at night, when the senses are alert and fears multiply. "There dwell many spirits that make for the wayfarers great and wonderful illusions to make them perish," he says. "For while any company of merchants or others is crossing the desert . . . , often it happens that they hear spirits malignant in the air, talking in a way that they seem to be their companions, for they call them sometimes by their names, and many times they make them, believing that they are some of them, follow those voices and go out of the right way so they are never reunited to their fellows and found, and news of them is never heard."

Afraid of being taken for a mere fabulist, Marco emphasizes the veracity of his description: "Again I tell you that not only by night does this appear, but often even by day men hear these voices of spirits, and it often seems to you that you hear many instruments of music sounding in the air, and especially drums more than other instruments, and the clash of weapons." At other times, the singing sands sounded like a "rush of people in another direction." Distracted travelers chased after the illusion, hoping to catch up with "the march of the cavalcade," only to find by day that they were hopelessly lost, tricked by spirits, "and many not knowing of these spirits come to an evil end."

Travelers who braved this unnerving stretch of the Silk Road developed techniques to defeat the dangerous illusion: "Those who wish to pass that way and cross this desert must take very great care of themselves that they not be separated from their fellows for any reason, and that they go with great caution; they must hang bells on the necks of their horses and animals to hear them continually so that they may not sleep, and may not be able to wander." Even in daylight precautions proved necessary: "Sometimes by day spirits come in the form of a company to see who has stayed behind and he goes off the way, and then they leave him to go alone in the desert and perish." At other times, these spirits "put themselves in the form of an army and have come charging toward them, who, believing they were robbers, have taken flight and, having left the highway, no longer knowing how to find the way, for the desert stretches very wide, have perished miserably of hunger."

To make sure that his readers understand that he is reporting fact, not legend, concerning the many deceptions wrought by the singing sands, Marco repeats, "They are wonderful things to hear and difficult to believe, which these spirits do; but indeed it is as is told, and much more wonderful."

Although Marco's account strains credulity, as if it were the result of too much sun and too little water, he was faithfully reporting a frequently observed phenomenon, "Singing Sands," caused by the action of wind on dunes. The resulting hum has been likened variously to the strumming of a mysterious harp, or booming, or chanting, and has been detected throughout Mongolia; in China, where it was known as "booming sand"; and even in South America. In the thirteenth century, the Chinese scholar Ma Duanlin said of this treacherous region: "You see nothing in any direction but the sky and the sands, without the slightest trace of a road, and travelers find nothing to guide them but the bones of men and beasts and the droppings of camels. During the passage of this wilderness you hear sounds, sometimes of singing, sometimes of wailing, and it has often happened that travelers going aside to see what these sounds may be, have strayed from their course and been entirely lost, for they were the voices of spirits and goblins"—just as Marco Polo describes. In the nineteenth century, Charles Darwin reported the same phenomenon in his account of the voyage of the *Beagle*. In Chile's Atacama desert could be found a hill known as El Bramador, "The Roarer" or "The Bellower." "As far as I understood," he wrote, "the hill was covered by sand, and the noise was produced only when people, by ascending it, put the sand in motion."

Even today, the Singing Sands shift in the wind, sending out their hypnotic howl.

AT THE NORTHERN EDGE of central China, the Polo company emerged from the perilous Desert of Lop into the remote province of Tangut, known as the Western State. About a century earlier, the region had declared independence from China, and now owed allegiance to the distant Kublai Khan. Marco found evidence of Nestorian Christianity even here, but Buddhism, the official religion of the Tanguts, prevailed. It was, as Marco notes, a place of intense devotion, filled with "many abbeys and monasteries."

For the first time, Marco took more than passing notice of the Buddhist "idols," and despite his reflexive attempt to dismiss them, they made a lasting impression. Some images extended "ten paces." They were fashioned variously of wood, earthenware, stone, or bronze, and, most impressively, they were "all covered with gold and very well worked and wonderfully." He even found a few good words for the "idolaters"—that is, the Buddhists—who "live more decently than the others, for they keep themselves from . . . sensuality and other improprieties." And yet, he notes, "if a woman invites them in love they can lie with her without sin, but if they first invite the woman they reckon it for sin. But I tell you that if they find any man who has lain with a woman unnaturally, they condemn him to death."

The more Marco considered "idol" worship, the more analogies to Christianity he found: "They make the festivals of their idols at different times as we do of our saints, and they have something like the calendar where the feasts of their idols are arranged on fixed days."

Entering deeper into the Buddhist ethos, he tried to explain the lunar calendar: "They have a moon calendar just as we have the monthly, and in this way they reckon the time of year. And they have certain moons when all the monks of the idolaters for anything in the world would not kill beasts nor flying birds, nor shed blood, for five consecutive days of the week, or four, or at least three, nor would they eat flesh that was killed in those five days, and they hold them in reverence as we Christians hold in reverence the Friday and the Sabbath, and other vigils."

Later, he perceived still more similarities between Buddhist and Christian forms of observance. "You may know quite truly that all idols have their proper days dedicated to them, on which days they make solemnities and reverence and great feasts in their names every year, as our saints have in the special days." Sacred and profane seemed to intermingle, indeed, to be interchangeable. It was all very baffling, and bracing, for the young Venetian.

MARCO'S DESCRIPTION of the size of Buddhist monasteries would leave Europeans in disbelief. Some establishments sheltered two thousand monks, "who serve the idols according to their custom, who dress more decently with more religious garments than all other men do." The monks "wear the crown of the head shaved and the beard shaved," he accurately notes, "beyond the fashion of laymen. They make the greatest feasts for their idols with greater singing and with greater light than were ever seen."

Outside the monastery walls, anarchy reigned. "The lay people can take up to thirty wives," Marco says. "He holds the first wife for the greatest and best. If he sees that any of his wives is old and is not good and that she does not please him he can well put her away and can take to wife the sister of the wife divorced, and do with her as he likes, and take another, if he wishes. Again, they take cousins for wives, and they are also allowed to take the wife of their father, except their mother, and also the wives of brothers or every other relation." Pondering this alternative morality, he concludes in disgust, "They live in this way like animals with no law."

In contrast to this sensual indulgence and anarchy was the life—"so very hard and rough"—led by the *sensin*, whom Marco calls "men of very great abstinence according to their custom." They did everything in their power to avoid sensual indulgence in any form; even the food they ate was as bland as possible, "nothing but semolina and bran, that is, the husks that are left from wheat flour," Polo learned. "They prepare it as we prepare it for swine; for they do take that semolina, that is, bran, and put it in hot water to make it soft and leave it to stay there some time till the whole head of grain is removed from the husk, and then they take it out and eat it washed like this without any substantial taste. And that is their food." Nor did their self-discipline regarding food end there: "They fast many times a year"—a small loss, considering how restrictive their diet was—"and eat nothing in the world but bran and drink water, and stay much in prayer, so that is a hard life beyond measure." No flicker of family life warmed this bleak existence of self-denial and spiritual devotion, for the monks "would not take a wife for anything in the world." Even their clothes, black and blue, made of the "commonest and coarsest sackcloth," seemed designed to inflict discomfort. As might be expected, they slept only on "very hard and cheap mats."

"They lead a harder life than any men in the world," Marco observes, more in despair than admiration.

AFTER CONTEMPLATING these instances of extreme self-denial, Marco considered the most repugnant practice of all: cremation. The custom, so alien to his sensibilities, paradoxically humanized its practitioners in his eyes; he realized that they fervently believed in the soul and in an afterlife. Having made this leap of imaginative identification, he entered into their spiritual life to the extent that he could. He noted the mourners' absolute dependence on the calculations of astrologers and necromancers, who, he tells us, determined the time of cremation and burial according to the time of birth: "When the necromancer or astrologer has heard it, he makes his divination by diabolical arts and says to his kinsmen when he has done his arts and seen under what constellation, planet, and sign he was born, the day and the hour that the body must be burned." The process could delay the burial for weeks, even months, during which time the deceased's family had to keep the body in their home, "waiting for the planets to be propitious to them and not contrary, for they would never make burning till the diviners tell them that it is good to burn."

To accommodate the astrologer's—and the planets'—demands,

family members constructed a painted coffin of thick boards, "well joined together," placed the body inside it, and sealed the coffin with pitch and lime, covered it with silk, and fumigated it with camphor and other spices so that "the body does not stink at all to those of the house." Each day that the body lay in residence, the family set out meals consisting of "bread and wine and flesh to eat and to drink just as if he were alive." There was no way to rid the house of this demanding guest until the planets permitted; anyone who defied the astrologer's ruling would "suffer great pain."

The family lavished care even after the corpse was removed from the house: "The kinsmen of the dead have made a small house of canes or of rods with its porch, covered with the richest cloth of silk and gold according to their power, in the middle of the road. And when the dead is carried before this house so adorned they are stopped and the men of the house place the body on the ground at the foot of the pavilion, and lay wine and flesh enough on the ground before the dead, thinking that the spirit of the dead is somewhat refreshed and receives strength from it, since he must be present to see the body burned."

Another custom, this one designed to guarantee the deceased's status in the afterlife, caught Marco's fancy. "When he is carried to the place where he must be burned," he says, "his kinsmen have painted images of men and women cut out of sheets of paper"—another technological innovation—"made from the bark of trees, and have the names of the kinsmen written so that their bodies are burnt, and horses and camels and sheep and other animals; and papers likewise in the form of money as large as bezants"—the coin of Byzantium. "And they have all of these things thrown into the fire and burnt with the body, and say that in the other world the dead man will have with him as many slaves and maids and horses and coins, and as many beasts and as many sheep as they have paper ones burnt for love of him that they place before the body, and so he will live there in wealth and honor."

BY THIS POINT in Marco Polo's narrative, a subtle but significant shift in tone has taken place, as though Marco had seized the pen from Rustichello's hand and begun to write down his adventures in his own words, rather than rely on an amanuensis. Until now, the narrator has engaged in a dutiful exercise in the pilgrimage genre. Henceforth, not even Rustichello's hand would restrain Marco, who sensed a greater purpose and depth to his narrative and his experience—something more epic, comprehensive, and nuanced, on the order of Herodotus's *Histories*, a compendium of vanished civilizations and fallen empires. Gradually, the *Travels* opened onto wider vistas in space and time suggested by the exhilarating landscapes spreading before him, as well as their enticing inhabitants.

The longer Marco spent among the people of Tangut, the more he cast off his shyness and prudery, and spoke freely about their lives, which in turn revealed his own sexual awakening. As his narrative continued, a new Marco Polo gradually emerged; he was less pious and self-effacing, and more eager to learn about and, by implication, participate in the unfamiliar but beguiling world all around him.

THE WOMEN of Kamul (now called Hami), which adjoined the province of Tangut, finally brought Marco out of himself. The people of the region as a whole struck him as wonderfully likeable children, freely sharing food and drink with "the wayfarers who pass that way." The men, "greatly given to amusement," passed their days in playing instruments and singing, in reading and writing, and in participating in "great bodily enjoyment," especially with travelers such as the Polos. But it was the women who utterly captivated Marco.

"These people have such a custom," he confides. "If a stranger comes to his house to lodge, [a man] is too much delighted at it, and receives him with great joy, and labors to do everything to please," instructing his "daughters, sisters, and other relations to do all that the stranger wishes," even to the point of leaving his house for several days while "the stranger stays with his wife in the house and does as he likes and lies with her in a bed just as if she were his wife, and they continue in great enjoyment. All the men of this city and province are thus cuckolded by their wives; but they are not the least ashamed of it. And the women are beautiful and vivacious and always ready to oblige." And one more thing can be assumed: they were ready to oblige young Marco Polo, just coming into manhood.

Yes, he admits, it could be said that this licentious behavior dishonored the women and men of Kamul, "but I tell you that because of the general custom which is in all that province; and is very pleasing to their idols when they give so good a reception to wayfarers in need of rest." Even more remarkable, the family unit remained intact: "All the women are very fair and gay and very wanton and most obedient to their husbands' order, and greatly enjoy this custom."

Although his description seems more fanciful than real, more ironic parable than reliable reportage, Marco is discussing a well-established custom of the region and an exception to "village endogamy," in which the people of the same community intermarry to preserve assets and bloodlines. Endogamy brings with it the hazard of incest and birth defects. Exogamy, or marriage outside the clan, refreshes a depleted gene pool. If the outsiders were nomadic, as Marco suggests, the replenishing of the gene pool would be accomplished without challenging the existing order. Lonely wayfarers like him would deposit their seed and move on.

THERE WERE, however, repercussions from the world beyond the isolated hamlets through which Marco and the other travelers were passing. The reach of the bloodthirsty Mongols, about whom Marco had heard dire reports, extended even to this remote mountain region. He repeats a disturbing account of the behavior of the area's former ruler, Möngke Khan, concerning exogamy, which in this part of the world took the form of inviting strangers to bed the wives of others.

As Marco reminds his readers, Möngke Khan, one of the grandchildren of Genghis Khan, had come to power in 1250, a little more than twenty years before Marco entered the lands controlled by the Mongols. During his brief reign, Möngke attempted to establish a reliable postal system, essential for the administration of a great empire. He restrained the military campaigns that had once wreaked havoc across thousands of miles of Steppe and mountainous regions alike. And he respected local customs. In the emerging Mongol society, women had more independence than their Western and Islamic counterparts. They served in the military, remaining hidden during combat but joining the fight if an emergency made that necessary. Under Möngke, all worshipped as they chose, and variations of Buddhism, Islam, and Christianity flourished.

But the khan's tolerance did not extend to the women of Kamul. The women's lustful behavior occasioned opprobrium rather than the incredulity and mirth that Marco displayed. Once Möngke learned of it, he levied "great penalties to prevent it." Wayfarers such as the Polos would have to stay in "public lodgings," not private homes, to prevent the "shaming" of the householders' wives.

Möngke had his way for three years, although the inhabitants of Kamul remained resentful. Matters worsened when their crops failed and sickness visited one household after another—misfortunes they took to mean they had to restore their customs if prosperity and health were to return. "They sent their ambassadors," Marco reports, "who took a great and beautiful present and carry it to Möngke and pray him that so great a wrong with so great loss to them, and danger, should not be done."

Möngke "joyfully" received the ambassadors of Kamul; he listened carefully to their plea and even appeared sympathetic to their plight. And then the khan spoke: "For my part I have done my duty; but since you wish your shame and contempt so much, then you may have it. Go and live according to your customs, and make your wives charitable gifts to travelers." With that, Marco says, "he revoked the order."

The ambassadors returned to Kamul "with the greatest joy of the whole people, and from that time till now they have always kept up and still keep up that custom."

MARCO TOOK PAINS to describe Möngke Khan as a wise and compassionate ruler, but in the historical record the khan emerges as an emotional and brutal martinet.

On one occasion, Möngke decided to punish seventy officers who he believed had plotted against him. The method of execution was traditionally Mongol: forcing stones into their mouths. In 1252, he sat in judgment on another group of subversives. One princess in particular, Ogul Gaimish, incurred his wrath when she refused to declare her loyalty to him. He ordered her hands and legs to be sewn up in a leather bag. He then stripped her naked to cross-examine her while she protested that no man except for a king had ever seen her in that condition. He declared both Ogul Gaimish and her mother guilty of trying to kill him by means of magic spells. As soon as he had pronounced his judgment, he ordered the two women rolled up in rugs and drowned. He also directed that Ogul Gaimish's two chief counselors be put to death.

SIXTEEN DAYS' march from Kamul across a "little desert," the Polo company came upon a natural wonder in the form of asbestos, which, like so much else in China, was scarcely known in the West. Nowadays, airborne asbestos fibers are notorious for their association with serious respiratory illness, including cancer, but in Marco's day, fabrics woven of asbestos were held in high regard as the equal of gold and fit for the burial shrouds of Eastern kings. Following the convention of the era, Marco called the substance "salamander," after the tiny, lizard-like animal that was supposedly impervious to fire. He immediately grasped the military implications of a fireproof material.

"In this mountain is found a good vein from which salamander is made that cannot be burnt if it is thrown into the fire," he reports. The salamander is neither beast nor serpent, he explains, and "it is not true that those clothes are of the hair of an animal that lives in fire, as they say in our country."

Marco tries to dispel the tenacious European belief that the sala-mander cloth had such a fantastic origin, explaining that he had become acquainted with a Turkish merchant named Çulficar, "who was very knowing in my judgment and trustworthy," and who had for three years supervised production of salamander—or asbestos—from these mountainside mines for the khan himself. To demonstrate just how far asbestos was from being the byproduct of a supernatural crea-ture, Marco furnishes a careful description of its manufacture. "When one has dug from the mountains some of that vein," he writes, "it is twisted together and makes thread like wool. And therefore when one has this vein he has it dried in the sun, and then when it is dry has it pounded in a great copper mortar," washed with water, "and only that thread like wool of which I told you stays on top of the water, and all the earth clinging there, which is worthless, falls off." The resulting thread was spun into cloth and towels. "When the towels are made I tell you that they are not at all white, and they are brown when they are taken from the loom. But when they wish to make them white they put them in the fire and leave them to stay there a space of an hour, and when it is taken out the towel becomes very white, like snow."

Expecting to be disbelieved, he insists, "I have seen it with my eyes put into the fire and come back very white." No fire-dwelling serpent is involved, and all the popular tales to that effect are nothing but "lies and fables." With such statements, Marco demonstrates that he could demolish old myths as readily as he generated new ones.

. . .

IN CAMPÇIO, yet another ill-defined stop along the Silk Road, the Polo company rested once again. The usually expansive Marco furnishes only this cryptic note concerning the extended interlude: "Master Niccolò and Master Maffeo and Master Marco stayed about one year in this city for their business, which is not worth mentioning."

By the time they mounted their camels and donkeys again, it was 1274, according to the Christian calendar. Marco was turning twenty. The Polos had been traveling the Sericulture Superhighway for three years, and they were still more than two thousand miles from their destination, the court of Kublai Khan.

CHAPTER SIX

The Secret History of the Mongols

In Xanadu did Kubla Khan
A stately pleasure dome decree:
Where Alph, the sacred river, ran
Through caverns measureless to man. . . .

WITH EVERY MILE that Marco Polo traveled along the Silk Road, he became ever more aware of the grandeur of the Mongol Empire, and the mystique surrounding the founder of the Mongol dynasty, Genghis Khan, reviled throughout Europe. Yet he has this to say concerning the ruthless warrior: "Genghis Khan was a man very upright: eloquent, and of great valor and of great wisdom and of great prowess." Continuing in this boldly revisionist vein, Marco insists: "I tell you that when this man was chosen for king he ruled with such justice and moderation that he was loved by all and reverenced not as lord but almost as God, so that when his good fame spread through many lands, all the Tartars of the world who were scattered through those strange countries willingly held him with reverence and obedience for lord."

Marco had seen for himself the havoc wreaked by the armies of Genghis Khan in Badakhshan and elsewhere—the cities lying in ruins, the houses burned to their foundations, the displaced populace living in exile while the Mongol invaders fed on their riches and infrastructure. But after three long years on the Silk Road, Marco had to express his hard-won admiration for the founder of the Mongol dynasty. To the young Venetian, only Alexander the Great approached Genghis in accomplishment.

Temüjin—Genghis's original name—was born in about 1162 into

one of Mongolia's ruling clans, and came of age amid feuding tribes. Rivals poisoned his father, and Temüjin became an orphan at the age of nine. As he matured, he familiarized himself with Mongol military tactics, such as raiding camps and stealing horses. He learned to wield patronage, and recruited allies known as *nökhör* to join him in his quest for power. To become a *nökhör* was a serious matter, for it meant renouncing allegiance to all tribes and kin in favor of a chosen leader. In a culture rife with betrayal, Temüjin's *nökhör* served him loyally.

By 1206, Temüjin's success in building alliances and in tribal warfare led to his becoming Ruler of All the Mongols, holding the title Genghis Khan. "Genghis" is said to derive from the Turkic word *tengiz*, which meant "the ocean," as if to suggest breadth and depth. And "Khan" simply means "emperor." A near contemporary, the Persian historian Vassaf al-Hazrat, whose name meant "the court panegyrist," ecstatically greeted the enthronement of Genghis as the Great Khan: "Ruby-lipped cupbearers poured wine in golden goblets and ravishing young ladies with glossy ringlets stood like statues by the throne of the Khan in tight and slinky dresses. Slaves with tulip cheeks knelt before the throne waiting on the dignitaries who performed the hand-kissing ceremony. A week of blissful feast and immense delight followed thus."

Genghis came of age amid a stark landscape of grassy Steppe and soaring mountains, frigid lakes, and the arid reaches of the immense Gobi Desert. He was surrounded by herds of cattle, and by sheep, camels, goats, and horses. Twice a year, the nomadic Mongols packed up and moved, on rolling carts by day, resting in portable tents by night, following their herds in search of grass and developing their hunting prowess.

As he matured, Genghis drew strength from his belief that the Mongol sky god, Mönke Tenggeri, had given him the superhuman task of unifying these disparate Mongol tribes and conquering other nations. In conquest, the Mongols acquired the customs of those they had subdued until it became unclear who had the upper hand. Although they were fierce warriors and skilled horsemen, and were brilliantly adaptable, the Mongols were few in number; yet they controlled populations ten, twenty, or thirty times greater. Ultimately the overextended Mongols could not rule their empire for long, but during their brief ascendancy they spread their culture and beliefs far and wide.

Genghis established Tenggerrism—the worship of Heaven—as the official religion of the Mongol Empire and appointed himself its chief representative. For the Mongols, the sky took precedence over all. It was greater than the mountains, greater than the rivers, greater, even, than the Steppe itself. It was life, it was spirit, and it was the source of universal power. Tenggerism was, above all, a unifying credo, inspiring the Mongols to conquer everything under Heaven—which meant, in practice, every corner of the world. In the process of carrying out their mandate, the Mongols became early practitioners of globalization, seeking to connect the entire world. They were conquerors and marauders, but more than that, they were unifiers.

Fired by his elaborate sense of destiny, and emboldened by his genius for military strategy, Genghis pursued a longstanding Mongol aspiration, the conquest of China, the Mongols' much larger and more powerful neighbor to the south and east. In his insatiable quest for more land to add to his empire, he subdued potential rivals—and there were many—among the Mongols, and built alliances with distant warlords. He then exploited the internal politics of China, playing one clique against another, using a mixture of diplomacy and war. The Chinese, who had seemed invulnerable, quickly fell before Genghis Khan's cunning generalship. He mastered the art of siege warfare, learning to take cities by any means, no matter how savage. His troops burned or starved out inhabitants. They employed giant slingshots or catapults such as mangonels and trebuchets, capable of hurling stones or flaming naphtha or even diseased corpses over the walls into the midst of terrified city dwellers trapped by their own defenses. "Sometimes they even take the fat of the people they kill and, melting it, throw it onto the houses," Carpini wrote, "and wherever the fire falls on this fat it is almost inextinguishable"—unless doused with wine, which few victims had the presence of mind to employ. "If it falls on flesh"—an even more horrifying possibility—Carpini calmly advised that "it can be put out by being rubbed with the hand"—a technique that escaped Marco Polo's notice.

Ill-equipped to repulse the determined Mongol adversaries, China became resigned to the Mongols' unifying influence and tried to make the best of the inevitable. In words that Genghis would have approved, Vassaf remarked, "As the rumors of his just rule spread to the horizons, the happy people of China and beyond, up to the Egyptian coasts and the far western territories, were honored to submit to his just rule." The bitterest of ironies informed this assessment.

Genghis Khan knew when to hold his strength in check, and he took pains to respect Chinese customs and religion. Where he was received relatively peacefully, he ordered his generals to proclaim religious freedom and to forbid wholesale slaughter. In the process, the Mongol invaders took on as many traits from the conquered as they imposed. They adopted Chinese dietary practices, clothing, legal procedures, and religious observances.

In 1227, as his vision of China unified under Mongol rule neared fulfillment, Genghis Khan died at the age of sixty-five, leaving his immense empire to his son Ögödei, along with a trove of lore unique in the world's literature.

The year after Genghis's death, a group of Mongol scribes produced *The Secret History of the Mongols*, an extraordinary compilation of Mongol history, ritual, folklore, and customs recorded in a mixture of Mongol and Uighur tongues. (The Uighurs are a Turkic people dwelling in Central Asia.) There were three to five major revisions of the work between 1228 and 1240, when a final compilation was produced. The original has been lost; an abridged Chinese transcript became the basis of subsequent versions of the *Secret History*.

Why secret? It contained stories about Genghis that the Mongols preferred to keep private, along with recommendations about governing best left to the powers that be. Even though the Mongols wanted to shield it from outsiders, they were all familiar with its laws and concepts, and among them it was known, simply, as their *History*.

Written in poetry and prose, the epic emerged from a shamanistic mind-set, connecting Heaven and earth, human and animal. The story begins: "Chinggis"—a more accurate transcription of the Mongol leader's name, which probably meant "strong"—"Qahan was born with his destiny ordained by Heaven above. He was descended from Boerte Chino, whose name means 'grayish white wolf,' and Qo' ai Maral, the wolf's spouse, whose name means 'beautiful doe,' who crossed the lake and settled at the source of the Onon River."

The narrative goes on to recount the elemental Mongol way of life, beginning twenty-two generations before Genghis. Of one hardy precursor, the *Secret History* records: "He saw a young female hawk catch and eat a black pheasant"—just the kind of spectacle Marco Polo later witnessed. "Using the tail hairs of his off-white, mangy-tailed, sore-ridden horse, with the blacked-striped back as a snare, he captured the hawk and reared it. When he was without food, he would lie in wait and kill wild beasts that wolves had cornered at the foot of the cliffs and shoot and kill them. Together with the hawk, he would pick up and eat what the wolves had left behind. So as the year passed, he nourished both his own gullet and the hawk's."

At times, the *Secret History* unfolds as if it were a saga of the American West, with its tales of horse rustling, sharp bargaining, and sudden displays of cunning and heroism, all set in the midst of a primeval landscape. But every incident and topic, from horses to hawking, struck a chord in the Mongol psyche, as the *Secret History* preserved the lifestyle embodied and codified by the warrior Genghis Khan.

As this collection of tales makes plain, ceaseless conflict shaped Mongol life—at first among siblings, and later among tribes—until Genghis Khan beat his rivals into submission and unified the realm. The *Secret History* tells of a symbolic battle among Temüjin, as the young Genghis Khan was known, and his half brothers over a "small fish," a mere minnow. Their "noble mother" ordered, "Desist. Why do you, older and younger brothers, behave in such a way toward one another? . . . Why do you not work together? You must cease to behave in such a way."

Temüjin and Qasar, his brother and ally, complained, "Only yesterday we shot down a lark with a horn-tipped arrow and they snatched it away from us. Now they have done the same again. How can we live together?" With that, the boys stomped out of the *ger*, mounted their horses, and went to avenge the theft, shooting arrows at the brothers who had tormented them. But when they returned, they confronted something far worse: their enraged mother. "You destroyers!" she cried, comparing them to wild animals:

> Like the *qasar* [wild] dog gnawing on its own afterbirth,
> like a panther attacking on a rocking mountain,
> like a lion unable to control its anger, . . .
> like a gerfalcon attacking its own shadow, . . .
> like a male camel biting the heel of its young, . . .
> thus you have destroyed!
> Apart from our shadows, we have no friends.
> Apart from our tails, we have no fat.

This last line referred both to the fat-tailed sheep on which they lived, and, by extension, to their kin. Thanks to the harsh discipline administered by his formidable mother, Temüjin eventually learned the lesson of cooperation and emerged as Genghis Khan, who transcended the internecine quarrels that marked Mongol history, and the Mongol psyche, to bring about a heavily guarded peace and stability.

THE MONGOLS believed that Genghis had come to them from the sky, and that after his death he returned to his home in the firmament. But his earthly dynasty continued after him. His grandson Kublai was born in relative obscurity, a circumstance that may have kept him out of harm's way, and he advanced not because he was the chosen successor to Genghis but because he was cunning and resourceful enough to maneuver his way to the pinnacle of the Mongol hierarchy. No rival posed a greater threat to Kublai than a young khan called Kaidu. Although the two were cousins, Kaidu "never had peace with the Great Khan," Marco says, and that is an understatement. The reason was simple enough: "Kaidu always demanded of the Great Khan that he wished his share of the conquest they have made." Kublai replied that he would agree, if Kaidu promised to "go to his court and to his council every time that he should send to see him." Kaidu refused "because he was afraid that he [Kublai] would have him killed."

Matters came to a head in 1266, when Kaidu attacked two of Kublai's barons, Kibai and Kaban, who had converted to Christianity. The opponents fought a tremendous contest involving 200,000 horsemen, with Kaidu emerging as the victor. "He grew in bombast and pride thereby," Marco says.

Several years later, Kaidu mounted a direct challenge to Kublai, riding with tens of thousands of horsemen to the Mongol capital of Karakorum, where a battle took shape, according to Mongol custom: "When the two sides were on the field drawn up and ready, then they were only waiting till they should hear the drums begin to sound loudly, one on each side." Once the drums sounded, "then they would sing and play their instruments of two strings very sweetly, and make great sport, waiting always for the battle."

The opposing sides let loose a hail of arrows, and when they drew closer, pummeled each other with clubs. Marco heard reports from those who had been there that "it was one of the most cruel and evil battles that ever was between Tartars. . . . The noise of people was so great there and the clash of swords and of the clubs that one did not hear God for the thundering of it." The battle amounted to a tragic waste of life, "for many men died thereby and many ladies were widows thereby and many children were orphans thereby and many other ladies were forever thereby in mourning and in tears—these were the mothers and the sweethearts of men who died there."

By the first light of dawn, a weary Kaidu surveyed the bloodied battlefield. Spies brought him troubling news: Kublai Khan was already sending a fresh army "to take and assail him." Kaidu gathered the exhausted remnants of his forces. "They mounted on horseback and set themselves on the way to return to their country," recounts Marco. Learning of the retreat, Kublai Khan "let them go quietly." Kaidu's army did not stop retreating until it reached Central Asia.

Later, Kublai Khan raged and insisted he would have put the rebellious Kaidu "to an evil death"—wrapped in a carpet and trampled by horses—had they not been blood relatives.

MARCO CASTS the Mongol conquests not as the merciless slaughter of thousands but as a fairy tale about the spontaneous emergence of the Mongol presence from the windswept Steppe: "When Genghis Khan saw that he had so great a multitude of most valiant people, he, being of great heart, wished to come out from those deserts and wild places and arrayed his people with bows and with pikes and with their other arms. . . . I tell you that so great was the fame of his justice and kindness that wherever he went everyone came to submit himself, and happy was he who was able to be in his favor, so that in very little time they conquered eight provinces."

In Marco's telling, Genghis Khan's conquests were marvels of peaceful subjugation: "When he had gained and taken the provinces and cities and villages by force, he let no one be killed or spoiled after the victory; and he put governors in them of such justice that he did them no harm nor took away from them their things." Moreover, Marco claims, "These people who were conquered, when they saw that he saved and guarded them against all men and that they had taken no harm from him, and they saw the good rule and kindliness of this lord, they went too gladly with him and were loyal to him." In this skewed version, their allegiance inspired Genghis to greater feats. "And when Genghis Khan had gathered so great a multitude of people that they covered the world, and saw that they all obeyed him faithfully and followed him, seeing that fortune so favored him, he proposed to himself to attempt greater things: he said to them that he wished to conquer a great part of the world. And the Tartars answered that it pleased them well, and they would follow him gladly wherever he should go."

MARCO'S PORTRAYAL of Genghis Khan's glorious rise omits disturbing details of the Mongol leader's murderous thirst for power in favor of an epic, and unreal, battle between the Mongol warrior and the Christian leader of the East, Prester John. ("Prester" is an archaic word meaning "presbyter," or priest.) But Genghis's great rival Prester John did not exist, despite the European conviction that he dwelled in Asia, or perhaps Africa, ruling a magical and wealthy Christian outpost. In fact, the tenacious myth of Prester John originated in the fertile imagination of monks, who composed a letter purportedly written by him and directed toward the forces of Christianity in the West. It contained much to gladden the hearts of Europeans living in fear of the Mongols, including a vow to "take Genghis in person and put him to an evil death."

Marco himself remained silent on the subject of Prester John's existence. He did not claim, as he often did of others, to have personal knowledge of the Christian leader. But that gap in his knowledge did not stop him from narrating a mythic battle between the forces of the East and the West—led by Genghis Khan and Prester John. Prester John loses his life in this battle, a development that Marco seems to savor rather than lament—further evidence that the Venetian had come to identify with the Mongols. Which Marco was the real one: the devout Christian on a papal mission, who dismissed all non-Christians as idolaters and worse? The enthusiastic admirer of the Mongols? Each represented a facet of his sensibility. For Marco, Christianity represented the established order, reassuring but also confining; the Mongols, in contrast, signified boldness, magic, and grandeur. For the young traveler, they embodied an intoxicating way of life and belief.

On the subject of Genghis's grandson Kublai, Marco became rhapsodic, and suddenly leapt ahead of his story. In his estimation, Kublai Khan was simply the greatest leader in history: "All the emperors of the world and all the kings both of Christians and Saracens also, if they were all together, would not have so much power, nor could they do so much as this Kublai Khan could do, who is lord of all the Tartars of this world."

True, Marco was expressing himself in the medieval tradition of the panegyric, or formal compliment; hyperbole was expected—indeed, required. Yet he could be acid when he wished, even when discussing the high and mighty, from the relative security of a Genoese prison. Rhetoric aside, it is apparent that the prospect of meeting this grand personage could only have filled him with a sense of excitement and high purpose. Everything the Polo company left behind in the West dwindled in importance before the majesty and color of Kublai Khan and his nomadic subjects, who had conquered China against all odds.

"AND SINCE we have begun to speak about the Tartars for you," says Marco, bursting with enthusiasm, "I will tell you many things of them." He begins by describing—quite accurately—the basics of their nomadic existence, a way of life akin to that of the Indians of North America, with whom they may have shared ancestry: "The Tartars commonly feed many flocks of cows, mares, and sheep, for which reason they never stay in one place, but retire to live in the winter in plains and in hot places where they have grass in plenty and good pasture for their beasts; and in the summer they move themselves over to live in cold places in the mountains and in valleys where they find water and woods and good pasture for keeping their beasts; and also for this cause, where the place is cold flies are not found nor gnats and suchlike creatures that annoy them and their beasts."

Marco takes his European readers inside the *ger*, the portable structure in which the Mongols dwelled: "They have their small houses like tents of rods of wood and cover them with felt; and they are round; and they always carry them on four-wheeled wagons wherever they go. For they have the wooden rods tied so well and orderly that they can fit them together like a pack and spread them, take them up, put them down, and carry them wherever they please. And every time they stretch and set up their house the door always opens toward midday." These structures constituted, in effect, a portable village, and Marco marvels at the Mongols' life on the fly: "They have beside this very beautiful carts with only two wheels covered with black felt that is so good and so well-prepared that if it rained all day water would soak nothing that was inside the cart. They have them brought and drawn by horses and by oxen and sometimes by good camels. On these carts they carry their wives and their children and all the things and food that they need. In this way, they go wherever they wish to go, and thus they carry everything that they need."

Once he grew accustomed to life in a *ger*, Marco noticed an unusual domestic arrangement. "The ladies buy and sell and do all the work that is needed for their lords and family and for themselves," he comments approvingly. "They are not burdensome for their husbands, and the reason is that they make much gain by their own work." The more he observed Mongol women at work, the more he admired their diligence and contribution to family life. They are, he says, "very provident in managing the family and are very careful in preparing food, and do all the other duties of the house with great diligence, so the husbands leave the care of the house to their wives, for they trouble themselves with nothing at all but hunting and feats of battle and hawking and falcons, like gentlemen."

Marco was instinctively drawn to the Mongols' method of hunting, designed both to find food and to afford sport on the limitless Steppe. "They have the best falcons in the world"—another slap at Europe, where falconry was recognized as the sport of the aristocracy and falcons were a source of pride to the nobility able to afford them—"and likewise dogs"—all of which allowed the Mongols an abundant supply of food. Marco's inventory of the Mongols' foods seems calculated to inspire envy in his European readers, who often hovered on the brink of famine: "They feed on flesh and on milk and on game, and also they eat little animals like rabbits, which are called 'Pharaoh's rats' "—in reality, these were a species of rodent akin to the prairie dog. "They eat even the flesh of the horses and of dogs and of mares and oxen and camels, provided that they are fat, and gladly drink camel's and mare's milk." Koumiss, the sour fermented beverage made from mare's milk, was a staple of the Mongol diet, and a bond between all warriors. Drinking it practically defined the Mongol way of life.

Koumiss is of ancient origin. Writing in the fifth century BC, Herodotus states it was known to the ancient Scythians, nomadic precursors to the Mongols, and it may have derived from the name of another ancient Asian tribe, the Kumanes. The action of two organisms, a yeast and a fungus, converted the carbohydrates in mare's milk into lactic acid and alcohol.

Marco came to enjoy this beverage, or at least tolerate it. At one point, he declares that the koumiss produced by one Mongol family tasted like white wine. He had no choice but to acquire a taste for it, because the Mongols drank little else; even in winter, when milk was scarce, they combined sour curd with hot water, beat the mixture, and imbibed it.

LIFE AMONG THE MONGOLS, for all its hardships, eventually won Marco's qualified admiration. Unlike the bawdy wives of Kamul, the Mongol women remained faithful to their husbands. "For nothing in the world would one touch the wife of another," he proclaims, "for if it happened, they would hold it for an evil thing and exceedingly vile." He proceeds to extol Mongol marital harmony: "The loyalty of husbands towards the wives is a wonderful thing, and a very noble thing the virtue of those women who if they are ten, or twenty, a peace and inestimable unity is among them." Instead of bickering, the women busied themselves with "selling and buying, . . . the life of the house and the care of the family and of the children"—all of which won young Marco's ringing (and, to Christian ears, stinging) endorsement. "In my judgment they are the women who most in the world deserve to be commended by all for their very great virtue."

Of course, the underpinning of this remarkable domestic concord was more complicated than Marco's account initially suggests. The women, he eventually reveals, certainly deserved their "praise for virtue and chastity because the men are allowed to be able to take as many wives as they please, to the very great confusion of Christian women. For when one man has only one wife, in which marriages there ought to be a most singular faith and chastity, or [else] confusion of so great a sacrament of marriage, I am ashamed when I look at the unfaithfulness of the Christian women, [and call] those happy who being a hundred wives to one husband, keep [their virtue] to their own most worthy praise, to the very great shame of all the other women in the world."

Having performed his investigation, he offers a careful description of the Mongol formula for marital success: "Each [man] can take as many wives as he likes, up to a hundred if he has the power to maintain them; and the men give dowries to the wives and to the mother of their wife to obtain them, nor does the wife give anything to the man for dowry. But you may know too that they always hold the first of their wives for more genuine and for better than the others, and likewise the children who are born of her. And they have more sons than all the other people in the world because they have so many wives, and it is a marvel how many children each man has." The polygamy extended to relatives. As Marco explains, "They take their cousins for wife and, what is more, if the father dies, his eldest son takes to wife the wife of the father, if she is not his mother, and all the women who are left by the father except his mother and sisters. He takes also the wife of his own brother if he dies. And when they take a wife they make very great weddings and a great gathering of people."

MONGOLIAN MARITAL and reproductive habits left a lasting mark. Juvaini, the Persian historian, noted: "Of the issue of the race and lineage of Genghis Khan, there are now living in the comfort of wealth and affluence more than 20,000. More than this I will not say . . . lest the readers of this history should accuse the writer of exaggeration and hyperbole and ask how from the loins of one man there could spring in so short a time so great a progeny."

According to contemporary genetic researchers, Juvaini did not exaggerate. One in twelve Asian men—that is, one in every two hundred men worldwide—carries a Y chromosome originating in Mongolia at the time of Genghis Khan. Geneticists believe that Genghis Khan's soldiers spread that chromosome as they raped and pillaged their way across Asia, replacing the DNA of the men they slaughtered with their own, by way of the children they sired. Some scientists have suggested that the Y chromosome persisting to this day came from Genghis Khan himself. (When a sperm's DNA joins with that of an egg, the Y chromosome exchanges almost no genetic material with its partner, the X chromosome, and remains largely free of mutations.) A group of Oxford University researchers evaluated genetic markers in men across Asia; 8 percent of those studied were virtually identical, meaning that the individuals were closely related, even though they lived thousands of miles apart. The geneticists concluded that the 8 percent were direct descendants of Genghis Khan. When the results of the study were published, the popular press, echoing Juvaini, took to calling Genghis Khan the greatest—or, to be more accurate, most prolific—lover in history.

· · ·

MARCO POLO became so enamored of the Mongols that he described their shamanistic beliefs with genuine appreciation rather than the disdain he reserved for most unfamiliar religious practices. He begins reassuringly: "They say that there is the high, sublime, and heavenly God of whom every day with censer and incense they ask nothing else but good understanding and health." He concedes that they worshipped idols, but says they devoted special attention to one god in particular, whom they called Natigai, a "god of the land who protects and cares for their wives and their sons and their corn."

Marco departed from his longstanding skepticism to study this worship of the idols. In his rendition, it bears an uncanny resemblance to Christian rites: "Each has in his house a statue hung on the wall of a room that represents the high and sublime god of heaven, or only a tablet set high on the wall of his room with the name of the god written there. Here every day with the thurible of incense they worship thus and lift up the hands on high, and at the same time gnashing thrice their teeth they ask him to give them long life, happy and cheerful, good understanding and health, and they ask him nothing more. Then also down on the ground they have another statue called Natigai, god of earthly matters. . . . With this god is his wife and children; and they worship him in the same way with the thurible and gnashing the teeth and lifting the hands, and of this one they ask temperate weather and fruits of the earth, children, and similar things."

In one important way, Mongol belief differed sharply from Christianity: "They have no consciousness and care of the soul, but are only devoted to nourishing the body and getting pleasure for themselves." Yet the Mongols did have their version of the soul. Marco writes that "they hold [it] to be immortal in this way. They think that when a man dies he enters immediately into another body, and, according as in life he had borne himself well or ill, going on from good to better or from bad to worse; that is to say, if he shall be a poor man and if he have borne himself well and modestly in life, he will be born again after death of the womb of a gentlewoman and will be a gentleman, and then of the womb of a lady and will be a lord; if he is the son of a knight and in life have borne himself well, at death he is born again of the womb of a countess . . . , and so always ascending until he is taken into God. On the contrary, if he shall have behaved ill, being the son of a gentleman he will be born again a son of a rustic, from a rustic he is made into a dog, always descending to lower life." By the end of this careful, respectful, and intimate description of Mongol worship, it is easy to imagine Marco swept along in the spiritual tide.

Although alert to their religious practices, Marco remained oblivious to the larger spiritual world of the Mongols, in which the figure of Natigai intervened between hearth and home and immense cosmic forces. The Mongols viewed their deities arrayed in a floating hierarchy. Over all hovered the supreme divinity, the Eternal Blue Sky, and just below that a pantheon of ninety-nine divinities, one of which was Marco's Natigai, the protector of women, of cattle, and of harvests.

With his description of Mongol religious beliefs, Marco set out to demolish the tenacious European image of the murderous Mongol savage. All wrong, according to Marco. Instead, he reports, "They speak prettily and ornately, they greet becomingly with cheerful and smiling face, they behave with dignity and cleanliness in eating"—if not in washing. "They bear great reverence to the father and mother. If it is found that any son does anything to displease them, or does not help them in their need, there is a public office that has no other office but to punish severely ungrateful sons whom they know have committed some act of ingratitude toward them." With such measures, Mongol society enforced its stability. Although Marco stopped short of endorsing the concept of a designated official to discipline ungrateful offspring, he looked on approvingly.

So much for piety. In reality, nothing excited Marco's admiration more than the Mongol warrior. Feared throughout the world, his kind specialized in horsemanship, rape, and destruction. The warriors seemed a glamorous and dangerous outlaw tribe, fiercely devoted to one another, consecrating their destiny to the pursuit of power. They lived strenuously and obeyed no one's laws but their own defiant code. To the genteel Marco, it seemed that they were more in touch with the forces of nature than their refined Chinese subjects. No wonder he fell under their sway.

His adulation overwhelmed the formal literary veneer applied by Rustichello. "The rich men and nobles wear cloth of gold and cloth of silk and under the outer garments rich furs of sable and ermine and vair [that is, variegated fur] and of fox and of all other skins very richly; and all their trappings and fur-lined robes are very beautiful and of great value," Marco tells his audience. "And their arms are bows and arrows and very good swords studded with iron, and some lances and axes, but they avail themselves of bows more than of any other thing, for they are exceedingly good archers, the best in the world, and depend much from childhood upon arrows. And on their backs they wear armor made of buffalo hide and of other animals very thick, and they are of boiled hides that are very hard and strong. They are good men and victorious in battle and mightily valiant and they are very furious and have little care for their life, which they put to every risk without any regard." Europeans trembled at the thought of these warriors; Marco Polo came so close to them he could see the glint in their eyes and smell their breath reeking of koumiss, and he became intoxicated.

Vastly outnumbered by those whom they sought to conquer, lacking a common religion or common tongue, the Mongols subjugated the entire Asian continent. It seemed impossible that they had accomplished this task, yet they had, within only a few years. For Marco, the reasons were written in the Mongols' wholehearted commitment to the warrior's life. These men, motivated by the single-minded desire to serve their lord at all times, seemed tougher and more resilient than their European counterparts. Their philosophy of conquest was simple and stark: all war, all the time. Everyone participated in the effort. "There was no such thing as a civilian," notes the historian David Morgan. Mongol forces drew from every stratum of society. In the words of Juvaini, the Mongol military was a "peasantry in the dress of an army, of which, in time of need, all, from small to great, from those of high to those of low estate, are swordsmen, archers or spearmen."

This concentration of purpose deeply impressed Marco. "When the army goes out for war," he observes, "more bravely than the rest of the world do they submit to hardships, and often when he has need he will go or will stay a whole month without carrying any common food except that he will live on the milk of a mare and the flesh of the chase, which they take with their bows." When necessary, "they stay two days and two nights on horseback without dismounting."

He concludes his description with unabashed hero worship: "They are those people who most in the world bear work and great hardship and are content with little food, and who are for this reason suited best to conquer cities, lands, and kingdoms." This hard but vital way of life was power incarnate, it was freedom, it was everything the young traveler desired.

As Marco repeatedly states, the size of the Mongol armies was staggering. "When a lord of the Tartars goes to war he takes with him an army of a hundred thousand horsemen"—an unheard-of number in Europe. Despite its size, the Mongol equestrian army followed remarkably simple principles of organization. The lord, or general, "makes a chief to every ten, and to every hundred, and to every thousand, and to every ten thousand, so that the chief lord has to take counsel with only ten men." So it went up and down the chain of command, each chief reporting on the actions of his ten underlings to the one chief above him. Under this system, the Mongols could launch an attack of an appropriate size on a plain, on a mountain, or in a valley; they even had a sophisticated network of spies who scouted remote roads and valleys before the army passed through, and in that way, "the army cannot be attacked from any side without knowing it."

And there were still more Mongol survival techniques to which Marco became privy. "They live at most times on milk," he reports, "and of horses and mares there are about eighteen for each man, and when any horse is tired by the road another is taken in exchange. They carry no food but one or two bags of leather in which they put the milk that they drink, and carry each a small pignate, that is, an earthen pot, in which they cook their meat." If they cannot take meat with them, he says, they kill animals as they go, then "take out the belly and empty it and then fill it with water; and then take the flesh which they wish to cook and cut it into pieces and put it inside this belly so filled with water, and then put it over the fire and let it cook, and when it is cooked they eat the flesh, cauldron and all."

Adhering to this strenuous, frugal lifestyle, Mongol warriors could go for days without eating cooked food or even lighting a fire. For sustenance, "they live on the blood of their horses; for each pricks the vein of his horse and puts his mouth to the vein and drinks of the blood till he is satisfied." They found other extraordinary uses for the blood of their horses. "They carry the blood with them, and when they wish to eat they . . . put some of it in water and leave it to dissolve, and then they drink it. And in the same way they have their dried mare's milk, too, which is solid like paste. It is dried in this way. They boil the milk, and then the cream which floats on top is put in another vessel, and of that, butter is made; because as long as it stays in the milk it could not be dried. Then the milk is put in the sun, and so it is dried. And when they go to war they carry about ten pounds of milk . . . in a little leather flask." Mixed with a little water, "this is their breakfast."

When circumstances permitted, Mongol cuisine featured more

variety and subtlety than a warrior's regime might suggest. Traditional recipes of this period included a medicinal concoction, Borbi Soup ("Reduce thirty or so sheep bones in one bucket of water until it is one-fourth the original amount of water, strain, skim oil from the surface, remove sediment, and eat as much as desired."); Russian Olive Soup ("Trim and cut up one leg of mutton, add five cardamoms, and shelled chickpeas. Boil, strain, add Russian olives, sliced sheep thorax, and Chinese cabbage or nettle leaf."); and Butter Skin Yuqba ("Finely cut mutton, sheep's fat, sheep's tail, Mandarin orange peel, and sprouting ginger. Add salt, sauce, and spices. Mix everything uniformly. To make skins, blend vegetable oil, rice flour, and white wheat flour."). Revealing a Turkish influence, noodles had entered the Mongol diet, often in combination with mutton, egg, sprouting ginger, sheep intestines, and mushrooms, the whole served in a clear broth seasoned with pepper, salt, and vinegar. Marco would not have been surprised to encounter noodles in Mongolia; long before his journey, this type of food had spread from Turkey along the Silk Road in both directions. Contrary to myth, Marco Polo did not introduce noodles to Italy; his anonymous predecessors had.

MARCO ACKNOWLEDGED the Mongols as masters of military strategy—on land if not at sea—not because they were brutal, but because they were subtly strategic. It came as a surprise to many Chinese and Europeans to learn that when the Mongols "come to battle with their enemies, in the field they defeat them as much by flight as by pursuit." The Mongols were not ashamed to be seen fleeing battle, but then they lured their adversaries into a culvert or onto a cliff where they closed in for the kill, felling them with the arrows they had saved for this moment. "When the enemy believe they have discomfited and conquered them [the Mongols] by putting them to flight," Marco writes, the warriors of the Steppe regroup and let fly arrows tipped with lethal poison, killing the enemy's horses. At this point the Mongols double back on their befuddled, exhausted adversaries to slaughter them.

Yet even as he wrote, Marco noted with regret that the purity of Mongol warrior life was passing—"now they are much debased"—undermined by the influence of "the customs of the idolaters," presumably Buddhists, whose influence was spreading rapidly through the region, and by Islam, also spreading quickly.

No matter what the opponents' faith, Mongol justice was swift, savage, and systematic. "If a man strikes with steel or with a sword, whether he hits or not, or threatens one, he loses his hand," Marco observes. "He who wounds must receive a like wound from the wounded." A petty thief received a beating for his transgression, "at least seven blows with a rod, or, if he has stolen two things, seventeen blows, or if three things, twenty-seven blows," and so on by increments of ten blows. "And many of them die of this beating." Anyone daring to steal a horse—the Mongols took care to brand them—or, for that matter, an ox, would inevitably die of all the blows he received in punishment, so to shorten the process, the malefactor was cut in two with a sword.

Clemency—what little of it there was—took a mercenary form. If a horse thief could afford to make ninefold restitution for his crime, he escaped with his life, if not his honor.

ONE MONGOL custom in particular astounded Marco: the marriage of dead children. He took pains to explain the elaborate rites to Europeans likely to dismiss them as grotesque fantasy. "When there are two men, the one who has a dead male child inquires for another man who may have had a female child suited to him, and she also may be dead before she is married; these two parents make a marriage of the two dead together. They give the dead girl to the dead boy for wife, and they have documents made about it in corroboration of the dowry and marriage."

When such a ceremony was complete, a necromancer—a shaman or magician who communicated with the dead—burned the documents, with the smoke announcing to the spirits of the dead the marriage of these two deceased children. A marriage feast ensued. Later, the families fashioned images of the dead newlyweds, placed them on a horse-drawn cart adorned with flowers, and paraded them throughout the land, until, when they were done feasting, they consigned the images to the flames, "with great prayer and supplication to the gods that they make that marriage known in the other world with happiness."

The two families bound by the marriage of their dead children exchanged gifts, even a dowry, as if bride and groom walked among them, erasing the boundary between life and death. Afterward, "the parents and kinsmen of the dead count themselves as kindred and keep up their relation . . . as if their dead children were alive."

But Marco is only warming to his theme, and he has something "really marvelous to put into writing." How could anything outdo the wonders he has already described? He has his answer ready: "We shall speak of the rule of the Great Khan and of his court, which in my judgment I hold, having searched out and seen many parts of the world, that no other dominion can be compared to." Not only that, but "I shall bind myself for certain not to say of it more than is according to the truth."

MARCO SPEAKS breathlessly of the "very wild" Mecrit people, nomads who domesticated and rode deer as large as horses; he enthuses over the kingdom of Ergiuul, with its "three races: there are some Turks and many Nestorian Christians, and idolaters [Buddhists] and some Saracens who worship by the law of Mahomet." Discussing the province of Sinju, he waxes rhapsodic over the oxen and cows "as large as elephants" that were "very beautiful to see, for they were all hairy except the back, and are white and black." Their wool, "more fine than silk" so impressed him that, he says, "I, Marco Polo, brought some of it here to Venice as a wonderful thing, and so it was counted such by all." Not only that, but the region "produced the best musk . . . in the world."

He was not alone in his fascination with musk; it was fabled throughout Europe as an ingredient in perfumes, aphrodisiacs, and potions of all kinds. Now Marco learned that the magical substance was actually obtained from an egg-sized abdominal gland of the male musk deer. He speaks of the musk he discovered in a "wild animal" resembling a gazelle. "The animal," he advises, "has deer's hair," but much thicker, feet as large as a gazelle's, and a tail like a gazelle's, "but it has four teeth, two below and two above, which are three fingers long and are very thin, and white as ivory, and go two upward and two downward." The Mongols, he notes, call the animals *gudderi.*

The secretion itself was reddish brown, with the consistency of honey, and a penetrating odor celebrated as a sexual lure. Marco precisely describes the Mongol method for obtaining musk: "The hunters sally forth at the full of the moon to catch the said animals; for when one has taken it he finds on it at the navel in the middle under the belly between the skin and the flesh a pustule of blood"—said to grow under the influence of the full moon—"which one cuts off with the whole skin and takes it out, and they dry in the sun. The blood is the musk from which comes so great an odor."

The musk gazelle so intrigued Marco that years later he returned to Venice bearing "the head and feet of one of the animals, dried, and some musk in the musk sac, and pairs of little teeth." The trophy served as a poignant reminder of the rich experiences in his past, but one that he could, with effort, re-create for his listeners from memory in his jail cell in Genoa.

About the region's people, Marco had decidedly mixed feelings; he seems to change his mind even as he speaks of them. They had small noses and black hair, and the men sported no beards, only a few chin hairs. The women were very fair, "well-made in all respects," with no hair anywhere, "except on the top of the head." Although he considered himself a worldly fellow, he was both fascinated and repulsed to discover that the men "delight themselves much in the sensuality and take wives enough, because their religion . . . does not hinder them, but they take as many as they can." Moreover, he says, "I tell you that the men seek beautiful wives rather than noble, for if there is a very comely and fair woman, and she is of low descent, yet a great baron or great man takes her to wife for her beauty and gives silver enough to her father and mother as they have agreed." Marco may have been thinking how such payments resembled Venetian dowries, which also transformed matrimony into a commercial transaction and a political alliance between families.

MOVING EAST, Marco Polo came to "the province of Tenduc," which he erroneously considered to be the former domain of the mythical Prester John. Relying on legends rather than facts, he explains that while the "greater part [of the inhabitants] are Christians," there are also people of mixed race (by which he means the offspring of parents of different faiths, or cultures). These people, known as *argon*, are "idolaters," presumably Buddhists and Muslims. Despite their mixed lineage, they, too, earn Marco's admiration: "They are the whitest men of the country and fine men more than the others of the country who are infidels, and more clever and better traders than can be found elsewhere in any province."

Marco stretches still further when he identifies the seat of Prester John as the "place which we call on this side in our country Gog and

Magog"—a far-fetched but, to Marco, credible reference to the biblical despot Gog, who ruled the land of Magog.

At this point in his narrative, Marco became hopelessly entangled in legends and fragments of ancient history. The usually reliable narrator of personal experience relied all too heavily on half-remembered histories and legends.

WHEN HE TURNED from history to hawking, Marco resumed his characteristic vigor and accuracy as an enthusiastic witness to his times. Hawking served as the sport of choice for both European and Mongol nobility, and Marco grasped its grandeur and status. Kublai Khan, he wanted his audience to know, visited this region each year to hunt. "He hawks with gerfalcons, and with falcons," Marco writes, "and takes birds enough with great joy and great festivity."

The Great Khan established himself during hunting season in a settlement of "several little houses made of wood and stone, where they stay the night, in which he has a very great number of cators, which in our language we call partridges, and quail kept." Moreover, "for their food, the Great Khan always has millet . . . and other seeds that such birds like sown over those hillsides in summer, commanding that none shall be reaped so that they may be able to feed themselves abundantly."

Kublai Khan's hunting camp, for all its rustic pleasures, served merely as a summer retreat. Three days' journey over the Steppe brought the Mongol ruler to his celebrated summer palace, Shang-tu— or Xanadu, as it became known in Samuel Taylor Coleridge's phantasmagoric poem "Kubla Khan."

DESPITE THE fantastic attributes for which it is known in the West, Xanadu was a real place, as solid as the ground underfoot, and Marco Polo came to know it well. "In this city," he tells his readers, "Kublai Khan made a vast palace of marble cunningly worked and of other fair stone." Here Marco beheld the sights whose mere description would inflame Coleridge's opium-besotted cortex.

Marco writes: "The halls and rooms and passages are all gilded and wonderfully painted within with pictures and images of beasts and birds and trees and flowers and many kinds of things, so well and so cunningly that it is a delight and wonder to see. From this palace is

Marco Polo: a traditional portrait
(Corbis)

The entrance to the Venetian *Arsenale*, by Canaletto (1732).
Here the Republic mass-produced warships.
(Art Resource)

Marco Polo commanded a Venetian galley similar to this
in the Battle of Curzola.
(Granger)

Pope Gregory X gives a diplomatic letter
to Niccolò and Maffeo Polo.
(AKG)

The departure of Marco Polo from Venice in 1271 depicted in a fifteenth-century illuminated manuscript.
(Imageworks)

The Psalter map of the world from Marco Polo's era
(Bridgeman)

In our own time as well as in Marco Polo's, travel on the Silk Road entailed months of hardship and grueling conditions.
(Yamashita)

Opposite top: A detail from the influential Catalan Atlas (1375) depicts the Polo company on their travels.
(Corbis)

The Pamir, also known as the "Roof of the World." Marco said the air was so thin that no birds flew.
(Corbis)

Marco Polo arrives in Hormuz,
near the beginning of his journey.
(*Art Resource*)

Opposite top: A Buddhist retreat along a remote
stretch of the Silk Road in the Gobi Desert. After
repeated exposure to Buddhism, Marco gradually
came to appreciate its philosophy.
(*National Geographic Society*)

The rugged Taklimakan Desert, which contained the most
challenging routes of the Silk Road. The name is said to mean
"Those who enter do not return."
(*Corbis*)

On bended knee, Niccolò and Maffeo Polo
offer a papal letter to Kublai Khan.
(Imageworks)

Kublai Khan bestows the *paiza*, a passport
permitting travel throughout the Mongol empire,
on the Polos.
(AKG)

built a second wall which in the direction opposite to the palace, clos-
ing one end in the wall of the city on one side and the other on the
other side, encloses sixteen miles of land. It is fortified like a castle in
which are fountains and rivers of running water and very beautiful
lawns and groves."

These elysian fields contained the splendid royal zoo. "The Great
Khan keeps all sorts of beasts there, that is, harts and bucks and roe-
deer, and has them given to the falcons and gerfalcons, which he keeps
in a mew. He does that often for his pleasure and amusement. In the
middle of the park where there is a most beautiful grove, the Great
Khan"—still envisioned only at a distance, not yet seen directly, but his
presence becoming more deeply felt with every passing mile—"has
made for his dwelling a great palace or loggia that is all of canes [that
is, bamboo] . . . and on top of each pillar is a great dragon all gilded
that winds the tail round the pillar and holds up the ceiling with the
head, and stretches out the arms, one to the right for the support of the
ceiling with the head, and the other in the same way to the left. . . .
The roof of this palace is also all of canes gilded and varnished so well
and so thickly that no water can hurt it, and the paintings can never be
washed out; and it is the most wonderful thing in the world to be
understood by one who has not seen it."

His powers of observation sharpening, Marco describes this marvel
of Mongol engineering, the edifice that Coleridge memorialized about
five hundred years later as Kublai Khan's "stately pleasure dome."
"The canes from which these dwellings are made are more than three
or four palms thick and are from ten to fifteen paces long. One cuts
them across in half at the knot, from one knot to the other, and splits
them through the middle lengthwise, and then a tile is made. Of these
canes that are so thick and large are made pillars, beams, and parti-
tions, [so] that one can roof a whole house with them and do all from
the beginning. This palace of the Great Khan, of which I have spoken,
was made entirely from canes. Each tile of cane is fixed with nails for
protection from the winds, and they make those canes so well set
together and joined that they protect the house from rain and send the
water downward."

Still more amazing, the entire elaborate structure was collapsible
and portable, just like the modest *gers* in which the nomadic Mongols
dwelled. This was, after all, a nomadic culture, on all levels. Marco
goes on: "The Great Khan has made it so arranged that he might have

it easily taken away and easily set up, put together and taken to pieces, without any harm whenever he wished, for when it is raised and put together more than two hundred very strong ropes of silk held it up in the manner of tents all round about, because, owing to the lightness of the canes, it would be thrown to the ground by the wind.

"And I tell you the Great Khan stays there in that park three months of the year, this is June and July and August, sometimes in the marble palace, and sometimes in the one of cane. The reason he stays there is that he may escape the burning heat, for the air is very temperate and good, and it is not very hot, but very fresh." Although Marco's language sounds wonderfully imaginative, and European audiences read it as a beguiling fantasy, his description derived from observation.

KUBLAI KHAN seemed to be a law unto himself, feared and omnipotent, capable of dazzling everyone in his realm, but he depended on soothsayers for important decisions. Marco reports: "When the Great Khan was staying in this palace, and there was rain or fog or bad weather, he had wise astrologers with him and wise charmers who go up on the roof of the palace where the Great Khan dwells when any storm cloud or rain or mist rose in the air, and by their knowledge and incantation dispose of all the clouds and rain and all the bad weather, while everywhere else the bad weather went on."

On second glance, Marco noticed there were actually two types of astrologers in the court, those from "Tebet" and others from "Chescemir" (presumably in present-day Pakistan), who were practitioners of black magic, and, it appeared, cunning manipulators of Kublai Khan. "They know devilish arts and enchantments more than all other men and control the devils," Marco says, "so that I do not believe there are greater charmers in the world. . . . They do it all by devil's art and make the others believe that they do it by their goodness and great holiness and by God's work." As if to announce their base character, "they go filthy and unclean, not caring for their own honor, nor for the persons who see them; they keep mud on their faces, nor ever wash nor comb themselves, but always go dirtily."

The astrologers from Chescimir—"this most evil race of necromancers and charmers"—were, in short, repugnant.

To demonstrate their malevolence, Marco relates a story certain to horrify his listeners: "When they know that a man is condemned to death for ill that he has done and is killed by the government of the land, that condemned man is given to them and they take him and eat him; but if he were to die of his own natural death, they [would] never eat him for anything in the world."

To demonstrate the full extent of their devilish powers, Marco spins a yarn that has transfixed listeners over the centuries: "When the Great Khan sits at dinner or at supper in his chief hall, at his great table, which is more than eight cubits high, and the golden drinking cups are on a table in the middle of the pavement on the other side of the hall ten paces away from the table and are full of wine and milk and other good drinks, then these wise charmers . . . do so much by their enchantments and by their arts that those full cups are lifted of themselves from the pavement where they were and go away by themselves alone through the air to be presented before the Great Khan, without anyone touching them.

"And when he has drunk, the cups go back to the place they set out." In case his listeners doubt this report, Marco insists that the exhibition took place in full view of the court: "They do this sometimes while ten thousand men look on, and in the presence of whomsoever the lord wishes to see it; and this is most true and trustworthy with no lie, for it is done at the table of the lord every day."

Marco reported the occurrence as if he had observed it himself. Perhaps his enthusiasm overwhelmed his common sense in this instance, or perhaps the charmers had temporarily managed to bewitch his senses, along with everyone else's.

AMONG ALL THE sights at the summer palace, nothing matched Kublai Khan's huge albino herds. "This lord has a breed of white horses and of mares white as snow without any other color, and they are a vast number"—more than ten thousand in the herd, according to Marco—as well as an equally impressive number of "very white cows." The milk supplied by these ethereal white mares and cows was considered so precious that "no one in the world dares drink of it except the Great Khan and his descendants," with the exception of "another race of that people of that region that are called Horiat." Long ago, says Marco, Genghis Khan accorded the Horiat that privilege "as a reward for a very great victory that they won with him to his honor." As a result, "he wished that they and all their descendants should love and should be fed on the same food on which the Great Khan and those of his blood were fed. And so only those two families live on the afore-mentioned white animals, and on the milk obtained from them."

Everyone else accorded special respect to the noble white beasts. Marco continues: "When these white animals go grazing through the meadows and forests and pass by some road where a man wishes to pass, one does them so great a reverence that if, I do not mean only the ordinary people but a great lord and baron were to see them passing there he would not dare for anything in the world to pass through the middle of these animals, but would wait till they were all passed, or would go so far forward in another direction, half a day's journey, that he would have passed them."

For the Mongols, the beasts had magical properties: "The astrologers have told the Great Khan that he must sprinkle some of this milk of these white mares through the air and on the land on the twenty-eighth day of the moon of August each year so that all the spirits that go by air and by land may have some of it to drink as they please." Once they do, "all his [the khan's] things may prosper, both men and women, and beasts and birds, and corn, and all other things that grow."

The worship of the white mares and their milk was commemorated in an annual festival, which took place on the day of the khan's departure from the summer palace, August 28. "On the day of the festival," Marco reports, "milk is prepared in great quantity in honorable vessels, and the king with his own hands pours much of the milk here and there to honor the gods. The astrologers drink the milk thus poured out." Having drunk deeply of the koumiss, king and court would fall into a drunken stupor.

FOLLOWING the feast came the sober departure from Xanadu and the disassembly of the summer palace. Marco says that Kublai Khan "has so planned it that he can make it and take it to pieces at his will very quickly; and it is all packed by pieces and is carried very easily where the lord commands." With that, the nomads took their leave.

The notion of a collapsible, portable summer palace made of bamboo or any another light, durable material that could be quickly dismantled and packed up and moved like so much furniture struck Europeans as improbable, yet it was just as Marco described. He only seemed to be living among primitive heathen warriors; in reality, he had found his way into a confluence of civilizations several centuries advanced over Western Europe. How to explain them all to his skeptical audience? Making the future credible exceeded even Marco's patience and powers of persuasion.

TRAVELING all this distance had proved extremely difficult, dangerous, and time-consuming for the Polos, and they felt secure in the khan's all-encompassing embrace. In time, they would realize that they had wandered unintentionally into a trap as large as Asia, but a trap nonetheless. Kublai Khan presented himself as an invulnerable emperor, practically a deity, but he was, in fact, a vain and vulnerable despot, and the Polo company's position within his empire was correspondingly precarious. Depending on his goodwill for their personal safety, they could neither renounce him nor flee him, not if they ever wanted to see Venice again. And if anything happened to him, they would be at the mercy of his enemies.

For the moment, Marco was too dazzled by his proximity to the most powerful ruler in the world to be concerned, for he had reached the heart of his story. "I will now tell you," he promises, "the truly amazing facts about the greatest lord of the lords of all the Tartars, the right noble khan whose name is Kublai."

FROM HIS privileged standpoint, Marco Polo urged his audience, Venetians especially, to study Kublai Khan's example of empire-building. His lengthy account can be read as a consideration of the question of how best to rule an empire, and in this way, it is the medieval equivalent of another Italian analysis of statecraft, *The Prince*, by Machiavelli. Marco found in Kublai Khan a master practitioner of the art—part warrior, part despot, and part sage. To the Venetian, Kublai Khan was a flesh-and-blood person, but also a towering figure on the order of Alexander the Great, a ruler capable of transforming the world and history itself. Kublai Khan was power personified— military, sexual, and spiritual.

"The people remain humble, quiet, and calm for half a mile round the place where the Great Khan may be, out of respect for his Excellency, so that no sound or noise nor voice of anyone who shouts or talks loudly is heard," Marco says of life in the Mongol palace. "Every baron or noble always carries a vase small and beautiful, into which he spits while he is in the hall, for none would have the courage to spit upon the floor of the hall."

In keeping with the refined atmosphere of the palace, visitors wore special footwear, "beautiful slippers of white leather that they carry with them." Marco explains that "when they are arrived at the court, if they wish to go into the hall, supposing that the lord asks for them, they put on these beautiful white slippers and give the others to the servants; and this, so as not to soil the beautiful and cunningly made carpets of silk, both of gold and of other colors."

And now it was time for the Polo company, clad in this splendid attire, to encounter the embodiment of opulence and authority, the leader of the Mongols, Kublai Khan.

"WHEN THE noble brothers Master Niccolò and Master Maffeo and Marco were come into that great city [Cambulac] in which the khan was, they go off immediately to the chief palace, where they found the Great Khan with a very great company of all his barons. And they knelt before him with great reverence and humbled themselves [until] they were stretching themselves out on the earth."

Prostrate before the omnipotent Mongol ruler, they waited in respectful but uneasy silence, until "the Great Khan made them rise and stand upright and received them with honor and made great rejoicing and great feasting for them." Kublai Khan eagerly engaged Niccolò and Maffeo in conversation, questioning them "about their life and how they had conducted it" during the years of their absence from the Mongol court. "The two brothers told him that they had done very well since they had found him in health and strength."

Having disposed of the preliminaries, Kublai Khan demanded to hear "what dealings" the brothers had had "with the chief Pontiff." Marco says that Niccolò and Maffeo "explained to him well and skillfully with great eloquence and order all they had done, being heard with great and long silence by the lord and all the barons, who wondered much at their great and long fatigues and at their great perils." When they concluded their account, they presented Kublai with the papal documents they had carried with them from Acre to Cambulac. The Mongol leader praised their "diligence" in accomplishing this superhuman task. But there was more.

With a Venetian flourish, "they handed him the holy oil that they had brought from the lamp of the Sepulcher of our Lord Jesus Christ from Jerusalem, which he had so much desired." The gift, so difficult to obtain, had its intended effect. Kublai Khan received the magical substance with "great rejoicing and held it very dear and ordered it to be kept with great honor and reverence, and nothing was ever more dear or welcome than that."

Next it was young Marco's turn. His father and uncle formally presented the young man to the Mongol leader. "The Great Khan, when he saw Marco, who was a young bachelor of very great and noble aspect, asked who he was," the reader is told. " 'Sir,' said his father, Master Niccolò, 'he is my son and your man, whom as the dearest thing I had in this world I have brought with great peril and ado from such distant lands to present him to thee for thy servant.' " One can imagine the youth's cheeks tingling with apprehension at the formality and intimacy of the occasion, as well as its significance, for his father had just committed him to the service of Kublai Khan.

"May he be welcome," said the Great Khan, "and it pleases me much."

BOOK TWO

Asia

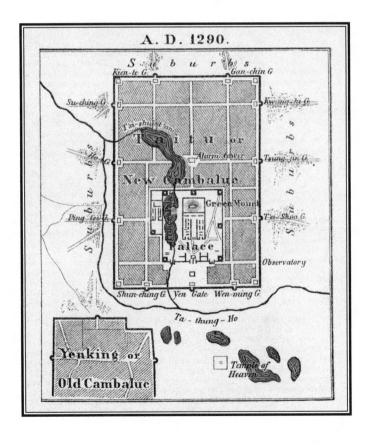

CHAPTER SEVEN

The Universal Emperor

I would build that dome in air,
That sunny dome! those caves of ice!

WINNING KUBLAI KHAN'S approval marked the decisive moment in young Marco's life; henceforth he stepped out of his elders' shadow and emerged in his own right. His exuberant, questing temperament proved the perfect match for the emperor and empire. So it was that the greatest ruler on earth saw promise in a keenly observant young traveler from the mysterious West. Together they freed Marco from his Venetian constraints, and under the khan's influence Marco began to evolve into the traveler remembered by history. For seventeen years, Marco Polo and Kublai Khan participated in a most unusual partnership as master and servant, teacher and disciple, and even father and son.

Marco declares that Kublai Khan held him "in great favor," and enlisted him "among the other honored members of his household, for which reason he was held of great account and value by all those at the court." The young Venetian, in turn, studied his unusual hosts. "While he stayed at the court of the Great Khan, this youth . . . , being of very distinguished mind, learned the customs of the Tartars and their language and their letters and their archery so well that it seemed a wonder for all," he says with characteristic lack of modesty. Before long, he had learned "several languages and four other letters and writings." Thus armed, he came to know Kublai Khan perhaps better than the khan knew himself, and to etch him in the Western consciousness for all time.

To Europeans, Kublai Khan, like his ancestors before him, was more of a demonic force than a person, and although Marco plainly stood in awe of the leader of the Mongols, he was also determined to give him a human face—itself an iconoclastic act.

"The great lord of lords, who is called Kublai Khan, is like this," Marco begins. "He is of good and fair size, neither too small nor too large, but is of middle size. He is covered with flesh in a beautiful manner; he is more than well formed in all parts. He has his face white and red like a rose; the eyes [are] black and beautiful; the nose well made and well set." The description was somewhat idealized; portraits of the khan in his maturity depict him as conspicuously fat and jowly, magnanimous-looking yet imposing.

Overwhelmed by this august personage, Marco portrayed him in exalted terms. "The title Khan means 'Great Lord of Lords,' and certainly he has a right to this title; for everyone should know that this Great Khan is the mightiest man, whether in respect of subjects or of territory or of treasure, who is in the world today," Marco said later, without exaggeration. "You should know that he is descended in the direct imperial line from Genghis Khan. . . . He is sixth in succession of the Great Khans of all the Tartars." Although Kublai Khan was in his early sixties by the time he received the Polo company on its second visit to Cambulac, he had, until recent years, lived a life fraught with danger, and had become khan as much by his cunning and courage on the field of battle as by accident of birth.

KUBLAI KHAN was the child of Genghis Khan's fourth son, Tolui, and a remarkable woman named Sorghaghtani Beki, who was largely responsible for forming the generous character of the future emperor. She raised the child in her husband's absence and imbued him with the mystic, all-embracing spirit that would mark his adult life.

After Tolui drank himself to death, Sorghaghtani showed her spirit of independence. She spurned a marriage proposal from Tolui's brother Ögödei, among others, and lobbied on behalf of her children's future. Her flair for politics, combined with her quiet self-determination, won her wide admiration. One of the era's wise men, the Syrian Gregorius Bar Hebraeus, the son of a Jewish physician who became a bishop and biblical commentator, said of Sorghaghtani, "If I were to see among the race of women another woman like this, I should say the race of women was far superior to men."

Sorghaghtani was a Nestorian Christian, and as a result Kublai Khan was far more appreciative of Christianity than the Europeans who reviled him would have suspected. Everyone, including Marco, was aware of her Christian faith, and for this reason, he believed he had some common ground with her son, the most exotic of rulers. But Kublai Khan's mother maintained a more elaborate spiritual life than her professed religion suggested. She actively encouraged religious toleration, partly out of conviction, and partly for political reasons. She embraced Buddhism and Taoism and Islam, all to gain the support of the populace ruled by her family. Even as she practiced Christianity, she donated generously to mosques and Muslim academies. And as she encouraged Kublai to learn to hunt like a Mongol, she insisted that he learn Uighur, one of several tongues adopted by the Mongols.

She was similarly enlightened in the administration of the affairs of the northern Chinese province that she ruled benevolently. Among the greatest challenges the Mongols faced in attempting to bring China under their control was the clash of two opposing ways of life: that of Chinese farmers versus that of Mongol nomads. Rather than force her Chinese subjects to adopt a nomadic way of life, based on the assumption of limitless but often useless land, Sorghaghtani permitted them to live according to their agrarian heritage; the result, for the Mongols, was a gratifying increase in tax revenues.

Kublai inherited the innovative aspects of his mother's approach to governing their Chinese provinces. He embraced her polytheism, which ensured the cooperation of their subjects, and promised economic accommodation. But as a young man, he had strayed far from home, and Mongol governors administered the provinces with a much heavier hand. They forced Chinese farmers to resettle, destroying fragile family structures; they imposed punitive taxes; and they exploited Chinese labor wherever they could. By the time these Mongol excesses came to Kublai Khan's attention, the Chinese had departed in droves.

Kublai tried to right the balance by replacing Mongol tax officials with Chinese equivalents, called "pacification commissioners." Over time, he welcomed more Chinese into his administration, and by 1250, some of the defectors had returned, conveying their conditional acceptance of Mongol rule.

. . .

RELYING ON FOREIGNERS to administer his empire, Kublai Khan gradually became the least Mongol of Mongol rulers; the Mongols often criticized him for abandoning Mongol ways and embracing Chinese civilization in all its manifestations—language, clothing, religion (that is, Buddhism), and government. There was some truth to the charge, because he enlisted counselors from all backgrounds. A monk named Hai-yün tutored Kublai in Chinese Buddhism. He gave Kublai's second son a Chinese name, Chinkim, "True Gold." Other Chinese followed suit, and soon the young Mongol leader was receiving instruction in Confucianism. Turkish Uighurs, Muslims, and Nestorian Christians all began appearing in his court and winning posts for themselves. By one count, Kublai relied on a council of forty advisers from these disparate backgrounds. Years later, when Muslims and Europeans who braved the Silk Road arrived in his court, it was only natural that Kublai Khan invited them to serve the Mongols. In time, he divided his subjects into four major segments. First came the Mongolians, entitled to the highest positions. They were followed by the so-called Colored-Eye People, meaning those from Persia and the Middle East. Then there were Northern Chinese, and finally Southern Chinese—the two most numerous but least influential groups.

Even as Kublai Khan mastered the intricacies of Chinese court life, he retained the ingrained Mongol tastes for portable housing, for hunting, for horsemanship, and for conquest. At times he feared he had become too reliant on his elite Chinese advisers, and he was heard to wonder if Buddhists and Confucians had hastened the end of other dynasties. His lack of fluency in Chinese prevented him from holding extended conversations with the Confucians all around him; if they wished to instruct him in Confucian doctrine, he relied on a Mongol interpreter. He sought to incorporate the world, but on his terms.

As a rising young ruler, Kublai oversaw four large separate households, each administered by one of his wives. Chabi, his second wife, outshone the others, both in popularity with their subjects and in her influence over her remarkable husband. They married in 1240, or shortly before, when Kublai Khan was about twenty-five years old. Chabi was devoted to Tibetan Buddhism; she donated her jewelry to Buddhist monasteries and soon inspired Kublai to turn to Buddhism as well.

· · ·

BELIEVING HE COULD overcome all differences—religious, linguistic, and more—through the force of his authority, Kublai Khan worked to strengthen his alliances within the Mongol Empire, and slowly proved his mettle as a leader. In 1252, he assisted his brother Möngke in conquering provinces in southwestern China. Within three years, records show, he charged a celebrated Chinese scholar with establishing schools to teach the Chinese language and sciences to Mongol children. In 1256, he assigned another respected Chinese scholar, Liu Ping-chung, to select a propitious site for the capital city of the Mongol Empire. His choice was Xanadu—a name that came to sound endlessly romantic and evocative to Westerners, but which simply meant "the Upper Capital," because it lay north of the winter capital in Cambulac.

Möngke's death in August 1259 cleared the way for Kublai's ascent. In May 1260, the Mongol barons gathered in a *khuriltai*, a convocation to select their next leader. Their deliberations led to Kublai's elevation to the position of "great khan." He was forty-five years old.

A MONTH after Kublai's election, his younger brother Arigh Böke rallied enough support among a coterie of disaffected Mongol barons to have himself declared "great khan" as well. From his stronghold at Karakorum, Arigh Böke vowed to undo Kublai Khan and his divided loyalties. Learning of his rival's intentions, Kublai suspended the military campaign in central China and conferred with his generals to devise a way to repel this challenge to his authority. They recommended that Kublai preside over a new election, in the interest of Mongol unity. As the designated successor, he was obligated to submit to an election by all the members of the family and the principal barons. The results of the vote were mixed; each rival had his devoted supporters, setting the scene for years of conflict among the competing Mongol barons and their followers.

To solidify his position, Kublai made a pact with China's dominant Song dynasty, whose prince pledged to serve Kublai Khan and to pay a generous annual tribute of 200,000 ounces of silver and 200,000 lengths of silk. On the advice of his Chinese advisers, he appealed to the Chinese populace, assuring them that his taxation rates would be lighter than those of his anti-Chinese rival, and he did whatever he could to identify himself with Chinese emperors in dress and custom.

The appeals worked, but Arigh Böke continued to harass Kublai Khan in Central Asia, or wherever he detected weakness.

The endless skirmishing took its toll on Arigh Böke's army. Disease and desertion and famine claimed many of his soldiers, and by 1264, Arigh Böke decided he had no choice but to surrender to Kublai Khan. Arriving in Xanadu, Arigh Böke appealed to his brother for mercy. The two brothers, until recently mortal enemies, embraced, and it is said that Kublai Khan tenderly wiped the tears from the eyes of his adversary.

Displaying the compassion for which he was known, Kublai Khan refrained from punishing Arigh Böke or his followers. Instead, Kublai banished his younger brother from his presence for a year, a measure that infuriated many barons, who were insisting on far more drastic measures. To appease his supporters, Kublai Khan conducted an inquiry designed to ferret out those who had inspired Arigh Böke to rebel. At last they settled on a hapless former adviser named Bolghai. Kublai Khan ordered Bolghai, along with nine other unlucky followers of Arigh Böke, to be executed.

In 1266, Arigh Böke himself died; he had been in robust health until his final illness, and suspicion arose that he had been poisoned to make way for Kublai Khan, but no conclusive evidence of wrongdoing surfaced. Kublai now ruled as the sole "great khan," although the support he enjoyed from lesser khans was tepid, at best. To foreigners like Marco Polo, he appeared to rule a unified Mongol hierarchy, but in reality his power over the empire was more tentative than outsiders assumed, as much the result of chance and circumstance as of military might or presumed virtue.

As emperor, Kublai immediately brought sweeping changes to the realm. In 1260, the first year of his reign, he ordered the Chinese to give up their coins, made of copper, gold, and silver, in favor of paper currency. And he replaced Chinese paper currency, which had been in existence since the ninth century, if not earlier, with its Mongol counterpart. Soon, three kinds of Mongol currency flooded China, one backed by silk, and the two others by silver. Despite Chinese resistance, the experiment worked.

The Mongol fiscal policies and technology, based on Chinese models and far advanced over Western counterparts, both impressed and baffled Marco, who struggled to comprehend financial concepts so unlike those of Venice. In his *Travels*, he extols the wonders of Kublai Khan's mint in Cambulac. "It is appointed in such a way," he says, "that the great lord has [mastered] the art of alchemy perfectly," by which Marco means that the mint enjoyed a license to manufacture wealth.

For the benefit of Europeans unfamiliar with paper currency, Marco clearly illustrates the procedure for printing money in Kublai's mint: "He makes men take the bark of trees, that is, of the mulberries of which the worms that make silk eat their leaves, and the thin skin that is between the bark and the wood of the tree." From that skin are made "sheets like those of paper. They are all black." After being cut into squares worth varying amounts, "all these sheets are sealed with the mark and with the seal of the great lord, for otherwise they could by no means be spent." In addition, each sheet is printed by hand with the mark of an official, and "if any were to counterfeit it, he would be punished." The marvel of this form of currency is that "each year [Kublai] has so great a quantity of them made that he could pay for all the treasure in the world, though it costs him nothing."

Marco tried to educate his skeptical European audience and persuade himself about the practicality and efficiency of Kublai Khan's paper money. He writes: "All the people and regions of men who are under his rule gladly take these sheets in payment, because wherever they go they make all their payments with them both for goods and for pearls and for precious stones and for gold and for silver; they can buy everything with them, and they make payment with the sheets of which I have told you." Equally impressive, the sheets of paper money "are so light that the sheet worth ten bezants of gold weighs not one."

IN HIS PASSION to reform, Kublai Khan welcomed craftsmen, artisans, traders, and merchants to his court, in a sharp break with Chinese practice. Muslims from the Middle East brought spices, camels, and carpets with them. Merchants brought luxurious silk and lacquer, not to mention rhinoceros horns, and incense, much of it designed to appeal to Muslim tastes.

Kublai Khan's treasury profited tremendously from this commercial activity. The Mongol government lent money at extremely low rates to the Mongol nobility while levying taxes on traders. No matter what type of transaction was involved, Kublai Khan's administration required that merchants exchange their own currency, usually in the form of valuable coins, and occasionally gems, into Mongol paper currency, as Marco Polo observes: "Many times a year the merchants come together with pearls and with precious stones and with gold and with silver and with other things, cloth of gold and of silk; and these merchants give all of these things to the great lord. The great lord calls twelve wise men . . . to look at those things that the merchants have brought and to have them paid with what it seems to them they are worth . . . with those sheets of which I have told you." If, perchance, "one has kept these sheets so long that they are torn and are spoilt, then he takes them to the mint and they are changed for new and clean ones."

Although Marco found it difficult to believe that paper currency could have real value, he saw—with his own eyes, as he was fond of saying—that it served as the basis of a flexible and practical economic system, and extended the Mongol Empire's economic influence over great distances. Paper money seemed to Marco a more potent invention than rockets or giant slingshots, and more persuasive than religion. It could even be considered Kublai Khan's hidden weapon of conquest.

THROUGHOUT HIS REIGN, Kublai benefited from a unique asset: Chabi, his principal wife, who yearned to become the empress of a unified Mongol realm, and who devoted her energies to sustaining her husband when he became ensnared by infighting among the Mongols. It was Chabi who summoned Kublai Khan from his battles with the Song dynasty to defend his throne. And it was she who insisted that Liu Ping-chung persuade Kublai Khan to abandon a plan to turn the Chinese agricultural land surrounding the capital city into pastures for Mongol horses. "You Chinese are intelligent," she told Liu Ping-chung. "When you speak, the emperor listens. Why have you not remonstrated with him?" Once the adviser interceded, Kublai Khan changed his mind, and left the Chinese farmland intact.

In court, where appearances mattered, Chabi set the fashion. Known for frugality, she collected discarded animal pelts and string, and other women soon followed her example. She took it upon herself to redesign the traditional Mongol headpiece, adding a visor to afford protection from the strong sun in China. She even devised a sleeveless tunic for combat.

Beyond her practical concerns, she shared with her husband a fascination with the Chinese emperor Taizong, who had reigned five centuries earlier, during the Tang dynasty. She encouraged Kublai to identify publicly with this revered figure as way of solidifying his identification with the Chinese people. Thanks in part to Chabi's advice and example, he managed to retain his position and his popularity with the Chinese, largely by imitation.

Kublai's manner of governing increasingly reflected Chinese approaches, especially those formulated by the Confucian scholar Jing Hao, who offered guidance concerning the principles of government. Yet Kublai clung to distinctive Mongol customs. Instead of relying on rigorous civil service examinations to select government officials, as the Confucians urged, he reserved the right to appoint his own choices, so that he would not run the risk of becoming overly dependent on the Chinese for the day-to-day operation of his administration. In this way, Kublai sought to blend his dynasty into the Chinese mainstream while maintaining a distinct Mongol heritage.

Kublai Khan became so adept at juggling these competing demands that he believed he could become all things to all people, the universal sovereign. He never quite achieved his aspiration; in Central Asia, various Mongol strongholds such as Persia and Russia claimed autonomy, although they paid lip service to the Great Khan in the east. Worse, as his reign continued, he presided over the disintegration of the Mongol Empire, even as he strengthened his base—and a very large and prosperous base it was—in China, where he continued his successful "pacification" of the Song, and its wealthy cities, especially the great prize of Hangzhou, located in the Lake District, the most sophisticated and scenic region in all of China.

Such was the thriving empire in which Marco found himself. His facility with languages commended him to Kublai, who dispatched him "as a messenger on some important royal business." Marco's first stop: a city that he called Caragian, a journey of six months from Cambulac.

The young emissary took pains to prepare for the assignment, and to distinguish himself from other messengers. After their travels through the Mongol kingdom, those messengers returned to Kublai Khan "and were not able to tell him other news of the countries where they were gone." Marco says that Kublai, in frustration, berated his couriers as "fools and ignorant, and said that he would like better to hear the new things and the customs and the usages of those strange countries than he did to hear those matters for which he had sent them; so Marco, who knew all this well, when he went on that mission, would fix his attention, noting and writing all the novelties and all the strange things that he had heard and seen according to the countries, going and coming, so that he might be able to recount them on his return to satisfy his wish." With that, Marco Polo the traveler and story-teller was born, and so was the self-promoter and braggart whom other Italians would come to label, with admiration and derision in equal measure, Il Milione, "the Million."

He saw himself, in contrast, as a conscientious emissary and chron-icler: "All things that Master Marco saw and did and with whatever he met of good or bad he put in writing and so told all in order to his lord." None of these field notes have survived, but it is believed that when he was imprisoned in Genoa he sent for them to assist in the composition of his *Travels*. Their particulars were etched in his memory.

Marco displayed an unexpected facility for conjuring distant, obscure worlds, making them seem both marvelous and comprehensi-ble to his audience. Kublai was his first assignment editor, his first and most important audience, and ultimately his most compelling subject. Marco describes how the back-and-forth between the two of them worked, revealing, incidentally, how impressed Marco was with him-self for pulling off this narrative feat: "When Marco returned from his mission he went before the Great Khan and reported to him all the affair for which he had gone. Then he told him all the novelties and all the things that he had seen on the road so well and cleverly beyond the wont of the other ambassadors who had been sent before that the Great Khan and all his barons were much pleased, and all those who heard him had great wonder at it and commended him for great sense and great goodness."

Aware of his own uncanny powers of perception, Marco lavishes praise on himself: "This noble youth seemed to have divine rather than human understanding." Throughout the Mongol court, "there was nothing more wonderful told than of the wisdom of the noble youth, and they said among themselves, 'If this youth lives for long, he cannot fail to be a man of great sense and of great valor.' " He can only sigh with recognition. "From this mission onward, they honored him not as a youth but as a man of very great age, and thenceforward the youth was called Master Marco Polo at court and so will our book call him in the future, though his virtue and wisdom deserve a much more worthy name than Master Marco. And this is really very right, for he was wise and experienced."

Kublai Khan's barons often tired of Marco's preening. To them, he seemed an obsequious stranger who had inexplicably charmed his way into their leader's affections. Marco recognized the jealousy he engendered at court. The Great Khan, he claims, "kept him so near to himself that many of the other barons had great vexation at it."

As HEIR to the throne of Genghis Khan, Kublai pursued his goal of becoming the "universal emperor," beginning in the spiritual realm. "He does the same thing at the chief feasts of the Saracens, Jews, and idolaters," Marco explains. "Being asked about the reason, Kublai Khan said, 'There are four prophets who are worshipped and to whom everybody does reverence. The Christians say their God was Jesus Christ; the Saracens Mohammed; the Jews Moses, and the idolaters Sagamoni Burcan [the Buddha], who was the first to be represented as God in an idol; and I do honor and reverence all four.' "

Of course, there were major differences among the four faiths cited by Kublai Khan, and in some ways their doctrines are not even compatible, let alone comparable. The Saracens' Islamic faith was resolutely monotheistic, while the Mongols promoted a shamanistic cosmology overflowing with deities and relying on religious tolerance. Beyond those theological differences loomed an unbridgeable cultural gap. The Muslims sweeping across Asia were intensely urban, putting down roots in cities, where they succeeded in commerce. The nomadic Mongols detested cities and destroyed those in their path. Even in the capital, Karakorum, the Mongols lived outside the walls, on the open Steppe, while Chinese, European, and Muslim inhabitants huddled within.

Kublai Khan ruled first by acknowledging differences, and then by leveling them. Although the khan felt most at home with Buddhism, which flourished all around him and was spreading quickly, he deftly persuaded Marco that of all these religions, Christianity took precedence. "The Great Khan showed he holds that Christian faith for the truer and better," Marco insists, "because he says that it commands nothing that is not full of goodness and holiness."

In their roles as "ambassadors to the Pope," Marco's father and uncle often asked Kublai Khan the obvious question: If he preferred Christianity, why not renounce all other faiths and declare himself a Christian?

"How do you wish me to make myself a Christian?" asked the khan. From his point of view, Christianity was but one more credo, and far from powerful in his realm. Even the sorcerers in his court had more influence. "You see the Christians who are in these parts are ignorant so that they do nothing and have no power," Kublai said, "and you see that these idolaters do whatever they wish, and when I sit at the table the cups that are in the middle of the hall come to me full of wine or drink . . . without anyone touching them, and I drink with them. They compel the storm to go in whatever direction they please, and do many wonderful things, and as you know their idols speak and foretell them all that they wish." In contrast to these potent shamanistic practices, Christianity, with its emphasis on redemption and rewards in an afterlife rather than the here-and-now, offered only a slender thread of hope. "If I am converted to the faith of Christ," Kublai Khan said, "then my barons and other people who are not attached to the faith of Christ would say to me, 'What reason has moved you to baptism and to hold the faith of Christ? What virtues or miracles have you seen of Him?'" Should sorcerers or shamans decide to cast an evil spell over him, or poison him, he did not believe the faith of Christ would be sufficient to save him.

IF EMBRACING Christianity threatened to weaken his hold on the Mongol Empire, rewarding the warlords, or "barons," who served him could only bolster it. Kublai Khan kept their loyalty with exceptionally generous rewards for their allegiance. Barons and lords who defended Kublai on the field of battle received "a great gift of gold and fair silver vessels and many fair jewels, and a superior tablet denoting authority." According to Mongol custom, Kublai Khan conferred the tablets according to a firm hierarchy. Those who commanded a hundred warriors received a silver tablet, those who commanded a thousand received one made of gold, "and he who has command of ten thousand has a tablet of gold with a lion's head." These lucky few were also lavishly rewarded with pearls, precious stones, and horses. And those who commanded a hundred thousand received gold tablets engraved with lions, falcons, the sun, and the moon.

Each tablet of authority conferred by Kublai Khan on one of his loyal barons carried the following inscription: "By the power and strength of the great God and of the great grace that he has given to our emperor, blest be the name of the Great Khan, and may all those who shall not obey him be slain and destroyed." Recipients also received "warrants on paper" explaining in writing their responsibilities and privileges.

The uppermost rank, those commanding 100,000 men, were highly conspicuous. By order of the khan, anyone of that rank who rode in public did so beneath a golden canopy "as a sign of great authority." Not only that, but during convocations, he was to sit in a silver chair. As an even greater sign of respect, the khan permitted his barons to ride whatever horses they wished; they could take them from commanders serving under them, not to mention from ordinary soldiers, and they could even ride those belonging to Kublai Khan. The honor conferred by the tablet of authority was great, and obedience to its tenets was absolute: "If any dared not to obey in everything according to the will and command of those who have those tablets, he must die as a rebel against the Great Khan."

DESPITE THEIR advanced warrior culture and astonishing record of conquests, the Mongols lagged behind the Chinese in technology, art, literature, architecture, philosophy, and dress. They even lacked a common language with which to administer their transcontinental empire. The Mongol court conducted business in a Babel of tongues; there were scribes for Mongolian, Arabic, Persian, Uighur, Tangut, Chinese, and Tibetan, among other languages. The scribes became adept at improvising multilingual written equivalents for the names and titles of Hindu deities, Chinese generals, Muslim holy men, and Persian dignitaries. To reach as many constituents as possible, court scribes translated Uighur—perhaps the most widely spoken tongue—into simplified Chinese characters, but this solution failed to resolve the complex communication quandary facing Kublai Khan and his ministers.

As a loyal servant of Kublai Khan, Marco relied on Mongolian, the tongue of the conqueror, or Persian, the lingua franca of foreigners in the Mongol court. For this reason, Marco frequently used Persian place-names in his account, not because he depended on Persian sources, as some skeptics have argued, but because he was following the accepted practice of the Mongol Empire.

In keeping with his aspiration to become the "universal emperor," Kublai sought to encourage a common written language for all the peoples of his empire. To bring order to the chaos of Mongol communication, he commissioned an influential Tibetan monk named Matidhvaja Sribhadra to devise an entirely new language: an alphabet capable of transcribing all known tongues. Endowed with prodigious intellectual gifts, the monk was said to have taught himself to read and write soon after birth, and could recite a dense Buddhist text known as the Hevajra Tantra from memory by the age of three. As a result of these accomplishments, he was called 'Phags-pa, Tibetan for "Exceptional One." Having arrived at the Mongol court in 1253 as an eighteen-year-old prodigy, 'Phags-pa later found special favor with Kublai Khan's principal wife, Chabi, and came to exert a profound influence over the court.

Although Kublai Khan professed to respect four distinct faiths, 'Phags-pa ensured that his Buddhist sect, the Sa-skya-pa, ranked first among equals. To the Chinese purist, the Mongol version of Buddhism was debased, corrupt; it derived from the Tantric Buddhism of Tibet, whose lamas, "Superior Ones," demonstrated a proficiency in sorcery that alternately delighted and intimidated the deeply superstitious Mongols and impressed the skeptical Marco Polo.

For a time, 'Phags-pa directed all spiritual matters at court, and even Kublai Khan deferred to him. In exchange for spiritual validation, he bestowed on the young monk a golden mandala said to contain pearls "the size of sheep droppings." When the two met for their mystical séances, 'Phags-pa sat above his pupil, and when conducting secular business, they traded places. The see-saw relationship was intended to demonstrate a harmonious balance between spiritual and temporal matters.

In 1269, 'Phags-pa, in fulfillment of his commission, presented Kublai Khan with a syllabic alphabet—that is, one in which symbols represent consonants and vowels—consisting of forty-one letters, based on traditional Tibetan. The new written language became known as "square script," owing to the letters' form. It was written vertically, from top to bottom, and from left to right, using these symbols:

Consonants

									Vowels
𖣔	ka	𖣔	tta	𖣔	pa	𖣔	zha	𖣔	ha	𖣔 i
𖣔	kha	𖣔	ttha	𖣔	pha	𖣔	za	𖣔	'a	𖣔 u
𖣔	ga	𖣔	dda	𖣔	ba	𖣔	-a	𖣔	qu	𖣔 e
𖣔	nga	𖣔	nna	𖣔	ma	𖣔	ya	𖣔	xa	𖣔 o
𖣔	ca	𖣔	ta	𖣔	tsa	𖣔	ra	𖣔	fa	𖣔 ee
𖣔	cha	𖣔	tha	𖣔	tsha	𖣔	la	𖣔	gga	
𖣔	ja	𖣔	da	𖣔	dza	𖣔	sha			
𖣔	nya	𖣔	na	𖣔	wa	𖣔	sa			

The system transcribed the spoken Mongolian tongue with more accuracy than its improvised predecessors, and even recorded the sounds of other languages, notably Chinese. Kublai Khan proudly designated this linguistic innovation as the language of Mongol officialdom, and he founded academies to promote its use. The Mongolian Language School opened the same year, and two years later, the National University. 'Phags-pa script appeared on paper money, on porcelain, and in official edicts of the Yüan empire, but scholars and scribes, devoted by sentiment and training to Chinese, Persian, or other established languages, resisted adopting it. Nor did Marco demonstrate familiarity with the new Mongol idiom.

In 1274, about the time the Polo company arrived in Mongolia, 'Phags-pa retired to the Sa-skya-pa monastery in Tibet, where he died in 1280. By that time, his version of Buddhism was falling into disfavor with the Mongols, and his clever script had failed to catch on, except among a small number of adherents who employed it on ceremonial occasions. It remained a worthy but failed experiment in artificial or constructed language.

KUBLAI KHAN's intimate life was as structured, and as extravagant, as other aspects of his empire. Marco's high position allowed him to become familiar with Kublai's extended family, which was large enough to make Europeans gasp in disbelief. "He has four women whom he holds always as his true wives, and the eldest son which he has of these four women ought to be lord of the empire by right when the Great Khan should die," Marco reports. "The [wives] are called empresses, and each is called also by her proper name. And each of those ladies holds a court by herself in her own palace; for there is none who has not three hundred"—in some versions of Marco's account, the number swells to a thousand, or even ten thousand—"girls [who are] very fair and amiable." In all, "they have very many valets and eunuchs, and many other men and women, so that each of these ladies has in her court ten thousand persons."

Drawing on his familiarity with Kublai, Marco dared to follow this august personage into the bedroom to glimpse his extraordinary sexual behavior. "Whenever he wishes to lie with any one of these four women, he makes her come to his room, and sometimes he goes to the room of his wife." As if they were not enough to keep him occupied, the khan had "many other concubines" at his disposal. Marco says that many came from the province of Kungurat, in Afghanistan, the home of a "very handsome and fair-skinned people; these women are very beautiful and adorned with excellent manners." They moved with uncommon suppleness, altogether feline, seductive, and alluring, and they dressed in a strikingly attention-snaring fashion, wearing a head-piece from which dangled long, glimmering strands of pearls, framing the face, and making the eyebrows into a sharp dark horizontal streak. The pearl headpiece focused their gaze until their dark eyes haunted the dreams of an emperor—or an impressionable young Venetian.

Like so much else in the Mongol court, the process of selecting concubines fit to serve the khan was highly ritualized. Every other year, Marco explains, "The Great Khan sends his messengers to . . . find him the most beautiful girls according to the standard that he gives them, four hundred, five hundred, more or less, as they think right."

Once assembled, the girls appeared before "judges deputed for this purpose, who, seeing and considering all the parts of each separately—that is, the hair, the face, and the eyebrows, the mouth, the lips, and the other limbs—that they may be harmonious and proportioned to the body, value some at sixteen carats, others at seventeen, eighteen, twenty." Only those fortunate girls awarded twenty carats or more were selected and ushered into the presence of Kublai Khan himself, where they submitted to the scrutiny of still more judges. The procedure yielded forty maidens valued at the highest number of carats and, as Marco puts it, "chosen for his own room."

Even these select girls had to undergo one final intimate inspection before they were deemed fit for Kublai Khan's bed. Under his direction, the "elder ladies of the palace . . . make them [the girls] lie with them in one bed to know if she has good breath and sweet, and is clean, and sleeps quietly without snoring, and has no unpleasant scent anywhere, and to know if she is a virgin, and quite sound in all things."

This description, as explicit as Marco dared to make it, is usually taken to mean that the barons' wives engaged in sex with the female recruits to break them in and train them in the arts of love. Those who passed this most intimate test of all, who were "good and fair and sound in all their limbs," were "sent to wait on their lord."

Every three days, six winners of this Mongol beauty contest were dispatched to Kublai Khan's quarters, "both in the room and in the bed and for all that he needs; and the Great Khan does with them what he pleases." When he finished, the exhausted girls departed, only to be replaced by a second shift of six. "And so it goes all the year that every three days and three nights they are changed until the number of those hundred is completed, and they stay for another turn."

During the orgies, Kublai Khan remained undisturbed by anyone except the young concubines. "If the lord has need of anything extraordinary, as drink or food or other things, the girls who are in the lord's chamber order those in the other room what they must prepare, and they prepare it immediately. And so the lord is not waited on by other persons, but by the girls." All the while, girls valued at fewer carats assisted other ladies in waiting, learning to sew and to make gloves, and "other genteel work."

The khan shared his surplus of women with his barons, earning the goodwill and cementing the loyalty of all his petitioners. "When any gentleman is looking for wives, the Great Khan gives him one with a very great dowry, and in this way he finds them all husbands of good position." As described by Marco, this intricate system of sharing sexual entitlements satisfied the needs of all the interested parties.

Marco realized that the arrangement required a remarkable degree of acquiescence on the part of Kublai Khan's subjects, who found a justification for losing their daughters in the irresistible movements of the planets. "Are not the men . . . annoyed that the Great Khan takes their

daughters from them?" Marco asks. "Certainly not." It was no shame
for a woman to be plucked from her town to serve the khan sexually,
but a form of royal recognition. "They think it a great favor and honor,
and are very glad that they have pretty daughters which he deigns to
accept, because, they say, 'If a daughter is born under a good planet
and with good fortune, the lord will be able to satisfy her better and
will marry her into a good position, which I should not have been able
to do.' "

KUBLAI KHAN believed that he was fulfilling Heaven's mandate to
produce as many heirs as possible. According to Marco's tally, Kublai
Khan sired twenty-two sons by his four wives, and twenty-five additional sons by his concubines. (His many daughters did not merit comment.) To hear the diplomatic Venetian tell it, every one of Kublai
Khan's male heirs possessed the father's courage and sagacity. And
every one wanted to be the next "great khan." Of them all, Kublai's
oldest surviving son, Chinkim, was expected to inherit the throne. He
had distinguished himself on horseback and in scholarship, and he was
popular with nearly everyone except for his direct rivals. Placed in
charge of the sensitive task of collecting taxes, he firmly opposed corruption, yet he was generous in providing assistance to families
afflicted by natural disasters such as drought and floods. In these
respects, he proved himself a worthy successor to his father.

According to the Persian historian Vassaf, "When Kublai approached his seventieth year, he desired to raise . . . Chinkim to the
position of representative and declared successor during his own lifetime; so he took counsel with the chiefs." The other khans, not surprisingly, declared that Kublai's proposal violated the precepts laid
down by Genghis Khan himself—Chinkim was not eligible to become
the "great khan" during his father's lifetime—but they did pledge to
support him after Kublai Khan's death. To the young Marco, it seemed
as if that day would never come.

But even Kublai Khan was mortal.

CHAPTER EIGHT

In the Service of the Khan

The shadow of the dome of pleasure
Floated midway on the waves;
Where was heard the mingled measure
From the fountain and the caves.

T HE SEAT OF Kublai Khan's power was "the great city called Cambulac," where he wintered over. This was a recent development in his empire. Ever since 1220, the Mongols, led by Genghis Khan, had considered Karakorum, on the Mongolian Steppe, to be their capital. Kublai Khan later decided to move the center of authority to the south, as if to superimpose Mongol might on Chinese civilization.

Kublai Khan chose a Muslim architect to oversee the construction of Cambulac, even though it was designed to demonstrate to the Chinese that Kublai's dynasty drew inspiration from them and identified with them. Work commenced in 1267. When it was completed several years later, the city featured eleven gates guarded by imposing three-story towers that served as observation platforms.

In the multilingual Mongol Empire, the new capital was known by several names. The Chinese called it Ta-tu, "Great Capital." The Turks knew it as Khanbalikh—which Marco spelled "Cambulac"—"City of the Khan." And the Mongols, adapting the Chinese name, called it Daidu. Today the city is known as Beijing.

BY THE TIME OF Marco's visit, the new city's eastern section was devoted to the study of astronomy, which held a special fascination for

Kublai Khan, with his capacious vision of the world. Kublai, inspired by a Persian center at Maragheh, Azerbaijan, renowned for its discoveries of celestial objects and for the sophisticated stargazing instruments devised there, had long wanted his own observatory.

To realize his vision, Kublai sent for a Persian astronomer, Jamal al-Din, who brought with him a trove of plans for state-of-the-art devices: the sundial, the astrolabe, celestial and terrestrial globes, and an armillary sphere—a skeletal celestial sphere with a model of Earth or the Sun in the center, often used for instruction. All of these mechanisms were more advanced than their European counterparts.

Modern astronomy in the West owes much to its Chinese and Arab precursors. In the traditional Chinese model, which the West eventually came to adopt, the equator is conceived as a circle around the globe, and the north pole as the uppermost point—a model that seems natural and obvious these days. European astronomers of Marco's time employed a different configuration, one based on the horizon and the Sun's motion through the heavens (the "ecliptic"). They gave the equator short shrift until Tycho Brahe, the Danish astronomer active in the late sixteenth century, adopted the Chinese approach, which had been in use at least since 2400 BC.

In the Chinese system, the heavens radiated from a central stem in twenty-eight distinct segments known as *xiu*, or lunar mansions. Each *xiu* had its complement of stars and constellations. For the Chinese, the heavens were orderly rather than random. As early as the seventh century—nearly a thousand years before their European counterparts—they observed that comet tails always point away from the sun; thus they anticipated the discovery of the solar wind. And they discovered craters on the moon long before Europeans, who, until the Copernican revolution, considered the moon, along with all other heavenly bodies, to be a perfect sphere.

In 1271, the year before Marco's arrival, Kublai Khan, recognizing the achievements of Persian astronomers, established the Institute of Muslim Astronomy. With the cross-cultural fertilization that would become typical of the Yüan dynasty, he enlisted the efforts of an esteemed Chinese engineer and astronomer, Guo Shoujing, who in turn employed Persian diagrams to build instruments and develop formulas to calculate a new Mongol calendar, similar to the Chinese lunar calendar. In the Mongol calendar, based on a twelve-year cycle, each year is named for a particular animal meant to characterize it: mouse, cow, tiger, rabbit, dragon, snake, horse, sheep, monkey, cock, dog, or pig. In this scheme, the year of the monkey exhibits simian traits; it is rambunctious and high-strung, a difficult year indeed.

The subtleties of Mongol and Chinese astronomy were lost on Marco, concerned as he was with earthly matters. Like other Europeans, the young man considered astronomy and astrology synonymous, and the refinements of Kublai Khan's astronomers failed to engage his curiosity. He was far more intrigued by the ubiquitous wizards and soothsayers. In Cambulac alone, he estimated, no fewer than five thousand "astrologers and diviners" plied their trade, according to their religious beliefs and cultural background—Muslim, Christian, or Chinese.

MARCO FAMILIARIZED himself with the various lunar calendars in use throughout the Mongol Empire. He reported that every year Christian, Muslim, and Chinese astrologers searched the heavens to watch "the course and arrangement of the whole year in this astrology according to the course of each moon. For they see and find what sort of weather each moon of that year will produce according to the natural course and arrangement of the planets and signs and their properties. Namely, in such a moon there will be thunders and tempests; in such, an earthquake; in such, thunderbolts, lightning, and many rains; in such, sicknesses and plagues and wars and infinite quarrels, and so on with each moon."

The astrologers gathered their celestial predictions into "little pamphlets into which they write everything that shall happen in each month that year"—the Asian version of *Poor Richard's Almanack*, the compendium of weather forecasts and other practical information assembled and published by Benjamin Franklin during the eighteenth century.

According to Marco, anyone planning "some great work"—a trip, a business venture—"will go to find one of these astrologers and say to him, 'See in your books how the sky stands just now, because I wish to go do such business or trade,' telling him the year, month, day, hour, and minute of his birth; because everyone as soon as he is born is taught about his nativity." After finding the planet under which his supplicant was born, the astrologer proceeds to "foretell him everything that will happen to him on that journey in order, and how his proposal will prosper in his doings, whether well or ill." A merchant such as Marco Polo might be cautioned to postpone his travels until a planet opposing trade moved out of range, or, to avoid its harmful influence, might be advised to leave the city by a gate facing away from the invisible planetary threat.

Marco's descriptions of "pamphlets" and "books"—although not found in all early manuscripts—confound skeptics of his presence in China who claim he never mentioned them. He was, in fact, aware of printing, but he overlooked the significance of this potent technology. His lapse is understandable because the invention of movable type lay almost two centuries in the future for Europe, and he could not have foreseen its role in disseminating the Bible and other important works. As a merchant, he immediately grasped the significance of paper currency, but books devoted to astrology remained a mere curiosity. For Marco, location was paramount, and no place on earth fascinated him more than Cambulac, the sudden center of Mongol civilization.

"THE PALACE IS square in every way," says Marco. "First, there is a square circuit of wall, and each face is eight miles long, round which there is a deep moat; and in the middle of each side is a gate by which all the people enter who gather here from every side. Then there is a space of a mile all around; there the soldiers are stationed. After that space is found another circuit of wall, of six miles for a side." The scale of this city, and its walls, was enough to make Marco's European audience gasp with astonishment. Instead of the quaint capital they may have imagined, a giant fortress rose as testimony to the strength of the Mongol Empire.

With this centralized capital, Kublai Khan attempted to alter the Mongol tradition, and the course of Mongol history, from nomadic to pastoral. The marvel of Cambulac and Kublai Khan's great experiment was that it worked. Marco witnessed this metropolis at its zenith, and he recorded a vivid description of Kublai's palace of the Mongols, a forerunner of the Chinese royal residence that came to be known as the Forbidden City, later built on the same site and incorporating some of the buildings and outdoor spaces that Marco had scrupulously chronicled. "At each angle of this wall, and in the middle of each of the faces, is a beautiful and spacious palace," Marco continues, "so that all around about the wall are eight palaces, in which are kept the munitions of the Great Khan, that is, one kind of trappings in each; as bridles, saddles, stirrups, and other things which belong to the equipment of horses. And in another bows, strings, quivers, arrows, and other things belonging to archery. In another cuirasses"—armor, especially breastplates—"corselets, and similar things of boiled leather."

A wall surrounded the entire complex, with "a great gate which is never opened except when the Great Khan comes out of it to make war." Kublai's palace, concealed within these walls, "is the greatest and most wonderful ever seen," a dwelling of unsurpassed luxury, shimmering and dreamlike in Marco's soaring description. "The walls of the halls and of the rooms are all covered with gold and with silver, and there are portrayed dragons and beasts and birds and fair stories of ladies and knights and other beautiful things and stories of wars, which are on the walls; and the roof is also made so that nothing else is seen there but gold and silver and paintings. The hall is so great and broad that it is a great marvel, and more than six thousand men would well feed there at once, sitting at table together. In that palace there are four hundred rooms, so many that it is a marvel to see them. It is so beautiful and large and rich and so well made and arranged that there is not a man in the world who would know how to plan it better nor make it." Although Marco seems to overstate yet again, he is accurately describing the size of the Mongol palace.

When he raised his eyes to the sky, he saw more wonders, which presaged the grandeur of the Forbidden City. "The roofs above are all red and green and azure and peacock blue and yellow and of all colors, and are glazed so well and so cleverly that they are bright like crystal, so that they shine very far round the palace. And you may know that the roof is so strong and so firmly put together that it lasts many years." He displays a thorough knowledge of the interior as well, writing, "In the part behind the palace there are large houses, rooms, and halls, in which are the private things of the lord, that is, all his treasure, gold, silver, precious stones, and pearls, and his vessels of gold and of silver; where his ladies and concubines stay, and where he has his affairs done conveniently and when he pleases; into which other people do not enter."

The grounds of this precursor to the Forbidden City offered a spectacular complement to the buildings. Where Venice consisted of treacherous canals and narrow, refuse-filled streets, the Mongol capital offered broad, clean, safe avenues; a sophisticated drainage system to channel rainwater for irrigation; and lakes and rivers generously stocked with fish—all combined with pleasing prospects at every turn. No wonder that Marco raves about "very beautiful large lawns and gardens and beautiful and good trees of different sorts of fruits in which are many kinds of strange beasts." To these creatures he gives special attention: "These are white stags, the animals that make the musk, roe-deer, fallow deer, and squirrels, and ermines, and many kinds of other strange beautiful animals in great abundance."

The landscape within the city walls also receives his praise: "The meadows have grass in abundance, because all the streets are paved and raised two cubits above the ground, so that no mud ever collects on them nor is the rain water caught there, but running through the meadows it fattens the land and makes the grass grow abundantly. At one corner . . . is a very large lake (of the earth from which was made the hill mentioned below), in which are many kinds of fish . . . and every time the great lord [Kublai Khan] wishes some of those fish he has them at his will."

There seemed no end to Cambulac's marvels. "Moreover," he writes, "I tell you that a great river flows in there and makes a kind of fish pond; and there the animals go to drink; and flows out of the lake afterwards, passing through a conduit near the said hill. . . . It is so planned that no fish can escape, and this is done and is closed with nets of iron wire and of brass both at the entry of the river into the lake and also at the exit. . . . There are also swans and other waterfowl."

The sights were marvelous, and Marco insisted that his audience believe his account down to the smallest detail.

THE SCIENCE OF urban planning, Marco hastens to inform his readers, was far advanced in China. He points out how the city of Cambulac consisted of broad main streets "drawn out straight as a thread," running from one gate to the next, and bordered by "stalls and shops of every kind." Wherever he looked, he saw beautiful inns, houses, and palaces. Behind it all, a rigorous logic ruled. "The city is laid out by squares, as a chessboard is, and is so beautiful and so skillfully planned that in no way would it be possible to tell of it." The plan was not merely esthetically pleasing; it was also intended to discourage criminal activity. Gates could be swung shut to isolate a street or square, and hiding places were scarce.

Marco thrilled to the striking of Cambulac's great "town clock" three times every evening, "so that none may go about the town after it has sounded." In fact, no one even dared to leave his house "except for the nurses who go for the needs of women in childbirth and physicians who go for the needs of sick men." And even these caregivers had to bring lanterns with them on their errands of mercy.

Sentries, a thousand of them at every gate, guarded the entire city against the depredations of robbers and marauders. "Besides this," Marco reports, "the guards always ride through the city by night, by thirty and by forty, searching and inquiring if anyone is going about the city at an unusual hour, that is, after the third sounding of the bell." The guards immediately arrested and jailed any suspicious person. "In the morning, the officials deputed for this examine him, and if they find him guilty of any offence, they punish him, according to the degree of it, with more or less blows of the rod, by which they sometimes die." All the while, within his gigantic palace, the khan and his wives, family retainers, and concubines slept in peace, and Marco felt more secure in this strange city than the average citizen did in Venice.

This utopian city planning stood in contrast to Marco's Venice, where sinuous streets and canals concealed vice and sedition, and where predators hid under bridges and in the shadows of irregular buildings. It is as though Marco were compiling astonishing bulletins from the future for the benefit of his countrymen, mired in the past. The future, he advised, was China.

IN HIS DESIRE to impress Europeans with the grandeur of the Mongol court, Marco told of feasts whose excess far exceeded their European counterparts. "When the Great Khan keeps his table in his hall for any great court and feast and rejoicing that he may wish to hold, he is seated in this way," Marco explains in three-dimensional detail. "For first the table of the great lord is set before his throne very high above all the others. He sits in the north part of the hall with the shoulders toward the tramontane"—the land beyond the mountains—"so that his face looks toward midday, and his first wife sits beside him on the left side, and on the right side, but at another table which is lower, sit his sons in lordly fashion, and likewise his grandsons, according to their ages, and his kindred and others who are connected by blood, . . . so low that I tell you their heads come to the feet of the great lord. . . . And it goes in the same way with the women, that at the feet of the first queen is the table of the other queens and of the younger children of the Great Khan; for all the wives of the sons of the great lord and of his grandsons and of his kindred sit on the left side, namely, of the empress, also more low; and next sit all the wives of the barons and of the knights, and they also sit lower." The pleasing arrangement means that the "great lord can see all the feasters, and they are always a very great number."

An incalculable number of revelers participated. At first Marco hesitates to offer an estimate, then he succumbs to temptation: "The greater part of the knights and barons eat in the hall on carpets, because they have not tables. And outside this hall are other halls at the sides; and in these royal banquets there sometimes feed more than forty thousand, besides those who are of the lord's court, who always come in numbers to sing and to make various sport. And many more times than ten thousand persons eat at the tables that are outside the great hall." Though sincere, Marco did not expect his readers to believe his figures, but he relished challenging Western ideas of Mongol life.

In the midst of this enormous festive hall stood a "most beautiful structure, large and rich, made in the manner of a square chest." Decorated with gilded carvings of animals, it contained a "great and valuable vessel in the shape of a great pitcher of fine gold that holds quite as much wine as a common large butt." It was surrounded by a number of smaller silver vessels containing "good spiced drinks," including the inevitable fermented mare's milk, supplemented with camel's milk.

The honored guests drank from "lacquered bowls" large enough to accommodate the thirst of eight or ten, using golden ladles. Once again Marco leaps ahead of his readers: lacquer was another technology raised to a high level of refinement in Asia, yet it was unknown in the West. Lacquer is, essentially, a sophisticated varnish made from resin extruded by an Asian sumac, *Rhus verniciflua*, known in China as the varnish tree. When the resin, similar to that of poison ivy, is layered as a thin film, it hardens into a tough skin, but only in the dark; exposed to sunlight, it remains tacky. Although Marco does not appear familiar with how lacquer was produced, he takes care to explain the vessel for Europeans unfamiliar with it: "The ladles are made like a gold cup with a foot and a golden handle, and with that cup they take wine from that great golden lacquer bowl and are able to drink." He says that there were so many of these "golden bowls" and "other things of great value" that "all those who see them are dumbfounded."

These exotic feasting customs could be confusing to the many "foreigners" who were guests at the court, so Kublai Khan obligingly assigned several of his barons the task of acquainting visitors with Mongol ways. "These barons go continually here and there through the hall asking those who sit at table if they want anything, and if any there wish for wine, milk, or meat, or anything else, they have it brought to them immediately by the servants."

Stranger still, those who served the khan food and drink had "their mouths and their noses wrapped in beautiful veils or napkins of silk and of gold, so that neither their breath nor their smell should come into the food and the drink of the great lord." Musicians, "of which there [were] a vast quantity," awaited the moment when the khan brought food to his lips, and then they began to perform. At that point, a boy presented a cup of wine to the khan, then walked backward three paces and knelt, whereupon "all the barons and all the other people who are there kneel down and make a sign of great humility; and then the great lord drinks." Even after all this ritual, feasting commenced only when the knights and barons in attendance brought food to their first wives.

The entertainment offerings were hypnotic. Dressed in iridescent attire, musicians played bewitching melodies on stringed instruments, lulling everyone present into a state of pleasant stupefaction. Mongolian music, so repetitive and insistent, was haunting and beguiling; it numbed the mind even as it awakened the soul with intensely pleasurable, even sexual sounds. The musicians were followed by highly theatrical, spectacularly costumed troupes of jugglers and acrobats, who in turn gave way to itinerant actors reciting poetry and soothsayers spouting whatever they pleased. "And all make great enjoyment and great festivity before the great lord," Marco comments, "and make much joy of it and laugh at it and enjoy it much."

MARCO REMINDED his audience that even in the midst of revelry, the Mongol barons observed a strict code of behavior. For example, two "great men like giants," each holding a rod in his hands, guarded every door to the feasting hall. The forbidding sight reminded everyone present that "no one is allowed to touch the threshold of the door, but he must stretch his foot beyond. And if by accident he touches it"—

a mere *accident*—"the guards take away all his clothes, and then again he must redeem them; and if they do not take his clothes, they give him as many blows as are appointed him." At least foreigners received a warning about this rule from the barons, who explained that touching the threshold was considered an ill omen. But the Mongols were realistic as well as superstitious; if any man became too drunk during the feasting to cross the threshold as he left the hall without tripping all over it, he was excused.

"And when it is all done, the people leave and each goes back to his lodging and to his house as he pleases."

KUBLAI KHAN, Marco explains, was born "on the twenty-eighth day of the moon of the month of September," according to the Mongol calendar. (This date is reckoned as September 23, 1215, in the modern calendar.) At that time, his grandfather, Genghis Khan, was busy laying siege to the city of Cambulac. Later, Kublai's birthday became the greatest feast of the entire lunar year. In preparation for the event, the khan dressed "in the most noble cloth of the purest beaten gold." In his honor, no less than twelve thousand barons emulated him by also dressing in silk and gold, although their clothes were not so valuable as the Great Khan's. Marco the merchant could not help but put a price on the festive attire. "Some of these robes," he calculated, "are worth ten thousand bezants of gold"—especially those with the pearls and gems sewn into them.

These cherished costumes went on display thirteen times a year, "for the solemn feast-days that the Tartars keep with great ceremony according to the thirteen moons of the year." They bore a total of 156,000 gems, by his estimate. "And when the lord wears any robe those barons and knights are likewise dressed in one of the same color; but those of the lord are of more value and more costly ornament." With frequent use, the raiment lasted ten years, at the very most. Then the costumes were retired.

INUNDATED with descriptions like these, Western readers assumed that Il Milione was engaging in embellishment to flatter Kublai Khan, or simply weaving fantasies to amuse himself. Yet the annals of the Yüan dynasty confirm the accuracy of Marco's eyewitness account, including the pearls sewn into the royal garments.

"The headdress and costume are made of fine black silk," begins the official description of Kublai Khan's exquisitely detailed wardrobe.

The top part of the headdress or ceremonial bonnet is a flat piece covered with the same cloth, and from which ribbons dangle. The outer garment is azure; it is lined with skin-colored cloth. Four ribbons encircle it with dragons and clouds. The opening of the bonnet or headdress is rimmed all around with a band of fine pearls. In front and behind are twelve pendants also made with twelve strung pearls. Left and right are two knots of raw yellow silk, from which hang tassels bearing earrings in jade and precious stones; strands of raw yellow silk, decorated with pearls, circle all the way to the top of the headdress. Dragons and clouds made of pearls sewn on with silk thread cover its surface. One can also see representations, here and there, of female swallows and small willows, and strings of pearls across the top form the picture of a river. The belt, to the right and left, descends to the floor. Flowers made of embroidered pearls are hidden in its knotted folds, as well as swallows and willows made of pearls. From two silk cords hang—or are fastened—all the pins that hold in place the dangling tassels of the headdress or crown; yellow strands of raw silk are employed to represent swallows and willows sprinkled with pearls. Jade pins are placed crosswise on the headdress or crown. . . . The under-garment is made of red or scarlet silk; it is cut like a skirt; it is decorated with a variety of embroideries, sixteen in number, arranged in rows; on each row there are two kinds of floating water-plants, one rice-stalk, two embroidered axes, and two Chinese characters. The ordinary garment or dress is of sheer white silk, edged with yellow leather thongs stitched with silk. The garment covering the knees (the upper-boot) is of red silk, and around the legs the red silk is elastic. Its shape is like that of a short skirt, at the top of which is embroidered a dragon with two bodies. . . .

The leggings are made of red silk. The shoes are made of silk with various decorations enriched with gold; they have two pairs of flaps, and are edged with stitching and with pearl ornaments. The stockings are made of fine red silk.

Here was the Kublai Khan whom Marco beheld. No wonder the glorious sight dazzled the impressionable young Venetian.

. . .

ON KUBLAI KHAN'S BIRTHDAY, Marco notes, all the "kings and
princes and barons who are subject to his jurisdiction" held feasts and
bestowed gifts in his honor. Some bearers requested large favors of the
khan, such as a domain to rule. Displaying his usual foresight, Kublai
appointed a committee to assign domains to worthy petitioners. Marco
again stresses that Kublai Khan's appeal transcended religious and cultural boundaries, especially on this day, when "all people of whatever
faith they are, all the idolaters and all the Christians or the Jews and all
the Saracens and all the other races of the Tartar people"—here Marco
appears to paraphrase a Mongol formula—"who are subject to the rule
of the Great Khan must make great petitions and great assemblies and
great prayers, each to the idols and to their God with great chants,
great lights, and great incense, that he may be pleased to save and protect them."

For all its detail, Marco's offhand account only hints at the actual
complexity of the Great Khan's birthday rites. Despite his immersion
in the Mongol lifestyle, Marco inevitably missed many subtleties, or
they eluded his memory when the time came to describe them to Rustichello. The section of the Mongol annals known as the "General
Ceremonial for the Receptions at the Mongolian Court" relates the
full story of Kublai Khan's extraordinary birthday festival.

"When the day of the reception arrives," reads the official account,

> the aides of ceremonies introduce those invited, starting at day-
> break, and conduct them to their assigned places. The "Chiefs
> of the Guards," all dressed in their special costumes, enter the
> great "room of rest." First, they take in their hand their ivory
> tablets (which each brought on his way to court) and make the
> prescribed genuflections. Then the "Informers of the Exterior"
> and the "Stewards of the Interior" enter and communicate the
> program that prescribes the formalities that must be observed
> during the ceremony. They bow, prostrating themselves, and
> rise. The emperor comes out of his interior apartments and gets
> onto his imperial chariot. Then cries are heard, together with
> the whips of the guardians. Three aides make the spectators
> align themselves left and right, and take them by hand to their
> places. The "Chiefs of the Guards" open the procession, pre-

ceded by heralds carrying hatchets, and they go outside of the "Room of the Great Light." The "Hatchet-Bearers" place themselves in front of the entrance and remain standing there, facing north, directing the crowd to prostrate itself; then they place themselves in the open apartments, east and west. This done, they conduct the crowd, in sections, outside the wall, to wait.

In the official account, Kublai Khan and his first wife, referred to as the emperor and empress, in Chinese fashion, ascend to their rest couch. At that moment, "cries of joy and lashes of whips are heard. Three arms heralds, carrying hatchets, open a passage through the crowd and return to place themselves east of the 'Steps of the Dew' "— the stairs leading to the palace.

There followed hours of carefully choreographed praying and bowing, led by the designated functionaries. For sheer size and complexity, nothing like this display existed in any European court of Marco's day, and he was properly awed. The ritual relied heavily on Chinese models, and sentiment among the Mongols accused Kublai Khan of exchanging basic Mongol ways, especially nomadism, for rarefied and very un-Mongol behavior. That was an exaggeration. Although he mastered the outward forms of Chinese court ceremonies with the help of Chinese advisers, who were imbued with tradition, he remained a Mongol at heart, and on the battlefield.

MARCO PERCEIVED the Mongol hierarchy as one based on performance in war rather than behavior within the confines of the court. Kublai Khan, he relates, "has chosen twelve very great and powerful wise men and barons to watch over whatever questions may arise about the armies, that is, to change them from the place where they are and to change the officers, or to send them where they see it is necessary" as well as "to make the distinction of the valiant and manly fighters from those who are mean and abject, promoting them to greater rank, and on the other hand demoting those who are of little use and cowardly." Accordingly, if a captain of a thousand men behaved badly in action, he was demoted to captain of a hundred, and if he behaved with great valor, he could be promoted to captain of ten thousand.

The twelve barons who made up the Great Court served directly under Kublai Khan. They formed a closely knit band, living together in Cambulac in a palace described by Marco as "large and beautiful and rich." Each of these barons had "for each province under his rule a judge and many writers or notaries under him, who all stay in this palace each in his house by himself."

MARCO ESTEEMED the same sense of logic and orderliness in the celebrated Mongol post system, a necessity for administering the diverse empire. "The manner of the messengers of the Great Khan is wonderful," he exults. Displaying even greater attention to detail than usual, he describes the intricate Mongol operation: "I assure you the messengers ride 200 miles in a day, sometimes even 250. Let me explain how it is done. When a messenger wishes to travel at this speed and cover so many miles a day, he carries a tablet with the sign of the falcon as a token that he wishes to ride posthaste. If there are two riders . . . , they tighten their belts and swathe their heads, and off they go with all the speed they can muster till they reach the next post-house twenty-five miles away." On arrival, he says, they change horses, and "without a moment's breathing space, . . . off they go again." It was thunder and lightning on the hoof.

Each road leaving Cambulac was named for the province to which it led. At a distance of twenty-five miles, the messengers reached a "post with horses" as well as a "very great palace . . . where the messengers and envoys of the great lord may lodge with dignity, and these lodgings have very rich beds furnished with rich silk cloths and have all the things that are right for exalted messengers." Even a king visiting one of these remote palaces would feel comfortable, Marco claims.

The principal function of the post was to stable fresh horses; each had no less than four hundred mounts at the ready, "that they may be able to dismount there, leaving the tired horses, and take fresh ones."

To Marco's eye, the complex system, with its many interdependent parts, worked flawlessly, transmitting vital information across great distances, as well as disparate cultures and languages. "In this way it goes through all the principal provinces and realms, cities and places of the great lord up to the borders of the neighboring provinces." Even off the main road, Kublai Khan had established smaller posts, thirty-five or even forty miles apart in remote areas. Marco claims that ten thousand of these posts, built at the khan's expense, dotted the landscape, each of them luxuriously furnished and capable of stabling twenty or so horses. These way stations provided safety and shelter for the footmen engaged in the essential task of directing messages to the proper recipients. The occupation called for a distinctive costume. "They wear a great and broad girdle all full round about of great balls, that is, of sounding bells, so that when they go, they may be heard from quite far."

Marco made a close study of these wonderful little outposts. He reports: "When the king wishes to send a letter by courier, the letter is given to one of the runners, and these go always running at great speed, and they go not more than three miles. . . . The other who is at the end of the three miles who hears him clearly by the bells coming from afar, stays all ready; and as soon as that one is come he takes the thing that he carries and takes a little ticket that the writer gives him and sets himself running and goes as far as the second three miles, and does just as the other had done. And so I tell you that in this way from these footmen the great lord has news from ten days' journeys in one day and in one night, for they go running by night as well as by day."

To cover longer distances, footmen yielded to horses trained for the task. "Messengers on horseback go expressly to tell the great lord news from any land which may be in rebellion against him." Each of these messengers carried special identification in the form of a tablet bearing the image of a falcon, as a sign that he wished to go "at express speed." The messengers "never have any but good animals and fresh for their needs. They take horses from the post, where they are ready for them, and if they are two, they set out from the place where they are on two good horses strong and swift; they bind up their belly and wrap up their heads, and set themselves to ride at full gallop to the utmost of their power, and gallop until they come to the next post at twenty-five miles, and then they find two other horses ready, fresh, and rested and swift."

Marco praised the system as a model of efficiency. "They mount so quickly that they do not rest themselves, and when they are mounted they set themselves immediately at full gallop, and do not cease to gallop till they are come to the next post; and there they find the other horses and men ready to change for the others, and they mount themselves as quickly and set themselves on the road. And so they do till the evening. And in this way," Marco concludes with vicarious pride and satisfaction, "messengers like these go two hundred and fifty miles in one day to carry news to the great lord speedily from distant parts, and also when there is need they go three hundred. And if it is a very grave case they ride at night; and if the moon does not shine, the men of the post go running before them with torches to the next post."

THERE WAS STILL more that Marco wished his readers to appreciate about Kublai Khan's splendid realm. Rows of towering trees marked the straight roads traveled by Kublai's messengers. Marco himself studied the sight as he followed in their tracks at a more leisurely pace. "The [trees] are so large that they can well be seen from very far," he reports. "The Great Khan has this done so that each may see the roads, and that merchants may rest in the shade, and that they may not lose their way either by day or by night when they go through desert places." And there was one other surprising benefit, according to Marco. "The Great Khan has [the trees] planted all the more gladly because his diviners and astrologers say that he who has trees planted lives a long time."

In the midst of surveying the Mongols' practical accomplishments, Marco pauses to praise the local rice wine, boiled and mixed with potent spices. He says it has "such a flavor that it is better than any other wine. It is clear and beautiful. It makes a man become drunken sooner than other wine because it is very hot." It is easy to imagine the young Venetian in an alcoholic daze gleefully admiring Kublai Khan's messengers, his trees, and all the other wonders of his realm—the perpetually burning stones, for instance.

Wherever he traveled in China, Marco came across "large black stones that are dug from the mountains as veins, which burn like logs." Everywhere, people put them to use. "They keep up the fire better than wood does," he notes. "If you put them on the fire in the evening and make them catch well, I tell you they keep fire all the night so that one finds some in the morning." These black stones gave off long-lasting, intense heat. They were so useful that Kublai Khan's subjects rarely resorted to burning wood, which was in short supply. "So great is the multitude of people, and stoves, and baths, which are continually heated, that the wood could not be enough" in a country where everyone bathed "at least three times a week, and in the winter every day if they can do so," in stark contrast to Mongols and Venetians.

The plentiful black stones making possible all this cooking, heat-ing, and bathing were lumps of coal, a source of energy that had been used throughout China for at least a thousand years. Yet in Marco's day, the notion of burning coal rather than wood for heat was practically unheard of in Europe. The existence of this black, dusty, carbon-rich substance had been noted at infrequent intervals throughout Western history, beginning with the Roman occupation of Britain and continuing to Marco's time, but not until the eighteenth century did coal become a common source of energy in European countries.

WITH TOUCHES LIKE THESE, Marco revealed Kublai Khan's splendid realm not as a static, remote fantasyland populated by savages, but as a vital state constantly on the alert for danger—an empire that never slept, where swift messengers moved by night if necessary, their way marked by reassuring rows of trees and lit by flickering torchlight. What could Venice do to equal such vigilance? So ran Marco's unspoken question. Could Venetians muster the same ingenuity, even if their lives depended on it?

The network of posts and messengers and fast horses reaching far and wide throughout the Mongol realm struck Marco as a grand achievement. "The greatest pride and greatest grandeur that any emperor has or might ever have," he exclaims. "A thing so wonderful and of so great cost that it could hardly be told or written." So wonderful, in fact, that it inspired Marco to deliver a stinging attack on Christianity.

WITH BLASPHEMOUS GUSTO, Marco explains to his readers that the key to maintaining this network of posts—and, by extension, the Mongol Empire—was the wonderful custom of polygamy. "If anyone were to doubt how there are so many people to do so many duties," he writes, "it is answered that all the idolaters and Saracens take six, eight, and ten wives each, provided that they can pay the expense, and beget infinite"—infinite!—"sons; and there will be many men of whom each will have more than thirty sons, and all follow him armed; and this is because of the many wives."

Nor did they starve, even with so many mouths to feed. Marco reports that they freely indulged their appetite for "plenty of victuals"—usually abundant grain combined with "milk or flesh." They also devoured "macaroni," a food that, contrary to Polo mythology, was already known in Italy. Their endless need for sustenance kept them busy. "With them, no land that can be ploughed lies fallow; and their animals increase and multiply without end, and when they go to the field, there is not one who does not take with him six, eight, and more horses for himself."

Christians could only envy the satisfying and fertile ways of these heathens. "With us," Marco laments, "one has but one wife, and if she is barren, the man will end his life with her and beget no son; therefore we have not so many people as they." It was now apparent where Marco's sympathies lay. He had become the most enthusiastic of converts.

Yet he saw the Mongols from a European perspective. Outwardly conventional, Marco subscribed to the medieval assumption that one's identity in life was determined by religion, place of birth, gender, social station, and birth order. In much the same way, he regarded the Mongol Empire as a fixed hierarchy with Kublai Khan at the top, and the khan's barons arrayed beneath him in predictable descending ranks. Marco and his collaborator stuck to their familiar categories even when experience strongly suggested otherwise. As nomads, the Mongols were less hierarchical than Marco suggested; their authority derived from their adaptability and their ability to take on the characteristics of the host culture in which they embedded themselves. Even though Marco was observant enough to describe their doing so, he remained at least partially oblivious to some aspects of their way of life. They were not simply the Asian equivalent of European nobility, but a drastically different type of society, living off the land, perpetually on the hoof, disconcertingly egalitarian and heterogeneous.

ON THE STEPPE, where the climate was harsh, and sustenance limited, Kublai Khan's ministers managed the food supply with a sensitivity unknown in Europe. When grain was abundant, they bought large quantities, which they stored for as many as four years. "When it happens that some grain fails and that the dearth is great," Marco reports, "then the great lord makes them take out some of his grain of which he has so much." Kublai sold grain to the needy at low prices for as long as the shortage lasted. And if famine threatened the populace, Marco says, Kublai Khan "does great charity and provision and alms to the poor people of Cambulac." Marco was referring to those families of six, eight, ten, or more crammed into one small dwelling, all with nothing to eat. In these dire cases, Kublai provided sufficient grain to feed them all for an entire year, if necessary.

Like other aspects of their government, the Mongols' welfare state was remarkably well organized. The afflicted families reported to officials appointed for this purpose. "Each shows a note of how much was given them in the past year for living, and according to that they [the officials] provide them [for] that year," Marco explains. "They provide them also with their clothes, because the Great Khan has the tenth of all the wool and silk and hemp of which clothes can be made." Drawing on a practice whereby all craftsmen were bound to give the khan the fruits of one day's labor every week, he was able to distribute clothing to the needy in winter and summer.

Marco recognized that among Europeans the Mongols carried a reputation for avoiding charity in any form. "The Tartars," he admits, "according to their customs, before they knew idol law, did no alms. When some poor man went to them they drove him away with abuse, saying to him, 'Go with the bad year that God gave thee, for if he had loved thee as he loves me, he would have done some good.' " According to Western beliefs, the Mongols let their hungry, sick, and elderly die—at least until Kublai Khan made public assistance part of his ruling style.

Wherever Marco looked, he found striking instances of Kublai Khan's innovative charity: "Those who wish to go to the court for the lord's bread daily can have a hot loaf; it is refused to none, but some is given to all who go, and it is sold to none." He estimates that twenty or thirty thousand people received their bread, as well as bowls of grain, every single day of the year. Based on this description, one can picture the Mongol indigent lining up at the distribution stations, their faces drawn with hunger, expectation, and anxiety, knowing that the loaf provided by Kublai Khan was all that stood between them and extinction. One can imagine the reverence these people felt for the beneficent ruler on whom their lives depended.

Kublai Khan reaped great loyalty for his good works. Marco asserts: "All the people are so fond of him that they worship him as God."

DURING MARCO'S TIME in the Mongol Empire, Kublai Khan extended his charity throughout his realm. Each year, he dispatched inspectors to check the grain supply. If an inspector should discover that rain, wind, caterpillars, locusts, or some other calamity has ravaged the crop, "he does not take the tax from them . . . for that season or that year, but he gives them his own corn from his granaries—as much as they need, that they may have it to sow and eat that year." In the winter, Kublai Khan "has inquiry made, and if he finds in some province a man whose animals are dead . . . , he has some of his own animals, which he has from the tithe of other provinces, given to him and sold to him cheaply and has him helped, and has no tax taken from him that year."

Nor did Kublai Khan's beneficence end with this gesture. On the largely treeless Steppe inhabited by Mongols and Chinese alike, lightning posed a constant hazard against which there was little defense. "If by accident lightning strikes some flock of ewes or sheep or other animals of whatever kind," Marco says, "be the flock as large as you like, the Great Khan would not exact tithe for three years. And equally if it happens that lightning strikes some ship full of merchandise, he does not wish any share of rent of it, because he thinks it a bad omen when lightning strikes anyone's goods." The reason for this leniency had more to do with superstition and fear of the unknown than with charity. "The Great Khan says, 'God hated him, therefore he has struck him with lightning,' and so he does not wish such goods struck by the divine to enter the treasury."

Fully in Kublai Khan's thrall, Marco emphasizes selfless motives on the part of the leader of the Mongols: "All his thought and chief anxiety is to help the people who are under him, that they may be able to live, work, and multiply their goods." At the same time, the Venetian never loses sight of the strict social order and rituals underlying Mongol family structure, agriculture, and military life.

NOWHERE WAS THE Mongol love of orderliness and opulence more evident than in their calendar. The Mongol New Year, which began in February, "by the Tartar computation," was called simply "White." In honor of the occasion, "Kublai Khan and his subjects dress themselves in white robes, both men and women." They did so, Marco explains, "because white dress seems to them lucky and good, and therefore they wear it at the beginning of their year so that they may take their good and have joy all year."

In their festive attire, Mongol barons bestowed still more presents upon the khan, "of gold and of silver and of pearls and of precious stones and of many rich white cloths," in addition to a hundred thousand (five to twelve thousand in some manuscript versions) camels and horses, all of them white. "And if they are not altogether white, they are at least white for the greater part."

Everyone embraced and kissed, exclaiming, "Good luck to you this year and may everything that you do turn out well." Kublai Khan then displayed his elephants, which were "quite five thousand, all covered with beautiful clothes worked richly in gold and in silk with many other beasts and with birds and lions embroidered." Each animal bore a coffer filled with items required for feasting, gold and silver utensils, and other trappings. His camels came next, draped in "very beautiful cloth of white silk." The glittering spectacle moved Marco to exclaim, "It is the most wonderful and beautiful sight that was ever seen in this world."

On the day of the White festival, all the prominent people of the realm appeared—kings, princes, dukes, marquesses, counts, barons, astrologers, philosophers, physicians, and falconers, along with other officials—to fill the "great hall before the great lord." Kublai Khan sat on a throne situated so that he could see them all. The overflow crowds arrayed themselves around the walls and prepared to worship there. Marco relates: "When they are all seated each in his proper place a great wise ancient man, as one might say a prelate, stands up in the middle and says in a very loud voice, 'Now all bow down and worship at once your lord.' And as soon as he has so said they all rise up and bow themselves immediately and bend the knee and put their foreheads on the ground and make their prayer towards the lord and worship him just as if he were their God. Then the prelate says, 'God save and keep our lord long with joy and gladness.' . . . And in such a way they worship him four times. And then, this done, they stand up and go all in their order to an altar which is there very well adorned, and on that altar is a red table on which is written with letters of gold and of precious stones of great value the proper name of the Great Khan."

Marco specifies that Kublai Khan presided over twelve thousand barons upon whom he bequeathed thirteen robes apiece, each robe of a different color and decorated with precious stones, as well as a belt "of crimson cunningly worked with threads of gold and of silver, very rich and very beautiful and of great value," and boots of similar luxury.

These statistics were simply too large for Europeans to credit, but Mongol and Chinese annals confirm their accuracy. The barons wore a different robe to each of thirteen great feasts throughout the lunar year. In all, Marco estimates that the Mongol court possessed "156,000 robes so dear and of great value."

They served as a backdrop for the singular spectacle of Kublai Khan presiding over his court. At feasts, "a great lion is brought before the great lord. As soon as he sees him, the lion throws himself down lying before him and makes signs of great humility, and seems to know him for lord. He is so tame that he stays thus before him, with no chain, lying quietly at the king's feet like a dog"—a sight that, Marco concedes, "makes one wonder."

THE PRONE LION before the khan reminded Marco of Kublai's immense appetite for hunting game in Cambulac during the clear, cold, dry winter months. According to custom, Marco notes, any game caught during this period, "wild-boar and stags and bucks and roe-deer and bears, lions, and other sorts of large wild beasts [must] be brought to him." These came in the form of entrails displayed on carts, as if to whet Kublai's appetite for the hunt, for he preferred to conduct his own hunting, employing leopards and lynxes "all trained to beast catching and . . . very good at the chase." Marco explains that the Great Khan relied on a "little dog for companion" during these exercises. For safety's sake, the lions were caged "because they would be too ferocious and ravening in the case of the beasts, nor could they be held. And it is necessary that they should be carried against the wind, because if the animals should perceive the scent, they would flee at once."

TWO BROTHERS, Bayan and Mingan, served as the khan's royal dog handlers ("called *cuiucci* in the Tartar tongue, which means 'master of the hunt'"), who maintained mastiffs, retrievers, and greyhounds. Each brother commanded an army of ten thousand men devoted solely to the khan's dogs, the handlers serving one brother dressed in red, and those serving the other in sky blue. "They are very great multitudes,"

Marco states. "One of these brothers, with his ten thousand men of one color, and with five thousand dogs (for there are a few who have not dogs), goes on one side of him to the right hand, and the other brother with his own ten thousand of the other color and with their dogs goes on the other side, to the left of him."

The brothers had to perform to high standards, because, as Marco explains, they were "bound by contract to give to the court of the Great Khan every day beginning from the month of October until the . . . month of March a thousand head between beasts and birds, excepting quails." The requirement kept them busy nearly around the clock, and when March arrived, they fell into a profound stupor to recuperate.

KUBLAI KHAN himself hunted on an equally grand scale, accompanied by "ten thousand falconers" and "five hundred gerfalcons, and peregrine falcons and saker falcons and other kinds of birds in very great abundance," in addition to "goshawks in great quantity to catch birds on rivers." His falconers were well trained and well equipped for the hunt, so as to reflect well on their lord and master.

Birds belonging to Kublai Khan carried a "little tablet of silver tied to their feet for recognition." If a bird strayed, it was immediately returned to its master, and the same rigorous policy applied to all the other paraphernalia of the hunt, horses and swords and other equipment. Anyone who found a misplaced item was "held for a thief" unless he promptly returned it to its rightful owner—in most cases a baron. According to Marco, the system, reinforced by drastic penalties, worked efficiently: "No things can be lost that are not soon found and returned."

Lesser citizens of the Mongol realm were not entitled to own or hunt with birds of prey: "No merchant nor any craftsman nor any citizen or villager nor any person, whoever he might be, dares keep any goshawk, falcon, nor hawking bird nor hunting dog for his pleasure through [out] all the domain of the Great Khan." Even Mongol barons and knights had to observe limitations set down by the khan. None "dares to hunt or hawk unless he is enrolled under the captain of the falconers, or has a privilege in this matter."

· · ·

ON THE MORNING of the hunt, the royal party proceeded along a road leading in a southerly direction from Cambulac toward the hunting grounds. Barons and lesser officials traveled on horseback, or walked, while Kublai Khan loomed over all atop one of his four elephants, which were adept at working their way through narrow passes. Befitting his station, he sat within an enclosure ("a beautiful wooden room," Marco calls it) decorated with the finest silk and beaten-gold ornaments. Kublai rarely strayed from his luxurious perch, Marco confides, because of the painful gout from which he suffered. All the while, twelve barons accompanied him, together with twelve attractive women. "There is no amusement in the world equal to it," Marco sighs.

Shielded by the drapes surrounding his private chamber, Kublai Khan conversed with his guests, as barons and knights rode alongside, acting as spotters. Whenever they saw cranes or pheasants overhead, they immediately cried out, "Sir, cranes are passing." At that, Kublai flung back the curtains and let loose his gerfalcon.

Looking up, Kublai and his minions squinted to see the streamlined creature streaking like a meteorite across the heavens, tucking its wings and diving until a hapless crane or other bird took notice and vainly tried to elude its attacker. The falcon's speed always won out, and as the two creatures collided, the falcon sank its razorlike talons into its stunned and helpless prey, engaging it in an intricate airborne dance of death. Locked in their fatal embrace, the birds plummeted to earth, and hunters galloped toward the spot where they fell to recover the falcon as it ravished its prey.

Lolling atop his elephant, Kublai Khan savored the spectacle of avian combat. "It is a very great amusement and a great delight to him," Marco attested, "and to all the other barons and knights who also ride round the lord."

FATIGUED from his hours of sport, Kublai Khan sought refuge amid the "beautiful and rich" tents and pavilions where his barons, knights, and falconers, together with their wives and concubines, numbering as many as ten thousand, congregated. Some of the tents were large enough to shelter a thousand knights, and each, regardless of size, had its door opening "toward midday," in accordance with Mongol custom.

The largest tent connected to the khan's private lodging, which consisted of two halls and a chamber. Marco left a sumptuous description of the furnishings of Kublai Khan's splendid dwelling on the remote plain: "Each hall has three posts of spice wood very well worked. They are all covered outside with lion skins that are very beautiful, for they are all striped with black and with white and with red. They are so well arranged that [neither] wind nor rain nor anything else can hurt those inside nor do harm to that skin, because they keep it off very well. And inside those halls and rooms they are all lined with ermine and with sable skins. These are both the most beautiful furs and the most rich and of greater value than any furs that may be. . . . The skin of the sable, as much as may be lining for one man's robe, is worth two thousand bezants of gold, . . . and the Tartars call it in their tongue 'the king of skins.' . . . The cords that hold the halls and the room are all of silk. They are of so great value and cost so much, these three tents, that a small king could not pay for them."

But Kublai Khan was no "small king." He was the emperor of the Mongols, the most powerful ruler alive.

IN FALCONRY, Marco Polo found striking similarities between East and West. In both cultures, falconry had been the sport of the nobility for more than a thousand years. A "swift dog and a splendid hawk," as one ancient Western phrase has it, were the perquisites of a well-equipped gentleman. Kings and commoners in Asia and Europe alike thrilled to the sight of a bird of prey soaring across a grassy plain as hunters below rode furiously toward their quarry.

Holy Roman Emperor Frederick II of Hohenstaufen was the most influential of all European falconry enthusiasts. In 1229, he returned to Europe from the Sixth Crusade with a retinue of skilled Arab falconers, who helped to spread the diversion across Europe. During the decades Marco Polo was abroad, Frederick compiled the sport's bible, *De arte venandi cum avibus*, or *The Art of Falconry*, among the earliest works to consider the anatomy of birds. His passion for falconry appears to have exceeded even Kublai Khan's; Frederick once lost an important military campaign because he decided to go hawking. Dedicated falconers understood his priorities.

.   .   .

IF MARCO EXPERIENCED disenchantment with Kublai Khan's excesses and lapses in judgment, he did not admit to it, but he realized that as long as he remained in China he was just another minion of a large-hearted but capricious ruler. Nor did he know how long he would stay. His father and uncle had planned to maintain their steady pace, deliver the message from the pope to Kublai Khan, and return with young Marco to Venice with their gems and silk and other valuable items. But now all three were ensnared in the intrigue of the Mongol court.

It had taken the Polos more than three years to travel from Venice to the court of Kublai Khan, but they came to realize that it would take much longer to return home. They would have to remain in China for as long as Kublai wished. Although he was nearing seventy, and was grooming his son to succeed him, he gave no sign of relinquishing power. And if he were to die suddenly, his death might pose a serious threat to the Polos, who would lose his personal protection and become vulnerable to the raw violence just below the surface in the Mongol Empire. So they were caught, privileged guests who were also prisoners in the largest kingdom on earth, doomed to serve the Great Khan for an incalculable length of time.

To survive in this strange land, Marco would have to find a way to make himself useful to the khan, and become a student not just of Mongol women and horsemanship but of the exercise of power. If he succeeded in making a place for himself, there was no telling how high he could rise. For all its peculiarities, Mongol society was open to foreigners who could be useful. He might wind up winning a lordship, or even the governorship of a wealthy province, as other trustworthy foreigners had done. He might rule over thousands as Kublai Khan's emissary, and even have his own court, with endless opportunities to enrich himself, or keep concubines for his personal pleasure. Or he might fall victim to crude Mongol justice, and never see his homeland again.

Just when it seemed Marco might have no place at all in the Mongol Empire, Kublai Khan sent him on the road to collect taxes and, more important, gather information about the realm, so much of which remained unexplored. Within the confines of the empire, Marco's occupation would bear an eerie similarity to his career before he encountered Kublai Khan: traveler.

CHAPTER NINE

The Struggle for Survival

Five miles meandering with a mazy motion
Through wood and dale the sacred river ran
Then reached the caverns measureless to man. . . .

MARCO POLO left Cambulac as Kublai Khan's emissary. Still in his early twenties, he went without his father and uncle, whom he ceased to mention as companions for this phase of his travels. As always he enjoyed the protection and the blessing of the khan, which guaranteed his safety—at the price of unending loyalty. Despite the challenges that lay ahead, he bristled with newfound self-importance, understandable in light of his destination: Hangzhou, the largest, wealthiest, most celebrated city in China.

He carried a golden *paiza* just as his father and uncle had done on their journeys on behalf of the Mongol Empire. This object was a foot long and three inches across, and was inscribed: "By the strength of the eternal Heaven, holy be the Khan's name. Let him that pays him not reverence be killed." Possessing it meant that Marco was designated as a very important person in the Mongol realm, and was able to make full use of the khan's extensive network of hostels, horses, and roads.

Draped along the shores of West Lake, Hangzhou presented the archetypal Chinese landscape of mountains soaring above a tranquil body of water that seemed to reflect Heaven itself. The metropolis was the traditional seat of the Song dynasty, and it had just been conquered by Kublai Khan's leading general, Bayan, at the time Marco was dispatched to help administer the khan's affairs. As a disinterested European, Marco was just the sort of official whom Kublai Khan preferred for overseeing the finances of a hostile or suspicious populace. Everything that Marco had seen since leaving Venice, even the wonders of Cambulac and the great Kublai Khan himself, served as a prologue to his voyage into the heart of China.

THE TWO CITIES were connected by one of the most massive public works in all of China, the Grand Canal, stretching over a thousand miles from Cambulac south to Hangzhou. The waterway served as a principal artery for Chinese (and Mongol) shipping and commerce. Its construction had been under way, in fits and starts, for centuries, but by the time of Marco's trip it was nearing completion. Although Marco does not supply a precise itinerary, he probably followed the Grand Canal for much of his journey to Hangzhou.

Leaving Cambulac, Marco encountered "a very beautiful stone bridge" that crossed a wide, swiftly flowing river, which led to the Ocean Sea. He estimated the bridge to be "three hundred paces long and eight paces wide," room enough for ten horsemen to ride abreast, clattering on the polished stone. "And it has twenty-four arches and twenty-four piers in the water supporting them," he says, "and it is all of gray marble and very well worked and well-founded." The bridge opened onto a vista as spacious as China itself. An impressionable young man could easily persuade himself that the world lay at his feet, and in a sense it did. The bridge, as much a spiritual symbol as an architectural wonder, evoked crossing over into a new realm, a new consciousness, even a new life. As he set foot on it, Marco may have sensed himself growing and changing with every step, as he passed beyond the Mongol stronghold into China itself.

Crossing the monumental bridge, he considered the care and ingenuity that had gone into its construction. "From one pillar to the other," he observes, "it is closed in with a flag of gray marble all worked with different sculptures and mortised into the columns at the side, through the length of the bridge to the end, so that people who cross may not be able to fall into the water." In all, he counted six hundred of these elegant pillars, each topped with a lion or similar animal, fashioned "of very fine marble."

Known today as the Marco Polo Bridge, this structure is essentially the same as the day Marco traversed it. Completed in 1192, it is also called the Guangli Bridge, and its stone span reaches across the banks of the Lugou River. Historical records indicate that the Lugou was "violent and flowed extraordinarily rapidly," but modern construction has diminished the current. The bridge witnessed one of the major engagements of the Second World War, when Japanese forces approached it during their campaign to conquer China.

THIRTY MILES from the bridge that would one day bear his name, Marco wandered through a charming landscape dotted with attractive, welcoming villages, seductive shade trees, "very fruitful cultivated fields," refreshing springs, and Buddhist monasteries, where the monks busied themselves weaving silk and fashioning gold jewelry. In a change from his rugged, hazardous journey to Cambulac four years earlier, Marco seems to have felt secure, and he received a courteous reception wherever he went. "There are very many fine inns or hostels in our manner," he notes with satisfaction, "where the wayfarers lodge, because of the multitude of merchants and strangers who come there."

Thereafter, Marco's account, likely drawn from the notes he brought back to Italy from China, becomes a fast-moving catalog of his "wayfaring" in the service of the khan. Marco traveled from one comfortable inn to another, always appreciative of the "beautiful" villages, cities, fields, and roads jammed with prosperous commercial travelers.

WHEREVER MARCO WENT, he encountered silk—and not just the fabric but the silkworms themselves, a great novelty to Europeans, and the mulberry trees on which they feasted. For centuries, Europe had known almost nothing about the art and science of sericulture; it was perhaps the most closely guarded secret in ancient history.

Even within China, the origin of silk was mysterious. Tradition credits Xi Ling-shi—a wife of the mythical Yellow Emperor, said to have ruled China in 3000 BC—with the introduction of silkworm cultivation and the invention of the loom. Although she was a phantom, silk was real; archeological digs have turned up silk threads, ribbons, and cocoons dating from 3000 BC, and a small ivory cup dating from 5000 BC contains images of spinning tools used for silk, as well as silk thread.

In China, a single cultivated species of moth became identified with silk, the blind and flightless *Bombyx mori*, whose ancestor *Bombyx mandarina Moore* fed on the leaves of the white mulberry tree. This silkworm's thread is composed of a filament that is rounder and smoother than those produced by other moths, and across the millennia, thanks to persistent Chinese sericulture, it evolved into the more specialized *Bombyx mori*.

This moth lays as many as five hundred eggs, each weighing no more than a gram or so, within a few days' time, and promptly dies. From that point, the story of silk can be told in a series of exploding numbers. An ounce of eggs eventually yields thirty thousand silkworms; the worms have one, and only one, source of food: the leaves of the mulberry tree. Those thirty thousand worms devour about a ton of mulberry leaves, and in turn produce twelve pounds of raw silk.

As the Chinese slowly perfected the cultivation of *Bombyx mori*, they learned to keep the eggs at 65 degrees Fahrenheit, and to raise the temperature 12 degrees to force them to hatch. Only then does the real work begin: feeding the worms fresh mulberry leaves, handpicked and carefully chopped, every half hour, around the clock, while maintaining a stable temperature. The worms quickly fatten in stacked trays stored in feeding huts; the sound of the munching creatures has been likened to heavy rain falling on a bamboo roof. At the same time, they must be protected from loud noises, drafts, and the odors of fish and meat and even perspiration; under ideal conditions, the coddled creatures can multiply their weight several thousand times, as they continually shed and change color.

To make their protective cocoons, the silkworms secrete a jellylike substance that hardens on contact with air. Over the course of three or four days, they spin a cocoon around themselves until they look like little puffy white balls about the size of a thumb. These are immersed in boiling water to loosen the silken filaments, which reach about half a mile in length, and the filaments, in turn, are gathered onto a spool.

There are two distinct types of silk cocoon. Cocoons of one type produce a filament about one-eighth the diameter of a human hair. The filament possesses tremendous tensile strength because of its molecular structure, known as a beta-pleated sheet, which looks like this:

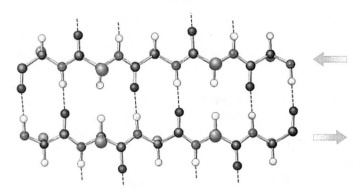

A single silk thread generally consists of five to eight of these filaments tightly wound together. After processing, the raw threads are ready for dyeing. Because dye fits neatly into the pleats, silk retains color far better than other natural fabrics can; colors look much richer and more vibrant on the sensuous surface of silk.

The other type of silk cocoon, much larger and fluffier, often goes by the name of Happy Family, because each cocoon contains two larvae. The filaments in this case are tangled together, and so are less valuable. Once it has been stretched over a form to dry, the silk is used for batting—warm, lightweight stuffing.

IN CHINA, the manufacture of silk was quintessentially women's work; in the spring, the reigning empress inaugurated the silk season as part of her official duties, and her female subjects followed suit, spinning and weaving and embroidering silk at home and in workshops. In silk-rich regions, three generations of women in the same family would feed and supervise the maturing silkworms. The production of silk, labor-intensive as it was—with spinning, weaving, dyeing, and embroidering—occupied half of China's provinces. Despite the ubiquity of silk manufacture, the key techniques of sericulture remained closely guarded by Chinese authorities; it was an offense punishable by death to reveal those secrets to foreigners, or to smuggle cocoons or even eggs beyond Chinese borders.

At first the wearing of silk was restricted to the emperor and his family. But over time, people from many classes of Chinese society took to wearing silk tunics, and silk eventually found a variety of industrial applications in fishing lines, strings for musical instruments, and silk-rag paper. By the time of the Han dynasty, 206 BC to AD 220, silk had become so widespread in China, and so deeply embedded in the Chinese economy, that it was a valuable commodity in itself, useful for paying debts. Farmers remitted taxes to the government in the form of silk they produced. The government in turn compensated civil servants in silk, and rewarded subjects for outstanding services in silk. Soon silk supplanted gold as a standard measure; rather than pounds of gold, value was calculated in lengths of silk. Eventually, silk became a form of currency, not only within China but also in settling debts with foreign nations. Silk became so much a part of the Chinese economy, way of life, and culture that 5 percent of Mandarin Chinese characters referred to some aspect of silk.

The Chinese monopoly on silk was eventually broken by competing countries. By 200 BC, the Koreans had mastered the rudiments of sericulture thanks to Chinese immigrants who brought the specialized knowledge with them. Five hundred years later, sericulture had spread along diverse "silk roads" to India, where it was embraced with the same vigor. Silk reached all the way to Rome, which became fascinated by the alluring textile. In about the fourth century BC, Roman accounts mention Seres, the semimythical Kingdom of Silk.

It is possible that the Roman legions first encountered actual silk at the Battle of Carrhae, near the Euphrates River, in 53 BC. It was said that the Parthians' vivid silk banners unfurling in the wind startled the Roman troops, who promptly fled the battlefield. Within only a few decades, nobles in Rome wore Chinese silks as a sign of status, much as Chinese emperors had done for thousands of years. The Roman emperor Heliogabalus, who reigned briefly in the third century AD, insisted on wearing only silk. And near the end of the fourth century, one Roman report noted: "The use of silk which was once confined to the nobility has now spread to all classes without distinction, even to the lowest."

Despite the inevitable dispersion of silk, the Chinese remained vigilant, and they succeeded in keeping the secrets of advanced sericulture to themselves until AD 550, when a pair of Nestorian monks appeared in the court of the emperor Justinian I with silkworm eggs concealed in their hollow bamboo walking sticks. In short order, the eggs hatched worms, the worms spun their cocoons, and *Bombyx mori* had come to the Byzantine Empire, bringing silk with it. Emulating China, the

Byzantine Empire attempted to monopolize the production of its silk, and to retain control over the secrets of sericulture. While Byzantine silk soon eroded the market for the ordinary Chinese variety, most luxurious Chinese textiles continued to dominate markets in Central Asia, and were prized wherever they could be found. Soon Persia joined India and the Byzantine Empire in the war for sericultural supremacy. But even as Chinese silk lost ground to lower-grade foreign competitors, it continued to bring in extensive revenues and to impart a sense of economic and cultural unity to the empire.

At the time of Marco Polo's stay, silk was just beginning to be produced in Italy, more than four thousand years after sericulture appeared in China. During the Second Crusade (1144–1149), two thousand silk weavers had migrated from Constantinople to Europe, and they disseminated trade secrets the Chinese had guarded for millennia. But for young Marco, silk remained an exotic novelty still identified with China.

THE JOURNEY continued to be idyllic until Marco came to a "province much wasted and destroyed," as he bluntly states, "by the scourge of the Tartars": Tibet. At this point in his travels, Marco had passed beyond the limits of European experience with Asia, and that is why it is occasionally difficult to determine the modern equivalents for the kingdoms and people he says he encountered. His trip to "Tibet" probably took him to the province of Yunnan in southern China, as well as to Burma, Vietnam, and vaguely defined regions to the north.

"Tibet" both fascinated and repelled Marco. As a merchant, he was intrigued with the spices—ginger and cinnamon, and still others he had never before seen, and failed to name—all growing in abundance. Amber appeared ubiquitous. Silk abounded. Coral, another medium of exchange, caught his attention, too. The locals, he says, "put it on the necks of all their wives and of their idols and hold it for a great jewel."

The region's anarchy and rampant superstition troubled Marco greatly, but he found himself succumbing to the spell cast by the powerful astrologer-magicians. He reports: "They do the most rare enchantments in the world, and the greatest marvels to hear and see, and all by devils' art, which is not good to tell in our book, because the people would be too much surprised." Once he has whetted his audience's appetite, Marco proceeds to tell exactly what these demonic astrologers were capable of doing. "They bring on tempests and lightning and thunderbolts whenever they wish and compel them whenever [they wish them] to cease, and do infinite wonders."

Returning to a subject that both fascinated and repelled him, Marco dramatizes in frightening detail the elaborate manner in which the conjurers attempted to exorcise the vulnerable sick: "When the magicians arrive, they ask about the manner of the sickness; then the sick persons tell them their ills, and the magicians begin to sound their instruments and to dance and leap until one of the magicians falls all on his back on the ground or on the pavement and foams at the mouth and seems dead. They say that the devil is inside his body, and he stays in such a manner that he seems dead. When the other magicians, of whom there were many, see that one of them is fallen in such a way as you have heard, they begin to speak to him and ask him what sickness this sick man has, and why he has it. One answers, 'Such a spirit has smitten him because he did him some displeasure.'

"The other magicians say to him, 'We pray thee that thou pardon him and that thou take from him for the restoration of his health those things that thou wishes to have.' "

Marco fearlessly probes the ecstatic spiritual life of these "Tibetans": "When these magicians have said many words and have prayed, the spirit who is in the body of the magician who has fallen down answers. If it seems the sick man must die, he . . . says, 'This sick man has done so much wrong to such a spirit and is so bad a man that the spirit will not be pacified by any sacrifice or pardon him for anything in the world.' This is the answer for those who must die.

"If the sick man must be healed, then the spirit in the body of the magician says, 'He has offended much, yet it shall be forgiven him. If the sick man wishes to be healed, let him take two or three sheep, and let him also make ten drinks or more, very dear and good.' . . . They have the sheep cooked in the house of the sick man, and, if the sick man is to live, so many of these magicians and so many of those ladies . . . come there. When they are come there and the sheep and drinks are made ready, then they begin to play and to dance and to sing."

At this point in Marco's account, one of the magicians collapses, "as if dead, and foams at the mouth." Those left standing beseech the "idol" to forgive and heal the sick man. At times, the idol responds in the affirmative, at other moments, he replies that the sick man "is not yet fully forgiven."

Having exacted still more tribute, "the spirit answers, after the sacrifice and all things commanded are done, that he [the sick man] is pardoned and he will soon be healed. When they have this answer, and have sprinkled broth and drink and have made a great light and great censing, believing that in this way they have given the spirit his share, they say that the spirit is on their side and is appeased, and they all joyfully send the sick man home, and he is made whole."

On occasion, the sufferer died after the magicians pronounced him healed. Nor did everyone who fell sick receive attention. A rite of this complexity was reserved for the wealthy, and took place only once or twice a month, according to Marco, who was ever attentive to finances, even where magic was concerned.

The individuals practicing these black arts, Marco insists, were deeply suspect, "bad men of evil habits." They looked the part, too, accompanied by the "very largest mastiff dogs in the world, which are as large as asses and are very good at catching all sorts of wild beasts."

In Tibet, Marco confronted the dark side of the Mongol conquest of Asia. To his credit, he describes in unflinching detail the havoc wrought by Kublai's brother Möngke, who, Marco flatly states, "destroyed [Tibet] by war." Following the path of Möngke's devastation, Marco experienced stabs of anxiety and dread the likes of which had not appeared in his account since his poignant description of crossing the Gobi Desert. The experience challenged his assumptions about the nature of the Mongol Empire and his small place in it. Alone in the desolate world, Marco had nothing more than his talismanic *paiza* to clutch for reassurance, a reminder of the comfort, indulgence, and grandeur of Cambulac and especially Kublai Khan, several thousand miles to the east. Even though the gold *paiza* conferred a special status on Marco as the khan's emissary, the object did nothing to dispel his sense of bewilderment at the chaos surrounding him, some of it caused by Möngke, some by the baffling and seemingly perverse nature of the Tibetans. All around him was evidence of the original Mongol culture—nomadic, predatory, its values utterly different from the charitable ethic that Kublai Khan championed.

Marco passed through a desiccated landscape drained of color and harmony, the somber aftermath of conquest. In disgust, he recounts what he saw in the "dilapidated and ruined" region: "One passes for twenty days' journey through inhabited places, through which a vast multitude of wild beasts roam, such as lions, lynxes, and other kinds; for which reason the passage is dangerous." But the dangers would only increase as he ventured ever deeper into Tibet.

Pop! Pop! Pop!

The explosive reverberation tearing through the curtain of night frightened Marco, as it did everyone else new to the region, and there was no escaping it. Eventually he found the explanation: "There are found in that region, and specially near the rivers, very wonderfully thick and large canes"—three palms around, he estimated, and fifteen paces long. "The merchants and other wayfarers who go through such country, when they wish to rest by night, take some of those canes with them and put them on a cart, and make a fire of them, because when they are in the fire, they make so great crackling and so great report that the lions and the bears and the other fierce beasts have so great a fear of it that when they hear those terrible reports they fly as far as they can, and would not try to come near the fire for anything in the world. And the men make fires like this to protect themselves and their animals from the fierce wild beasts of which there are so many."

Marco knew just how to perform this critical task: "One takes some of these canes all green and makes great bundles of them in the evening, and puts them on a fire of logs at some distance from the camp. . . . And when these canes have stayed awhile in this great fire, then feeling the heat they are twisted this way and that and split in half, popping terribly as they split, and then make so great a report that it is heard well ten miles off by night."

Pop!

The noise was so loud, Marco claims, that anyone unaccustomed to hearing it "becomes all terrified, so horrible a thing is it to hear." Indulging his taste for whimsy, he claims that the unsuspecting traveler might even "lose his senses and die" from the cacophony. Marco recommends an equally unlikely remedy against this possibility: stuff the ears with cotton, then bind the head, face, and even clothing until the newcomer becomes accustomed to the popping canes.

The horses' reaction to the noise presented a serious problem. They became "so violently frightened" that they broke "halters and all other ropes" and fled from it. Neophyte merchants such as Marco learned to take precautions against losing their mounts this way; the proper method to prevent horses from bolting was to fetter their feet. Experienced merchants plying the route brought shackles with them for just this purpose. In time, the horses became conditioned to the racket, and no longer needed to be hobbled every time the canes were set ablaze.

To MARCO'S EYES, marriageable young women of Tibet were as blighted as the region, sullied by "an absurd and most detestable abuse" contrary to the laws of nature. He observes: "No man [there] would take a maiden for wife for anything in the world, but every man requires in her whom he wishes to take to wife that she shall first have been known by many men, and they say that they are worth nothing if they are not used and accustomed to lie with many men." As if obsessed, Marco repeats variations on the theme: virgin brides were displeasing to the gods worshipped by these people; having many lovers was proof that a bride-to-be was, in fact, desirable; and the value of a bride increased according to the number of men who have sampled her delights.

Merchants such as Marco who strayed into the region fell prey to the villagers' schemes to secure bedmates for local young women. "When they perceive that some caravan of merchants or the people of other strange lands pass through that country and have stretched their tents for lodging," Marco says, "then the old men of the villages and of the hamlets bring their daughters to these tents; and these are by twenty, and by forty, and by more and by less according to the number of foreigners so that each one has his own; and give them to the men who will take them, one vying with another in begging the merchants to take his daughter, that they may . . . lie with them."

Marco's dispassionate account of these bizarre proceedings suggests that the young women of the region failed to suit his fancy and that the commercial nature of the transaction dismayed him. However, that did not deter him from describing the practice in full: "Then the men take them and enjoy themselves with them and keep them as long as they wish there, but cannot take them with them to another place, nor to another district, forward or backward. And then when the men have done their will with them and they wish to go, it is the custom for him to give some jewel, or some other token to that woman with whom he has lain, so that she can show proof and sign when she comes

to be married that she has had a paramour. In such a way it is the custom for each girl to have more than twenty tokens on her neck to show
that many men have lain with her." A girl adorned in this manner was
"received by her parents with joy and honor," Marco says. "Happy is
she who can show that she has had more presents from more
strangers." Yes, he reluctantly admits, "young gentlemen from sixteen
years to twenty-four"—his age group—"will do well to have as many
of these girls at their will as they should ask for and should be begged
to take without any cost."

Marco often demonstrated that he was no prude, but sex Tibetan
style offended his sensibilities. Seeking the moral high ground, he
reminds his European audience, and himself, that these people were
"idolaters and extremely treacherous and cruel and wicked, for they
hold it no sin to rob and to do evil, and I believe they are the greatest
scoundrels and the greatest thieves in the world."

Nevertheless, their women were very eager in bed.

THE WOMEN of the adjacent province, Gaindu, appeared even more
bizarre to Marco than did the daughters of Tibet. The men, Marco
relates, did not "regard it as villainy if a foreigner or other man shames
him at pleasure with his wife or with his daughter or with his sister or
with any woman whom he may have in his house." More astonishing,
he "regards it as a great good when [a foreigner] lies with them."
Indeed, the man of the house "strictly commands" his wives and
daughters to make themselves available to travelers such as Marco, and
removes himself "to his field or to his vines and does not come back
there so long as the stranger stays in his house. And I tell you that
many times [the foreigner] stays there three days or four, eight and
sometimes ten, and lies in bed enjoying himself with the wife of that
wretch or his daughter or sister or whoever he shall wish." All the
while, he hangs his hat in the window or displays it in the courtyard as
a sign that he is inside. "And the cuckold wretch, so long as he sees that
token at his house, does not dare go back at all, knowing that the
stranger is there, lest he should hinder him in his pleasures." More surprising still, after the visitor departs, the master of the house returns to
find "his family all joyful and happy, and rejoices with them, making
them tell all the entertainment they made for the stranger, and all with
joy give thanks to the gods."

Although he enjoyed titillating his audience with this lurid description, Marco denounced the practice as a "vile custom" outlawed by Kublai Khan—not that anyone in this remote region paid much attention to the remote leader's edicts.

Marco hints that the practice caused him keen embarrassment as he left Gaindu. Families inhabiting the "rugged places of the mountains near the roads" extended their peculiar form of hospitality to itinerant merchants, who repaid their kindness with a bit of fabric "or other thing of little cost." Marco probably did just that, but ran afoul of his hosts. He relates that when such a merchant mounted his horse to depart, the man of the house and his wife mocked him and shouted curses: "See what you have left to us that you have forgotten!" they cried. "Show us what you have taken of ours!"

And with these words of derision ringing in his ears, the unsettled foreigner galloped away.

MARCO PAUSED just long enough to take note of an eye-catching bush that he took to be a clove. Not knowing quite what to make of it, he diligently reports that it "has twigs and leaves like a laurel in manner. . . . The flower it makes is white and small as in the clove, when it is ripe it is dusky black." M. G. Pauthier, the nineteenth-century French scholar and editor, concluded that Marco meant Assam, or black tea—an especially interesting observation because it had long been assumed that the Venetian, despite all his years in China, never mentioned tea. Other commentators retorted that Marco was actually talking about the aromatic cassia tree, whose bark provides cinnamon. That is a less likely explanation because almost in the same breath Marco mentions cinnamon, implying that it was quite different from this particular flower.

Most likely, Marco was describing tea without realizing what it was. Unlike the Chinese, the Mongols drank koumiss and rarely sipped tea. No wonder Marco was unfamiliar with it.

JUDGING FROM HIS familiarity with Mongol commerce, Marco probably served as a tax collector for Kublai Khan, and most likely he collected revenues from salt, a vital commodity in the empire. Kublai frequently gave this task to foreigners who roamed the empire in his employ, and Marco was a good candidate for the assignment: throughout his account, he discusses the uses and economics of salt with ease and authority.

Earlier in the *Travels*, he had spoken of paper money, and silk money, about which Europeans would remain deeply skeptical. Now he would take up money in the form of salt, a concept still more baffling to Western sensibilities. Marco explains how this sort of currency was produced in the region: "They take salt water and have it boiled in a pan . . . for an hour [until] it becomes stiff like paste, and they cast it into a mold, and it is made into shapes . . . that are flat on the underside and are round above, and it is of a size that can weigh about half a pound." The salt cakes were placed on fire-heated stones until they dried. "On this sort of money they put the seal of the lord; nor can money of this kind be made by others than the officers of the lord."

Once he became familiar with the intricacies of trading these homemade hard salt cakes for gold, Marco realized they presented an opportunity to acquire a substance whose intrinsic value he fully appreciated. Throughout "Tibet," he saw merchants "go through mountains" to reach remote hamlets where they traded salt cakes for gold to "make vast gain and profit, because those people use that salt in food, and also buy things that they need. But in the cities they use almost nothing but the broken pieces of the coins in food, and spend the whole coins." One can sense Marco's wonder at this odd transaction, in which both sides came away with the item they believed they needed. The government salt monopoly, it seemed to him, was virtually a license to print, or in this case boil and bake, money.

MARCO next turned his attention to a place he called Karagian, his rendering of the Turkish name for the modern Chinese province of Yunnan.

Although ruled by Kublai Khan's son Temür, Karagian offered scant reassurance for the unsuspecting merchant traveler. It was a land where quantities of "very great adders . . . very hideous things to see and to examine" lurked in the swampy muck. The creatures were ten paces long, and thick as a man. Barely containing his disgust, Marco endeavors to portray these brutes: "They have two short legs in front near the head, which have no feet, except that they have three claws, namely, two small and one larger claw made sharp like a falcon's or a lion's." The creature's massive head was the stuff of nightmares, with its two shining eyes, each the size of "four dinars." As for the mouth, Marco would have his audience believe that it was "so large that it would well swallow a man [or] an ox at one time," tearing its victim to shreds with "very large and sharp teeth." In sum, says Marco, "it is so very exceedingly hideous and great and fierce that there is no man nor beast that does not fear them."

The monsters were, of course, neither adders nor serpents, but crocodiles. Marco resolutely outlines how to catch one of them without getting eaten alive. Hunters, he explains, "put a trap in the road by which they see that the adders are usually gone toward the water, because they know they must pass there again. They fix a very thick and strong wooden stake so deeply in the ground—that is, in the road of those adders, on some sloping bank by which the path descends— that . . . none of the stake is seen; in which stake is fixed a sword made like a razor or like a lance, and it projects about a palm above the stake, very sharp and cutting and always sloping toward the approach of the serpents. And he covers it with earth or sand so that the adder does not see it at all. And the hunters put very many such stakes there in many places. . . . When the . . . serpent comes down the middle of the road where the irons are, it strikes them with such force that the iron enters it by the breast and rends it as far as the navel, so that it dies immediately. When they see them dead, the crows begin to clamor. One knows by the noise of birds that the serpent is dead, and then [the hunters] go there to find it."

The hunters risk their lives, Marco explains, for the animals' medicinal value: "When they have taken it, skinning it immediately, they draw the gall from the belly and sell it very dear. It is much prized because great medicine is made of it, for if a man is bitten by a mad dog, and one gives him a little . . . to drink in wine, . . . he is healed immediately. And again, when a lady cannot give birth and has pain and cries aloud, then they give her a little of that serpent's gall in drink, and then the lady gives birth immediately. . . . The third virtue is that when one has any eruption like a boil or other worse thing that grows upon the body, then one puts a little of this gall on it, and it is healed in a few days."

No matter how grotesque the crocodile's appearance, its meat was prized as a delicacy. "They sell the flesh of this serpent because it is very good to eat and they eat it very gladly," Marco reports. And the reptile even helped, in its awful way, to protect humans from other predators by devouring the newborn cubs of wolves, lions, and bears "while their parents cannot defend them."

Through arduous study, Marco came to realize that the crocodile, for all its ferocity, could be an unexpected ally in the daily struggle for survival.

As an emissary of Kublai Khan, Marco familiarized himself with the Mongols' bloody attempts to subdue Karagian. The region was home to various tribes far removed from the refinements of Chinese civilization. Despite their very distinct and insular character, the tribes acknowledged arm's-length Chinese rule during the Qin (221–206 BC) and Han dynasties, but ultimate power remained in local hands, with tribal chieftains, who lived by their own codes. Chinese inhabitants were few and far between, obvious outsiders in the province.

By the time of the Tang dynasty (AD 618–907), a kingdom known as Nanzhao had emerged as the dominant political and cultural power in the area, and it unified the disparate warlords, bringing a measure of sophistication to this otherwise primitive area. At its peak, just before Marco's arrival, Nanzhao sheltered artisans who produced elegant fabrics woven from cotton and silk. The kingdom also provided salt—perhaps Marco's reason for visiting in his capacity as a tax assessor—as well as gold. For a time, China's policies encouraged Nanzhao to prosper, in part as a buffer against aggressive tribes in neighboring areas, but during the Song dynasty (960–1279), Chinese power declined. By the time Marco presented himself at the Mongol court, Kublai Khan was determined to bring this distant kingdom into line with a strenuously applied Pax Mongolica, but the tenacity of Nanzhao's warlords promised to make doing so a very difficult task, with the prospect of only partial success.

Although Marco says the inevitable combat occurred in 1272, the date is incorrect, the result either of a faulty manuscript or of his own flawed attempt to convert it from the Mongol lunar calendar to the European Julian system. According to reliable Chinese sources, the events occurred in 1277, just before Marco arrived in the region. In any case, when he came on the scene, memories of the spectacular carnage were still fresh, and it seemed as if the neighing of horses and the thrumming of arrows had only just subsided.

As Marco learned, Kublai Khan's pacification of the region came at the cost of a series of bloody and spectacular battles. In this varied, often mountainous terrain, the Mongols were out of their element, and they relied on local mercenaries for support. Their forces met with fierce resistance from a local warlord, whom Marco calls the king of Mien—that is, Myanmar, or Burma—and Bengal. This warlord, determined to repel Kublai Khan's forces, vowed to "put them all to death in such a way that the Great Khan shall never wish to send another army against him."

IN PREPARATION for battle, the king of Mien and Bengal assembled a force of two thousand "very large" elephants "well armed and prepared for war." Each carried a "castle of wood, very strong and very well made and planned for combat." And each castle, or howdah, contained "at least twelve men well armed to shoot arrows and fight." In addition, the king's army deployed "sixty thousand armed men on the ground, between those on horses, and [those] on foot."

This tremendous army—its horses, elephants, men, and followers, all of them led by the king himself—pursued the forces of Kublai Khan until it was just three days' journey away, and there the troops pitched their tents to gather strength for the battle to come. The Mongol general Nescradin led an army of just twelve thousand horsemen, whom he exhorted to do their utmost in battle. He tried to convince them that the soldiers serving the king of Mien and Bengal, though overwhelming in number, were "inexperienced in arms and not practiced in war." Therefore, he said, the Mongol troops "must not fear the multitude of the enemy but trust in their own skill that had already been tried in many places [and] in so many enterprises that their name was feared and dreaded not only by the enemy but all the world." If they lived up to their valorous reputation, they would win a "certain and undoubted victory."

According to Marco, Nescradin could be as shrewd as he was eloquent. He took care to station his men on a great plain beside a dense jungle—too dense for the king's elephants to enter. If by chance the beasts approached, Nescradin planned to send his Mongol troops into the jungle "and shoot arrows at them in safety."

EUROPEANS habitually dismissed elephants as ineffective and dangerous in battle, even though they were the largest animal on land. But in
Asia, tamed elephants had played a role in military conflicts for thousands of years. They carried heavy loads for armies on the march; in
battle, they charged at fifteen miles per hour, although they had difficulty coming to a halt. A herd of stampeding elephants could crush
enemy forces, who found themselves defenseless before the onslaught.
Elephants terrified horses and camels, which turned and ran away.
Their size afforded a great advantage to soldiers stationed on top of
them; javelin throwers and archers could hurl their weapons from a
great height into fleeing enemy forces on the ground. They did have
drawbacks—a badly wounded elephant could thrash about wildly and
menace its own army—but they were more than a match for the bold-
est Mongol horsemen.

THE TWO SIDES took each other's measure for several days, while
Mongol military intelligence went to work. Mongol spies learned the
length of the arrows used by the enemy, and made sure that their own
warriors' arrows were shorter, so as to be incompatible with the
enemy's in battle. That way, the enemy would be unable to reuse them
in bows designed for a longer weapon.

The Mongol arrow combined aerodynamic elegance with surgical
precision. It was three feet long and perfectly balanced, with three
rows of feathers at the butt for stability in flight. On occasion, the
Mongols poisoned the tips, or dipped them in salt or another substance designed to inflict maximum pain. The deadly missile symbolized the Mongols' mastery of military technology, and, coupled with
their horsemanship, foretold success in combat.

With the battle about to begin, both sides approached within a mile
on an open plain, where the enemy king "posted his battalions of elephants and all the castles and the men above well armed for the fight."
Behind them were thousands of soldiers on horseback, which he had
arranged "very well wisely, like the wise king that he was, . . . leaving a
great space between. And there he began to inspire his men, telling
them that they should determine to fight bravely because they were
sure of victory, being four to one, and had so many elephants and castles that the enemy would not be able to look at them, having never
fought with such animals."

The instruments signaling the commencement of battle sounded, and the king himself took off on horseback in the direction of the waiting enemy.

The Mongol forces observed the king and his troops approaching, but did not move until the two armies were face to face. When there was "nothing wanting but to begin the battle, then the horses of the Tartars, when they saw the elephants, were terrified in such a way that the Tartars could not bring them forward toward the enemy, but they always turned themselves back," with the king's forces in pursuit.

Nescradin ordered his men to dismount and to lead their horses into the surrounding jungle and tie them to trees; then he urged them to take up their bows and arrows "of which they knew well how to make use, better than any people in the world." They advanced in unison on the elephants and began to shoot their arrows directly at the creatures' heads. "They shot so many arrows at them with so great vigor and shouting that it seemed a wonderful thing," Marco says. "Some of the elephants were severely wounded and killed in a short time, and many of the men, also."

At the same time, the king's soldiers perched in their castles "drew arrows also on the Tartars very liberally, and gave them a very vigorous attack. But their arrows did not wound so gravely as did those of the Tartars, which were drawn with greater strength." And the Mongols, Marco informs his audience, "defended themselves very bravely." Arrows flew so thick and fast that the elephants received wounds "on every side of the body."

The pressure on the king's elephant-borne forces mounted until the animals "felt the pain of the wounds . . . that came in such numbers like rain, and were frightened by the great noise of the shouting," Marco says. "I tell you that they turned themselves in rout and in flight towards the people of the king with so great an uproar that it seemed like the whole world must be rent, putting the army of the king of Mien into the greatest confusion." The panicked elephants charged this way and that "till at last in terror they hid in a part of the wood where no Tartars were, with such impetuosity that those who guided them could not hold them nor bring them in another direction." The elephants blindly plunged deep into the jungle, smashing the castles high upon their backs into the trees, "with no small slaughter of those who were in the castles." The Mongols watched the disoriented elephants wander off, beyond any hope of recovery.

. . .

THEN NESCRADIN turned his attention to the suddenly unprotected king of Mien and Bengal. The Mongol soldiers mounted their horses "with great order and discipline" and advanced on the king, "who was not a little frightened when he saw the line of elephants scattered."

The king stood his ground, despite his weakening position, as the warring troops finally engaged in hand-to-hand combat "with such vigor, with such slaying of men, with such spilling of blood, that it was a wonderful thing." Marco reports that the king's troops "bravely" defended themselves with their arrows, "and when they had . . . drawn all the arrows, they laid hands on swords and on clubs of iron and ran upon one another very fiercely."

The superbly equipped Mongol forces were destined to prevail in hand-to-hand combat. The warriors rode into battle wearing their version of chain mail: metal squares attached to flexible animal skin. The Mongol suit of armor featured a mirror over the heart, in the belief that mirrors could deflect and even destroy evil forces, such as enemy spears, simply by reflecting them. The warriors also wore a vest made of finely worked mesh, to prevent arrows from piercing the flesh, and carried hooks designed to grab on to an enemy's chain mail so as to drag that warrior to the ground. Even their boots were adapted to the rigors of the Steppe, with upturned toes to create an air pocket as insulation against frostbite.

Marco describes the ensuing carnage in an eloquent crescendo: "Now one could see hard and bitter blows given and received with swords and with clubs; now one could see knights killed, and horses; now one could see feet and hands and arms cut off, shoulders and heads; for you may know that many fell to the ground dead and wounded to death. The cry and the noise there were so great that one did not hear God thundering. The fighting and the battle was very great and most evil on all sides; but yet you may know with no mistake that the Tartars had the better of it, for in an evil hour was it begun for the king and for his people, so many of them were killed that day in that battle.

"At last the king of Mien, seeing that it was impossible to make them stand or to resist the attack of the Tartars, the greater part of his army being either wounded or dead, and all the field full of blood and covered with slain horses and men, and that they were beginning to turn the back, he, too, set himself to fly with the remainder of his people.

"When the Tartars saw those that were turned in flight, they went beating and chasing and killing them so evilly that it was a pity to see, for they were for the most part dead. And the Tartars had the victory."

MARCO FAULTS the ill-starred king of Mien and Bengal, who should have "waited for them in a wide plain where they would not have been able to bear the charge of the first armed elephants; and then with the two wings of horse and foot he should have surrounded them and destroyed them." Such an outcome was not to be. The Mongol army came away from the battle with a great prize, more than two hundred elephants. Those elephants were far from the dumb beasts Marco had once taken them for; he now claimed that "the elephant has greater understanding than any other animal that is."

In the end, Marco pays tribute to the victors, his Mongol masters: "This day's work was the cause of the Great Khan winning all the lands of the king of Mien and Bengal, and making them subject to his rule."

Unlike the regions around Cambulac, Karagian was Mongol in name only. Despite the Pax Mongolica imposed on it, the southwestern province remained treacherous, even for the most experienced traveler. Marco had painstakingly mastered his survival skills, but peril awaited him at every turn.

CHAPTER TEN

The General and the Queen

Could I revive within me
Her symphony and song,
To such a deep delight 'twould win me. . . .

WHEREVER HE ROAMED in these remote provinces, Marco Polo found examples of the natural order of things overturned: astrologers conjuring up tempests at will; salt employed as money; householders inviting strangers to lie with their wives, sisters, and daughters; deadly serpents yielding life-saving medicine—a dizzying succession of curiosities and paradoxes.

No group better exemplified the region's topsy-turvy customs than certain inhabitants of "Uncian," thought to be western Yunnan. The men were lazy, self-important, and mostly useless, or, as Marco puts it, "gentlemen, according to their notions. They have no occupation but warfare, the chase, and falconry. All work is done by women, and by other men whom they have taken captive and keep as slaves." Yet something about this otherwise disreputable group caught Marco's attention. Expectant parents practiced couvade (the word derives from the French for "to hatch"). As he describes it, "When the ladies have been confined and have given birth to a child, they wash him and wrap him up in clothes, and the lord of the lady gets into the bed and keeps the infant that is born with him and lies in the bed forty days without getting up except for necessary duties. All the friends and relations come to see him and stay with him and make him great joy and enter-tainment. They do this because they say that his wife has borne great fatigue in carrying the infant in her womb."

The new mother, meanwhile, went straight back to work. "As soon as she has given birth to the child, she gets up from the bed and does all the duty of the house and waits on her lord, taking him food and drink at the time he is in bed, as if he himself had borne the child."

No wonder Marco's first audiences believed he had made up this custom for the sake of amusement. He described behavior so extreme, so fantastic, that he seemed to be satirizing imaginary heathens just to divert his listeners. But he was not inventing, and couvade as described by Marco Polo has been observed by anthropologists in such diverse places as Africa, Japan, India, and North and South America (among native populations), and among the Basques in Europe. The matter became the subject of medical inquiry in 2002, when two Canadian researchers, Dr. Katherine E. Wynne-Edwards and Dr. Anne Storey, studied saliva and blood drawn from expectant fathers, looking for hormonal changes during their partners' pregnancies, and noticed changes in the men's level of the hormone prolactin. This was highly unusual because prolactin is a female hormone involved in milk production. They also found that a form of estrogen, normally present at low levels in men, attained much higher levels in the men studied. The findings suggested that the men's bodies were subtly imitating the adjustments taking place in their pregnant partners' bodies—that is, the doctors concluded that "men are experiencing hormonal changes associated with parenthood and that those changes are similar to maternal changes."

MARCO'S JOURNEY through what is now called Myanmar became more challenging and exotic with every step. In the *Travels*, he conveys the unnerving sense of passing through a dreamscape that remained solid so long as he was present, and then swiftly returned to the shadows from which he had momentarily rescued it. He writes of journeying for days on end through the jungle, "where there are elephants enough and unicorns enough and many lions and other strange wild beasts. There are no men nor dwellings."

The unicorn, of course, was a mythical symbol of purity or virginity, resembling a horse with a horn protruding from its forehead. Powder derived from the horn was reputed to have magical curative properties, affording protection from epilepsy, poisoning, and other afflictions. Yet Marco mentions this wonderful creature only in passing, as if it were part of the scenery. And it probably was, for what he meant was the considerably less elegant, yet entirely real Asian rhinoceros, with a horn protruding from its forehead. The horn is made from keratin, the fibrous protein found in hair. The animal's lack of magical properties, not to mention its ungainliness, may account for Marco's lack of interest in the sighting.

Refusing to be distracted by myth, Marco preferred to pay strict attention to the practice of poisoning. Inflamed by stories he had heard, he imagined a "stranger" very much like himself, "a handsome man, and gentle," who "came to lodge in the house of one of these of this province," where the inhabitants "killed him by night either by poison or by other thing so that he died." The murder took place "so that the soul of that noble stranger might not leave the house," and so that the occupants might derive good fortune from it. It is easy to conceive of Marco afraid to sleep, or even to eat, for fear of succumbing to the evil designs of his hosts.

This hideous practice persisted until the coming of the Mongols, who inflicted "great punishment" on those who killed strangers for their souls. Marco attempted to reassure himself that the practice had been eliminated long before his arrival, but he worried that it might resume at any time. He notes that men and women alike, "specially those who purpose to do evil, always carry poison with them so that if by chance anyone is caught after something has been committed for which he ought to be put to torture, before he will bear the pains of the lash he puts poison into his mouth and swallows it, that he may die through it as soon as possible." The local authorities had prepared a dreadful antidote. Marco says that "dog's dung is always at the ready so that if anyone after being taken were to swallow poison, one may immediately make him swallow dung in order that he may vomit the poison." And he assures his skeptical audience that "it is a thing very often tried."

AFTER PAINTING a picture of the dread he experienced in the hinterlands, Marco heaps praise on the ancient capital city of Pagan, although it is doubtful that he actually visited it. Nevertheless, he had heard of the opulent burial site of the kingdom's deceased ruler.

In terms usually reserved for Kublai Khan, Marco describes the ruler as rich and powerful, and "loved by all," and he repeats a story he had been told about him: "This king, when he approached death, commanded in his will that there should be . . . a monument like this, that on his tomb should be made two towers, one of gold and one of silver." One of the towers, Marco explains, was made from "the most beautiful stone" covered with plates fashioned from gold "one finger thick." Because of the gold exterior, "the tower did not seem to be of anything but gold alone." The gleaming monument, says Marco, extended "ten paces high." Atop the column sat a "round ball" containing "gilded bells that sounded every time the wind struck them." Its mate, the silver tower, was equally impressive, and was topped with silver bells.

By implication, nothing in Europe equaled the towers' grandeur.

MARCO CONSOLED himself with the thought that the formerly rebellious region had been conquered by Kublai Khan's forces, and in a highly unusual fashion. It seems that the khan prepared for the incursion by summoning the "jesters and acrobats" of his realm and dispatching them to Mien along with the soldiers. He promised to provide them adequate leadership for the campaign, and they, in turn, would obey his commands.

The Mongol army, accompanied by jesters, quickly conquered the city of Pagan, where they were confronted by the two towers, one gold, the other silver, the mere sight of which diminished their arrogance. "They were all astonished at them," Marco relates, and "told the Great Khan about the likeness of these towers and how they were beautiful and of very great value; and that if he wished they would take them down and send him the gold and the silver. The Great Khan, who knew that the king had built them for the welfare of his soul, that one might remember him after his death, said that he did not wish that they should be taken down at all, but said that he wished them to stay in such a manner as that king who had made them planned and appointed."

This show of respect for a fallen enemy impressed Marco, who states that "to this day, the towers are adorned and well guarded," and makes the questionable assertion that "no Tartar touches a thing of any dead man" because Mongol custom considers it "a very great sin to move anything belonging to the dead." It was true, however, that Kublai's deference was of a piece with his policy of encouraging local beliefs in lands conquered by his army. The Mongols realized that if they left intact the indigenous character of regions they overran, the inhabitants were far more likely to cede political control in order to preserve their spiritual identity.

As Marco resumed his travels through Asia, he experienced the once-static culture in a time of rapid transformation, making and unmaking itself as Kublai Khan incorporated one distant kingdom after another into his empire.

SOME LOCAL CUSTOMS proved too extreme for the Mongols to absorb, as Marco found in a province near Bengal. There, he says, "the people all in common, men and women, are painted or pricked with the needle all over their flesh . . . in a color of blood on their faces and all over their flesh of cranes and eagles, of lions and dragons and birds and of many other likenesses different and strange, so that nothing is seen not drawn upon and not scratched. They are made with the needles very cunningly and in such a way that they never come off by washing or nor by any other way. They also make them on the face and on the neck and on the belly and on the breast and on the arms and on the hands and on the feet, legs, and all over the body in this way."

Marco must have cringed as he described the tattooing procedure in excruciating detail. It began with the tattoo artist, or "master," drawing "patterns, so many and such as he shall please . . . with black over the whole body," whereupon the subject "will be bound feet and hands, and two or more will hold him, and the master, who practices no other art, will take five needles, four of them tied together in a square, and the fifth placed in the middle, and with these needles he goes pricking him everywhere according to the drawing of the patterns; and when the pricks are made, ink is everywhere immediately drawn over, and then the figure that was drawn appears in those pricks. But the men suffer so much pain in this that it might be thought enough for purgatory." Not surprisingly, "very many of them die while they are being so painted, for they lose much blood."

Although Marco participated eagerly in many local customs, there is no indication that he submitted to this ordeal.

VENTURING DEEPER into the jungle, toward what is now Vietnam, Marco found himself among tribes whose "valiant men of arms" wore only skimpy loincloths made from the bark of trees. The region was so

Kublai Khan, emperor of
the world's largest
land-based empire
(Granger)

Kublai Khan's wife Chabi,
an influential partner
during his reign
(Granger)

Kublai Khan dining, surrounded by wives and barons
(AKG)

Opposite top: One of the many statues arrayed like supernatural sentries along the Marco Polo Bridge *(Courtesy of the author)*

Opposite bottom: The Marco Polo Bridge, leading from Cambulac (Beijing). The Venetian crossed this impressive stone bridge to begin his journey across China in the service of the khan. *(Courtesy of the author)*

The city of Quinsai (Hangzhou) as depicted in the fifteenth-century *Book of Marvels*, based on Marco's lavish description of what was then the largest city in the world
(AKG)

The Venetian traveler dressed in Mongol finery
(Art Resource)

in the West at the time of Marco Polo's journey.
(Imageworks)

A Chinese banknote
(Bridgeman)

Kublai Khan employed Westerners as tax
collectors to administer his empire, and
Marco Polo likely found himself
in this role.
(AKG)

Kublai Khan hunting atop elephants
(AKG)

Kublai Khan's generosity to the poor, as recounted
by Marco Polo and portrayed in this illuminated
manuscript, impressed Western minds.
(Art Archive)

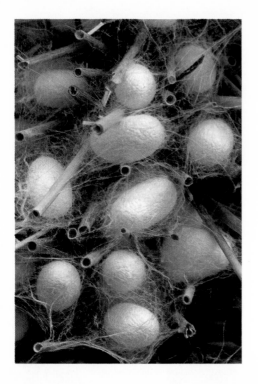

Silkworms, one of the principal
sources of Chinese wealth
(Imageworks)

Haunting representations of
the Buddha outside Quinsai
(Hangzhou) deeply impressed
Marco, who had initially
dismissed them as idols.
(Courtesy of the author)

alien that the prevalence of paper currency bearing the seal of the Great Khan came as a reassuring reminder to Marco that he was still in the Mongol Empire, and still enjoying the protection of his *paiza*.

Nothing else offered Marco much comfort in a land where lions were rarely seen but often heard. It was so dangerous, he says, that no man could dare to sleep at night outside the house "for fear of them, for the lions would eat him immediately." The lions were so rapacious that merchants (like Marco) were forced to sleep in simple craft on the river, and even then their safety could not be guaranteed, for if they were not far enough from shore, "the lions go to them, jumping into the water and swimming up to the boat." Once there, "they take a man from it by force and go their way and eat him." To prevent this horror, the merchants made every effort to "anchor in the middle of the river, which is very broad."

To defend themselves against lion attacks, Marco explains, the merchants formed a symbiotic partnership with fierce "dogs"—actually wolves—"with the courage and strength to go and attack the lions." The "dogs" fought in pairs, and they offered serious protection against the king of the jungle. Marco says that a man alone on horseback, armed with a bow and arrow, and with two such "dogs," could kill a lion: "When it happens that they find a great lion, the dogs, which are brave and strong, as soon as they see the lion, run upon him very bravely, encouraged by the man, one in front and the other behind. And the lion turns toward the dogs, but the dogs are trained so well to protect themselves and so agile that the lion does not touch them; and the lion looks at the men and not the dogs. And so the lion goes flying. But the dogs, as soon as they see that the lion is going off, run behind him barking and howling, and bite him in the legs or in the tail, and the lion turns very fiercely and would kill them, but cannot catch them, because the dogs know well how to protect themselves. . . . The lion is much frightened by the great noise that the dogs make, and then he sets himself on the road, escaping the noise of the dogs, to go into some thicket, or to find some thick tree against which he can lean his back, to show his face to the dogs so that they cannot worry him from behind. . . . He goes off step by step—not by any means would he run—because the lion is not held by fear, so great is his pride and the extent of his spirit. While the lion is going off in this way by degrees, the dogs go biting him all the time behind, and the man with the bow shoots at him. When he feels himself bitten, the lion turns this way and

that towards the dogs, but the dogs being able to draw back, the lion
returns to pass on his way. When one sees this, he lays hand to his boy
(for they are very good archers) and gives him some arrows, both one
and two and more and so many that the lion is wounded with arrows
and weakened by loss of blood that he falls dead before finding a
refuge. . . . [Lions] cannot defend themselves against a man on horseback who has two good dogs."

IT CAME as a relief to the wayfaring Marco to turn from the strain of
lion hunting to the mechanics of harvesting salt, his stock-in-trade as
Kublai Khan's tax assessor. In the city of Cianglu, yet another remote
outpost of the Mongol Empire, he observed with a fine appraising eye
local miners digging for veins of salt in the earth, and laboriously pil-
ing the salt into great mounds. "Over these mounds they throw water
in plenty, so much that the water penetrating through them goes to the
bottom of the mound of earth, and then they take and collect that and
put it in great jars and in great cauldrons of iron, and make it boil.
When it is well boiled and purified by the force of the fire, they leave it
to cool, and then the water thickens and they take it and salt is made
from it—very beautiful and white and fine."

The locals produced enough salt to sell quantities to other
provinces, deriving "great wealth" from the sale. At the same time,
Kublai Khan received "much revenue and profit from it," thanks to the
diligent efforts of foreign tax collectors like Marco.

IN THE RECENTLY conquered province of Tundinfu—a place-name
sometimes taken to refer to Yen Chau in Vietnam—Marco resumed
his investigation of the intimate lives of young women. He found those
in the area refreshingly "pure" and "able to keep the virtue of modesty," in contrast to women of other places who opened their beds, if
not their hearts, to travelers. In fact, the women of Tundinfu sound
downright severe, for they neither danced nor skipped nor frolicked,
nor did they "fly into a passion." Unlike other girls he had encountered, these virtuous creatures did not lurk behind windows, staring at
passersby, and they abjured "unseemly talk" and "merry-making." On
the rare occasions when they ventured beyond the sanctuary of their
homes, they were accompanied by their mothers, and they avoided

"staring improperly at people." Their broad bonnets restricted their field of vision and focused their attention on the road ahead. It went without saying that they paid "no attention to suitors." So modest were these young women that they refrained from bathing in pairs.

Their entire lives were arranged to protect them from any disturbance or violation; otherwise, the girl in question would not be able to marry, or, as Marco puts it, "if the opposite [of virginity] is found, the marriage would not hold." Since this was a serious legal matter, the interested parties—the father of the bride and the bridegroom—took extreme measures to confirm the girl's virginity.

"When the bonds and agreements have been duly made," reports Marco, "the girl is taken for the test of her virtue to the baths, where there will be the mothers and relations of herself and of the spouse, and on behalf of either party certain matrons specially deputed for this duty who will first examine the girl's virginity with a pigeon's egg. And if the women on behalf of the bridegroom are not satisfied with such a test, since a woman's natural parts can well be contracted by medicinal means, one matron will cunningly insert a finger wrapped in fine white linen into the natural parts and will break a little of the virginal vein so that the linen may be a little stained with virginal blood. That blood is of such a nature and strength that it can be removed by no washing from cloth where it is fixed. And if it be removed, it is a sign that she has been defiled, nor is that blood of her proper nature. When the test has been made, if she is found a virgin, the marriage is valid; but if not, not. And the father of the girl will be punished by the government according to the agreement that he has made.

"You ought to know that for the keeping of this virginity, maidens always step so gently as they walk that one foot never goes before the other by more than a finger, because the privy parts of a virgin are very often opened if she take herself along too wantonly."

Marco notes parenthetically that Mongols "do not care about this sort of convention; for their daughters ride with them, and their wives, whence it may be believed that to some extent they suffer harm"—with none the worse for the disturbance. Clearly, this was a more realistic approach to the issue of virginity.

WHILE IN TUNDINFU, Marco lost a cherished ring, and his attempts to recover it opened his eyes wider than ever before to the possibilities of Buddhism. Here he found "eighty-four idols, each with its own name," but this time he did not dismiss this form of worship. He faithfully reports that "the idolaters say that an appropriate power has been given to each idol by the supreme God, namely to one for the finding of things lost; to one for the provision of fertility of lands and seasonable weather; to one for the helping of flocks; and with regard to everything."

Marco naturally felt drawn to the idols capable of locating lost items. Resembling twelve-year-old boys, they were decorated with "beautiful ornaments" and were tended around the clock by an old woman. Anyone seeking to retrieve a lost item, he notes, appealed to this woman, whereupon she advised burning incense. Only then would she speak on behalf of her inanimate charges, saying, "Look in such a place and you shall find it." If the item was stolen, she would answer, "So-and-so has it. Tell him to give it to you. And if he shall deny, come back to me, for I will make him certainly restore it to you." And this is what Marco did and heard in pursuit of the lost ring.

He reports that the old woman's charms, in combination with the idols' powers, worked wonders beyond the mere retrieval of lost or stolen goods. A woman who refused to return a stolen kitchen knife, for instance, might find that it "cuts off her hand, or [she] falls into the fire, or another misfortune happens to her." A man might wind up accidentally cutting off his foot with a stolen knife while chopping wood, or breaking his arms and legs. "Because men know by experience that this happens to them because of denials of thefts, they give back what they have stolen immediately."

To hear Marco tell it, the old woman frequently communicated with the mischievous spirits. They "produce whispering in a sort of thin and low voice like a hissing. Then the old woman [gives] them many thanks in this way: she raises her hands before them, she will gnash her teeth three times, saying something like, 'Oh, how worthy a thing, how holy, and how virtuous.' And she will say to him who has lost horses, 'You may go to such a place and you will find them'; or, 'Robbers found them in such a place and are leading them away with them in such a direction, run, and you shall find them.' And it is found exactly as she has said."

There was a catch: a bounty had to be paid. "When the lost things are found, then men reverently and devoutly offer to the idols perhaps an ell of some fine cloth," such as silk. This was exactly Marco's case, and proudly he reports, "I, Marco, found in this way a certain ring of mine that was lost," and he hastens to add, "not that I made them any offering or homage."

WHEN MARCO RESUMED his travels throughout southwestern China, adventures awaited him at every turn, more than he could stuff into his comprehensive account. "Do not believe we have treated the whole province of China in order," he warns his audience at this point in his account, "not indeed a twentieth part; but only as I, Marco, used to cross the province, so the cities that are on the way across are described, passing by those that are at the sides and through the middle, to tell of which would be too long."

"THIS PROVINCE OF MANZI," says Marco, picking up where he left off, "is a very exceedingly strong place. All the cities of the kingdom are surrounded with ditches full of water broad"—the length of a crossbow shot, he estimates—"and deep." By Manzi, Marco meant the realm of the wealthy and sophisticated Song dynasty, which even Kublai Khan had long avoided, preferring to conquer other, more vulnerable regions of China. But the men of Manzi were not the courageous warriors that Marco, or the Mongols, supposed them to be. In 1268, they scattered before Kublai's forces, or quietly surrendered "because they were not valiant nor used to arms."

After the defeat, Marco made it his business to find out exactly how the khan's men had come to defeat the local king, a supposed tyrant named Facfur, "who took delight in nothing but war and conquest and making himself a great lord."

In reality, Facfur had little stomach for fighting, preferring peaceful commercial pursuits; he was precisely the kind of enlightened, semidivine monarch Kublai Khan aspired to be. And for that reason, Facfur was vulnerable to the rapacious Mongol forces. By coincidence, King Facfur's astrologers had informed him that under no circumstances would he lose his kingdom unless he were attacked by a man "with one hundred eyes." This prediction had comforted the king, "because he could not think that any natural man could have a hundred eyes." He was destined to be proven wrong. As it happened, Kublai Khan's forces included an exceptional officer by the name of Bayan Hundred Eyes, who would prove to be Facfur's nemesis.

Born in 1236, Bayan was a young man at the time of the campaign.

He had joined Kublai Khan's household as a retainer, and in this capacity he exhibited formidable administrative skills, impressive bearing, and dynamic communication. Bayan was married, but Kublai terminated his marriage and gave him a new, highly placed wife named Besüjin. Profiting from his elevated social status, Bayan quickly rose through the allied Mongol-Chinese ranks, forming alliances with the Confucian faction; in 1260, he joined the military, serving first as an administrator, and then as a commander whose leadership ability favorably impressed his superiors and disarmed potential rivals. A statesman and soldier, Bayan mastered Chinese literary forms, and he dutifully wrote military poetry in honor of the Mongol forces. Kublai Khan bestowed the highest praise on him, confiding to one of his sons, "Bayan combines in his person the talents of a general and of a minister. He is trustworthy in everything." He concluded, "You must not treat him as an ordinary person." Bayan had become the indispensable man of the Yüan dynasty.

When Kublai Khan determined that the time was right to attack the Song, he placed Bayan in charge of 200,000 cavalry supplemented by the Chinese infantry, as well as a navy of 5,000 vessels manned by 70,000 sailors. Leading his massive force, Bayan circled one city in southern China after another—five in all—demanding that the people lay down their arms and surrender to the Great Khan, but everywhere he went, he met with stubborn, silent resistance from the resolute Chinese. When he came to the sixth disobedient city, Bayan lost all patience and "took it by force and skill, causing all who were found in it to be killed." Energized by victory, he led his troops on a campaign of burning and pillaging, taking twelve cities in quick succession. "Then the hearts of the men of Manzi trembled when they heard this news."

With military control of the entire province, Bayan readied himself for the ultimate conquest, Hangzhou, the richest prize in all of China, or, for that matter, anywhere in the world, and the home of a million and a half people. No other city rivaled Hangzhou for opulence, beauty, or sophistication, or for progressive and generous government.

WITH HIS celebrated concern for the poor and dispossessed and his abundant charity, King Facfur embodied the wealthy city's altruistic spirit. Exhibiting a newfound appreciation for Facfur, Marco insisted that the good king's deeds merited a memorial, and that the king's subjects loved him more than they had loved any previous king of the city, "because of the great mercy and justice of which he was master."

Facfur championed the cause of children abandoned by their mothers, and he devised an efficient system of welfare and adoption on their behalf. "In that province," says Marco, "they cast out the child as soon as he is born. The poor women who cannot feed them nor bring them up for poverty do this. The king had them all taken, and caused to be written for each one in what constellation and in what planet he was born. Then he had them brought up in many directions and in many places, for he had nurses in great abundance. When a rich man had no child, he went to the king and had himself given as many as he wished and those who pleased him most." If an adopted child's biological parents underwent a change of heart, and wished to have it back, they could, so long as they documented that the child was theirs. Otherwise, the infant remained under the king's protection until marriage. When the adoptees reached marriageable age, the king performed mass marriages, and generously "gave them [the newlyweds] so much that they could live in comfort."

Facfur was similarly generous with housing, ensuring that every dwelling, whether it sheltered rich or poor, "was both beautiful and great." In this beneficent environment, petty crime was unknown, or so Marco claims: "The city was so safe that the doors of the houses and shops and stores full of all the very dear merchandise often stayed open at night as by day and nothing at all was found missing there." And here, in contrast to so much of the Mongol Empire visited by Marco, "one could go freely through the whole kingdom safe and unmolested by night also by day."

At the moment, the king and queen of Hangzhou were in residence amid their lavish court, "and there he [Bayan Hundred Eyes] drew up his army in order before it." Overwhelmed by the might of the Mongol army, Facfur summoned his astrologers to inquire how he could have suffered this overwhelming defeat, and they explained that his adversary bore the name Bayan Hundred Eyes. The prediction had come true.

King Facfur "feared greatly, and he left that city with many people and entered into . . . a thousand ships loaded with all his goods and wealth and fled into the Ocean Sea, among the impregnable islands of India, leaving the city of Quinsai [Hangzhou] to the care of the queen, with orders to defend herself as well as she could, for, being a woman, she would have no fear of death if she fell into the hands of the enemy." At that point, to the surprise of everyone, the queen, "who was left in the city with a great people," displayed her mettle in the face of the Mongol onslaught. She "bestirred herself with her military leaders to defend it as well as she could like the valiant lady she was."

The queen held her ground until she received a simple but unnerving piece of intelligence from her astrologers: a commander named Hundred Eyes was destined to prevail. When she learned that the general laying siege to the city was known by this name, "her strength failed altogether, for it immediately caused her to remember the aforesaid astrology that said that none but a man with a hundred eyes would take the kingdom from them." With that revelation, "the queen gave herself up immediately to Bayan. And after the queen surrendered to the Great Khan, and the chief city of the kingdom, all the other cities and villages and all the remainder of the kingdom gave themselves up without mounting any defense."

She and her husband met with sharply differing fates. "The queen who surrendered to Bayan was taken to the court of Kublai the Great Khan. And when the great lord saw her, he had her honored and waited upon in costly fashion like the great lady she was." All the while, King Facfur languished in exile on an island off the coast of India until his death, far from the bountiful kingdom he had once ruled with such enlightened generosity.

UNTIL HE encountered Facfur's example, Marco had embraced Kublai Khan as the ideal ruler. True, Kublai Khan displayed impressive generosity toward the poor late in his life, but Facfur's passion for social and economic justice far exceeded the Mongol leader's. A careful reading of Marco's flattering description of Facfur suggests that Marco flirted with the idea that he, rather than Kublai, was the greater of the two—a judgment based on generosity of spirit rather than military might.

The change in Marco's thinking reflected his shifting vantage point. When Marco was in Cambulac, Kublai Khan seemed a brilliant sun outshining all other sources of light, but the farther the Venetian ventured to the fringes of the Mongol Empire in performance of his duties as a tax collector, and the more instances of Mongol violence—

including the slaughter of women and children—he witnessed or heard about, the more disillusioned he became. At one time, the Mongols had appeared more sympathetic to Marco than their enemies, but as he observed them brutally enforcing their empire's rule, having himself sampled the refinement of China, a long, slow disillusionment with the Mongols quietly set in. That disillusionment informed his narrative, even as he struggled to maintain his allegiance to the warriors of the Steppe.

IF MARCO's habitual tendency to gild his experiences appears suspect, he goes beyond the limits of plausibility when he describes how he played a heroic, pivotal role in the siege of the Siang-yang-fu, a "large and splendid city." At least, that is the way he tells the story. Chinese annals contradict his version. The siege actually occurred in 1273, while Marco was languishing in Afghanistan, recovering from an unspecified illness, two years before he reached the court of Kublai Khan. In the case of the siege of Siang-yang-fu, Marco's imprecision in converting dates from the Chinese to the European calendar does not account for the discrepancy, nor does the possibility of omitted text, because he emphatically places himself, his father, and his uncle at the center of the action.

According to Marco, Siang-yang-fu held out against the forces of Kublai Khan while much of China surrendered. Protected by a large, deep lake, the city was vulnerable to attack on only one side, the north. While resisting the Mongols, the inhabitants of Siang-yang-fu arranged to have ample provisions smuggled in over the lake; as a result, the Mongols were unable to starve them out. After three years of trying and failing to take the city, the Mongol army was "greatly enraged" and wished to leave.

Marco launches into a series of astonishing assertions, beginning with an offer that he, his father, and his uncle made to assist in the siege. Since describing his departure from Cambulac in the service of the khan, Marco had ceased to mention his father and uncle, creating the impression that he ventured forth alone while they remained close to Cambulac to pursue their trading business. More suspect, the offer to help with the siege violates the underlying premise of the narrative. Previously, Marco observed history in the making but scrupulously avoided portraying himself as affecting the course of events. Now, in contrast, he was presenting the Polos as heroes of the siege. "We will find you a way by which the town will surrender immediately," they supposedly proclaimed.

Marco claims that the Mongol army accepted the offer and relayed it to Kublai Khan, who endorsed the plan. And he proceeds to show his family out of character, as combat-hardened warriors familiar with the latest Mongol military technology. He depicts the Polo company going to see Kublai Khan—highly unlikely, since the Great Khan was thousands of miles distant—and offering to "find a device and engine that the city would be taken and that it would surrender." He explains parenthetically that the device was a mangonel, essentially a large and powerful catapult "that would throw into the town stones so great and heavy and from so far that they would confound all they would reach, killing the people and ruining the houses." In the medieval fashion, Marco refers to the mangonel as an engine, meaning artillery that did not rely on gunpowder. Indeed, the mangonel derived its force from a torsion bundle—a length of rope wrapped around a rotating beam, or epizygis.

At first, Marco says, the Polos' offer to employ a European-style mangonel baffled the Mongol leaders. "They all wondered greatly because . . . in all those parts they do not know what mangonels are, nor engines, nor trebuchets [a smaller device relying on a counter-weight rather than a torsion bundle], for they did not use them, nor were accustomed to use them in their armies." Nevertheless, the Mongols were "very glad and astonished" by the audacious plan.

The technology of which Marco speaks was familiar in Europe; by AD 50, the forces of the Roman Empire deployed similar catapults, known as onagers, to lob rocks over fortress walls; Alexander the Great had also used them in his military campaigns. In medieval Europe, the mangonel served as a mainstay of armies laying siege to fortresses and castles because it could hurl huge stones or fireballs more than a thousand feet, causing considerable damage to otherwise impervious fortress walls. Marco portrays Kublai Khan as eager to use the mangonel in the siege, if only because it was "a new and strange thing."

The Polo company made preparations with the help of two European assistants (mentioned nowhere else), one identified as a German, the other as a Nestorian, who were "good masters of this work." Marco claims he ordered them to construct two or three engines capable of throwing large stones, and in only a "few days," they fashioned three "very great and very fine mangonels according to the orders of the brothers, each of which threw the stones that weigh more than three hundred pounds each, and one saw it fly very far; of which stones there were more than sixty."

There followed a demonstration of the siege engines for the benefit of Kublai Khan himself, "and others," who came away mightily impressed. Immediately thereafter, the Great Khan ordered the mangonels "put on boats and carried to his armies, which were at the siege of the city of Siang-yang-fu." Soon the mangonels were backed up by trebuchets, portable but equally destructive siege engines. Marco alleges, "they seemed to the Tartars the greatest wonder of the world."

With gusto, he describes the European machinery's devastating effect on the Chinese fortress. "When the trebuchets were set up before the city of Siang-yang-fu and drawn, each one threw a stone of three hundred pounds into the town. The stone that the mangonel first shot struck into the houses and broke and ruined everything, and made great noise and great tumult."

Under attack from the strange engines, the inhabitants of Siang-yang-fu panicked. "Every day they threw a very great number of stones, by which many were killed. And when the men of the city saw this misfortune, which they had never seen nor heard [before], they were so dismayed by it and so alarmed that they did not know what they ought to say or do," Marco gloats, "and they believed that this was done to them by enchantment, for it seemed that the bolts came from the sky." Surrender became inevitable. "They wished to give themselves up in the way that the other cities . . . had done, and . . . were willing to be under the rule of the Great Khan. The lord of the army said he was quite willing for this. And then he received them, and those of the city gave themselves up like other cities."

Marco boasts about the role that he and his family had supposedly played in the Mongol victory: "And that happened by the kindness of Master Niccolò and Master Maffeo and Master Marco Polo, son of Master Niccolò Polo, as you have heard. This solution . . . increased the fame and credit of these two Venetian brothers in the sight of the Great Khan and all the court."

The Mongol victory at Siang-yang-fu remains one of the outstanding tales in Marco's account, but with its departure from the facts as recorded in Chinese annals, its unusually bellicose tone, and its chronological impossibility, it also remains the episode most open to question. Nevertheless, the military contest did occur, and the annals indicate that the Mongols did, in fact, employ "foreign engineers" to lay siege to the city. Marco, however, could not have been among them. To give Marco his due, it is possible that his father and uncle participated in some phase of the siege on their previous trip. Yet at least three early manuscripts of the *Travels* fail to mention the siege at all. It seems more likely that this stirring episode was added by Rustichello, seeking to aggrandize the role played by the young tax collector and his elders in the making of the Mongol Empire. Even if the romance writer played false with history, he accomplished his literary aims.

As MARCO veered back toward the east, heading for Hangzhou, he traveled the rivers of China. Although he was familiar with the sight of the canals of Venice teeming with watercraft, nothing had prepared him for the sight of the immense Qiantang River, as it is known today, "pursuing its course . . . more than a hundred and twenty days' journey before it enters the sea, into which river enter infinite other rivers, all navigable, which run in different directions and swell and increase their turns to such a size." The sheer size of the river—actually an estuary—inspired Marco to state, with accuracy, that it flowed through "so many regions, and there are so many cities upon it," that watercraft traveling along contained cargo "of greater value" than on "all the rivers of Christendom," and, on further thought, of greater value than on "all their seas."

He cites a source for his claim: inspectors who "keep account for their lord" told him that more than five thousand watercraft traveled on the river each year, but he did not simply take their word for it. He asserts: "I tell you that I saw there at one time when I was in the city of Singiu fifteen thousand boats at once that all sail by this river, which is so broad that it does not seem to be a river but a sea." The number referred to vessels in just one city, as difficult as Europeans would find that to believe.

Marco was particularly attentive to waterborne commerce because, it appeared, "the chief merchandise that is carried upon this river is salt, which the merchants load in this city and carry through whatever regions are upon this river, and also inland." As a tax assessor, he was doing his job, following the salt, but he also noted that boats did a brisk trade in wood, charcoal, hemp, "and many other different wares with which the regions near the seashore are supplied." The abundance was enough to overwhelm even the most jaded merchant of Venice.

These boats enthralled him—not just their number, but their variety, and their construction. Patrolling the docks, he took advantage of his position to study their construction and fittings at close range, as if plotting his eventual escape from the Mongol Empire aboard one of them. "They are covered with only one deck and have only one mast with one sail, but they are of great tonnage," he reports. And he describes their rigging with great detail and expertise: "All the ships have not all the tackle of ropes of hemp, except indeed that they have the masts and the sails rigged with them. But I tell you that they have the hawsers, or, to speak plainly, the tow-lines of nothing else but of canes, with which the ships are towed upstream by this river. . . . Each of these ships has eight or ten or twelve horses which tow it through the river against the stream, and also with it."

One day, perhaps, a similar ship might carry him from China to Venice and freedom.

CHAPTER ELEVEN

The City of Heaven

So twice five miles of fertile ground
With walls and towers were girdled round. . . .

"W HEN ONE is gone riding for three days, then one finds the most noble and magnificent city that for its excellence, importance, and beauty is called Quinsai, which means the City of Heaven," Marco Polo records. "It is the greatest city that may be found in the world, where so many pleasures may be found that one fancies himself to be in Paradise."

Marco had arrived at the apogee of Chinese civilization, a city so advanced, so beautiful, so filled with sensual pleasures that he would scarcely be able to convince skeptical Europeans that it was not some insubstantial vision, but as real as Venice. Like Venice, Quinsai was built around a series of canals in which boats of every type jostled against each other. No wonder Marco believed that he had arrived in a more highly evolved version of his native city.

Hangzhou, as the city is known today, captivated Marco as did no other place in Asia. For the first time, he encountered the grandeur of China at its most advanced, unspoiled by the Mongols. In Quinsai, he arrived at a breathtaking future, as unreal to him as some science fiction fantasy would be to a time traveler of today, yet it was tangible and vital. For once, he saw himself not just as a wayfarer but as an explorer, and he set out take the measure of this urban marvel. "I, Master Marco Polo," he proclaims, "was in this city many times and determined with great diligence to notice and understand all the conditions of the place, describing them in my notes."

The inhabitants of Quinsai resisted opening hearth and home to a foreigner such as Marco, who, in their eyes, represented the invading

Mongols. Also, he had never acquired an understanding of Chinese. As a result of those barriers, much of the city's inner life, spiritual and sexual, eluded his inquiry. Yet his curiosity impelled him to learn more about the city and its people than any other European before him.

He never offered a full account of why he went to the great capital, or what duties he performed there. Most likely, he served as a tax assessor and collector not long after Kublai Khan's trusted general, Bayan, conquered the city. In some versions of the *Travels*, Marco claims that he held the post of governor of Hangzhou, and skeptics of his account have seized on this as a prime example of his tendency to inflate his experience outrageously. Yet in other versions, Marco says only that he visited the city repeatedly in his capacity as a tax assessor, and sat on a city council. Both assertions are plausible. In any event, his dazzling descriptions of the city speak for themselves.

How did a Venetian manage to infiltrate and decode the immense, advanced, and complex city? His forays into alien cultures often yielded mixed results, yet his account of Quinsai demonstrates a mastery of detail and uncanny accuracy. The answer is that he received expert help, as he explains: "I will follow the account of it [Quinsai] sent in writing by the queen of the realm to Bayan, the conqueror of the province, when he was besieging it. This was for him to pass on to the Great Khan, so that, learning of its magnificence, he might not let it be sacked or laid waste." In other words, Marco enjoyed access to the flow of Mongol intelligence about the city. He is silent concerning the language of this valuable document. It may have been in Persian, which he knew well, or in one of the Mongol tongues with which he was familiar. In either case, his consideration of Quinsai is more than a patchwork of quotations; he brought his own observations to bear, so that he could confidently state, "It is all true, as I, Marco Polo, later saw clearly with my own eyes."

MARCO LAUNCHES INTO a fervid account of Quinsai, a city "so large that in circuit it is . . . a hundred miles around or thereabouts, because the streets and canals in it are very wide and large." Proceeding to bring this unknown metropolis to life for his skeptical Western readers, he says, "Then there are squares where they hold market, which on account of the vast multitudes that meet in them are necessarily very large and spacious."

The more Marco pondered this metropolis, with its canals and

bridges and constant waterborne traffic teeming with commerce on a
scale that his readers would not have believed possible, the more eloquent his reportage became. "It has on one side," he continues, "a lake
of fresh water [West Lake] that is very clear, and on the other there is
an enormous river which, by entering by many great and small canals
that run in every part of the city, both takes away all impurities and
then enters the lake. . . . This makes the air very wholesome; and one
can go all about the city by land and by these streams. The streets and
canals are so great that boats are able to travel there conveniently and
carts to carry the things necessary for the inhabitants."

Marco stumbles when he comes to estimate the number of bridges
in the City of Heaven: "There is a story that it has 12,000 bridges,
great and small, for the most part of stone, and some are built of wood.
And for each of these bridges, or for the most part, a great and large
ship could easily pass under the arch of it; and for the others smaller
ships could pass. But those that are made over the principal canals and
the chief streets are arched so high and with such skill that a boat can
pass under them with a mast, and yet there pass over them carriages
and horses, so well are the streets inclined to fit the height." The actual
number of bridges in Quinsai came to 347, not 12,000 as Marco states,
a discrepancy that would furnish the doubters with ammunition. But as
the context makes clear, "12,000 bridges" is not meant to be taken literally. He simply wants to impress upon readers that there were more
bridges in Quinsai than he could tally, more, even, than in Venice.
"And let no one be surprised if there are so many bridges," he goes on,
"because I tell you that this town is all . . . lagoons as Venice is, and also
all surrounded by water, and so it is needful that there may be so many
bridges for this, that people may be able to go through the town both
inside and out by land."

Nor were bridges the only engineering marvel of Quinsai. The
city's enormous moat was "perhaps forty miles long." Marco relates
that it was made "by order of those ancient kings of that province so as
to be able to draw off the river into it every time that it rose above the
banks; and it serves also as a defense for the city, and the earth that was
dug out was put on the inner side, which makes the likeness of a little
hill that surrounds it."

Marco again strained credulity with his description of Quinsai's
sprawl, although it was entirely accurate. "There are ten principal
open spaces, besides infinite others for the districts, which are square,

that is, half a mile for a side," he writes. "And along the front street of those there is a main street forty paces wide, which runs straight from one end of the city to the other with many bridges that cross it level and conveniently; and every four miles is found one of those squares such as have two miles (as has been said) of circuit."

He took note of Quinsai's celebrated Grand Canal—"a very broad canal that runs parallel to the street at the back of the squares"—without realizing that he was gazing upon the longest artificial waterway in China. The Grand Canal connected major rivers from Quinsai to Cambulac, a distance of a thousand miles. It was an ancient artery, at least a thousand years old by the time Marco visited. Originally a casual network of waterways, the Grand Canal became a unified entity after an inspection tour undertaken by Emperor Yang Ti of the Sui dynasty in AD 604. Over the next six years, three million laborers expanded the Grand Canal, largely by hand. The sacrifice was enormous; half the workforce perished, and eventually the Sui dynasty collapsed as a result. But the canal survived.

BY EUROPEAN STANDARDS, Quinsai's varied population was as incredible as its size. Marco tells of a profusion of people and goods that would have amazed those accustomed to life on a more intimate scale: "Three days a week, there is a concourse of from forty to fifty thousand persons who come to market and bring everything you can desire for food, because there is always a great supply of victuals; of game, that is to say, of roebuck, red-deer, fallow-deer, hare, rabbit, and of birds, partridges, pheasant, francolin, quail, fowl, capon, and more ducks and geese than can be told; for they rear so many of them in [West] Lake that for one Venetian groat"—a thick silver coin of modest value, whose name derived from the Italian *grosso*, or large—"may be had a pair of geese and two pair of ducks."

As Marco wandered past the market stalls, rubbing shoulders with enough shoppers to populate several European cities, he marveled at the profusion of goods on display, the likes of which he had never seen in the West—"all sorts of vegetables and fruits, and above all the rest immense pears, which weigh ten pounds apiece, which are white inside like a paste, and very fragrant; peaches in their seasons, yellow and white, very delicate."

The abundance of fresh produce available was exceeded only by the

quantity of fish. Each day, Marco reports, it arrived fresh from the
"Ocean Sea up the river for the space of twenty-five miles," all of it
supplemented by equally succulent fish from West Lake, although this
was not as desirable, "because of the impurities that come from the
city" polluting the lake water. "Whoever saw this quantity of fish
would never think that it could be sold, and yet in a few hours it has all
been taken away, so great is the multitude of the inhabitants who are
used to live delicacies; for they eat both fish and flesh at the same
meal."

DESPITE MARCO'S tendency to embellish, the City of Heaven was
emphatically real. Contemporaneous accounts by outsiders who managed to reach Quinsai all emphasized the city's overwhelming size,
prosperity, and beauty, and acclaimed Quinsai the greatest in all the
world.

The Persian historian Vassaf, writing about Quinsai in 1300,
described very much the same city Marco experienced and loved—its
great size, broad streets, and abundance.

> Quinsai, which is the principal city of the country of Matchin
> and which seems a paradise of which the sky forms the ground,
> extends in length so that its circumference is approximately
> twenty-four *parasang*s [about fifteen kilometers]. Its pavement is
> made of baked bricks and stones; it contains many houses and
> buildings built in wood and decorated with beautiful paintings
> of all kinds. From one end of the city to the other three post sta-
> tions have been established. The largest of the streets is, it is
> said, three *parasang*s in length, and contains sixty pavilions of a
> uniform architecture, sustained by pillars of the same propor-
> tions. The revenue from the tax on salt amounts daily to 700
> *balich*s of *tchao* [paper money]. The number of people who exer-
> cise different professions is truly prodigious: it has been calcu-
> lated that there are thirty-two thousand cloth dyers; one can
> judge from that about the other kinds of industry. Seven hun-
> dred thousand soldiers and an equal number of inhabitants are
> recorded in the offices of numbering and on the registers of the
> chancellorship. In addition, the city contains seven hundred
> temples which resemble fortresses, each inhabited by a number

of priests without faith, monks without religion, as well as by a multitude of workers, guards, servants, idolaters with their families and people of their suites. All these men are not mentioned in the census, and they are not subject to the payment of taxes and levies. Forty thousand soldiers are devoted to guarding the city and serving as sentinels.

Confirming Marco Polo's impressions, Vassaf wrote:

For the comfort of this immense population, boats and barks of all kinds circulate continually on the waters in such a great number that imagination cannot conceive an idea of it, and the more so because it would be impossible to calculate their numbers.

A very different visitor, Odoric of Pordenone, a Franciscan friar, arrived forty years after Marco Polo's time, and, like Marco, cast off all restraint in describing the wonders he experienced there.

It is the greatest city in the whole world. It is a hundred miles around, and in all this great space there is no empty area which is not fully inhabited by people; and there are many houses which have ten families or more; this city has many suburbs and more people than any other city. It has ten principal gates, and adjacent to each of its gates are eight large cities, much larger than the city of Venice; and from these gates to these cities, run continuous roads, so that a man can well go six or eight days and it will seem that he has only gone a little way, because he will always have gone among towns and houses.

Like Marco, Odoric saw Quinsai as the Asian Venice, but bigger and better.

This city is located on a low plain, between lakes, seas and swamps, like the city of Venice. There are more than seven thousand bridges, and at each bridge there are people guarding it on behalf of the Khan.

Odoric estimated that Quinsai was home to 850,000 households, which made for a population of over a million and a half, just as Marco claimed. "Whoever would write of this city would fill a great book," the friar concluded, unaware that Marco Polo's chronicle had already fulfilled this prophecy. "But in brief it is the greatest that there is in the world and the most noble."

The most celebrated traveler in the Muslim world, Ibn Battutah, is said to have arrived in Quinsai in 1340, more than fifty years after Marco. By that time, the City of Heaven had become even larger, with a more visible European population, including prominent Jewish and Muslim communities. "We entered the said city, which is divided into six towns; each has its separate wall, and a great wall circles all of them. In the first town live the guards of the city with their commander," he wrote.

> The next day we entered the second town through a door called the Door of the Jews; this town is inhabited by the Israelites, the Christians, and the Turks, adorers of the sun; they are very numerous. The Emir of this town is Chinese, and we spent the second night in his house. The third day, we made our entry into the third town, and this is occupied by the Moslems. It is beautiful; the markets here are disposed as in the Islamic countries; it contains mosques and muezzins; we heard the latter call the faithful to midday prayer when we entered the town.

The ethnic variety of Quinsai, unremarked by earlier visitors, reflected the ascendancy of the Mongols, who invited "the Israelites, the Christians, and the Turks" to settle and trade in the great city.

THE CITY OF HEAVEN'S celebrated joie de vivre centered on the numerous public bathhouses and their courtesans. The locals, both men and women, availed themselves of the cold-water baths, "recommended for health," as Marco slyly notes, while foreigners made use of the hot baths, where alluring serving maids offered their clients more than simple hygiene. These women, reeking of "sumptuous perfumes," he says, "are very clever and practiced in knowing how to flatter and coax with ready words and suited to each kind of person, so that the foreigners who have once indulged themselves with them can never forget them. . . . It comes to pass that when they return home they say they have been to Quinsai, that is, the City of Heaven, and count the hours until they be able to return there."

Combining a market and a brothel, Quinsai also had the air of a perpetual carnival. One memoirist who came of age there never forgot the man who trained his fish to perform.

> He has a large lacquer bowl in front of him in which swim turtles, turbots, and other fish. He beats time on a small bronze gong and calls up one of the creatures by name. It comes immediately and dances on the surface, wearing a kind of little hat on its head. . . . There is also an archery expert who sets up in front of the spectators a big wheel a yard and a half in diameter, with all sorts of objects, flowers, birds, and people painted on it. He announces that he is going to hit this or that object, and having started spinning it rapidly, he shoots his arrows through the midst of the spectators. He hits the exact spot he has declared he will hit. He can even score a hit on the most precisely defined spots of the spinning target, such as a particular feather in a particular wing of a bird.

The memoirist wandered in a daze among snake charmers blowing on little pipes, luring their hideous charges from the bamboo baskets where they coiled in darkness; and a Taoist monk who carried a trap filled with multicolored shellfish, which he claimed he had hypnotized. Boxers abounded, as did chess players, poets, writers of light verse, acrobats, and magicians. A Chinese record of the era lists five hundred and fifty-four performers who appeared at court, grouped into fifty-five categories, including kite flyers and ball players, magicians and singers, impressionists, archers, and bawdy raconteurs.

THE GREAT rectangular palaces looming over this frenzied activity caused Marco to tilt his head upward, to take in their lush gardens, "and nearby them, houses of artisans who work in their shops." He writes that "at all hours are met people who are going up and down on their business, so that to see a great crowd anyone would believe that it would not be possible that victuals are found enough to be able to feed it; and yet every market day all the squares are covered and filled with people and merchants who bring them both on carts and on boats, and all is disposed of."

He sensed the order underlying this apparent chaos, the existence of twelve principal crafts or trades: "And each trade of these twelve has twelve thousand stations, that is to say, twelve thousand houses for each." Each house contained "at least ten men to exercise those arts, and some fifteen, and some twenty, and thirty, and some forty." Taken together, the men's commercial activities generated a staggering amount of wealth, more than Marco expected any European to credit. "There are so many merchants, and so rich, who do so much, and so great trade, that there is not a man who could say or tell the truth about them that should be believed, they are so extraordinary a thing." Generating unimaginable wealth, these princes of commerce did not work "with their hands," but all lived "as delicately and cleanly as they were kings and barons." And the women of Quinsai were equally refined, "very delicate and angelic things," in Marco's estimation. These ethereal creatures were "very delicately reared," and they dressed "with so many ornaments of silk and of jewels that the value of them could not be estimated." He was awed by the inhabitants' splendid homes, "very well built and richly worked." He breathlessly reports, "They take such great delight in ornaments, paintings, and buildings, that the sums they spend on them are a stupendous thing."

In describing the inhabitants, Marco gropes for superlatives: "The native inhabitants of the city of Quinsai are peaceful people through having been brought up and habituated by their kings, who were of the same nature. They do not handle arms nor keep them at home. Quarrels or any differences are never heard or noticed among them. They do their merchandise and arts with great sincerity and truth. They love one another so that a district may be reckoned as one family on account of the friendliness that exists between the men and the women by reason of the neighborhood. So great is the familiarity that it exists between them without any jealousy or suspicion of their women, for whom they have the greatest respect; and one who should dare to speak improper words to any married woman would be thought a great villain. They are equally friendly with the foreigners who come to them for the sake of trade, and gladly receive them at home, saluting them, and give them every help and advice in the business they do."

NO MATTER HOW festive Quinsai seemed, it was a city under military occupation. The inhabitants, Marco says, "do not like to see soldiers, nor those of the Khan's guards, as it seems to them that by reason of them they have been deprived of their natural kings and lords."

Despite his allegiance to Kublai Khan, Marco came to consider the
Mongol presence in Quinsai a stain upon the fine silken fabric of Chinese society. No less than sixty thousand Mongol guards were billeted
throughout the city, ostensibly to protect its wooden houses from the
ravages of fire; in reality, they formed an army of occupation. "After
the Great Khan took the city," Marco relates, "it was ordered that on
each of the twelve thousand bridges ten men are on guard night and
day, under a covering, that is, five by night and five by day. And these
[men] are to guard the city that none should do evil things, and that
none should dare think of treason, nor make his city rebel against
him."

The khan's zealous sentries "never sleep, but always stay on watch."
Each of their huts contained a "tabernacle with a large basin and a
clock," by which they marked the passing of the hours with military
precision. Some guards patrolled the city streets, not to preserve safety
but to spot minor infractions and make life miserable for those responsible. Should anyone "keep a light lit or fire after the hours allowed,"
he would be severely punished. The guards' presence was sufficiently
intimidating to keep everyone indoors, even when self-preservation
dictated otherwise. Should a fire break out, "no dweller in the city
would have the courage to come out of the house at nighttime nor to
go to the fire, but only those to whom the goods belong go there and
these guards who go to help, and they are never less than one or two
thousand."

Any fire, no matter how insignificant, imperiled everyone in the
city built of wood. "It would run the risk of burning half the city,"
Marco reports. In response, the guards maintained a sophisticated
alarm system. On a nearby hill stood "a timber tower commanding the
whole city," and on that tower was hung "a great wooden board, which
a man holds and strikes with a mallet to signal in case of fire." In practice, the guards on the watchtower sounded the alarm at any hint of
"tumult or uproar" reaching their ears from the city below.

Marco's precise observations about the danger of fire in daily life
find confirmation in records showing that nearly every year brought a
fire emergency. During the thirteenth century, the city suffered especially devastating losses in 1208, 1229, 1237 (thirty thousand homes
burned in this conflagration), and finally 1275, on the eve of the Mongol occupancy. Perhaps the most severe loss occurred on April 15,
1208, when a fire broke out in the district occupied by the govern-

ment. Over the course of the next four days more than 58,000 houses burned across an area of three square miles, causing countless fatalities. In the succeeding months, the government billeted more than five thousand people left homeless in various Buddhist and Taoist monasteries, and even in boats floating on West Lake. No wonder Quinsai took few precautions against invaders from distant lands, such as the Mongols, when fires close to home proved a much deadlier menace.

Merchants stored their wares in fireproof buildings. Owned by wealthy families and the local nobility, the warehouses occupied lots surrounded by sinuous water channels, which protected them from flames and robbers alike. The owners rented them out by the month, charging hefty fees but including a night watchman in the bargain. Despite these precautions, city dwellers lived in constant fear of sudden infernos, and the tiniest show of sparks, a fast-spreading rumor, or a sound, however soft, resembling the alarm on the watchtower could set off a panic. And if a fire did break out, looting posed an additional hazard. When caught, the "fire followers," as the looters were known, faced swift and sure justice under martial law.

In the same spirit of protection and oppression, the Mongol guards detained anyone who ventured abroad late at night. They dispatched the poor and crippled to public shelters and hospitals, but if the object of their scrutiny was healthy, they compelled him "to do some work."

THE MONGOLS insinuated themselves into Quinsai, as they did with other prize cities they had conquered, by replacing Chinese notes with their own paper money. Marco observed Mongol notes being minted. "One takes the innermost bark of the mulberry tree and lays it together and makes of it the same as one does with us, paper of which one makes sheets, as one does our paper," he reports. "The sheets one tears after the shape of a penny on which one prints the stamp and mark of the Great Khan. The money is taken for everything that will buy and sell."

Next, the Mongols constructed their own style of roadway through the heart of the city. "Because the couriers of the Great Khan could not travel quickly with horses over paved streets," Marco explains, "a part of the street at the side is left without pavement for the sake of the couriers." The couriers mingled with the city's ordinary traffic, which consisted of "long carriages covered and furnished with hangings and cushions of silk, in which six people can sit."

Even in occupied Quinsai, life continued as before. Military skills and technology mattered less than commerce, literature, drama, poetry, painting, crafts, or charitable pursuits. Here the Mongols, their lust for conquest for its own sake apparent to all, confronted a superior civilization, and their response was paradoxical yet predictable: they emulated those whom they conquered, hoping to rise to the level of their subjects. The result was the most civilized and elegant of war zones.

MARCO SAMPLED the temptations offered by the numerous "boats and barges" skimming across the surface of West Lake, "for enjoyment and to give one's self pleasure; and in these there can stay ten, fifteen, and twenty, and more persons, because they are fifteen to twenty paces long with broad and flat bottoms, so that they sail without rocking on either side."

The exquisite West Lake vista resulted from centuries of careful maintenance. Nine miles in circumference, and only nine feet deep, the lake served as the focal point for the city, the quintessential Chinese landscape, and the inspiration for countless works of art. It symbolized the soul of China, and was guarded like the national treasure that it was. Military patrols, unmentioned by Marco but noted in other sources, conducted constant surveillance of West Lake to maintain tranquility and hygiene, lest it become fouled with spoiled food and waste. It was strictly forbidden to deposit refuse in the lake, or even to attempt to cultivate common plants such as the lotus or water chestnut. As Marco, or any other pleasure seeker, floated out on the water of West Lake, the crowded city receded, and the surrounding mountains loomed ever larger, while the eye was constantly drawn to the striking pagoda erected on Thunder Point three hundred years before Marco's arrival. This soaring octagonal tower, 1 70 feet high, seemed to connect Heaven and earth.

The idyllic setting served as the perfect backdrop for the women of Quinsai. "Every one who likes to enjoy himself with women or with his companions takes one of the boats," Marco notes. And the boats are "always kept adorned with beautiful seats and tables and with all the other furniture necessary for making a feast." In his description, they resemble the elegant gondolas plying the canals of Venice, only grander, and more luxurious. "Above, they are covered and flat, where men stand with poles that they stick into the ground (for the lake is not more than two paces deep) and guide the barges where they are ordered. The covering on the inside part is painted with different colors and patterns, and likewise all the barge; and there are windows round about that they can open and shut, so that those who stay seated . . . may be able to look this way and that and delight the eyes with the variety and beauty of the places to which they are taken." The result is refined euphoria, "for their mind and care is set on nothing else but bodily pleasure and enjoyment in feasting together."

The concept of recreation for the masses was as new to Marco as it would have been to his readers, and he portrays an entire city in the thrall of pleasure: "Barges like these are found on the lake at all times with people who go for enjoyment; for the inhabitants of this city never think of anything else after they have done their work or business but to spend part of the day with their ladies, or with courtesans."

MARCO HINTS that the women of Quinsai—courtesans and others— were bolder and more sensually aware than their Western counterparts. True enough: by Western standards, Quinsai fostered an outré culture in which sexual behavior often centered on female pleasure. It was believed that whenever a couple had intercourse, the woman should, if possible, experience orgasm; the man, however, was encouraged to reach orgasm only on special occasions, the better to preserve his vital essence—his semen. In addition, male masturbation was strongly censured as a waste of semen, but female masturbation was subtly encouraged. Sex toys designed to aid women in reaching orgasm were common in Quinsai and were widely discussed and written about in popular sex manuals, usually in the form of spurious dialogues involving historical figures.

"The Biography of Emperor Wu of the Han Dynasty" was over a thousand years old by the time of Marco's arrival in Quinsai, but it was still quoted in more recent sex primers. One passage addresses the timeless issue of male potency, and offers a commonsensical solution.

The Yellow Emperor said, "Sometimes it happens that in the exercise of coitus, my Jade Stalk does not want to rise. When that happens, I turn red from the shame of humiliation, and my brow becomes moist with sweat. However, as I burn with blazing desire, I shake my member with my hand, so that it might

rise. Please instruct me as to what to do on such an occasion."
The Plain Girl said: "What Your Majesty inquires about is a
common suffering of all people. This is [because they forget]
that every time a man wishes to copulate, there is a certain order
of things that must be followed. In the first place, the man must
harmonize his mood with that of the woman, and then the Jade
Stalk will rise."

A complementary passage addresses the female orgasm.

The Yellow Emperor said, "How can one know that the woman
is near orgasm?" The Plain Girl said: "Woman has the five signs
and the five desires, and moreover the ten ways of moving her
body during the act. The five signs are as follows: First, she
grows red in the face. Then the man can slowly press near. Second, her nipples become hard, her nose moist. Then the man
may slowly insert his penis. Third, her throat becomes dry, and
she sucks back her saliva. Then the man may begin to thrust
slowly. Fourth, her vagina becomes moist. Then he may sink his
penis deeper. Fifth, her vaginal emissions drop between her buttocks. Then the man may move freely."

The Plain Girl was nothing if not outspoken.

"By the five desires one can judge women's response. First, if her
thoughts desire the union her breathing will become irregular.
Second, if her vagina desires the union her nostrils will distend
and her mouth open. Third, if her vital essence wants to be
stirred she will move her body up and down. Fourth, if she
wants to fulfill her desire, the liquid emitted from her vagina
will soak her clothes. Fifth, if she is about to reach orgasm, she
will stretch her body and close her eyes."

The Plain Girl also suggested provocative positions for sexual intercourse, with names like the Turning Dragon ("the woman is turned
onto her back"), the Tiger's Tread ("the woman leans forward on her
hands and knees with her buttocks raised"), and the Monkey's Attack
("the man raises her legs until her knees touch her breasts and her buttocks and the lower part of her back hang in the air")—this last said to

cure or prevent a hundred ills. And so on through other positions, including Overlapping Fish Scales and the Fluttering Phoenix.

Even in the City of Heaven, sexual expression had its limits. Kissing, considered an intimate part of sexual intercourse, was strictly forbidden in public. Male homosexuality was discouraged, though its female counterpart was tolerated, and even expected. The underpinnings of this seeming inequity had to do with the Chinese concept of yin and yang, female and male essence, and the emphasis on preserving the all-important but limited yang. It was considered necessary for the male to guard against excessive ejaculation, which would deplete his sexual energy. Prolonged arousal was held to be preferable to simple ejaculation. In this scheme of things, male homosexuality was judged a waste of yang, and thus out of harmony with the balance of nature.

As they attempted to exert social control over Quinsai, the Mongols sought to restrain sexual expression among the populace, especially women. T'ao Tsung-i, a Yüan dynasty chronicler, sternly cautioned against relying on the questionable advice contained in "Art of the Bedchamber," an ancient but still-popular anthology of Chinese sexual practices and philosophy. He identified no fewer than nine types of professional women who wreaked havoc on a household: the Buddhist nun, the Taoist nun, the female astrologer, the female go-between, the sorceress, the female thief, the female quack, and lastly the midwife. "Few are the households that, having admitted one of them, will not be ravaged by fornication and robbery," he warned. "The men who can guard against those, keeping them away as if they were snakes and scorpions, those men shall come near the method for keeping their household clean."

Pamphlets specifying various types of scandalous behavior that corrupted a family's moral standing circulated among households. The guides warned against the hazards of "violent debauch," or rape; "crazed debauch"; "predestined debauch," or romantic love; "proclaiming debauch," or boasting; and "idle debauch." Even the production of erotica, a staple of Chinese intimate life, earned censure. Only prostitutes escaped the new wave of censorship invading the city; their trade, if anything, flourished in the face of it.

If Marco was aware of these sexual politics, he did not refer to them in his account. Nor did he mention that other prominent feature of Chinese domestic life, foot binding. Skeptics have cited its omission as evidence that he did not visit China, or at least Quinsai. There are reasonable explanations for the lapse. Women with bound feet remained sequestered indoors, and Marco may not have been aware of them, or of the custom. Furthermore, the practice may have fallen out of favor during his time in Quinsai. The women he did observe carefully—courtesans at the public baths and on West Lake—had to be ambulatory to perform their tasks. The Venetian did take note of Quinsai's many eunuchs—who occupied prominent places in the government bureaucracy—but only in passing.

MARCO PREFERRED to focus on public affairs, especially Kublai Khan's systematic approach to the occupancy of Quinsai, and the harvesting of its wealth. "After he had reduced to his obedience all the province of Mangi [Quinsai], the Great Khan has divided it into nine parts," Marco observes, "so that each is a great kingdom. But . . . all these kings are there for the Great Khan and in this way, that they make each year the report of each kingdom separately to the factors of the great lord, of the revenue, and of all things. In this city of Quinsai dwells one of these nine kings, and is lord of more than a hundred and forty cities, all very great and rich." Yet the king coexisted with the occupying Mongol forces, which seemed to Marco a model of restraint. He points out they "are from Cathay, good men at arms, for the Tartars are horsemen and do not stay except near the cities that are not in marshy places, but in those situated in firm and dry places where they can take exercise on horseback."

Along with them, Marco was a highly appreciative, sophisticated, and well-intentioned intruder, but an intruder nonetheless; yet he expressed no remorse about helping himself to the Mongol spoils of conquest, only wide-eyed appreciation of Chinese culture. He became yet another invader conquered by his more sophisticated and civilized subjects.

DAILY LIFE IN QUINSAI, although punctuated by pleasure, left little time for rest. The giant city began stirring well before dawn. "About four or five in the morning," an observer noted, when bells of the Buddhist and Taoist monasteries have rung, hermit-monks come down from the hills surrounding the town and go about the streets of Quinsai beating their strips of iron or their wooden resonators in the form of a fish, announcing everywhere the dawn. They call out what the weather is like: "It is cloudy," "It is raining," "The sky is clear." In wind, in rain, in snow, or in freezing cold, they go out just the same. They also announce any court reception to be held that day, whether a grand or a little or an ordinary audience. In this way, the officials in the various government departments, the officers of the watch, and the soldiers whose names are on the list for the watch-towers, are all kept informed and hurry off to their offices or their posts. As for the monk announcers, they go round the town collecting alms on the first and fifteenth of each month as well as on feast days.

To a Venetian, the scene was familiar, though reenacted on a grand scale.

Audiences with King Facfur, in the days before the Mongols sent him into exile, took place at six in the morning, or even earlier. By seven, the day was considered well advanced, and the sound of drums reverberated throughout the city, announcing the time. Noise was constant; bureaucrats' offices came to life with the harsh ringing of a gong or the startling ping of wooden clappers. Any government employee who was tardy or absent would be beaten.

Although Marco refers to the phenomenon only in passing, printed books and other written materials abounded in Quinsai, almost two hundred years before the invention of movable type in Europe. Movable type existed in and around Quinsai in many forms, including clay, wood, and tin. Wood-block printing, already in use for more than three hundred years in China, was widely dispersed; it was employed especially for Buddhist sutras and other sacred texts. Because calligraphy is an integral part of Chinese arts and letters, and the Chinese written language at the time contained about seven thousand characters, handwritten manuscripts flourished side by side with books and pamphlets.

Drama thrived, as did poetry, which appeared in public places as if composed by the hand of nature. One popular stanza, credited to Tai Fu-ku, reflected mournfully on the Mongol occupation of this splendid city:

> *Athwart this ridge where down below the rolling river runs,*
> *My house in the clouds looks out over mile after mile of*
> *   brooding sadness.*
> *How bitterly I wish that mountains blocked my wandering gaze.*
> *For northwards, far as the eye can reach, our conquered land*
> *   seems endless.*

Another poet, Hsieh Ao, brooded on the sight of his beloved city occupied by alien invaders in his poem "On Visiting the Former Imperial Palace at Quinsai (After the Mongol Conquest)":

> *Like an ancient ruin, the grass grows high: gone are the guards*
> *   and the gatekeepers.*
> *Fallen towers and crumbling palaces desolate my soul.*
> *Under the eaves of the long-ago hall fly in and out the swallows*
> *But within: Silence. The chatter of cock and hen and parrots*
> *   is heard no more.*

The abundance of printed material—of poetry and sacred texts and almanacs and guides to sexual fulfillment, of Confucian philosophy, of ghost tales and legal codes—eluded Marco's usually observant eye. He offered some cursory observations concerning Chinese dialects, drawing analogies to European tongues, but, at the same time, he felt that Chinese was alien to him, despite his important official position in Quinsai. "I tell you that those of this city have a language for themselves," he says. "Through the whole province of Mangi [Quinsai], one speech is preserved and one manner of letters; yet in tongue there is difference by districts, as if, among laymen, between Lombards, Provençals, Frenchmen, . . . so that in the province of Mangi the people of any district can understand the idiom of the people of the next."

In market squares, shopkeepers opened for the day's business, setting out their goods to lure buyers; bazaars came to life as merchants hawked their wares, or stood by as silent sentries of commerce. And on the main thoroughfare known as the Imperial Way, tiny cafés served pungent concoctions such as deep-fried tripe, aromatic chunks of duck and goose, and freshly steamed pancakes prepared in dark, makeshift kitchens. The slaughterhouses providing them with meat had been busy since three o'clock in the morning. Crowds jammed the squares to sample the wares of street peddlers, who offered hot towels for the face and rejuvenating pills for the circulation.

By late afternoon, the pace of work in Quinsai slowed and the day drew to a close. Officials quietly streamed to their homes. The late afternoon and early evening were given over to reading, to composing literary works (something of an obsession in this hyper-refined city), playing chess, boating on West Lake, and sampling the delights of the courtesans and singing girls. These houses of pleasure stayed open until the fourth drumbeat reverberated through the dim streets: two o'clock in the morning. A few smaller markets and noodle shops did business long into the night, as Quinsai slowed but never slept. Night watchmen, ever vigilant against the twin evils of thieves and fire, patrolled the streets, but excuses from this duty were so common that the roster of absentees was called simply "the list of stomach pains."

Unnoticed by Marco, but crucial for understanding the tempo of city life, is the fact that Quinsai's work "week" lasted ten days, followed by a single day of rest. A city official had the right to observe but one vacation with his family every three years; it varied in length from a fortnight to a lunar month.

The only real respite in this arduous schedule occurred when an official's mother or father died. According to Confucian custom, the bereaved family member took a mandatory sabbatical of three years' duration, devoted solely to personal pursuits such as calligraphy, painting, and literature, all intended to stimulate reflection on the profound changes taking place in his life and to prepare him to take his place in nature's inflexible order.

Ordinary workers did not have the benefit of even these vacations; they toiled constantly throughout their lives.

FESTIVALS afforded relief from the press of work and the obligations of family, and the greatest of all was the Chinese New Year. Within the lunar calendar, the date ranges from January 15 to February 15, and the celebration lasts the better part of a month. A snowfall during preparations for the New Year was taken by all as a good omen; the leisured few fashioned snow lions for all to admire and rode on horseback around West Lake to admire the spectral scenes of snow and ice. In kitchens throughout the city, special rice dishes were prepared to propitiate domestic deities; the feasting ended with a concoction of red beans, which was shared even with pet dogs and cats.

In the commercial environment of Quinsai, shopkeepers, especially pharmacists, tried to benefit from the holiday. They decorated their stores with colorful streamers, painted images of heroic figures from Chinese folklore and history, and paper horses. To attract customers to their establishments, they distributed little packages of good-luck charms, while in the chilly streets, the ubiquitous peddlers worked the crowds, pushing a popular decorative thistle and firecrackers made of small shafts of bamboo filled with gunpowder (yet another technology unknown in the West). Even the beggars put on a show, impersonating popular deities and beating gongs.

The celebrations began to build to a climax on New Year's Eve, when housekeepers swept and washed their doorsteps, took down last year's images of deities, and affixed new wooden amulets to the doors and red streamers above the lintel. At night, the occupants withdrew to their quarters to offer flowers, incense, and food to the gods in hopes of having a good year. These domestic customs may have been shrouded from Marco's view, but everyone in Quinsai was aware of the huge New Year procession, which started at the Imperial Palace, with masked soldiers carrying wooden swords, as well as flags of yellow, red, black, white, and green, all of them fluttering in the damp winter air. The procession wound its way through the broader streets of the city, seeking to replace the evil influences of the outgoing year with the virtues and hopes of the incoming one.

On New Year's Day, King Facfur burned incense and prayed fervently for a good harvest, peace, and prosperity; delegates from every corner of his realm came to pay their respects and offer tributes.

Still more days of observance followed, enough to occupy two full weeks, until the Festival of Lanterns began, signaling the real commencement of the New Year. For three glorious days and nights, gluttony and drunkenness ruled, while those citizens who were able to do so competed to acquire or make spectacular lanterns. The most highly prized came from Suchow; they were multicolored, round, and decorated with illustrations of animals, flowers, people, and landscapes, and were more than four feet in diameter. Other types of lanterns were fashioned from beads and feathers, gold and silver, even pearls and jade. Some, operated by a small stream of water, slowly turned; others resembled the boats gliding across West Lake.

As the festivities dragged on, drinking increased, and the revelers ended by donning white garments for nocturnal strolls in honor of the New Moon. By dawn, the public clamor had died away and the streets were empty. In the wake of the celebration, a few scavengers armed with modest lanterns combed the squares and avenues in search of lost hairpins, jewelry, and other valuable items.

The New Year celebrations lasted even longer in the Imperial Palace. Workmen erected a brilliantly decorated scaffolding 150 feet high to hold musicians on one level, and athletes and gymnasts on another, just below. The women of the palace danced with young eunuchs wearing turbans. After the show, the palace women—that is, courtesans and serving women—made a mad dash for the peddlers, who were delighted to sell their goods at a large premium.

IN THE CITY OF HEAVEN, astrology ruled, and the rigorous Chinese bureaucracy applied it ruthlessly and systematically. "As soon as the infant is born in this province, the father or the mother has the day and the minute and the hour that he was born written, and in what sign and in what planet, so that each knows his nativity," Marco relates. With these files on record, any inhabitant of the city consulted an astrologer before setting off on a long journey or undertaking a betrothal. For once, the skeptical Marco seems impressed with the expertise of the astrologers, acknowledging them as "wise in their art and diabolical enchantment, so that they really tell the men many things to which they give much faith."

For Marco, the prevalence of astrologers in Quinsai offered a rare glimpse into the inner lives of the city's inhabitants. He concludes that "the men of the province of Mangi are more passionate than other people, and for anger and grief some very often kill themselves. For it shall happen that some one of these shall give a blow to some other or pull out his hair or inflict some injury or harm upon him, and the offender may be so powerful and great that he is powerless to take vengeance; the sufferer of the injury will hang himself from excess of grief at the door of the offender by night and die, doing this to him for the greater blame and contempt. . . . And this will be the greater reason why he hung himself, namely that this rich and powerful man should honor him at death in order that he may be likewise honored in the other world."

MORE THAN ANY other feature of the City of Heaven, King Facfur's castle epitomized Quinsai's outsized scale and sophistication, but the landmark had lately fallen into decline, as Marco learned when he made the acquaintance of a "very rich merchant of Quinsai, . . . who was very old and had been an intimate friend of King Facfur and knew him all his life, and had seen the palace." The merchant inspired Marco's imagination with tales of the luxury palace. But having visited it, Marco relates that "the fine pavilions are still as they used to be, but the rooms of the girls are all gone to ruin and nothing else is seen but in traces. In the same way, the wall that encircled the woods and gardens is fallen to the ground and there are no longer either animals or trees."

With the old merchant's help, Marco resurrects for his readers "the most beautiful palace where King Facfur lived, whose predecessors had a space of country enclosed that was surrounded for ten miles with very high walls and divided into three parts." Within the castle, guarded from the eyes of the world, were the king's personal harem— "a thousand girls whom the king kept for his service"—who coexisted peacefully with the queen of the realm.

The girls of the harem, Marco says, entertained both king and queen with elaborate erotic games involving the animals and lake within the walls of the enclosure: "Sometimes he [the king] went with the queen and some of the girls for recreation about the lake on barges all covered with silk, and also to visit the temples of the idols."

Later, the frolicking commenced: "The other two parts of the enclosure were laid out with woods, lakes, and most beautiful gardens planted with fruit trees, where were enclosed all sorts of animals, that is, roe-deer, fallow-deer, red-deer, hares, rabbits; and there the king went to enjoy himself with his damsels, some in carriages and some on horseback, and no man went in there. And he made the damsels run with dogs and give chase to these kinds of animals; and after they were tired, they went into the woods that faced one another above the lakes, and leaving the clothes there they came out of them naked and entered the water and set themselves to swim some on one side and some on the other, and the king stayed to watch them with the greatest delight."

Amid his tale of sensual abandon, Marco conveys a strict warning: "Sometimes he [the king] had food carried into those woods that were thick and dense with very lofty trees, waited on by the damsels. And with this continual dalliance with women he grew up without knowing what arms might be—which in the end brought it about that through his cowardice and incompetence the Great Khan took all the state from him with the greatest shame and disgrace."

The powerful moral was not lost on Marco, who took it as a cautionary tale for the people of Quinsai, whom he perceived as dangerously prone to self-indulgence. One day, he relates, "a fish was found lying on the dry land across the bed of the river that was something wonderful to see, for it was a hundred paces long, but the bulk by no means corresponded to its length. It was indeed all hairy, and many ate of it, and many of them died." Marco claims to have seen the head of this giant, poisonous fish on display in a "certain temple of idols"— that is, a Buddhist temple. And the annals confirm the event, recording that a hundred-foot-long whale was indeed stranded in shallows of the Fu-ch'un River near Quinsai in 1282, followed soon after by another cetacean. The annals also show that foragers placed ladders against one of the stranded creatures, climbed onto its back, and butchered it for food—a daring act that, as Marco tells his listeners, turned out to be a lethal mistake, for they all died from eating the flesh.

FINALLY, Marco gets down to business: the city's lucrative salt monopoly. He calculates the revenue of "the salt of this town" and moves on to sugar, claiming that the value of the province's sugar was "more than double that which is made in all the rest of the world." That was not all: the "spicery . . . is without measure." And they all contributed to the khan. "All the spiceries pay three and a third percent; and of all goods they pay also three and a third percent. And from the wine that they make of rice and of spices they have a very great revenue also, and from charcoal. And from all the twelve crafts . . . they have, each craft, twelve thousand stations; from these crafts they have very great revenues, for they pay duty on everything."

He reveals how trade worked in Quinsai: "All the merchants who carry goods to this city by land and carry them away from it to other parts, and those also who carry them away to sea, pay in the same way—a thirtieth of the goods . . . , which takes three and a third percent; but those who carry merchandise to it by sea and from far countries and regions, as far as from the Indies, give ten percent. Moreover, of all the things that grow in the country, produce coming both from animals and from the land, and silk, a tenth part is applied to the lord's government." Not surprisingly, this revenue "amounts to untold money."

Marco assures his readers that the khan had one object when he collected these tremendous revenues, the well-being and safety of the people of his empire: "For the great profit that the great lord has from this country he loves it much and does much to guard it carefully and to keep those who dwell there in great peace." In practice, that meant he used the revenues to pay for the mercenaries to occupy the cities and towns of the province, especially Quinsai. Marco puts this exploitation in the most favorable light: "The Great Khan has all those revenues spent on arms that guard the cities and countries, and to alleviate the poverty of the cities."

MARCO'S SOJOURN in the City of Heaven ended abruptly, inexplicably. He gives no reason for his departure, not even a date for this watershed event. Perhaps his tenure as an official of the Mongol government terminated with an embarrassment, a charge of corruption, or a jealous rival getting the better of him. In any event, he found himself expelled from Quinsai and its myriad pleasures, no longer a tax assessor, and once more a wayfarer.

He took comfort in reuniting with his father and uncle, and in resuming his former identity as a private merchant. Trekking with them through "mountains and valleys," he arrived in South China, where the people, although idolaters—that is, Buddhists—were "subject to the rule of the Great Khan" and so posed no obvious threat to the traveler in their midst. But to his disgust, Marco realized that "they eat all coarse things and they also eat human flesh very willingly, provided that he [the deceased] did not die a natural death." Their preferred meat came from those who died by the sword, rather than from disease, and, Marco says, they considered this "very good and savory flesh."

The warriors' battle costumes were as fearsome as their eating habits: "They have their hair cut off as far as the ears, and in the middle of the face they have themselves painted with azure like the blade of a sword." In keeping with their wrathful visage, they were "the most cruel men in the world," for, Marco notes, "I tell you they go all day killing men and drink the blood, and then they all eat them." Worse, "they are always eager about this." Their presence was sufficient to distract Marco from the lions roaming the mountain escarpments. From time to time the animals leapt upon wayfarers like Marco and made a meal of them. He found a semblance of safety from these dangers by joining a caravan of merchants, predominantly Buddhists and silk traders. No matter what their religion, they guided Marco through the region unharmed, if not untroubled.

LION TRAPPING was common in the area, and Marco set about learning the technique as a matter of survival. The requirements were simple enough: parallel trenches and, as bait, an unlucky dog. When deployed correctly, they produced dramatic results.

"Two very deep pits are made one beside the other," he writes. "It is true that between some ground is left perhaps for the width of one ell; and on the other side of the pits a high hedge is made, but nothing at the ends. At night, the owner of the pits will tie a little dog on the ground in the middle, and leaving him there will go away. Then the dog tied like this, when left by the master, will not cease to bark; and the dog shall be white. The lion, hearing from whatever distance thence the voice of the dog, will run to him with much fury, and when he shall see him gleaming white, wishing to leap hastily to catch him, will fall into the pit. In the morning, the master of the pits will come and will kill the lion in the pit. Then the flesh will be eaten up because it is good, and the skin will be sold, for they are very dear."

Marco also recorded a way to capture a type of fox that he called a *papione*, which gnawed on sugarcane, damaging that valuable crop. Here is his recommended method for catching these four-legged pilferers: "They have great gourds that they cut in the knob at the top, making a mouth for the entry of a width calculated so that one of the *papiones* may put his head in with force." To make certain that the *papione* would not damage the neck, the hunters drilled holes around it and threaded twine through the openings to strengthen it. To entice *papiones* to the gourd, the hunters placed a wad of tempting fat at the bottom, and distributed the traps around the perimeter of the caravan. "When the *papiones* come to the caravan to take something away, they perceive the smell of the fat in the gourds and go up to them, and, wishing to put their heads in, cannot. But pressing violently from greed for the food inside they force the head to enter. Then, being unable to draw it out, they lift and carry with them the gourds because they are light; and then they do not know where to go."

The poor creatures wandered blindly until the merchants caught them.

. . .

IN THE CITY that Marco called Fugiu, his uncle Maffeo struck up a friendship with a "certain wise Saracen"—that is, a Muslim—and remarked to him about a "certain manner of people whose religion no one understands." These were not Buddhists, from the looks of things, because there were no Buddhas, or idols, in evidence. Nor did they appear to be Muslims. Neither were they Zoroastrians, for they did not worship fire. One can see Maffeo suggesting to the wise Saracen, "May it please you that we go to them and speak with them; perhaps we will learn something about their life." So they went, solely from curiosity, but their questions unsettled the objects of their inquiry, who feared that the three curious merchants were plotting to "take away their religion from them."

"Do not be afraid," Maffeo and Marco urged, "for we did not come here for your harm at all but only for good and the improvement of your condition."

They returned the next day, slowly ingratiating themselves with the locals, "asking them about their business," until they came upon the answer to the riddle. These secretive and suspicious people were, after all, Christians, "for they had books, and these Masters Maffeo and Marco reading in them began to interpret the writing and to translate from word to word and from tongue to tongue, so that they found it to be the words of the Psalter"—the Book of Psalms.

Astonished by this discovery of lost Christians in China, they asked how they came by their faith. "From our ancestors," the locals replied.

Inspecting one of their temples, the merchants saw "three painted figures, who had been three apostles of the seventy who had gone preaching through the world; and they said that they were those who had taught their ancestors in that religion long ago, and that that faith had already been preserved among them for seven hundred years"— that is, since the sixth century—"but for a long time they had been without preaching and so were ignorant of the chief things." Their curious allusion to three apostles refers, perhaps, to Peter, James, and John, who accompanied Jesus on particularly exalted and disturbing occasions, such as the Agony in the Garden of Gethsemane. The origins of this isolated sect's faith were lost in time, yet Marco acknowledged their connection.

"You are Christians and we are likewise Christians," Maffeo and

Marco declared. "We advise you to send to the Great Khan and explain to him your state, that he may come to know you and you may be able freely to keep your religion and rule." The mysterious Christians, although accustomed to living among hostile "idolaters," followed this bold suggestion and dispatched a delegation of two men to Kublai Khan.

Marco and Maffeo told the men to present themselves to a "certain man who was head of the Christians at the court of the Great Khan." But the request, rather than smoothing the petitioners' way to recognition as Christians, inspired masses of Buddhists to claim them as their own. There followed a "great argument in the presence of the lord. Finally, the lord being angry, making all go away, ordered the messengers to come to him, asking them whether they wished to be Christians or idolaters." The petitioners timidly replied that if the Great Khan would not take offense, they wished to be considered Christians, like their ancestors. Kublai Khan approved, insisting that they all "must be addressed as Christians."

With that assurance, they made their full strength known. The sect, far from being a small band of spiritual nonconformists, included "more than seven hundred thousand families," says Marco, all of them now safely assigned to the Christian camp, their identity officially confirmed, and their right to worship guaranteed by Kublai Khan and the might of the Mongol Empire.

Having helped to usher these lost Christians into the Mongol fold, Marco was again left to his own devices, doomed to wander the Silk Road to the end of his days in the service of Kublai Khan—or so it seemed. He could not have imagined what lay in store for him, as events occurring thousands of miles away began to shape his destiny.

CHAPTER TWELVE

The Divine Wind

And 'mid this tumult Kubla heard from far
Ancestral voices prophesying war!

O F ALL THE descriptions of places Marco Polo included in his *Travels*, none prompted more disbelief among Europeans than his fantastic account of "an island that is called Çipingu."

Reverberating with improbable battles, storms, and sudden reversals of fortune, his portrayal of this remote kingdom appeared to be an elaborate flight of fancy. For all his far-fetched tales about China, the place at least existed in the European consciousness, even if it was largely a blank. But Çipingu, surely, was wholly fictitious; it did not even appear on Western maps. Biblical lands such as Gog and Magog had more credibility in Europe than the strange islands that made up Çipingu—later known as Japan.

The skeptics were not entirely to blame. Although Marco's words provided his incredulous readers with their first account of the island nation, his rendering was beset by imprecision, for he never visited it. He wrote about the world of the Japanese with such vigor and confidence that it seemed as if he were recounting his firsthand impressions, yet nowhere in his account of Japan did he claim, "I, Marco, saw these things," as was his custom with China and the Mongols. Instead, he offered intelligence and hearsay of a high order, the authorized Mongol view of its enigmatic, tantalizing, and intimidating rival to the east.

JAPAN SEIZED Marco's imagination because Kublai Khan, always keen for fresh territories to bring into his realm, proposed to conquer the island nation across the sea. It seemed the unlikeliest of goals. The Mongols, for all their ferocity, were not sailors; they were warriors on horseback, and overextended warriors at that, barely able to manage their land-based empire. Not even Kublai Khan could rule the entire world, yet his goal was to do exactly that, to become the "universal emperor" mediating between Heaven and all the peoples below. During Marco's years in Quinsai, Kublai Khan became consumed with the idea of conquering Japan. But that grand ambition proved to be the Mongol leader's undoing.

The fall came about quickly. In 1279, when Marco was still in Quinsai, Kublai Khan was at the zenith of his power, his career capped by his conquest of the realm of the Song dynasty, China's former stronghold. Only two years later, the arc of his reign suddenly altered. His wife Chabi died. Along with Kublai's mother, Chabi had served as an architect of his career, especially in the early years when he struggled for power. Now that she was gone, Kublai was no longer restrained by her shrewd judgment, and he embarked on one destructive action after another, as if determined to tear his empire apart.

In his grief, Kublai Khan became an alcoholic (not an uncommon affliction among the Mongols), gained an unhealthy amount of weight, and suffered from gout and other, less specific ailments. Entering his dotage, he slowly lost his grip over the empire. In attempting to demonstrate that he remained the Great Khan, he decided to pursue his most reckless scheme, the conquest of Japan. He had become so addicted to empire building that he believed that if the Mongol Empire could not grow, it would die. Marco was the witness and, for centuries, the sole Western source of information about this mysterious conflict with an obscure but mighty island nation.

Kublai failed to consider the immense difficulties posed by attempting to conquer this distant country, so different from the peaceful and often disorganized tribes the Mongols had terrorized and subdued. The Japanese, Marco recognized, were as fierce and as cruel as the Mongols, yet they were a more sophisticated society. Most important of all, they were protected by the sea, with which the Mongols had little expertise, luck, or confidence. Kublai Khan would slowly and painfully learn that the Mongols might be masters of the Steppe, but on the water, they were as vulnerable as their feeblest prey.

. . .

"ÇIPINGU is an island to the sunrising that is on the high seas," Marco begins. "It is an exceedingly great island. The people of it are white, fair-fashioned, and beautiful, and of good manners. They are idol-aters"—that is, Buddhists. "They are ruled by their own king and pay tribute to no other, and they have no lordship of any other men but themselves. Moreover, I tell you that they have gold in very great abundance, because gold is found there beyond measure"—so much gold, according to Marco, that "they do not know what to do with it." Furthermore, "ships are rarely brought there from other regions, for it abounds in all things."

Marco discusses Japan, the island nation he had never visited, in respectful tones. "According to what the men who know the country say," he explains, the island's ruler "has a very great palace that is all covered with sheets of fine gold. Just as we cover houses and churches with lead, so this palace is covered with fine gold," worth so much that "no one in the world . . . could redeem it." He reports that its many rooms are covered with tiles, all of them "two fingers" thick, and made from pure gold. "Large white pearls" reportedly could be found in abundance in Çipingu, and even red ones that had great value and beauty. And they were ubiquitous; it was said that "the mouth of every-one who is buried" contained a large shimmering pearl. No wonder Marco found it difficult to convince listeners that he was reporting the truth.

He was not far off. Japan *was* immensely wealthy, with abundant pearls and silver (but not gold). If not literally true, Marco's conviction that Japan possessed more gold than any other place in the world can be understood as an allegory of the island's cultural, intellectual, and spiritual wealth—the riches of a highly developed civilization. In dis-tant Çipingu, Marco implied, even the heavens obeyed the emperor's will.

Coveting Çipingu's treasure, Kublai Khan "wished to have it taken and subjected to his rule," no matter how difficult that would be to accomplish. At first he tested the resolve of the Japanese by dispatch-ing emissaries to the shogun regent, Hojo Tokimune, to demand that the Japanese pay taxes to the distant, unseen Kublai Khan. Not sur-prisingly, the incredulous Japanese court spurned them. Redoubling his efforts, Kublai Khan launched an invasion—in 1274, but the sea posed hazards for which the Mongols were not equipped. The fleet made landfall on Kyushu Island; the warriors disembarked and set about destroying villages and a holy shrine. After the Mongol forces returned to their ships, a devastating storm assaulted the fleet, claiming thirteen thousand lives.

Kublai Khan responded to the loss by stubbornly sending another delegation, demanding peaceful surrender. This time, the Japanese executed the entire delegation. Expecting the worst, they then dispatched an army of samurai to Kyushu. The samurai spent five years building a stone wall to repel the next Mongol invasion, should it ever come.

DESPITE ALL THE SETBACKS, Kublai remained determined to conquer Çipingu. In keeping with his practice of sharing authority with various ethnic groups in his empire, he relied on three military leaders, one Mongol, Hsin-tu; one Chinese, Fan Wen-hu; and one Korean, Hong Tagu, the commander in chief. He committed 100,000 warriors representing a coalition of Mongol, Chinese, and Korean forces, as well as paper money and armor. He amplified these resources with still more arms and with ships in such quantities that his demands drew complaints from suppliers, who strained to fill his orders for weaponry.

The triumvirate of leaders adopted a sophisticated strategy for the assault, relying on two separate forces, which would eventually merge into one army of conquest. At the same time, the Chinese became preoccupied with premonitions that the heavens opposed the expedition. Omens proliferated; there were reports of a sea serpent, and of seawater reeking of sulphur. Amid the insecurity, the commanders disagreed with one another, and the Chinese fleet failed to appear as scheduled. Unwilling to wait any longer, the Mongol invasion force began its attack on June 10, 1281.

TWO WEEKS LATER, the fleet approached Kyushu and made landfall close to the wall built by the Japanese to repel invaders. The Chinese arrived late, planning to join forces with the Mongols and Koreans. During the ensuing weeks, the Japanese confidently fought the invaders to a standstill. The wall frustrated the Mongol armies, as intended, and Japanese troops killed as many members of the disorganized invading force as they could before retreating to safety. The Mongol and Chinese military leaders became embroiled in distracting disputes; by some accounts, the Chinese, who had little sympathy for the Mongol invasion of Japan, failed to muster a properly warlike attitude.

All of these events were known to Marco, at least in their rough outlines, and he narrates them molto agitato.

Kublai Khan dispatched "two of his most famous barons with a very great number of ships and men on horses and on foot" on a naval expedition that quickly came to grief, as Marco explains. The barons sailed from Hangzhou, and after "many days" at sea, their fleet reached the island nation. Disembarking, the barons and their men explored the plain stretching before them, and then ravaged defenseless hamlets in the name of Kublai Khan. "They took many men in a castle that they took by storm on that island, and because they [the Japanese forces] had not been willing to give themselves up, the two barons commanded that they all be killed and that the heads of all should be cut off . . . except those of eight men . . . who, being in the hands of the Tartars and being struck with many blows of the sword, there was no way that they could kill them."

The Mongols paused in amazement at their captives' defiant behavior. Only on very close examination did the sword-wielding Mongols learn of the protective mechanism that enabled the Japanese to cling to life despite repeated blows of the blade to the neck and extremities. "This happened by virtue of precious stones that they had. For, this being a marvel to all the Tartar host, those eight were stripped naked and searched and they had each of them a stone sewn into his right arm, between the flesh and skin, so that it was not seen outside. And this stone was so charmed and of such virtue that as long as one might have it, he could not die by iron." Once the barons discovered the impediment, they immediately executed the soldiers by other means: "They have them clubbed with thick wooden clubs, and they died immediately. When they were dead, they have those stones taken from the arms of each, as I have told you, and hold them very dear." The practice of inserting subcutaneous stones or even precious metals such as gold to afford protection in battle, while new to the Mongol barons, was actually widespread in Asia.

The swift Mongol victory proved deceptive. Despite their august reputations, Kublai Khan's barons fell victim to petty disputes and jealousy, "and the one did nothing for the other."

After two months of conflict, the invasion, which Kublai Khan had once expected to unfold with the efficiency for which the Mongols were famed, had reached a standstill.

IN MID-AUGUST, nature intervened in a manner that the Japanese would come to regard as predestined. As the bickering continued among the Mongol leaders, a typhoon was building. Marco observes that such storms could do "great harm to that island." For once, he is far from exaggerating: the storm altered the course of Asian history. The Japanese called it *kamikaze,* "Divine Wind."

A typhoon, or tropical cyclone, is a violent, low-pressure storm occurring in late summer and early fall in the western reaches of the Pacific. For the storm to develop, the topmost layer of water must exceed 80 degrees Fahrenheit. At that temperature, seawater evaporates, only to be absorbed by the atmosphere. As the warm, moist air rises in a giant column, the air pressure beneath it falls. Air moves from high-pressure regions to low-pressure regions, creating downward gusts of wind—the genesis of a storm.

Storms vary around the globe. In the Northern Hemisphere, Earth's rotation causes wind to swirl counterclockwise. In the Southern Hemisphere, winds move clockwise. The influence of Earth as it rotates on wind flow is known as the Coriolis effect, and that is what made all the difference to Kublai Khan's proud fleet. The intensity of the Coriolis effect grows steadily greater the farther from the equator the storm-to-be happens to be located. To produce even a modest hurricane or cyclone, a low-pressure area must be more than 5 degrees of latitude north or south of the equator. For this reason, cyclones rarely form closer to the equator.

A cyclone in formation can be fragile as well as powerful. Wind shear—a difference in speed and in direction between the winds circulating at the upper and lower elevations—can make it or break it. Winds of just one speed enable the warm inner core of the nascent storm to stay intact, but wind shear can topple the storm or blow its top in one direction and its bottom in another. However, if conditions are just right, the cyclone takes on a churning life of its own. In the seas surrounding Japan, conditions frequently are right to breed such tempests; in fact, the typhoon is the most common natural disaster to afflict Japan.

. . .

THIS MID-AUGUST typhoon arrived nearly unheralded. At first, observant mariners in Kublai Khan's fleet may have noticed a distinctive swell, about three feet high, on the ocean's surface, coming along frequently, every ten seconds or so. A day later, the swells were a menacing six feet high, and they were traveling rapidly across the surface of the water. But there was still no storm in sight; the skies remained clear, the wind calm. Only the swells, relentlessly increasing in size and in speed, foretold disaster.

Another day passed, and the swells reached nine feet in height.

Three days after the telltale swells began to appear on the ocean's surface, the first obvious signs of an approaching storm could be seen. As the swells increased in size and velocity, cirrus clouds gradually filled the sky. The wind, thus far calm and unremarkable, picked up slightly. An experienced sailor would have known that a typhoon was approaching and taken evasive measures, but the Mongols had no plan for responding to the warning signs, if they even noticed them. Within hours, the wind was driving the swells at an even greater rate, and the sky had darkened perceptibly. Whitecaps proliferated, as did streaks of foam on the water's churning surface. The wind was now thirty or forty knots strong; merely standing in the open was difficult. The clouds sank lower and darkened as the wind surpassed sixty knots, sending branches and loose objects flying and signaling the arrival of a full-blown typhoon. Every wave that crashed into the shore carried unusual force and destroyed all barriers to its progress. Low-lying land began to flood. Despite the dire conditions, the storm had yet to reach the peak of its violence.

Nearly four days after the first swells appeared, the wind speed approached a hundred miles an hour—more than eighty knots—and relentless rain formed stinging horizontal needles. Surging seas submerged high-tide marks on land. Not a soul could stand outdoors unassisted. Wind uprooted trees and bushes and hurled them through the air. At sea, the wind sliced off the tops of waves, and a white spray covered the water's boiling surface. As the eye of the storm approached, the horizontal sheets of rain became even heavier. Flooding increased, and the wind exceeded ninety knots. Along the shore, fifteen-foot-high waves crashed against the rocks. When the eye arrived, the winds slackened, at first imperceptibly, later markedly. The sky brightened, and it seemed that the storm, impossibly strong only minutes before, had played itself out. The air turned warm and humid, and unnaturally calm. The sun was visible, and glistening white clouds formed a circular wall around the storm's eye: a sinister impersonation of tranquility. And then, ever so slightly, the wind picked up, and walls of clouds swept into view, heralding the return of the storm, as awful as before.

Those caught in the storm barely noticed when it began a slow retreat. A half day after the eye passed overhead, the wind, still over sixty knots, slowly abated, and the ocean, once ready to overflow the land entirely, returned to its customary levels.

A full day after the eye had passed, the clouds began to break up, and the high waters, retreating from land, exposed the damage they had wrought. Small whitecaps and massive waves still dappled the water's surface as the sea began to give up its dead. Within hours, the cirrus clouds dissipated, the sky cleared for real, and the sun shone with unaccustomed brilliance. But the air remained unsettled, imbued with pungent brine, the stink of rotting vegetation torn from the sea floor, and bloated floating carcasses.

The typhoon cycle had ended, while somewhere in the western Pacific, new typhoons were breeding.

THE WINDS BLEW so long and hard, says Marco, that "a great part of those of the army of the Great Khan could not bear it." The Mongols soon decided to flee the typhoon for their lives. "If they did not leave," Marco explains, "all their ships would be broken up." They quickly gave up any idea of conquest, even of hamlets. "Then they all went into their ships and left the island and put out to sea so that not one of their men remained on land."

Four miles off Çipingu, "the force of the wind began to increase, and the multitude of the ships was so great that a large quantity of them was broken up with one another; but the ships that were not crushed by others but were scattered about the sea escaped shipwreck." Some ships sought refuge on "another island, not too large and uninhabited," only to be "driven thither by the wind and wrecked on that island, to which many of those who were shipwrecked escaped with pieces of planks and swimming." Meanwhile, "others who could not reach the island perished."

The *kamikaze* had done its work, destroying the Mongol fleet, and Kublai Khan's bold plan ended in humiliation and defeat.

·   ·   ·

A FEW DAYS LATER, "when the violence of the wind and the fury of the stormy sea was stilled," the Mongol leaders launched a large-scale operation to rescue "all the men who were of position, namely, captains of hundreds, thousands, and ten thousands." Not everyone was saved, "there being so many," and "afterward they departed and set their sails toward home."

Those survivors who found safety on the island—Marco claims there were thirty thousand souls, but the actual number was but a fraction of that figure—realized they had been abandoned by their own army and they faced a gruesome ordeal. "When they saw themselves on that island in such danger, and they were so near to Çipingu, these all held themselves for dead, having no victuals, or little, saved from the ships, nor arms, nor any good plan, and had great vexation because although they escaped from the storm they were in no less peril, for they see they cannot escape [the island] and come to a safe port because their ships were all wrecked and broken up." To drive home their desperation, "the ships that escaped the storms of the sea were going off without helping them, with great speed and as fast as they could toward their country, without making any show of turning back to the companions to save and help them."

The survivors "all held themselves for dead because they did not see in any way how they could escape."

Japan celebrated as the emperor and his subjects realized that the Divine Wind had destroyed their enemies. They regarded the event as Heaven's assurance that their nation would remain inviolate, and the emperor's reign intact.

AS THE STRANDED MONGOLS faced the prospect of a slow death by starvation, their immediate situation worsened. Patrolling the waters off Çipingu, Japanese sailors rescued several Mongols, who revealed that the remainder of their forces had taken refuge on the uninhabited island four miles from Japan's coast. The Japanese proceeded "straight to the island with a vast number of ships well armed, and with a great multitude of men, and with little order and less wisdom all climb down immediately onto the land to take those remaining on the island. And when the thirty thousand saw their enemies come upon them, they went into a wood near the harbor." From their hiding places, the Mongols watched the Japanese wander about the island "like those who feared nothing and knew little of such work." Believing the Mongols were too weak to move or pose a threat, they did not even trouble to leave watchmen on their waiting ships.

There was a hill in the middle of the island, "and when their enemies came hastily to take them," the Mongol warriors made a pretence of flight. They zigzagged their way across the island until "they came to the ships of their enemies and, not finding them occupied by any of the army, they climbed up there immediately." To their astonishment, the ships were "empty and unguarded." Once in possession of the ships, the Mongols "immediately hoisted the sails and left the island and like very valiant men went to the other great island of the enemies." The desperate Mongols, once given up for dead, effected a stunning reversal of fortune.

ARRIVING AT ÇIPINGU, the Mongols quickly disembarked, as if they were Japanese soldiers; they carried with them "the standards and ensigns of the lord of the island." In disguise, they marched directly for "the capital city," where they were taken to be returning soldiers. "So they [the inhabitants] opened the gates and let them enter into the town."

Once within the city gates, the disguised Mongols "found no men there but [only] old ones and women," whom they "drove out." Then they "took the fort as soon as they were in it and chase all people out . . . except only some fair young women who were there, whom they kept to serve them."

Marco brings his story to an eloquent climax: "When the lord and the people of the island saw that they had lost their city and their fleet, and . . . when they had learned of the taking of the city and the fathers or sons driven out and the women kept, to their extreme disgrace, and especially the king, they wished to die of grief, knowing that so great a mistake with their extreme disgrace of the fatherland came about not through the power of the enemy but only through lack of prudence."

AFTER THIS DISPLAY of ritual self-castigation, the Japanese, drawing on inexhaustible reserves of strength, mounted another defense against the invaders. Marco relates that "brave citizens encouraged the king, saying that this was not a time to lament, but to put themselves all of one mind to avenge themselves of so great an injury."

The Mongols executed their plan with renewed vigor. "They came back to their island with other ships, having found many of them about those harbors, because owing to the vast multitude of ships, the Tartars, who were only thirty thousand, and also like men who flee, had not been able to remove them all. So having gone on board as best they could, they carried themselves over to the island." Although the Japanese surrounded the Mongols, the trapped invaders held the women of the island hostage, "so that none would be able to go there nor to come out without their consent and will."

The standoff between the Mongols occupying the city and the Japanese trying to retake it lasted seven months. Throughout, the Mongols "took pains day and night to find out how they could make this affair known to the Great Khan that he might send them help," but the Japanese captured all their messengers, no matter how great their stealth and daring.

All the while, Kublai Khan remained ignorant of the protracted contest taking place in his name. "The Tartars day and night did not cease to attack the people of the island with very great damage and loss. And when they saw that they could not do this that they proposed by any device, and seeing that they lacked food and that they could hold out no longer, then finally they made agreement and truce with those outside, and gave themselves up, saving their persons in such a way that they must stay there all the days of their lives."

IT FELL TO the combatants to negotiate a peace, as Marco carefully explains: "The islanders who for very many years had not had war and bore it very ill, and especially the loss of their women who were in the hands and power of their enemies, believing that they would never have them again, when they saw that the Tartars were willing to give them back the place and the women, joyful and satisfied with so great an offer all with one voice constrained the king to make peace on the terms offered. And so it was observed and the peace was made and the place returned to the king."

Marco told a remarkable tale, but it is impossible to verify. Unlike other aspects of Kublai Khan's failed siege of Japan, this suspiciously sweet denouement lacks corroboration in other sources. Yet his account fits so neatly with what is known of the failed effort that it is likely based on historical fact, and lost sources, all related con brio.

ALTHOUGH A significant portion of Kublai Khan's forces survived, his campaign to bring Japan into the Mongol fold ended in the worst disgrace of his reign, threatening his prestige and throne. To the deeply superstitious Mongols, the entire episode, and especially the intervention of the Divine Wind, suggested that the heavens had turned against the emperor's designs.

Kublai looked for scapegoats, and they seemed to be everywhere. Learning of the bickering and resentment among his generals, Kublai "immediately made them [the Mongols] cut off the head of one of the barons who was captain of that army who had fled so evilly, and the other he sent to the desert island named Ciocia, where he had many people destroyed for grave offenses." The dishonored leader, never named by Marco, died the death of a traitor to the Mongols. "When he [Kublai] sends anyone to the aforesaid island to be killed," Marco says, "he causes his hands to be very well wrapped round with skin of a buffalo lately flayed, and to be tightly sewn; and when the skin is dried it is shrunken round the hands so that by no means can it be moved from them, and so he is left there to end with a death of agony because he cannot help himself and has nothing to eat, and if he wishes to eat grass he must crawl on the ground. And in this way he made the baron perish."

AGAINST THE ADVICE of his councilors, Kublai Khan prepared for a third invasion of Japan.

In 1283, two years after the *kamikaze* demolished the Mongol fleet, the shipyards of southern China sprang to life once more, obeying the Great Khan's orders to build five hundred new battleships. Two years later, the Khan demanded the same contribution from the Manchurians of northern China. The Chinese protested Kublai's warlike excesses, as did his own advisers. Opposition to the undertaking became universal, and in 1286 Kublai Khan reluctantly abandoned his visions of conquest.

·   ·   ·

AFTER THE ROUT in Japan, Kublai Khan never regained his political power or his diplomatic dexterity, and the entire Yüan empire suffered from diminished prestige. Kublai's modern biographer Morris Rossabi observes: "The failures shattered the Mongols' mantle of invincibility in East Asia." And everyone took note. "One of the principal under-pinnings of their power—the psychological edge of terror they held over their opponents—was badly shaken, if not dislodged."

In defeat, Kublai Khan retreated from reality. He passed his days and nights feasting on boiled mutton, eggs, raw vegetables in pancakes, koumiss, and beer. He became depressed and obese. Portraits of the Great Khan in old age show him grown as fat as a Buddha, but not nearly so happy. How could he rejoice with his empire collapsing all around him, his favorite wife and son both dead, and his reputation in tatters? He sought relief from his political and physical ills in a variety of miracle cures, everything from drugs to more drinking to the incan-tations of shamans from as far away as Korea. None of the spells proved efficacious, and his drinking became still more excessive. The expansive yet shrewd monarch who had once greeted Marco Polo and his father and uncle had given way to a sad and self-pitying old man whose weaknesses encouraged his enemies.

Marco looked on in dismay as the Great Khan, along with the entire Yüan dynasty, nearly succumbed to the subversive designs of a single highly placed individual.

HIS NAME WAS AHMAD, and he had risen from obscurity to become the most powerful Muslim official during Kublai Khan's long reign. Ahmad specialized in finance, an area in which the Mongols lacked expertise, and he cunningly turned his influence and high status to tremendous personal profit. He had the arrogance of a minister secure in his sovereign's trust. He was Kublai Khan's gatekeeper, feared and secretly despised, who bullied everyone at court and held them at bay, at least for a time. While the khan was devoting his energies to brilliant military conquests, his minister was conducting a reign of terror in the palace.

Ahmad made himself indispensable to the khan, yet remained an outsider because he was a Muslim. Although Kublai declared the prophet Muhammad to be one of the empire's four spiritual beacons, he himself preferred to keep Muslims at arm's length. Skilled in finance and trade, Muslims had their uses, Kublai believed. And they were considered more trustworthy than the Chinese, if only because they were beholden to the Mongols, in the same way that Marco was. Of the many Muslims who energetically served Kublai Khan, none rose higher or posed a greater threat to the Mongol rule of China—and the Polo family's secure niche within it—than Ahmad. In his hunger for power, he came close to toppling the Yüan dynasty.

Marco observed Ahmad's rise and fall firsthand; he knew the principals and was able to describe their bewilderment at the thought of one man—an outsider, no less—nearly toppling Kublai Khan. The entire affair was heavily documented in Mongol and Chinese annals, and was described by the Persian historian Rashid al-Din in 1304, not long after the events transpired, but it was unknown in the West. Marco Polo's account marked the first time that Europeans heard of the power-hungry Ahmad and the dangerous machinations of the Mongol court.

TRADITION HOLDS that Ahmad hailed from a region south of Tashkent that the Mongols conquered fifty years before the Polo family traveled to China. The region, largely Muslim, was populated by Iranian and Turkic ethnic groups. Ahmad first appears in historical records as the retainer of a prominent member of the Quonggirat tribe who happened to be the brother-in-law of Genghis Khan. Later, he attracted the attention of Kublai, who came to rely on him for financial administration. In his account, Marco speaks of Ahmad as "a clever and strong man, who had great influence and authority with the Khan, who was so fond of him that he had every liberty."

The theme of their collaboration was centralization, an approach that was utterly foreign to the nomadic Mongols, who had devised strategies for controlling sprawling regions with a minimum of bureaucracy. Kublai Khan, in contrast, labored to consolidate his empire by emulating the Chinese. While Kublai sought new worlds to conquer, Ahmad patiently restructured finances from one end of the empire to the other. He won appointment as commissioner of the imperial granary, and in this capacity established the Office for Harmonious Purchase; the idea was to buy grain at a fixed price to hold in reserve against the possibility of war and famine. In practice, the Office for Harmonious Purchase, along with a sister institution, the Office for Regulated Management, simply confiscated goods for the Mongol court. Ahmad made sure that Kublai Khan and his barons had everything they needed to live in their magnificent and self-indulgent style.

BY 1262, Ahmad had won promotion to the Secretarial Council, another Mongol stronghold, and appointment as commissioner of transportation throughout the empire. He lobbied to increase the salt tax, a potent source of revenue, and to buttress the central government's grain reserves. Although he managed to consolidate his financial control over the Mongol realm, he bridled at having to answer to the council itself. For twenty years, Ahmad did battle with the council, trying to overrule it, circumvent it, marginalize it—anything that would make him answerable to Kublai Khan alone. His great adversary was the Chinese bureaucrat Chang Wen-ch'ien, who insisted on a strictly observed hierarchy in government. Time and again, Chang Wen-ch'ien persuaded the khan to keep the council's powers intact.

Two years later, Ahmad won appointment as a director of political affairs for the Secretarial Council and, even more impressive, controller of the Imperial Treasure. He knew more about the finances of the Mongol Empire than anyone else, and exercised more power over it than anyone, with the exception of the khan. While Kublai Khan was engaging in sexual gymnastics with six concubines at a time, Ahmad was overseeing the administration of the empire's finances. But Ahmad also maintained a large harem to which he constantly added by tendering lucrative government jobs in exchange for women he fancied. Husbands offered him their wives, and fathers their daughters, in return for coveted appointments.

Marco sharply observes: "There was no fair lady with whom, if he wanted her, he did not have his will, taking her for his harem if she was not married, or otherwise making her consent. When he knew that someone had a pretty daughter, he had his ruffians who went to the father of the girl, saying to him, '. . . Give her for wife to Ahmad, and we will make him give you a governorship or an office for three years.' And so he gave Ahmad his daughter." In these transactions, Ahmad always got his way, both with the khan, who would agree to the appointment, and with the girl in question, who had no other choice.

AHMAD'S INFLUENCE waned in 1264, when his followers became involved in a violent melee that, from a distance, resembled an insur-

rection. The resulting scandal shook the Yüan dynasty to its foundations. Ahmad was tried, found guilty of being unable to control his followers, and punished with a severe beating. In the khan's uproarious
court, corporal punishment in the form of canings and beatings was
standard procedure for disciplining government officials, the Mongol
equivalent of a censure or reprimand.

The irrepressible Ahmad rebounded from this humiliation to win
an appointment as the chief of a new agency, the Office for Regulating
State Expenditure. Once again he was in his element, issuing official
complaints about the poor quality of linen produced in Manchuria and
the inadequacy of the gold and silver foundries of Chen-ting and
Shun-t'ien. Having learned of the production of asbestos, as reported
by Marco Polo, the agency dispatched officials to nationalize the
asbestos industry. Ahmad's approach was stark: the Mongol government would take the lion's share of everything. Indeed, no new source
of potential revenue was too small to escape his notice. When he
learned that silver was being mined in a remote location in the district
of Shang-tu, he recommended that tin, an inexpensive by-product of
the smelting process, should be sold, and the revenue paid directly to
the government.

All the while, Ahmad schemed to consolidate his power. In 1270,
Kublai appointed him director of political affairs for a new council
directing the empire's finances in the face of intense opposition from a
coalition of respected Mongol and Chinese opponents, including Hsü
Heng, a revered scholar and bureaucrat. Ahmad had his way again, and
once he secured this post, he skillfully played on the divisions among
his political enemies. Confronted with the prospect of another inquiry
and beating, he deflected the blame to a lesser official, who became the
scapegoat.

Wielding more influence than ever, he now presided over a growing ménage of four wives and forty concubines, not quite enough to
overshadow his master's retinue, but an impressive demonstration of
the status he enjoyed. At the same time, he secured a prestigious post
for his son Husain, as if laying the groundwork for a rival dynasty.

WHEN MARCO POLO first arrived at the Mongol court, all the elements of Ahmad's financial control and Kublai Khan's military conquests appeared to mesh flawlessly.

In January of 1275, Mongol forces ranged along the Yangtze River and put the remnants of the Song dynasty's army to flight. Kublai Khan, his brain trust of Chinese scholars, and Ahmad met regularly to discuss the prospect of harvesting the wealth of the new additions to the empire. At issue was the matter of currency. Ahmad, renowned as a skillful debater, was in favor of replacing Song currency with the paper currency recently disseminated by the Yüan dynasty. Chinese officials argued that the Mongol commander, Bayan, had just promised the conquered region that Song currency would continue to circulate under Mongol control. They insisted that if Kublai Khan ordered otherwise, the Mongols would lose credibility. The Chinese wise men disagreed among themselves about the best course, and Ahmad, exploiting their dissension, prevailed. Yüan currency flooded the conquered Song territories, and to make matters worse, Ahmad imposed a punitive rate of exchange of fifty to one in favor of Yüan notes. At a stroke, the Chinese economy for the region was dismantled.

Once he had won this victory over Kublai Khan's Chinese advisers, Ahmad maneuvered to reduce their influence at court. He ended the longstanding Mongol policy of free trade and local taxes in favor of imposing onerous central taxation. He replaced Chinese officials, whom he feared and distrusted, with Muslims. He took his lead from Kublai Khan, who relied on skilled foreigners to help administer the realm. Ahmad, for his part, made it seductively easy for Kublai Khan to rely on him to look after the government bureaucracy and provide the luxurious furnishings calculated to appeal to the khan's weakness for opulence, while stifling dissent by any means necessary. Nor was Ahmad the only beneficiary of the policy of employing foreigners; the Polo company owed its favored position in the Mongol court to that practice, and Marco in particular owed his entire improbable career in the service of the khan to it.

As AHMAD SOLIDIFIED his power, rumors circulated at court that he wanted even more. Everywhere Ahmad looked, he saw enemies, and he dealt with them all. With slight exaggeration, Marco insists that "whenever he [Ahmad] wished to put anyone whom he hated to death, whether justly or unjustly, he went to the khan and said to him, 'So-and-so deserves death because he has offended your Majesty in this manner.' Then the khan said, 'Do what pleases you.' And immediately he had the man put to death."

In reality, Ahmad's machinations were more subtle. For example, when Bayan, the Mongol commander, arrived home in victory, local officials attempted to give him a jade belt buckle from the Song to commemorate his triumph. In a gracious gesture of modesty, Bayan declined the gift, saying he could take nothing personally from the Song.

Displaying a talent for subversion, Ahmad falsely accused the honorable general of stealing a jade cup, and ordered an investigation. So deeply was Kublai in Ahmad's thrall that the emperor blindly ordered an inquisition. Despite Ahmad's scheming, Bayan escaped conviction, although a cloud of suspicion hung over him because the cup itself could not be located. Ahmad tried again to neutralize his potential rival by claiming that Bayan had needlessly massacred Song soldiers. He was no more successful in this attempt than in his previous campaign of slander, but with each charge leveled against him, Bayan the war hero lost stature at court until he no longer posed a serious threat to Ahmad.

Ahmad was more ruthless with other critics. Ts'ui Pin, the Chinese leader of an anti-Ahmad group, complained that Ahmad had established unnecessary government agencies to give his many relatives lucrative and influential government jobs, despite his pledge not to engage in nepotism. For a brief time, Ts'ui Pin had his way, and he forced Ahmad's relatives—even his son Husain—off the government payroll. But Ahmad then arranged for Ts'ui Pin to be investigated. An inquiry concluded that Ts'ui Pin and two other conspirators had stolen grain from the government and cast unauthorized bronze seals to enhance their own power. In 1280, they were found guilty; all three were executed.

By then, Husain had returned to his former government post, established a new government bureaucracy himself, and doubled taxes in the wealthy Quinsai region. Ostensibly, the taxes financed distant Mongol military campaigns against Burma, Japan, and Java. All the while, he fended off charges of greed and indifference by claiming that local officials engaged in corrupt reporting and outright theft of grain supplies.

Throughout these controversies, Ahmad enjoyed the naïve trust of Kublai Khan, as always more interested in glorious military conquests and sensual indulgence than in the minutiae of finance and administration.

. . .

AFTER BAYAN'S DEATH the jade cup in question surfaced, proving his innocence. A chastened Kublai Khan realized how close to complete defeat Bayan had come at Ahmad's hands, with the khan himself an unwitting accomplice. But Kublai Khan did nothing to restrain Ahmad's reign of political terror.

IN CONTRAST, Kublai Khan's son and heir apparent, Chinkim, loathed Ahmad with a passion. Of all his adversaries, Ahmad feared only Chinkim, who was spared the rigged inquisitions that brought down others. He was frequently on record denouncing the Muslim financial mastermind. Chinkim spoke not only for himself but also for the Chinese scholars and courtiers hovering around the khan; indeed, as time passed, he became strikingly sinicized, speaking Chinese and wearing traditional Chinese clothing. One of his closest associates had been Ts'ui Pin, brought down by Ahmad. Chinkim had even dispatched officials at the last minute to prevent the execution, but they had arrived too late. Now he wanted bloody revenge.

No matter how much Chinese culture he absorbed, Chinkim remained true to his Mongol roots. During one confrontation, he struck Ahmad so hard that the minister could neither open his mouth nor speak for a week. When Kublai asked how Ahmad had come to sustain his injuries, the Muslim was afraid to point the finger at the khan's son, and pretended that he had fallen from his horse.

On another occasion, Chinkim attacked Ahmad in the presence of Kublai Khan, who, astonishingly, seemed to take no notice of the fracas.

By now, Ahmad was afraid for his life. To shield himself from Chinkim's wrath, he pleaded with Kublai Khan to establish a high court of justice, in the hope that it would intercede. But Kublai refused, viewing the proposed body as a virtual duplicate of one already in existence.

Ahmad's reign of bureaucratic terror lasted just a bit longer; he spent much of the next two years raising taxes to the breaking point and plotting to destroy his Chinese critics. If Kublai Khan ever suspected something was awry, he gave no indication; in fact, he promoted the feared Muslim minister again, this time to the position of vice chancellor. Ahmad was now more powerful than ever.

.   .   .

AHMAD DEFTLY PUNISHED his enemies in the Mongol court, but
his rapaciousness sowed hatred beyond its confines. During an obscure
military campaign in a northern province of the Mongol Empire, a
Chinese soldier and ascetic named Wang Chu happened to encounter
a Buddhist monk named Kao, who claimed to be skilled in magic. For
a time, Kao marched with the Mongol army, but when his spells failed,
he was mustered out. If not capable of working magic, he did demonstrate a flair for the macabre. To persuade the world of his death, he
spread rumors and even killed a man, whose corpse he dressed as if it
were his own. Once Kao and Wang Chu came together, they discovered their shared loathing for Ahmad, and they hatched a wild scheme
to assassinate him.

Whether they acted alone or as instruments of a larger clandestine
conspiracy remains an open question. The record suggests they were
loners, but Marco insists that the Chinese whom Ahmad had
oppressed "planned to assassinate him and to rebel against the rule of
the city." In Polo's feverish retelling, Wang Chu emerges not as an
ascetic but as a man "whose mother, daughter, and wife Ahmad had
violated," a man acting out the will of the Chinese, who despised
Ahmad.

In the early months of 1282, the ascetic soldier and the devious
monk conspired to insinuate themselves into Kublai's court. Wang
Chu worked up documents supposedly from Chinkim ordering him to
report to the prince's palace. It was all a deception, because Chinkim
himself was nowhere to be found.

Next, Wang Chu approached Ahmad, bearing false reports of
Chinkim's imminent arrival at his palace. Ahmad and other dignitaries
would be expected to greet him properly out in front.

Marco, drawing on unofficial sources and gossip, explains that they
planned a much larger conspiracy: they were to signal with torches to
others spread across the land to "kill all those who have beards, and
make the signal with fire to the other cities that they should do the
like." Since the Chinese were beardless, those with beards would have
been Mongols, Muslims, and Christians.

The two conspirators had raised a ragged little army of a hundred
or so men to help carry out the plot. Under cover of darkness, they
approached the palace on horseback, lighting their way with an
impressive display of lanterns and torches. Occupying a prominent
position in their midst, the monk Kao rode high on his horse, doing his
best to impersonate Chinkim arriving at his palace.

At the same time, Ahmad was entering the city gate on his way to meet Chinkim and happened to meet a "Tartar named Cogatai, who was captain of twelve thousand men with whom he kept continual guard over the city," according to Marco Polo, whose account of these events deserves attention because he claimed to be close at hand.

"Where are you going so late?" Cogatai asked Ahmad.

"To Chinkim, who is this moment come."

Cogatai was understandably suspicious. "How is it possible that he is come so secretly that I have not known it?"

Historical records suggest that as he drew up, Kao, still posing as Chinkim, summoned the soldiers on guard to approach, a move that suddenly exposed Ahmad. Lying in wait, Wang Chu withdrew a substantial brass bat from his sleeve, leapt at Ahmad, and beat him to death.

Marco offers a more sophisticated insider account of the assassination: "The moment that Ahmad came into the palace, seeing so many candles lighted, he knelt down before Kao, believing he was Chinkim; and Wang Chu who was there ready with a sword cut off his head. And seeing this, Cogatai, who had stopped in the entry of the palace, said, 'Here is treason'; and immediately shot an arrow at Kao, who was sitting on the seat, and killed him." (In the historical record, Kao survived a bit longer.)

Cogatai ordered that "anyone found outside his house be killed on the spot" and proceeded to slaughter Chinese on the assumption that the two assassins had worked closely with the local populace. And the barbarism spread quickly to other cities.

WITHOUT LEADERSHIP, the uprising soon played itself out. Within days, Wang Chu and Kao gave themselves up to the authorities, proclaiming themselves heroes for ridding the empire of the wicked Ahmad.

On May 1, 1282, both conspirators were quartered—their limbs pulled off by horses walking in opposite directions—and beheaded as punishment for their deed.

Just before he was executed, Wang Chu cried out, "I, Wang Chu, now die for having rid the world of a pest. Another day, someone will no doubt write the story for me."

· · ·

WHEN NEWS OF Ahmad's assassination reached Kublai Khan, the supreme ruler reacted with alarm and uncharacteristic decisiveness. He traveled to Shang-tu and ordered a thorough investigation. Expecting to learn of the perfidy of Ahmad's murderers, Kublai instead heard tales of Ahmad's treachery; now that the minister was gone, those whom he had harmed came forward to describe his flagrant dishonesty and abuse of power.

Indignant at these revelations, Kublai prosecuted Ahmad's followers, his children, and other members of his clan. Within weeks it was decreed that anyone who had offered his wife or daughter to Ahmad in exchange for a government post should be removed from office, and all property that he had confiscated returned to its rightful owners. In all, 714 government appointees were dismissed, according to official records.

In June, the Yüan dynasty tallied Ahmad's staggering assets, which included more than 3,700 camels, oxen, sheep, and donkeys. His slaves were freed, his property was claimed by the state or given away. Marco vigorously narrates Kublai's relentless retaliation: "He ordered Ahmad's body to be taken from the grave and flung in the street to be torn to pieces by dogs. And those of his sons who had followed the example of his evil deeds he caused to be flayed alive." And Rashid al-Din, the era's leading historian, adds a few grisly details of his own, revealing that Kublai, enraged even after Ahmad's death, ordered the minister's body to be "dragged from his grave, that a rope be tied to his feet and that he be hanged at the cross-roads in the bazaar; over his head they drove wheels."

RETRIBUTION PERSISTED long after Ahmad had disappeared from the scene, largely because the culture of corruption that he created remained. According to Chinese custom, executions occurred in the fall, and when the season arrived, four of his sons, including Husain, as well as a nephew, were dispatched; to deepen the disgrace, their bodies were pickled. All Ahmad's followers were blacklisted. The government compiled a catalog of his crimes and announced it in cities and towns throughout the empire so that all would know his evil deeds and treachery. Most of the hundreds of government offices he had established were dismantled, and the excesses associated with his administration, such as harsh treatment of prisoners, were curbed.

Ahmad's personal effects included bizarre items that gave clues to his inner life and suggested he was not the conventional Muslim that Kublai Khan believed him to be. His closet held a pair of tanned human skins, and the eunuch who had cared for him told an alarming tale: Ahmad would from time to time place them on an altar and mutter mysterious invocations. Equally troubling, he owned a silk scroll depicting a provocative image of mounted soldiers surrounding a large tent and attacking the unseen occupant, perhaps the khan himself. Marco took these items as proof that "Ahmad so bewitched the khan with his spells that the khan gave the greatest belief and attention to all his words, and did all that he [Ahmad] wished him to do."

Revelations such as these inspired Kublai Khan to purge Muslims from his court, as Marco relates: "When he recalled the cursed sect of Saracens [Muslims], by which every sin has been made lawful to them and that they can kill whoever is not of their law, and that the cursed Ahmad with his sons had not for this reason reckoned that they committed any sin, he despised it much and held it in abomination." From that time forward, says Marco, Kublai Khan ordered that Muslims must conduct themselves "according to the law of the Tartars, and that they must not cut the throats of animals, as they did, to eat the flesh, but must cut them in the belly."

Ahmad's legacy bedeviled Kublai Khan and the Yüan court. Courtiers wondered aloud how such a power-mad schemer could have flourished in their midst for so many years, and questioned why his critics had remained silent until his death suddenly loosened their tongues. There was an outstanding reason for Ahmad's steady ascent: he brought critical financial and bureaucratic skills to government. He imposed a uniform currency on a fragmented society, formalized taxation to pay for Kublai Khan's expensive military campaigns, and partly succeeded in his goal of indoctrinating all of China with the revolutionary idea that a central Mongol authority administered the entire country.

One unresolved question about this enigmatic tyrant remains. Did Ahmad plan to carry out a palace coup, or did he expect to prosper indefinitely while remaining subordinate to Kublai Khan? If he had led such a coup, the advent of Muslim rule over China would have dramatically changed the course of Asian history. Not even Marco Polo ventured a guess about that prospect. For Marco, Ahmad's fall marked a coming of age. He had arrived at the Mongol court as a young man enthralled with the larger-than-life figure of Kublai Khan, whom he regarded with undisguised hero worship. His account makes it seem that he could not believe his good fortune in establishing rapport with the powerful ruler. But the Ahmad affair demonstrated to Marco, and to the Mongol world, that Kublai Khan, for all his military prowess and enlightened domestic policies, was capable of making errors of judgment serious enough to threaten the empire itself.

FOR MORE THAN thirty years, the complementary skills of the warrior khan and the bureaucrat had permitted the Mongol Empire to flourish. The sumptuousness of the Shang-tu summer palace (Xanadu) reflected the tastes of Kublai Khan and the organizational skills of Ahmad. For all its excesses, their collaboration might have lasted even longer, had Ahmad known how to win the affection or respect of the Chinese people whom he ruled, and not just their fear.

Kublai Khan turned to a man whom he believed would be a safe choice to succeed Ahmad. His name was Sanga, and he was a Uighur, a member of a Turkic tribe. But he soon ran into trouble when a jealous rival told Kublai about Sanga's supposed treachery. Kublai Khan disciplined the errant minister with a Mongol-style beating.

Sanga held his ground, and Kublai turned his wrath on the informant, who insisted that he was simply trying to warn the khan of danger. The khan held an inquiry and learned from a trusted Persian aide that Sanga was stockpiling pearls and gems at the expense of the government. When the khan asked to share in this hoard, Sanga protested that he had no such riches. The khan arranged for Sanga to be distracted briefly, and during that time the Persian retrieved not one but two caskets stuffed with valuable pearls.

"What is all this?" Kublai Khan asked his minister. "You have so many pearls, but refuse to give me even a few. Where did you get these riches?"

Sanga awkwardly explained that he had collected them from Muslims governing provinces throughout China. His answer infuriated the khan.

"Why did they bring me nothing? You bring me trifles and keep the most precious items for yourself."

"They were given to me," Sanga insisted, and offered to return them, if his lord and master wished.

Unimpressed, Kublai Khan condemned Sanga to be put to death by having his mouth filled with excrement. The Khan seized the hoard of gems and executed several of Sanga's Muslim loyalists. Kublai had learned the lesson of the Ahmad uprising only too well. But he had eliminated one threat only to face others, as adversaries crowded him on all sides.

KUBLAI KHAN'S next challenge came from his detested "uncle," Nayan, who was determined to become the Great Khan, at Kublai's expense. While still a young man, Marco Polo says, Nayan had become "ruler of many lands and provinces, so that he could easily raise a force of 400,000 horsemen." Having an army of this size at his disposal inspired dreams of glory: "He resolved that he would be a subject no longer."

Although Nayan was a Nestorian Christian, as were many of his followers and soldiers, Marco's sympathies clearly lay with Kublai Khan in this contest. But the conflict between the two warlords was in no sense a religious crusade. Nayan wanted power, and to acquire it he formed an alliance with another insubordinate member of the Mongol royal family, Kublai's subversive nephew Kaidu, whom Marco describes as the khan's "bitter enemy" and a perpetual menace to stability in Asia. "I assure you," he says, "that Kaidu is never at peace with the Great Khan, but maintains constant warfare against him." Marco despaired at the havoc this troublemaker had wrought over the years. "Kaidu has already fought many battles with the Great Khan's men," he says. Even though Kaidu had lost all the battles, he clamored for his share of Kublai Khan's hard-won victories. To hear Marco tell it, Kublai would have obliged if only Kaidu had promised to appear at Cambulac whenever summoned. But Kaidu was "afraid for his life if he went," and Kublai Khan maintained 100,000 "horsemen in the field" to contain his adversary.

In 1287, Nayan and Kaidu concocted a plot to attack Kublai simultaneously from opposite directions and force him into submission. "When the Great Khan got word of this plot," Marco relates, "he was not unduly perturbed; but like a wise man of approved valor he began to marshal his own forces, declaring that he would never wear his crown or hold his land if he did not bring these two false traitors to an evil end."

Within only twenty-two days, Kublai assembled an army consisting of 260,000 cavalry and 100,000 infantry, but the forces arrayed against him were larger still. "The reason why he confined himself to this number was that these were drawn from the troops in his own immediate neighborhood," Marco reports. Kublai commanded some twelve additional armies, but they were "so far away on campaigns of conquest in many parts that he could not have got them together at the right time and place." If he had summoned all his guards on duty in distant parts of his empire, "their numbers would have been past all reckoning or belief." But such measures would have been too slow and too public; Kublai preferred speed, "the companion of victory," and secrecy to "forestall Nayan's preparations and catch him alone."

CHINESE ANNALS confirm Marco's account of this matter, and they suggest that Kublai was willing to sacrifice Bayan by sending him on a hazardous intelligence-gathering mission. With Bayan at close range, "Nayan conceived the plan of kidnapping him; but Bayan, informed of his plans, was able to escape and returned to the emperor."

At the same time, other Mongol barons in northwestern China, learning of Nayan's rebellion, sided with him, and as the annals relate, "the emperor was very afflicted." Acting on the advice of a military official, Kublai Khan dispatched an envoy to try to talk sense into the upstart barons, now known as the confederates. Although the envoy was able to persuade them that their cause was doomed, Nayan refused to surrender. Rather, he formed allegiances with other leaders, who supplied him with troops. Kublai Khan's forces surrounded their encampment. Eventually a "small, secret expedition" consisting of only a dozen "intrepid and determined men" under the command of a Chinese officer penetrated the enemy.

Although Kublai Khan won this contest, he had not succeeded in eliminating Nayan, whose power and ambition seemed to gain strength from the Mongol efforts to contain it.

ALTHOUGH MARCO wished to persuade his audience, and himself, that Kublai Khan was a wise and beloved leader who ruled the empire by virtue and the mandate of Heaven, the Venetian's account occasionally betrays an opposing point of view—that the khan could be a wily despot who ruled China and rival Mongol clans by cunning and military force. "In all of his dominions," Marco admits from the safe remove of his prison cell in Genoa, "there are many disaffected and disloyal subjects who, if they had the chance, would rebel against their lord." To prevent local insurrection, Kublai Khan rotated the occupying armies every two years, as well as the captains in charge of them.

Maintaining large standing armies across the length and breadth of China cost Kublai Khan dearly. Marco relates that the troops, in addition to receiving regular pay, "live on the immense herds of cattle that are assigned to them and on the milk that they send into towns to sell for necessary provisions." In time, the armies drained both the Mongol treasury and Chinese natural resources. The Mongols were stretched too thin to rule all of China, especially by force, and while they displayed amazing dexterity with their messenger service, and their admirable (if necessary) respect for local languages, religions, and customs, they presided over barely controlled chaos. Marco was fortunate to travel across China during the years of the Pax Mongolica, when the Mongols maintained a delicate balance between Chinese nationalism and Mongolian imperial ambitions. This state of affairs meant that travelers along the Silk Road enjoyed relative safety, especially in the Mongol strongholds in the north, where marauders who often terrorized traders were kept at bay. But as Marco came to realize, the status quo could not last, because Nayan expected to rule China himself.

DRAWING CONFIDENCE from the predictions of astrologers, as was his habit, Kublai Khan assured himself that his cause would be successful. Only then did he lead his forces—now reckoned at 400,000 horsemen—into battle against Nayan. Fortune once again favored Kublai Khan, as Marco points out: "When they arrived Nayan was in his tent, dallying in bed with [one of] his wives, to whom he was greatly attached." Nayan had felt so secure that he had not troubled to post sentries or send out patrols.

Without warning, the Great Khan appeared. "He stood on the top of a wooden tower, full of crossbowmen and archers, which was carried by four elephants wearing stout leather armor draped with clothes of silk and gold. Above his head flew his banner with the emblem of the sun and moon, so high that it could clearly be seen on every side. His troops were marshaled in thirty squadrons of 10,000 mounted archers each, grouped in three divisions; and those on the left and right he flung out so that they encircled Nayan's camp in a moment. In front of every squadron of horse [men] were five hundred foot-soldiers with short pikes and swords. They were so trained that, whenever the cavalry proposed a retreat, they would jump on the horses' cruppers and flee with them; then, when the retreat was halted, they would dismount and slaughter the enemies' horses with their pikes." The Mongols' false retreats proved highly effective.

Nayan's troops, nearly equal to the khan's in number, straggled into their battle formations, to the accompaniment of drums, songs, and martial music produced by a two-stringed instrument. The two sides rode into battle, Kublai Khan's banners with his sun-and-moon insignia flying, and Nayan's standard displaying the "Cross of Christ."

After lengthy delays, "the two armies fell upon each other with bow and sword and club, and a few with lances." They clashed in a "bloody and bitter battle," complete with "arrows flying like pelting rain." Beneath them, "horsemen and horses tumbled dead upon the ground."

Marco pays tribute to Nayan's troops, claiming that the men stood ready to die for their leader, "but in the end victory fell to the Great Khan." Seeing that he had lost the battle and his fiefdom along with it, Nayan tried to flee, but he and his generals were all captured, and they eventually surrendered. Kublai condemned Nayan to death according to Mongol custom. "He was wrapped up tightly in a carpet and then dragged about so violently, this way and that, that he died," Marco reports. "Their object in choosing this mode of death was so that the blood of the imperial lineage might not be spilt upon the earth, and the sun and the air might not witness it, nor the limbs of Nayan be touched by any animal."

KUBLAI KHAN received the show of loyalty that was his due. Barons from four provinces arrived to swear obeisance. But instead of submission and unity, Marco relates, ugliness quickly ensued. "Saracens, idolaters, Jews, and many people who do not believe in God made fun of the Christian faith and of the sign of the Holy Cross that Nayan had carried on his banner."

When word of this blasphemy reached Kublai Khan, "he called to him the chief Saracens and Jews and Christians and spoke evil to those who made fun of it before him and before the Christians, and rebuked them severely, saying to them, 'If the Cross of Christ has not helped Nayan, it has done reasonably and justly, because he was disloyal and a rebel against his lord.' " For this reason, Kublai Khan said, he deserved to die.

With that, Kublai Khan "called many Christians who were there and began to comfort them, saying that they had no reason or occasion for shame . . . , for Nayan who came against his lord was both disloyal and treacherous, and so there is great right in that which happened to him." Although the Christian followers of Nayan remained suspicious of Kublai Khan, they were relieved, and perhaps surprised as well, that he did not "tempt them from their faith, but they stayed quiet and in peace."

HAVING SECURED his power in China, Kublai Khan stumbled anew when he undertook a series of military skirmishes in Southeast Asia, provoking war where there had been stability and amity. He then repeated the Japanese disaster by attempting to conquer another island stronghold, Java.

Marco relates the Mongol invasion of Java with confidence, once again giving his European readers their first account of political struggle in a land they never knew existed. His account represents a remarkable feat of intelligence gathering on his part; even though his comprehension of events was partial and inevitably colored by the Mongol perspective, he remains generally accurate throughout.

Located south of Malaysia and Sumatra, in the Indian Ocean, Java is so distant from China that Marco probably never reached its shores, but he gathered stories to transmit to the West—the first accounts of this distant kingdom to reach Europe. "According to what the good sailors say who know it well," he states, "this is the largest island in the world, for it is indeed more than three thousand miles around." And it abounded in the most valuable commodity in the medieval world: spices. "They have pepper and nutmeg and spikenard and galingale and cubebs and cloves and all dear spicery that one could find in the world." From the sound of things, trade was brisk—"Unto this island come great numbers of ships and merchants who buy many goods there and make great profit," Marco says—but it excluded the emissaries of Kublai Khan, who "can never have it subjected to his rule because of the long way and for the danger that it was to sail there."

Despite the hazards, Kublai did send envoys, led by his personal ambassador, Meng Ch'i, to visit Java's ruler, King Kertanagara. The emissaries survived the voyage—at least, Marco tells of no shipwrecks or other losses en route—and upon reaching the Javanese court, they made the same outrageous demands that had once been made of the Japanese, insisting that the king submit unequivocally to the unseen khan across the sea. Kertanagara responded with a shocking insult: he branded the ambassador's face.

To a Mongol ruler, there could be no greater insult than the disfigurement or murder of an ambassador. Seizing on this new incitement to war, Kublai Khan made ready for the invasion of Java with the zeal he had once brought to preparations for the invasion of Japan. Failing to heed the lessons of past failures, he appointed three commanders to carry out the task. One was a Mongol, Shih-pi, the commander in chief; the second a Chinese, Kao Hsing, appointed field general; and the third a Uighur, I-k'o-mu-ssu, charged with providing ships.

In 1292, the new Mongol invasion force departed. It was as grand as its predecessors: a thousand ships, twenty thousand men, a year's supply of grain, and forty thousand ounces of silver to buy supplies en route—all of it ruinously expensive.

Kertanagara's intelligence gave him ample warning of the assault, but he made the fatal mistake of committing all of his troops to the distant Malay Peninsula, where he believed the Mongols would land. Suddenly vulnerable in his homeland, Kertanagara found himself embroiled in a local rebellion. His clever rival, Jayakatwang, took advantage of the king's weakness, sent in troops, and slaughtered Kertanagara.

That was not quite the end of Kertanagara's influence. His wily son-in-law, Prince Vijaya, assumed the vacant throne and offered to submit to Kublai Khan if the Mongols would assist in putting down the Javanese uprising. To this end, Vijaya promised detailed maps describing the rivers and ports of Java. The Mongol leaders accepted the offer and pursued the upstart Jayakatwang, whom they captured and executed, much to Vijaya's satisfaction.

Just when it seemed that the Mongols had carried off a great strategic success, Vijaya made an apparently simple request: two hundred unarmed men to accompany him to the kingdom of Madjapahit, where, he declared, he would formally submit to Kublai Khan's envoys. Eager for this prize, the Mongols gave Vijaya his wish. But during the march to Madjapahit, Vijaya revealed his true purpose. His soldiers mounted a surprise attack against the unarmed Mongol escorts, and pursued Mongol forces in the region. They boldly attacked the Mongol general, Shih-pi, who barely escaped with his life. Shih-pi ordered a humiliating retreat to his ships that cost three thousand lives.

Safely on board his command ship, Shih-pi debated with the other Mongol leaders about the best means to punish Vijaya for his treachery, but they were unable to reach an agreement. Instead they sailed home to China and disgrace. Although the expedition returned with interesting Javanese artifacts—the horn of a rhinoceros, a reliable map and census of Java, and a letter from Bali written in gold characters—they were, unmistakably, a vanquished fleet.

The repercussions would be felt all the way back to Kublai Khan's court.

BOOK THREE

India

ABOUT A.D. 1300

Iceland

Greenland

Scotland   Den

Ireland   Engld

Poland

ATLANTIC OCEAN   France

Markland   Spain   Hungary

Vinland   Portugal   Gr

Mongol Empire

Zipangu

Mohammedan States

India

Abyssinia   Ceylon   Chinese Sea

Arab Settlements   INDIAN OCEAN

CHAPTER THIRTEEN

The Seeker

And all should cry, Beware! Beware!
His flashing eyes, his floating hair!

As the Yüan dynasty trembled, Marco carefully distanced himself from his one-time mentor, Kublai Khan. To hear the Venetian tell it, his primary motive for leaving the court and all its intrigues was his insatiable desire to see more of the world than anyone before him. He presented this new phase of his travels as a case of urgent wanderlust. He had fallen under the spell of India, and had arranged for Kublai Khan's permission to visit.

Marco, like other Western wayfarers of the era, remained vague about what he meant by "India." Europeans often referred to "the Three Indias" or to a "Greater" and a "Lesser" India—all rather flexible terms. Each writer or traveler reconfigured "India" to suit his purpose or preconceptions, and Marco was no exception. In any case, India was for him a byword for escape more than an actual place on the map.

En route to India, Marco the overland explorer metamorphosed into Marco the navigator, as might be expected of a gentleman of Venice, the empire by the sea. As a remedy for his malaise, he discovered, nothing surpassed the ocean. Marco reveled in blue water's therapeutic buoyancy, expansiveness, and sense of freedom.

"We shall begin first of all to tell about the great ships in which the merchants go and come into Indie," Marco announces. These were sophisticated vessels of Arab and Chinese design, constructed of fir and pine, and fitted with a broad deck. For his European readers, accustomed to primitive sailing vessels, the surprise was their sheer size. The ship on which he sailed featured sixty cabins, each sufficient for a merchant to "stay comfortably." It was equipped with a rudder, four masts, and four sails. "They often add . . . two masts more, which are raised and put away whenever they wish," Marco reports. The larger ships boasted as many as thirteen holds, "so that if it happens by accident that the ship is staved in any place"—by a rock, for instance, or an aggressive whale "in search of food"—the injured craft would stay afloat.

Six centuries before Herman Melville's *Moby-Dick*, Marco described how an Arab ship survived a deadly encounter with a cetacean. "If the ship sailing by night [and] making the water ripple passes near a whale, the whale, seeing the water glisten as it moves, thinks there will be food for it, and, moving quickly forward, strikes against the ship and often staves the ship in some part. And then the water entering through the hole runs to the bilge, which never remains filled with anything." Here Marco mentions a piece of nautical technology unknown to Europeans: a watertight hold. It was nothing short of an engineering marvel. "And then the sailors find out where the ship is staved, and then the hold that answers to the break is emptied into the others, for the water cannot pass from one hold to another, so strongly are they shut in; then they repair the ship and replace the goods that have been removed. They are nailed in such a way; for they are all lined, that is, two boards, one above the other, . . . [and] they are, in the common speech of our sailors, caulked both outside and inside, and they are nailed with iron pins."

Relying on his study of Arab shipbuilding methods, Marco describes a technique for making craft watertight, one that would have been of great interest to the shipbuilders of Venice's Arsenal. "They are not pitched with pitch, because they have none of it," he says. "I tell you that they take lime and hemp chopped fine, and they pound it all together, mixed with an oil from a tree. . . . And with this thing, they smear their ships, and this is worth quite as much as pitch."

Not only were the Arab ships better engineered and safer than their Western counterparts, they were so large that Marco could not resist another opportunity to dazzle his audience with statistics. The vessels were operated by between 150 and 300 sailors, and they carried far more cargo than anything afloat in Venice. Ships of bygone days had been larger still, before a series of storms, or what he termed "the violence of the sea," made harbors and coastlines too shallow to accommodate "those great ships, and so they are now made smaller; but they are [still] so large that they carry five thousand baskets of pepper, and some six thousand."

The great vessels also had "tenders" large enough to carry a thousand baskets of pepper. Flourishing his nautical expertise, Marco explains precisely how the tenders were deployed in this distant land: "They help to tow the great ship with ropes, that is, hawsers, when they are moved with oars, and also when they are moved with sails if the wind prevails rather from the beam, because the smaller go in front of the larger and tow it tied with ropes; but not if the wind blows straight, for the sails of the larger ship would prevent the wind from catching the sails of the smaller."

Such maneuvers were undertaken to bring the larger vessels in for refurbishing. "When the great ship . . . has sailed a year or more and needs repair, they . . . nail yet another board over the two all round the ship, and then there are three of them and they also caulk and oil it." This arduous procedure was repeated as necessary until there were six layers of boards, at which point "the ship is condemned and they sail no more in her on too high seas but [only] in near journeys and good weather." In the end, Marco says, "they dismantle and break them up."

DESPITE THEIR superior technology, the sailors of India slavishly followed bizarre nautical superstitions. Marco was startled to learn how they predicted the outcome of a voyage. A ship, a strong wind, and a hapless drunk were required.

"The men of the ship will have a hurdle, that is, a grating made of wickerwork, and at each corner and side of the hurdle will be tied a cord, so that there will be eight cords, and they will all be tied at the other end with a long rope," he explains. "They will find some stupid or drunken [man] and will bind him on the hurdle; for no wise or sane man would expose himself to that danger. When a strong wind prevails, they set up the hurdle opposite the wind, and the wind lifts the hurdle and carries it into the sky and the men hold it by a long rope. . . . If the hurdle makes for the sky, they say that the ship for which that proof has been made will make a quick and profitable voyage, and all the merchants flock to her for the sake of sailing and going with her. And if the hurdle has not been able to go up, no merchant will be willing to enter the ship for which the proof was made, because they say that she could not finish her voyage and many disasters would afflict her. So that ship stays in port that year." Marco notes this behavior as dispassionately as an ethnologist observing an unusual tribal custom.

Having seen and experienced so much more of the world than other Europeans, he brought a mature sense of judgment, tolerance, and skepticism to bear on his experiences in India, etched in bulletins from the farthest reaches of the globe.

INDONESIA

At the outset, Marco describes Indonesia as having eight kingdoms, six of which he visited, "namely, . . . the kingdoms of Ferlec, Basman, Sumatra, Dagroian, Lambri, and Fansur." Perhaps the most primitive was Basman, whose inhabitants had "no law except like beasts." He remarks, "They are claimed by the Great Khan, but they make him no tribute because they are so far off that the people of the Great Khan will not go there."

It was an enchanted kingdom, stocked with a varied bestiary including elephants, unicorns, "and specially of a kind of black goshawk." Once again, Marco's "unicorn" was the Asian rhinoceros, as his gruesome description makes clear: "It has the hair of the buffalo; it has the feet made like an elephant. It has one horn in the middle of its forehead very thick and black. And I tell you that it does no harm to men and beasts with its horn, but only with its tongue and knees, for on its tongue it has very long spines and sharp; so that when it wishes to hurt anyone it tramples and presses him down with the knees, afterward inflicting the harm with its tongue."

The "monkeys" of Basman were even more disturbing. "In this isle there is a kind of monkey which is very small and has a face that is altogether like the face of men, and they have other parts of the body resembling them. So they say these monkeys are men and deceive others." The monkeys provided cruel sport, according to Marco. "Now the men who are hunters take such monkeys as those and boil them and strip them all bare of all hair with a certain ointment, and fix and leave them the long hairs in the chin in place of beard and on the chest, and paint the skin with some color to make it like human skin. And when the skin is dry, the holes where the hairs are fixed are shrunken [so] that it seems as if they grew there naturally. And the feet and hands and the other limbs which are not quite like human limbs they stretch and reduce and fashion them by hand to the human likeness. Then they have them dried and put them in wooden molds with salt and smear them with saffron and with camphor and with other things that they may not decay, in such a way that they seem to have been men. And they sell them to merchants who carry them through the world for profit and give men to believe that there are men so small."

Marco was talking not about monkeys but about pygmies—"men so small"—generally defined as humans less than sixty inches tall. Although frequently associated with Africa, pygmy communities or their remains have been found in Indonesia and throughout Southeast Asia. Asian pygmies have been labeled Negritos, in contrast to the name given to the pygmies of Africa, Negrillos, but both names have lately fallen into disfavor. Even today, the origins of pygmies are not fully understood. It is believed, but has not been proven, that all pygmies share a common ancestry, and common DNA, and in general, pygmy communities remain apart from the dominant community in which they live.

Sumatra.

The monsoon season arrived with him, to his dismay: "I myself, Marco Polo, stayed with my companions for about five months because of the unfavorable weather which we had, which forced me to stay there, and contrary winds which did not let us go our way."

During his layover, Marco remained confined with two thousand other stranded travelers, who took up residence in five temporary wooden structures—"there is much timber here," he explains. He asserts that he assumed a leadership role in defending the travelers against rising floodwaters during those five rain-sodden months. But Marco had assigned phantom heroic roles to himself in the past, and may have done so in this case. "Toward the island I caused great ditches to be dug round us," he says, "of which the ends finished on either side upon the shore of the sea, for fear of beasts and of those bad beast-like men"—ravenous cannibals, it seems—"who gladly catch and kill and eat men."

With the crisis behind him, Marco reveals that experienced merchants traded at a safe distance with the cannibals for food and other necessities for survival, especially rice and fish, for which he exhibited a fondness born of the fear of starvation, declaring it "the best fish in the world." He passed the time drinking the local wine to ease the boredom and fear. "They have a kind of tree of which they cut off the branches," he notes, "and from the branches flows water . . . which is wine. One puts a trough or very large jar at the stump that is left on the tree where the branch is cut off, just as they catch the sap of the vines. . . . Those branches drop [wine] very quickly, and in a day and night it is filled, and it is very good wine to drink, like our local wine."

Dagroian.

When the rainy season ended, Marco groggily exchanged the shelter of wine-producing trees for the road leading to the next kingdom. There he came across appalling rituals for dealing with the sick, who were examined by "magicians"—seers who predicted whether the afflicted "must recover or die."

The lucky ones were spared any further attention, and left to recover, but those pronounced doomed were subjected to a primitive form of euthanasia, followed by a banquet of cannibalism: "Some of these men who know how to kill sick persons most easily and gently come and press down the sick man who will soon be dead and . . . suffocate him immediately, and kill him before the time of his death. And when he is dead they cut him up and have him skillfully cooked. All the relations of the dead come and have a friendly feast together and eat him up stump and rump after he is cooked and roasted."

Marco recorded these customs in horrifying detail, conveying the cannibals' reverence, and perhaps fear, of the souls of the dead. "They eat and suck out also the marrow inside the bones, leaving no moisture or fat in them at all," he goes on. "They do this because they do not wish any atom of him to remain, so that it may not decay. For they say that if there were to remain any substance in the bones, that it would make worms, and the worms would die at last for want of food. . . . After they have eaten him, they take the bones and put them in a casket of stone, and then they carry them and hang them in great caves of the mountains in such a place that no beast or other evil thing could touch them."

Marco proclaims his revulsion: "This is a very evil way and bad custom, and so it is a very cruel and evil people."

Fansur.

As he recounts his travels through Indonesia, Marco ceases to extol the grandeur of the Mongol Empire and concentrates on his preoccu-

pation with food. By the time he arrived in the kingdom of Fansur—
the word means "camphor"—he was so ravenous that he ignored the
region's celebrated natural resource in favor of bread made from the
sago palm. Preparing it was simple enough: the locals opened the trunk
of a mature sago and ground the pulp into a starchy substance that they
washed, sieved, pulverized, and then baked into dense, nearly tasteless
loaves that he claims were "very good to eat." In fact, he says, "the
bread of that flour is like barley bread and of that taste."

He invites his readers to visualize him feasting at last: "I, Master
Marco Polo who saw all this, tell you that we ourselves tried it sufficiently, for we often ate them [the loaves]." He became so enamored of
sago flour that he gathered a supply to take with him on his travels. "I
took some of this flour to Venice with me," he confides, but it is difficult to imagine Venetians sharing his enthusiasm for it.

CEYLON

"Noble and good rubies are produced in this island," Marco has heard.
Even more enticing, "the king of this province has the most beautiful
ruby in all the world." Marco describes it with authority, because, he
says, "I, Marco Polo, was one of the ambassadors and saw the said ruby
with my eyes; and when that lord was holding it in his closed hand, it
projected below and above the fist, which the lord put to his eyes and
to his mouth." Marco makes the ruby sound larger still: "It is about a
large palm long and quite as thick as the arm of a man. And it is the
most splendid thing in the world to see. It has no flaw in it. It is red like
fire."

Kublai Khan had declared that he must have it, and so, Marco
reports, "the Great Khan sent his messengers to this king, . . . saying
that he wished to buy this ruby, and that if he would give it to him, he
would have the value of a city given him for it." It would not be easy to
obtain the ruby, for "the king of Seilan said that he would not give it
for anything in the world, because he said that it belonged to his ancestors, and for this reason he couldn't have it"—words that Kublai Khan
could not tolerate or understand.

With stories such as these, Marco acknowledges that even Kublai
Khan, the mightiest ruler in the world, was mortal, and, even more
painful, was rapidly losing his powers.

INDIA AND THE GULF OF ADEN

Maabar.

Here, in "the noblest and most rich [province] in the world," Marco felt that he was in his element, for once. He found himself among wealthy merchants trading for pearls, which could be found in the shallow waters just off the mainland. "In all this gulf there is no water more than ten or twelve paces deep, and in some places there is some that is not more than two paces. In this gulf the best pearls are taken," he reports. Drawing on his experience with the precious commodity, Marco explains the process of harvesting and selling pearls, all of it little changed from the earliest accounts two thousand years before. "There will be several merchants who will form a company and agreement together and will take a large ship specially fitted out for this on which each by himself will have a room fitted and furnished for him, and in it a tub full of water and other necessary things."

During the short harvesting season, April to May, the ships sailed to a "place where the scallops are found in greater number, which is called Bettala, which is on firm land. And from there they go into the sea . . . , sixty miles straight toward midday, where they cast their anchors, and then from their large ships enter into those small barques. . . . There will be many ships like this"—as many as eight thousand, according to other contemporaneous accounts—"because it is true that there are many merchants who pay attention to this fishing; and they make many companies. All the merchants who are associated on one ship will have several boats that will tow the ship through the gulf. The small boats carry the anchors of the large boats to land. They [employ] many men who can swim well, clever pearl-fishers for hire, with whom they make agreement by the month; that is, they give them so much for the whole month of April till mid-May or so long as the fishery lasts in the gulf."

Harvesting posed hazards, especially "great fishes" ready to strike and kill the fishermen. The merchants protected themselves with "magicians" known as "braaman, who with their enchantments and diabolical art control and stupefy those fishes so they can hurt no one. Because this fishing is done by day and not by night, those magicians make spells by day that they break for the following night."

At last "the ship is anchored and the men who are in the small barques . . . leave the barques and go under the water some four paces and some five, up to twelve, and stay under water as long as ever they can; and when they are at the bottom of the sea, they find on it scallops that men call sea oysters, and bring them up in a little bag of net tied to the body."

Marco proceeds to describe the timeless process of extracting pearls: "These scallops are indeed split and are put in the aforesaid tubs full of water that are on the ships, for the pearls are found in the flesh of those scallops. And while they stay in the water of the tub, those bodies decompose and rot and are made like the white of an egg, and then they float at the top and the pearls stay on the bottom clean." When Marco avers that "the pearls that are found in this sea are distributed through all the world," he does not exaggerate.

The inhabitants of Maabar adorned themselves lavishly with the pearls they acquired. At times, that was *all* they wore. "There is no need of a tailor or stitcher to cut and sew cloth because they go naked at all times of the year," Marco notes, with the exception that "they cover their natural parts with a little cloth." The king of the realm was distinguished by a broad gold collar studded with "large and beautiful pearls and . . . precious stones," including rubies, sapphires, and emeralds. From his collar hung a long "cord of thin silk" strung with exactly 104 choice pearls and rubies, the number of precious stones determined by the 104 prayers the wearer uttered each day. The king also wore pearl-studded golden bracelets—"a marvel to see"—covering his arms and legs, and even his fingers and toes. Marco estimated these gems to be "worth more than a good city." The king jealously guarded his treasures, "commanding that all those who have beautiful pearls and good stones must bring them to the court; and that he will have twice as much as the cost." The offer enticed merchants like Marco, as well as the king's subjects, to "take them gladly to the court because they are well paid."

As always, sexual excess preoccupied the Venetian, who revealed that the king had five hundred wives. "As soon as he sees a beautiful lady or girl then he wishes her for himself and takes her to wife," Marco states. "In this kingdom are women very beautiful of themselves; and besides this they make themselves beautiful in the face and in the whole body."

Despite the ease with which he acquired wives, this privileged king had resorted to an "unfitting" deed to win a "very beautiful woman" who happened to be his brother's wife. Undaunted, the king "took her from him [his brother] by force and kept her many days for himself. His brother, who was a prudent man and wise, showed no sign but suffered him in peace and made no quarrel with him." There was an extraordinary reason for his reticence: "He was many times on the point of stirring up war against him because he [the king] had taken his wife from him, but their mother used to show them her breasts and say, 'If you stir up a quarrel between you, I shall cut off my breasts that nourished you.' And so the trouble was stayed."

The king had much else to occupy his thoughts—countless children, for one thing, and a large, fanatically devoted retinue of servants. Coming of age when the legacy of feudalism still retained its power, Marco understood the bond between lords and servants—after all, he had been the vassal of Kublai Khan for nearly two decades—but the ties between this king and his servants were another thing entirely, as Marco relates. "When the king dies and his body is burnt in a great fire, then . . . many of the company and also of all these barons who were his faithful ones . . . throw themselves into the fire together with the king of their free will, and are burnt with the king to bear him company in the other world; for they say that since they have been his companions in this world, they ought to be so and to serve their lord in the other, also." This startling custom afforded Marco his first exposure to suttee, widely practiced through the world he now explored. "When a man is dead and his body is being burnt, his wife throws herself on the fire herself and lets herself burn with her lord," he marvels, adding that the "ladies who do this are much praised," while those who refrained from self-immolation invited scorn.

The kingdom's approach to criminal behavior diverged sharply from Western conventions as well. "When a man has done a crime such that he must die and that the lord wishes to have him killed, then he who must be killed says that he wishes to kill himself for the honor and for the love of such an idol. The king tells him he is quite willing for this."

Marco depicted the ritual punishment that followed with macabre flourishes: "All the relations and the friends of this one who must kill himself take him and put him on a chair and give him twelve swords or knives well ground and sharp, and tie them round his neck, and carry him through all the city, and go saying and crying, 'This very valiant man is going to kill himself for the love, honor, and reverence of such an idol.' " When the procession comes to a halt at the appointed place, "then he who must die takes a knife and cries with a loud voice, 'I kill myself for the love of such an idol.' After he has said these words, he strikes himself with the knife in the middle of the belly. . . . He gives himself so many blows with these knives that he kills himself." In another version, perhaps even more gruesome, he places the knife "at the back of his head and drawing it violently to him cuts through his own neck, for that knife is very well sharpened, and dies in the very act."

Having shocked his audience, Marco offhandedly comments, "When he is killed, his relations burn the body with great joy and with great festivity, thinking that he is fortunate."

Madness, he implied with a stern Venetian squint, resided in the eye of the beholder.

MARCO ALSO ACQUAINTED his audience with the curious *ciugi,* or yogis, devout Indians distinguished by their "great abstinence" and the "strong and hard life" they led for "love of their idols."

Their appearance was arresting: "They go naked without wearing anything above so that their natural parts are not covered, nor any member." Marco says that they worshipped the ox and most of them carried "a little ox of copper or of bronze gilded in the middle of their foreheads." They burned ox dung, then anointed themselves with the ashes "with great reverence . . . as Christians do with holy water." They ate nothing green, believing that all living things, including plants and leaves, have souls, and they slept naked on the ground "without keeping anything whatever in the world neither below nor above." It was a "great wonder" they did not all die from the practice. To complete the harshness of their lives, "they fast all the years and drink water and nothing else."

The yogis confronted sexuality in their "churches" or "abbeys," where they enacted bizarre rites that Marco describes with lascivious relish. When one of their number who served their "idols" died, the candidates for successor entered the abbey and tested their steely self-control against the warm, sweet caresses of various maidens. "They [the maidens] touch them both here and there in many parts of the body," Marco says, and "they embrace and kiss them and put them in the greatest pleasure in the world. . . . If his member is not moved at all except as it was before the maidens touch him, this one is counted

good and pure and they keep him with them, and he serves the idols."
As for a candidate unable to resist the maidens' touch, "if his member
is moved and rises, this one they do not keep at all but drive him away
immediately from the fellowship of the monks for ever and say they
refuse to keep a man of self-indulgence with them."

OBSERVING THESE outlandish customs, Marco neither judged them
nor recoiled in horror. He remained objective, if baffled, always
absorbed by the astonishing variety of behavior on display in the
provinces through which he traveled. Beneath the welter of observations he offered his audience, he moved ever farther from the touch-
stone of his youth, Christianity, into the realm of Buddhism.

He fastened on Saint Thomas, one of the twelve apostles, as the
chief point of comparison between Christianity and Buddhism. In
both Aramaic and Greek, the saint's name means "twin," and John
11:16 identifies him as "Thomas who was called the Twin." Alone
among the disciples, Thomas doubted news of the Resurrection—this
is the origin of the phrase "doubting Thomas." (Only when Thomas
touched Jesus's wounds did he become a fervent believer.) The subject
of a large body of apocryphal literature, including the Acts of Thomas,
he was said to have been martyred in AD 53 in Madras, India, on what
later came to be known as Mount Thomas.

As Marco traveled through India, his thoughts turned occasionally
to this martyr as to no other figure in Christianity. "The body of Master Saint Thomas the Apostle, who endured martyrdom for Christ in
the province, is buried in . . . Maabar . . . in a little town, for there are
no men at all, and few merchants, nor do merchants come there
because there is no merchandise that they could well take away from it,
and also because the place is much out of the way." So Marco heard, and
he could not resist going there. Years before, in Armenia, he had missed
what he believed was his chance to confirm the presence of Noah's Ark
on Mount Ararat; now he had an opportunity to confirm the existence
of an apostle, and this time he was determined to pursue it.

He made the pilgrimage in the company of both Christians and
Muslims. "I tell you the Saracens of that country have great faith in
him and say that he was a Saracen"—an affecting but illogical assertion, because Thomas's life and works predated Islam by several
centuries. Nevertheless, those Saracens "say that he was a very great

prophet and call him *aviarun* in their tongue, which means 'holy man.' " Marco's confusion about Thomas's identity may reflect a blending of religious traditions in the region, or it may reveal his own misunderstanding of what he had been told.

No matter who the "holy man" had been in life, his burial place was rife with mystery and miracles. Trees produced nuts—Marco calls them "Pharaoh's Nuts"—that furnished both food and drink. "They have an outside shell on which there are as it were threads that are used in many things and avail for many purposes. Under that first shell is a food on which a man feeds sufficiently. It is indeed very savory and sweet as sugar, white as milk, and is made cup shaped like the outer shell. And in the middle of that food is so much water that a phial would be filled, which water is clear and cold and of a very perfect taste," says Marco, plainly amazed. The mysterious nuts were, of course, coconuts.

The very earth, rich and red, contained magical healing properties. "The Christians who go there on pilgrimage take of the earth of the place where the holy body of Saint Thomas was killed and reverently carry that earth into their country and give a little of this earth, mixed with water or other liquid, to the sick to drink when he might have quartan fever or tertian fever"—that is, malaria—"and as soon as the sick man drinks it he is healed by the power of God and of the saint."

Marco declares that he himself "carried some of this earth to Venice with him and healed many with it." Marco the merchant did not assume the mantle of healer naturally. While it is entirely possible that he returned to Venice with a sample of the magical soil, there are no reports of his employing it to cure others, nor was it listed among his effects. More likely, his amanuensis Rustichello or a pious translator of the manuscript added this flourish to portray Marco as a man of faith.

HE WAS, IN FACT, BECOMING more spiritually inclined. No longer did Marco Polo dismiss the hundreds, and then thousands, of images of Buddha he encountered—wooden statues, stone carvings, illustrations—as idols. Now he plunged into the history of this singular figure in an attempt to fathom the Buddha's mysterious appeal.

The first stirrings of Buddhist sympathies in Marco may have come from his contact with the Mongols, who were succumbing to Buddhism in ever-increasing numbers. They had originally encountered it from their neighbors to the west, the Uighurs, but the Uighurs' version of Buddhism issued not from India but from Tibet. Steeped in magic rituals, this form spread east along the Silk Road to Cambulac and reached Kublai Khan, who endorsed it, as he did the other major belief systems in his empire. In India, Marco encountered a more ancient form of Buddhism, and he found it intoxicating. Ever the chameleon, he altered his persona once more: Marco the Mongol became Marco the Buddhist.

MARCO SET HIMSELF the task of educating his Western audience about the Buddha's significance. The traveler's portrayal of his encounter with Buddha conveyed a suggestion of destiny, as if Marco had come all this distance to meet the great teacher who would bestow a sense of purpose and clarity upon his wayfaring. The Buddha's coming of age resembled Marco's, and the Venetian merchant naturally identified with the spiritual journey of the Indian sage. Marco offered an account of the Buddha's life that was drastically simplified, yet heartfelt rather than dismissive or condescending. He provided his earliest audiences with their first exposure to the Buddha and the Buddhist mystique.

Marco called the Buddha by an unusual name: Sagamoni Burcan, "the Divine Buddha." The first part is his transcription of S'akyamouni, a Sanscrit term meaning "the religious saint of the royal family of S'akya." The second part comes from a Mongol term, *burkhan*, meaning "god," "divine being," or "saint."

"This Sagamoni was the first man to whose name idols were made," Marco explains, proceeding to describe him as "the most holy and best man who ever was among them."

Marco continues: "He was the son of a great king, both rich and powerful. And this his son was of so good life that he did not wish to hear any worldly thing, nor did he wish to be king. And when his father saw his son did not wish to be king . . . he was [in] very great vexation at it. He offered him a very great offering, for he told him that he would crown him king of the kingdom and he should be lord of it at his pleasure.

"His son indeed said that he wanted nothing. And when his father saw that he did not wish to rule in any way in the world, he had so great vexation in it that he nearly died of grief. It was no wonder, because he had no more sons than this one, nor had he any to whom he should leave the kingdom after his death. The king after deep thought . . . made him move into a very beautiful palace and gave him thirty thousand very beautiful and winning maidens to serve him, and commanded them to play with him all day and all night, promising the one who would be first to induce him to lie with her that she would be his wife and queen."

The maidens did as ordered. They played, danced, and sang. They "served him at table and made him company all day." And still the son refused to be moved to "any act of self-indulgence" and continued to lead a virtuous life and retain his singular innocence. "I tell you," Marco says, "that he was so delicate a young man that he had never gone out of the palace of his father in his youth nor had ever seen a dead man nor any other who was not sound in his limbs, for the father let no old and no decrepit man go before him." That state of innocence could not endure.

"Now it happened that this young man, having leave of his father to go out with a very fine company, was riding one day along the road through the city and then he saw a dead man whom they were carrying to bury, and he had many people following. He became all dismayed at it. So he asked immediately of those who were with him what thing it was, and they told him it was a dead man.

" 'What?' said the son of the king. 'Do all men die?'

" 'Yes, truly,' they said.

"Then the young man said nothing and rode on very thoughtful. After this, he had not ridden far before he found a very old man bent down with age who could not walk and had no teeth in [his] mouth, but had lost them all through great old age. . . . The youth said, 'How from youths do they become old and bent like this?' To whom the servants answered, 'Sir, all those who live long in this world must become old like this man and then die.' And then, when the son of the king had well understood about the dead and about the old, he went back to his palace frightened and all astonished."

Marco recounts this story with more conviction and precision than he brought to other spiritual episodes. Of all the legends he heard during his travels, the story of the young son's response to the death and decay of the world around him had the greatest resonance. He continues: "He went off to the mountains very great and out of the way seeking still the rough and wildest places and stayed there all the days of his life very uprightly and chastely, and led a hard life, living on roots and herbs and wild fruits and made very great abstinence, just as if he had been a Christian."

For Marco, this account of the privileged young son's life marked the point of contact between East and West, between the Christian faith and the Buddhist worldview. More than that, it prompted him to dare to elevate the central Buddhist system to the same level as Christianity, as heretical as that idea would seem in Venice. Nevertheless, he hammers the point home: "For truly, if he had been Christian he would have been a great saint with our Lord Jesus Christ for the good life and pure that he led."

Marco pauses, and then brings the story to its conclusion: "When this son of the king died, he was carried to the king, his father. When he saw him dead, whom he loved more than himself, there was no need to ask if he has vexation and grief; he almost went out of his senses. He made great mourning, with bitter lamentation of all the people. Then he had an image made in his likeness all of gold and precious stones and made it honored by those of the land with the greatest reverence and worshipped as their god."

A change in the narrative's pitch signals that although Marco was willing to embrace the Buddha, he remained skeptical concerning the doctrine of reincarnation: "They said that he was God, and they say it still, and also that he was dead for eighty-four times; for they say that when he died the first time that he became a man, and then he revived and became an ox, and revived and became a horse, and thence an ass, and so they say that he died eighty-four times, and every time they say that he became an animal, either a dog or other thing, but at the eighty-fourth time they say he died and became a god; and him the idolaters hold for the best god and for the greatest that they have."

MARCO'S VERSION of Buddhism was heavily influenced by the Mongol interpretation of the Buddha as a potent source of magic. But Marco also put a personal slant on the Buddhist traditions he encountered in India, seeking both an idealized father figure who would not abandon him as his own father had done years before, and a cynosure who transcended the carnality and mortality of Kublai Khan. Ever elusive, the Buddha filled this exalted role, and appreciation of Buddhist precepts liberated Marco from his past.

In the realm of the Buddha, nothing was shocking or blasphemous—

a change in perspective that marked the first revolution in Marco's consciousness since his illness in the poppy fields of Afghanistan. This time, his enlightenment was entirely natural, yet bewildering. He verges on confessing that, for once, language is inadequate to explain his expansion of consciousness. In India, his powers of description lag behind his experience. No longer does he relive his adventures for the benefit of his readers, performing the task of imagining for them. Instead, he offers sketches for an uncompleted canvas. He seems to be soul-searching and thinking aloud rather than re-creating his experiences for one and all. All the glorious battles and alluring concubines on which he had lavished attention fade in significance before the spiritual journey unfolding before him and his newest, and greatest, discovery: himself.

IN HIS ACCOUNT of Ceylon, Marco had referred in passing to a steep, inaccessible mountain at whose peak stood a "monument" to Adam, or so he had heard from both Christians and Muslims. But after paying lip service to this traditional interpretation, he immediately moved on to the Buddhists' interpretation of the "sepulcher." No matter who was commemorated in this remote location, all faiths agreed that it consisted of the "teeth and the hairs and the bowl"—that is, the food bowl—of a venerable figure. Marco carefully noted that he did not agree with those who insisted Adam's remains would be found there, "for our scripture of the holy Church says that he is in another part of the world. The decision of this I wish to leave to others."

In 1281, Kublai Khan learned from Muslims who had visited this mountaintop that the remains of Adam could be found there. "He says therefore to himself that it is necessary for him to have the teeth and the bowl and the hair." This wish, no matter how unrealistic, was in keeping with Kublai Khan in his dotage. As he did on many other occasions, "he sent an embassy to the king of the island of Ceylon to ask for these things." It was just the kind of expedition that Marco himself might have been selected to join, if at that point he had not been maneuvering to go home, and he describes it with an insider's appreciation.

Three years later, the emissaries reached their quarry. As Marco relates, "[They] exerted themselves so much that at last they have the two molar teeth which were very thick and large, and again they had some of the hair and the bowl in which he [the revered person] used to eat. The bowl was of very beautiful green porphyry. When the messengers of the Great Khan had these things of which I have told you, they set themselves on the road and go back to their lord. When they were near to the great town of Cambulac, where the Great Khan was, they made him know that they were coming and bringing the holy things for which he had sent them." Kublai received the items gratefully, and paid particular attention to the bowl, having heard that if food for just one person was placed in it, "five men would have enough from it." Seeking proof, he ordered it filled with a portion fit for one, and then declared that it did, indeed, feed five—or so Marco says. He tells the story of the magical bowl with obvious skepticism, although he refrains from labeling Kublai Khan as credulous, even while raising the possibility.

WHEREVER MARCO TRAVELED along India's coast, the "fervent heat" tormented him. "The sun is so hot that one can scarcely bear it there," he complains. "Even the water is so hot that if you were to put an egg into some river when the sun is shining brightly on it, it would be cooked before you were gone at all far, just as in boiling water." Despite the oppressive climate, merchant ships from the four corners of the earth converged to trade.

Exotic and terrifying creatures populated the region, and they were "different from all the others in the world," according to Marco. There were "black lions" (probably panthers); beautiful "parrots" as white as snow, with red beaks and feet (Marco apparently had another bird in mind, for which he lacked a name); peacocks larger than any to be found in Venice; hens bigger and better than any he had ever encountered; and fruit, the likes of which he had never seen, and which he could not name. For once, the variety of flora and fauna rendered Marco Polo speechless.

Melibar.

Upon reaching this "great kingdom to the west," Marco posts an urgent warning concerning the scourge of pirates. He denounces them as "great robbers of the sea" and describes their modus operandi, apparently from anxious personal experience: "Most of the ships of these evil corsairs are parted hither and thither to wait for and find ships of the merchants who pass by." He says that they are so adept at catching their prey that "no merchant ship may pass that is not taken, for they go together in companies of twenty or of thirty ships of these corsairs and form a great line on the sea." Anchored about five miles apart, "twenty pirate corsairs control over one hundred miles of open water with this strategy."

The hunt went on day and night. "As soon as they [the pirates] see any merchant ship they make a light of fire or smoke for a signal, and they all collect together and go there hard and take everything." The cargo consisted of items as varied and valuable as copper (used for ballast), silk, and pepper, spikenard, cloves, and other spices concealed aboard the unlucky ships. As a merchant, Marco realizes that his colleagues "know well the way of these evil corsairs and know well they are bound to find them," so "they go many together and so well armed and so well prepared that they have no fear of them when they find them, for they defend themselves bravely and very often do them great harm."

Occasionally, the pirates ensnared one of the merchant vessels, taking the goods aboard but sparing the lives of the men, whom they taunted by saying, "Go home to gain some other goods, so you will give them to us again!"

Goçurat.

Here the pirates were even more "cruel and evil" than elsewhere. Cringing with empathy for the victims, Marco tells how they "seize the merchants and beside taking the goods from them, torture them and put a ransom on their persons; and if they do not quickly pay the ransom, they give them so great torments that many die of it."

Nothing that Marco had seen, not even among the Mongols, notorious for their savagery, affected him as deeply as the reports of the torments inflicted on merchants by Arab pirates. Waxing increasingly indignant on the part of his fellow merchants, he describes the lengths to which the merchants would go to prevent their tormentors from succeeding. If they are carrying pearls and other precious stones, he says, "they swallow them that they may not be snatched from them by the pirates," and thus manage to keep some of their goods.

But the pirates are "infected with evilness," Marco warns, "for you may know that when these wicked corsairs take some ship of the merchants and find no stones and pearls, they give them to drink a certain drug called tamarind and seawater, so that the merchants go much below and pass or vomit all that they have in belly."

A long-lived, massive tree, the tamarind is distinguished by graceful, feathery dark-green foliage that withdraws by night. Lost in this profusion are the tamarind's flowers, which harbor abundant cinnamon-brown pods that are as long as a banana and contain acidic flesh and soft seeds. As they mature, the pods fill out, the juicy, acidulous pulp turns brown or reddish-brown, and the seeds harden. Tamarind is used as a staple in Indian food and medicine, and the pirates described by Marco made it into a powerful purgative. The seawater the merchants ingested caused them to vomit, bringing up some of the items they may have swallowed, while any items that had passed farther down the alimentary canal mixed with the tamarind bulk and passed out in the stool.

"The corsairs have all that the merchants pass collected and have it searched to see if there are pearls or any other precious stones," Marco explains, with mingled sympathy and disgust. "The merchants can in no way escape without losing everything if they were taken." Either way, the pirates claimed their loot and inflicted a humiliating lesson on the merchants in the process. "Now you have seen . . . great malice," Marco snorts, as he considers these maritime thugs.

Tana.

Marco implies that he has visited the place, without insisting on it. His casual handling of his sources of information becomes increasingly apparent as he traces his course through India, relying ever more heavily on secondhand information. Whether or not he stretched a point to include it in his travels, Tana suited his theme: the dangers of piracy to merchants and the India trade, otherwise so profitable. Here pepper and incense abounded, as did buckram and cotton. "Great trade is done there and ships and merchants go there in plenty," he informs his public, "and the merchants who come there with their ships bring and carry in with them several things; these are gold, silver, and brass, and many other things that are necessary to the kingdom from which they trust to profit and gain."

Here, too, pirates infested the waters, earning another rebuke from the Venetian: "Many corsairs come out from this kingdom, who go about the sea doing great harm to the merchants." Oddly, they plied their nefarious trade in collusion with the king of Tana, in exchange for horses, which his kingdom needed. "The king has made this agreement with the corsairs that they are pledged to give him all the horses that they take." At the same time, "all other goods, both gold and silver and precious stones, belong to the corsairs." In the face of this corruption, damaging to merchants throughout India, the Venetian could only lament, ". . . this is an evil thing, and it is not kingly work."

Socotra.

Marco's yearning for the sea, and, by extension, the voyage home, prompted him to sail across the Indian Ocean to the island of Socotra, at the entrance to the Gulf of Aden.

Part of an archipelago of much smaller islands, Socotra seems to stand alone as it rises out of the sea on massive coral banks. Home to an ecosystem that had been isolated for millions of years, the island held many biological rarities. The Venetian had just entered a biologist's dream in which about one-third of the plants and animals surrounding him were found there and only there; the unique specimens included land crabs living at more than two thousand feet above sea level, rare birds, and a profusion of exotic reptiles. The most celebrated of the island's flora was the Dragon's Tree, whose astringent resin was used to treat wounds. So impressed was Marco by the island's flora and fauna, its giant lizards and fanlike Dragon Trees standing in isolation against the infinite sky, that he came to declare it "the most enchanted place on earth."

To his delight, Marco discovered that this remote but strategically located outpost supported thriving tuna and whaling industries, which appealed to his mercantile instincts. The whale was well known, if poorly understood, in Europe. For centuries, the giant mammal had furnished meat, blubber, and teeth to northern Europeans. Whalebone was especially prized for fashioning weaving tools, gaming pieces, and chopping blocks. In the eleventh century, an Arab traveler wandering far from home discovered that people living on the islands off the coast of England used whale bones, not wood, for construction. Whaling was a popular pursuit in Scandinavia as well as Ireland.

Marco explains how Arabs caught their whales, and how merchants turned a handsome profit from the creature's by-products. He begins with the procedure for preparing tuna, used as bait. "The tuna is very fat, and they cut it into pieces and place it in large vases or jars and put in salt and make much brine," he says. "This done, there will be perhaps twelve who will take a small ship and, putting on board this fish with all the brine or salt broth of the fish, will go out to sea. And then they will have some remnants of torn pieces or of other cast-off things, and they will soak these leavings tied in a bundle in the brine that will be very fat, and afterward they will throw them into the water; and they will be tied to the little ship with a rope. They will then hoist sail and will go all day wandering through the high seas hither and thither; and wherever they pass the fat that is in the brine leaves as it were a path on the water."

Marco was astonished by the whale's endurance—"If it happens that they pass by a place where a whale is, or by some means the whale perceives the scent of the fat of the tuna, [the whale] follows that track . . . for a hundred miles"—and its vulnerability. When the hunters reached their elusive prey and threw it "two or three pieces of tuna," the whale, on devouring the bait, was "immediately made drunk as a man is made drunken with wine."

The bravest whale hunters clambered out of their craft onto the back of the slippery wet beast and attempted to balance themselves. One held a "stake of iron barbed at the end so that if it is fixed in, it cannot be pulled out because of the barb." At the first opportunity, one of the hunters "will put the stake on the head of the whale and another will strike the stake with a wooden mallet and will immediately fix it all in the head of the whale. For the whale through drunkenness hardly feels the men who stand on it, so that they can do whatever they wish."

By "stake," Marco meant a harpoon; once it was fixed, the stage was set for the wildest of rides. "When the whale plunges and flees, it drags the boat to which the rope is tied after it. If it seems to succeed in drawing the boat downward too much, then another barrel with another flag is thrown out, because it cannot draw the barrels under water, and so it is so tired by dragging them after it that in the end it is weakened by the wound and dies."

At the moment of the whale's death, the small vessel following the beast approached; the men tied the whale securely to their craft and towed it to "their island or to one that is near them, where they sold it. They took the ambergris"—a waxy excretion of the whale's intestines—"out of the belly," and "many butts of oil from the head." Marco estimated that one whale produced a thousand pounds of oil.

Whale by-products were just one feature of Socotra's abundant marketplace. In the course of his strolls along the waterfront, Marco noted

Marco Polo's vivid and occasionally misinterpreted descriptions of his travels
inspired this medieval artist to depict dragons in China.
(Granger)

A rendering of the city of Pagan,
whose gold and silver towers so impressed Marco Polo
(Imageworks)

Kublai Khan attacks his rival, Nayan.
(AKG)

Right: Kublai Khan's mighty fleet tried to extend the
Mongol Empire with repeated attempts to conquer
Korea and Japan, but came to grief.
(Corbis)

Saint Thomas, whose exile fascinated Marco Polo, in a
dramatic portrait by Caravaggio (1601–1602)
(Bridgeman)

A European depiction of a Mongolian ship foundering at sea.
Marco barely escaped with his life from a shipwreck during
his journey home.
(Bibliothèque Nationale de France)

Marco Polo's last will.
In his careful allocation
of resources, he proved to
be a diligent merchant
until his final hour.
(Bridgeman)

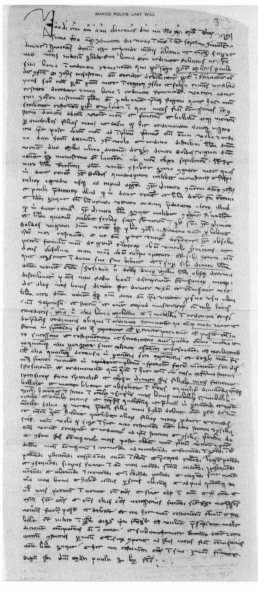

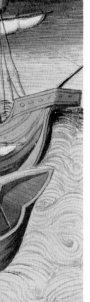

Left: Mongol forces attempt to take Japan in this illustration
from the *Book of Marvels*. Until Marco Polo wrote of the epochal
struggle at sea, Europe knew nothing of it.
(Bridgeman)

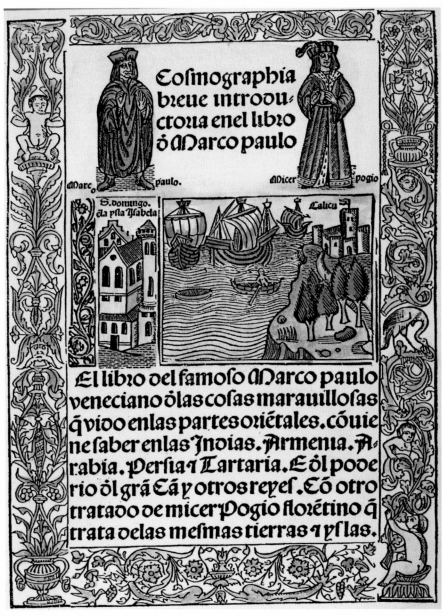

Cosmographia breue introdu-ctoria enel libro ὸ Marco paulo

Marco paulo. Micer pogio.

S. domingo. ὸla ꝑ́la Ꝺ́sabela. Calicu.

El libro del famoso Marco paulo veneciano ὸlas cosas marauillosas ꝗ vido enlas partes orie̅tales. co̅uie ne saber enlas Jndias. Armenia. A-rabia. Persia ꝗ Tartaria. E ὸl pode rio ὸl gra̅ Ca̅ y otros reyes. Co̅ otro tratado de micer Pogio flore̅tino ꝗ trata delas mesmas tierras ꝗ yslas.

Frontispiece of an early published edition
of Marco Polo's *Travels*

(Granger)

Frontispiece of an early
published edition of
Marco Polo's *Travels*,
Nuremberg, Germany,
1477
(Granger)

Fra Mauro's renowned map
of the world (1459) drew on
Marco Polo's account
(Corbis)

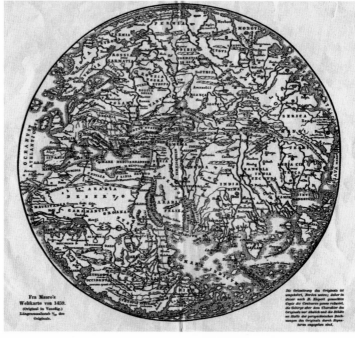

Venice in the eighteenth century, by the prolific artist
Canaletto (Giovanni Antonio Canal)
(Art Resource)

that "many ships come to this island with many merchants and with many wares that they sell in this island, and carry away again with them of the things that are in the island, of which they make great gain and profit." Amid the abundance, piracy flourished openly: "Corsairs come to this island with their ships when they have made their cruise, and make camp there and sell all the things that they have stolen at sea." Most everyone on the scene knew about the pirates, and most everyone looked the other way, including Christians who were aware that "all those things are robbed from idolaters and from Saracens." At the same time, Marco says, the Christians "hold that they can lawfully buy them all gladly," and so they financed the pirates whom they condemned.

In these lawless waters, magicians, charmers, and necromancers all practiced their versions of extortion, meeting with much criticism but little interference. The archbishop himself "does not wish them to do those enchantments and forbids as much as he can and chastises and admonishes them for it, and says it is a sin." But, Marco adds with a sigh of resignation, "it avails nothing because they say that their ancestors did them of old." And so the archbishop "bears with it so far." Even the threat of excommunication had no effect on the necromancers' practice of black arts.

According to popular belief, which Marco uncritically repeats, the magicians dared to defy the pirates: "If any of the pirates were to cause any loss to the island, they detain them with their enchantments so their ships can never freely leave this island till that which was taken has been wholly replaced. I tell you that if a ship may be going with sails set and have a good wind and fair enough on her way, they will make another contrary wind come to her and will make her turn back to the island." These enchanters could just as easily quiet the sea, or, if it suited their fancy, summon a devastating storm.

To ADVANCE HIS ACCOUNT, Marco Polo increasingly drew on information gathered from reasonably reliable sources such as merchants, traders, and local officials during his coastal travels, rather than on personal experience. Although he did not set foot in them, the regions with elaborate mating and marital customs, and varieties of worship, seem designed to appeal to his lurid taste and overheated imagination, especially the pair of islands known as Male and Female.

Male, he informs his readers with as much confidence as he can muster, was a Christian land populated mostly by men. "When [an inhabitant's] wife is pregnant, he does not touch her afterward until she has given birth, and from the time when she has given birth he leaves her again without touching her for forty days. But from forty days onward he touches her at his pleasure. . . . I tell you," Marco asserts, "that their wives do not live in this island, nor any other ladies, but they all live in the other island that is called Female. And you may know that the women never come to the island of the men, but when it comes to the month of March the men of this island go off to this island of Women and remain there for three months, these are March, April, and May." During that time, the men "take great enjoyment and pleasure" with their wives, then afterward they return to their bachelor quarters on Male Island, to "plant, harvest, and sell their produce."

The islands were about thirty miles apart, and couples learned to incorporate child rearing into their domestic arrangements. "Their children which are born to their mothers nourish in their island, and if it is a girl, then the mother keeps her there till she is of the age to be married, and then at the season marries her to one of the men of the island. Yet it is true that as soon as they are weaned and the male child has fourteen years, his mother sends him to his father on their island." To Marco, the plan made for careful, considered child rearing and respectful, cooperative relations between the sexes. "Their wives do nothing else but nourish their children," he observes, "for the men supply them with what they need. When the men come to the women's island, they sow grain, and then the women cultivate and reap it; and the women also gather any fruit, which they have of many kinds in that island." In light of the excesses of sensuality and asceticism he had witnessed, the inhabitants of Male and Female islands had, in his view, evolved a satisfying, if strenuous, design for living.

ALTHOUGH BRIEF in comparison with the long years Marco spent in China, his sojourn in India prompted a spiritual transformation. Marco had begun his travels wanting only to reach Kublai Khan's court in one piece; later, he sought to travel and comprehend all of China, and then India. En route, he evolved from apprentice merchant and traveler (and bumbling student of history) to pilgrim and explorer of the spirit. By this late point, his inner lens had opened wide enough to take in all humanity, or so he believed. Yet nothing had prepared him for the spectacle of the river of the plains, the Ganges, the holiest river to the Hindus—perhaps the holiest river on earth.

The Ganges was not the longest river in Asia—at fifteen hundred miles, it was surpassed by many others—but from its origins in the Himalayas to its final destination in the Bay of Bengal, it was the most revered, as Marco acknowledged. He probably visited the river during January or February, when the celebrated bathing festival known as the *mela* took place; during the ceremony of purification, pilgrims from afar immersed themselves in its waters. "Both men and women wash themselves twice a day in the water," he says, "their whole bodies, that is, morning and evening." Refusing to wash was tantamount to heresy. He observes with fascination: "Naked they go to the river and take water and throw it over their head, and then they rub one another."

The obsession with cleanliness took many other forms. "In eating they use only the right hand, nor with the left hand do they touch anything of food. And all clean and beautiful things they do and touch with the right hand, for the office of the left is only about unpleasant and unclean necessities like cleansing the nostrils, anus, and things like these. Again, they drink with cups only, and each with his own; nor would anyone drink with the cup of another. When they drink they do not put the cup to the mouth, nor with those cups would they give to drink to any strangers."

THE LOCAL SYSTEM of justice struck Marco as equally stringent, but far from illogical. He says that if a debt goes unpaid, and the debtor makes empty promises to fulfill his obligation, "the creditor is able to catch the debtor in such a way that he is able to mark a circle round him, [and] the debtor will not leave that circle unless he shall first have satisfied the creditor or shall make him a proper pledge and bond that he shall be wholly satisfied the same day." If the debtor attempted to flee without paying, "he would be punished . . . with death as a transgressor of right and of the justice established by the lord."

In Marco's hands, the following tale becomes an intriguing study in commercial conflict: "And this Master Marco saw in the king, being in the kingdom on the way home. For when the king himself was bound to satisfy a certain foreign merchant for certain things had from him, and though many times asked by the merchant had often on account of inconvenience fixed a later date for payment, the merchant, because the delay was hurtful to him on account of his business, being ready one day while the king was riding about the place immediately surrounded the king himself with all his horse with a circle on the ground. And when the king saw this, he let his horse go no farther, nor did he move himself from the place before the merchant had been wholly satisfied." The sight surprised onlookers, who exclaimed, "See how the king was obedient to justice." And the king replied to them, "I who established this just law, shall I break it because it was against me? No, I am bound before others to observe it."

THE MINGLING of religious observance and fertility rites drew Marco's curiosity. He became aware of multitudes of young girls who visited monasteries where they sang and danced to entertain the idols, that is, the images of various divinities, and to feed the monks and priests dwelling within; the custom continued, he says, until the girls took husbands. He found the girls slim and surpassingly lovely: "These maidens . . . are so firm in flesh that none can by any means take hold of them or pinch them in any part," except that "for a small coin they will allow a man to pinch them as much as he can." On the basis of hints he drops, one can imagine the Venetian merchant staring, considering, and finally parting with a coin, or several, to satisfy his curiosity and his libido.

The maidens' behavior raised an urgent question: "Why do they make these entertainments for the idols? Because the priests of the idols often say that the god is vexed with the goddess, nor is one united with the other, nor do they talk together. And since they are angry and vexed, unless they are reconciled and make peace together all our affairs will be contrary and will go from bad to worse because they will not bestow their blessing and grace."

In the service of this goal, "the damsels go . . . naked except that they are covered in the natural parts, and sing before the god and goddess. For the god stays by himself on one altar under one canopy and the goddess stays on another altar by herself under another canopy, and those people say that the god often takes his pleasure with her and they are united, and that when they are vexed they do not join together. Then these damsels come there to pacify him, and . . . begin to sing, dance, leap, tumble, and make different entertainments to move the god and goddess to joy and to reconcile them, and thus they say as they make entertainment, 'O Master, why are you vexed with this goddess and do not care for her? Is she not beautiful, is she not pleasing?" This plea was accompanied by some astonishing gyrations. "She who has said so will lift her leg above her neck and will spin round for the pleasure of the god and goddess. And when they have solaced enough they go home. And in the morning, the priest of the idols will announce as a great joy that he has seen the god and goddess together and that peace has been made between them, and then all rejoice and are thankful."

NO MATTER HOW diligently Marco tried to come to terms with the people and practices he witnessed, India remained surpassingly strange and constantly challenging to the Venetian traveler. He observes that "certain animals by the name of tarantula" infested homes; these hideous carnivorous arachnids were everywhere, even overhead, startling him. They resembled "lizards that climb up by the walls," and they had "a poisonous bite and hurt a man very much." They even screamed, or so Marco claims.

To make matters worse, he considered tarantulas bad omens for merchants. "When some people were trading together in a house where these tarantulas are, and a tarantula may cry to the merchants there above them, they will see from what side of the merchant, whether of the buyer or of the seller, namely whether it cries from the left side or from the right, from the front or back, or over the head, . . . they know whether it means good or ill; and if good, they finish the dealing, and if it mean ill, that dealing is never begun. Sometimes it means good for the seller and bad for the buyer, sometimes bad for the seller and good for the buyer, sometimes good for both or bad for both; and they guide themselves by that."

To sleep safely amid such peril, he relied on the inhabitants' clever apparatus. "The men have their very light bed of canes so contrived that while they are inside, when they wish to sleep they draw themselves up with cords near to the ceiling and tie themselves there. They do this indeed for the sake of escaping the tarantulas that bite much and fleas and other insects, and also for the sake of catching the air to do away with the heat that reigns in those parts."

Travelers such as Marco also employed their suspended beds to safeguard their valuables. "When men are traveling in the night and may wish to sleep (for on account of the lower heat they make their journey by night rather than by day), if they have a bag of pearls or other treasure they will put the bag of pearls under the head and sleep there, nor does anyone ever lose anything by theft or otherwise. And if he does lose [it], it is made good to him immediately provided that he has slept on the street." If he has not slept on the street, "evil is presumed against him, for the government says, 'Why didst thou sleep off the street unless because thou hadst proposed to rob others?' Then he is punished, and the loss is not returned to him."

AFRICA

Zanzibar.

"A very exceedingly great and noble island," Marco declares. "It is two thousand miles around."

For once, he had strayed into a territory with an abbreviated history. The island's first inhabitants apparently had emigrated from the African mainland and reassembled in small villages reminiscent of those in Africa. Soon they were confronted with Arab traders, who may have been aware of the island even before it was settled. Skillful and courageous sailors, the traders caught the monsoon winds to speed them across the Indian Ocean, and they found a makeshift harbor where the town of Zanzibar now stands. Eventually they settled there, as well, and interbred with the African emigrants. Not long before Marco's arrival, the emerging Zanzibar community established a ruler, the Jumbe. Although he was neither a great warrior nor bold leader, he helped to give the island a semblance of political unity.

Despite oft-repeated claims that the first European to visit Zanzibar was Vasco da Gama in 1499, Marco, according to his account, set foot on the island about 205 years before the Portuguese navigator sailed into its harbor. If true, Marco was the first European to do so—or at least the first to write about Zanzibar. Marco's account captures Zanzibar in its precolonial state, as a primitive and isolated island capable of startling even the experienced Venetian traveler.

Once there, he feels as if he has entered another world, a very menacing one. The men are all "very large and stout," so much so that if they were as tall as they are stout, they would "seem without doubt to be giants." Nevertheless, he says, they are "immensely strong, for they carry a load for four other men who are not of the island. And this is no wonder, for I tell you that [each one] eats food for five men of another country." These superhumans "are all black and go naked except that they are covered in their natural parts"—much to his relief—"for they have them very large and ugly and horrible to see." Even their hair takes him aback, "so curly and black like pepper that it could hardly be made to stretch out with water." And their faces startle him to the point of trauma: "They have so great a mouth and the nose so flat and turned upward the forehead, and beards, and nostrils so thick that it is wonderful. They have large ears, thick lips, turned outward, and eyes so large and so bloodshot and so red that they are a very horrible thing to see; for whoever should see them in another country would say of them that they were devils."

The women of this land strike Marco as repulsive, "a very ugly thing to see," he states. "They have great mouths and large eyes and large, thick, and short noses. They have breasts four times as large as other ordinary women, which adds to the ugliness. They are black as a mulberry and of great stature." And they also "look like devils."

Marco's exceptionally harsh and racist portrayal of the Zanzibaris raises questions about its authenticity. He may have been conflating tales of nearby East Africa with accounts of Zanzibar, recklessly embellishing as he went. But after venting his spleen, he softens his characterization, as if to make amends, by acknowledging a common interest. "They are great merchants," he says, "and do great trade." With this endorsement, he implies that, first impressions notwithstanding, the inhabitants are fully human. To his way of thinking, trading virtually defines their humanity.

Elephants were bred on the island, and the local merchants made "a great trade of the tusks." Fascinated, Marco includes a graphic account of elephant breeding rites: "When the bull elephant wishes to pair with the female elephant, he hollows out a great pit in the ground until he may put the female elephant there turned over in the manner of a woman because she has the natural parts far toward the belly, and the bull elephant mounts upon her as if he were a man."

The island's inhabitants, whom Marco considered "good fighters" and "strong"—though not "in proportion to their size"—relied on the elephants in battle, equipping them with "castles of wood" covered with the "skins of wild beasts and with boards." Outfitted in this manner, they could hold "sixteen to twenty men with lances and with swords and with stones." Marco says that to prepare the elephants for battle, the warriors "give them plenty to drink of their wine . . . so that they make them half tipsy, and they do this because they say that when an elephant has drunk of that drink it goes more willingly and becomes more fierce thereby and more proud and is of much better worth for it in the battle."

Marco insists, without proof, that the elephants were preyed upon by an even larger beast, the "grifon bird." Those whom he asked about the strange creature likened the grifons to "immeasurably great" eagles. He reports: "They say it is so great and so strong that one of these birds, without the help of another bird, seizes the elephant with its talons and carries it off high into the air. Then it lets it drop to the ground so that the elephant is all broken to pieces, and then the grifon bird comes down upon the elephant and mounts up on it and tears it and eats it and feeds itself upon it at its will." It is a sight he would dearly love to see, but the best he can do is convey what he has heard of the improbable spectacle.

ALTHOUGH MARCO did not visit Ethiopia—did not even claim to have done so—the oversight did not stop him from offering a few more nuggets. He speculated that Prester John, the legendary Christian ruler, might live on in this remote African territory. Relying heavily on hearsay, Marco claims, "The greatest king in all the province is Christian and all the other kings of the province are subject to him."

There were six kingdoms, he reported, three of them Christian, and three Saracen—that is to say, Muslim. "I was told," he says, "that all the Christian people of this province have three golden marks on their faces in [the] form of a cross that they may be known as more noble by others, that is, one on the forehead, two on the cheeks; and the mark that is on the forehead stretches from the forehead to the middle of the nose, and they have one of them on each cheek. And these marks are made with hot iron, and they make them when they are small, and it is for their second baptism with fire, for when they are baptized in water, then . . . those marks of which I have told you are made." He also states that "many Jews" inhabit Ethiopia, "and these also bear like marks on their faces, but Jews have two marks, that is, one long line on each cheek." As for the Saracens, they have "only one such mark alone, that is, from the forehead to the middle of the nose. And they do it with the hot iron."

Ethiopian religious customs held special interest for Marco, for the land had been home to his spiritual beacon, "Master Saint Thomas the glorious Apostle." The saint's disciple recounts with fascination that Thomas had preached in Ethiopia "and after[ward] he converted some of this people with his preaching and miracles to the Christian faith" before he went to the "province of Maabar in India where, after he had converted infinite people, he was killed, and his most holy body is."

Although Marco looked warmly on Ethiopia's Christian king and people, and longed to see nearby Aden, he admitted that, were he to visit, he would be ostracized, because "merchant Christians are much hated in this kingdom, for the [inhabitants] do not wish to see them, but hate them like their mortal enemies." That realization came as something of a shock. He had gone to considerable lengths to persuade himself, and others, that he was a Mongol official, a Buddhist student, a gentleman wayfarer. All the while, he had engaged in a search for his identity, trying out the roles of a businessman, storyteller, adventurer. Yet those around him saw through his various guises and regarded him simply as another "merchant Christian." No matter how far he traveled, even to the ends of the earth, or how well he adapted to his changing surroundings, even to the point of persuading himself that he had become someone else, he had yet to transcend himself.

Marco Polo had reached the end of his personal quest and of Kublai Khan's protection. He had seen the world, or what was known of it. But how would he find his way home?

CHAPTER FOURTEEN

The Mongol Princess

A damsel with a dulcimer
In a vision once I saw. . . .

A S KUBLAI KHAN entered a slow, painful decline, Marco and his father and uncle desperately sought release from service. With each passing year, it seemed more likely that they would not live to see Venice again. Worse, if Kublai Khan died while they were still in China, their *paizas*—and their lives—would be worthless. They might fall victim to his enemies, or whoever seized the throne and wished them out of the way. So a timely release from service was a matter of life and death.

Marco describes the circumstances behind their deliverance from glorified servitude with considerable care, tracking the course of a fond wish as it developed into an obsession and, finally, a plan. "When Master Niccolò, Master Maffeo, and Master Marco had stayed with the Great Khan at his court [for] many years," he begins, "they said among themselves that one day they wished to go back to their . . . native country, for it was now high time to do so. Though they found themselves very rich in jewels of great value and in gold, an extreme desire to see their native land again was always fixed in their minds; and even though they were honored and favored, they thought of nothing else but this." Marco summarizes their plight in a manner that is both poignant and realistic: "Seeing that the Great Khan was very old, they feared that if he were to die before their departure they might never be able to return home, because of the length of the way and the infinite perils that threatened them; though they hoped to be able to do this if he were alive."

When he judged the moment to be right, Marco's father, Niccolò, seized his chance. "One day, seeing that the Great Khan was very cheerful, [he] took occasion to beg of him on his knees in the name of all three leave to depart to their home, at which word [the khan] was all disturbed and answered, 'Why do you wish to go to die on the way? Tell me. If you have need of gold I will give you much more of it than you have at home, and likewise every other thing for which you shall ask.' "

The khan promised to advance them "whatever honors they might wish" to guarantee their loyalty. His words implied that he considered the Polo company bound to him for life, if not for eternity.

On bended knee, Niccolò argued, "That which I say is not for want of gold, but it is because in my land I have a wife and by the Christian law I cannot forsake her while she lives."

Kublai Khan considered this carefully worded appeal. "On no condition in the world am I willing that you depart from my realm," he answered, "but I am well content that you go about it where you please."

Still frustrated, Niccolò, pleaded, as Marco put it, "very sweetly," for formal permission to quit the kingdom, only to be undone by his family's longstanding loyalty to the Mongol leader. "The Great Khan loved them so much, was so much pleased with their deeds, and kept them willingly about him, that for nothing in the world did he give them leave." Only now did the Polos realize that Kublai Khan might consider their departure a sign of his diminishing power; at this volatile point in his reign, he could not afford that challenge.

WHEN IT SEEMED that negotiations had reached a standstill, Kublai Khan, inspired by the unlikeliest of circumstances, the effort to find a successor for a distant queen, devised a solution that saved face for all parties.

As Marco reports, "It happened that the Queen Bolgana, who was wife of Argon, died." Argon, or Arghun as he was sometimes known, was the "lord of the Levant," a western kingdom loosely affiliated with the Mongol Empire. At the same time, Argon had been locked in a fierce quarrel with his uncle Acmat Soldan, who had converted to Islam and committed the outrage of stealing his brother's wives. Argon vowed to avenge this wrong and kill Acmat Soldan, who in turn vowed to kill him, but not before torturing him. The two spent years at war with each other, and eventually Argon won out.

For the sake of maintaining a semblance of stability in the empire, Kublai Khan was prepared to oversee the line of succession in this distant kingdom. Marco explains that on her deathbed, the queen had expressed the wish "that no lady might sit on her throne nor be wife of Argon if she were not of her line." Then, he continues, "Argon took three of his barons"—Oulatai, Apusca, and Coja by name—and sent them "very grandly as his messengers to the Great Khan with a very great and fair company in order to ask that he should send him a lady who was of the line of the Queen Bolgana . . . to marry him."

The three emissaries completed the hazardous mission to Kublai Khan, who "received them most honorably and made joy and feasting for them. Then, since King Argon was his very great friend, [Kublai sent] for a lady who had Cocacin for name, who was of the lineage they desired." This was the Mongol princess known to history as Kokachin. She was seventeen years old, "very fair and amiable," and she instantly won the emissaries' approval. Her name, which meant "blue like Heaven," has often been taken to indicate that her eyes were blue, which would have been highly unusual among the Mongols. More likely, her eyes were dark, and the name, like many Mongol names, included a color, in this case blue, suggestive of Heaven.

Kublai commanded the three barons, "Take her to Argon your lord, for she is of the family he seeks, so that he may take her safely to wife."

In Marco's telling, their journey sounds like a fairy tale, but it is replete with the awkwardness of reality, beginning with a false start. "When all things necessary had been made ready and a great brigade to escort with honor this new bride to King Argon, the envoys, after taking leave of the Great Khan, set out riding for the space of eight months by that same way they were come." Soon enough, they encountered trouble. "On the journey they found that by a war newly begun between certain kings of the Tartars the roads were closed, and not being able to go forward they were obliged against their will to return again to the court of the Great Khan, to whom they related all that had befallen them."

The reversal of fortune provided the Polo company with a slender chance to escape the Mongol Empire, as Marco explains. "At the same time the ambassadors were come for that lady, Master Marco returned with a certain embassy from India, who was gone as ambassador of the lord and had been or passed through the kingdom of Argon." Marco was overflowing with mesmerizing tales as he described "the embassy and the other different things that he had seen on his way and how he had gone through foreign provinces and very strange seas, and [he told] many wonderful new things of that country."

By virtue of his extensive travels, Marco possessed impressive credentials as a worthy guardian for the young princess on her journey to King Argon. "The three barons who have seen Master Niccolò and Master Maffeo and Master Marco, who were Latins"—that is, Christians—"and wise men, had very great wonder. And when they heard that those [the Polos] had a wished to depart, then they thought and they said among themselves that they wished that they may go with them by sea; for their intention was to return to their country by sea for the sake of the lady, because of the great labor that it is to travel by land. . . . On the other hand, they would gladly take them [the Polos] as their companions in this journey because they knew that they had seen and explored much of the Indian Ocean and those countries by which they must go, and"—the narrator proudly adds—"especially Master Marco."

Marco's professed expertise in sailing enabled him to secure a commitment from Kublai Khan. "As Marco who had sailed to those lands had said, his Majesty should be content to do them this kindness that they should go by sea, and that these three Latins, that is, Niccolò, Maffeo, and Marco, who had experience in sailing the said seas, must accompany them to the lands of King Argon."

Even with this point in their favor, Kublai Khan, a latter-day Pharaoh, still resisted the idea of letting the Polo company go. "Nevertheless, as he could not do otherwise, he consented to all that they asked of him."

Displaying the humanity that originally drew Marco to him, Kublai Khan "made them all and three come before him and spoke to them many gracious words of the great love that he bore them, and they should promise that when they had been some time in the land of Christians and at their home, they would return to him." The Polos, eager to be on their way after years of delay, agreed to this promise without any intention of keeping it. Timing was critical. As was apparent to all, Kublai Khan was nearing the end of his life. They had no choice but to leave now, under any terms they could negotiate.

The bargain they struck with the Mongol ruler did not allow them complete freedom; Kublai Khan could claim that he had dispatched the Polo company on just another mission in the service of the empire. But no return was planned. Once they completed their task, the Polos would be free to go.

IT WAS NOW 1292, and Marco Polo was a man of thirty-eight, having spent seventeen years in the service of Kublai Khan. He no longer had occasion to masquerade as someone other than a merchant of Venice, even though he was most memorable, and most convincing, when he pretended to be someone else, a replica capable of surpassing the original. Confined within the limits of his own identity, he was diminished. By way of compensation, he no longer had to play the role of dutiful son serving an extended, strenuous apprenticeship to his father and uncle, or that of the charming protégé of the most powerful ruler on the face of the earth. He was simply the itinerant, observant merchant, impressed by ingenuity, dismissive of folly, susceptible to the temptations of the flesh, and moved by faith. The mature Marco cast a cold eye on the dealings around him, seeing these machinations for what they were, not for what his fertile imagination might take them for.

Despite his disillusionment, Marco was intoxicated by the prospect of returning home. Later, when he came to tell his story, he seems to have intended to describe this turning point in his travels twice, as if to underscore its importance. But his manner of handling it was odd. He devoted a significant part of the prologue to narrating the episode in considerable detail rather than summarizing it. In fact, the description of his departure from Kublai Khan's court was by far the longest entry in the prologue, and the space devoted to it suggests that Marco regarded it as the most noteworthy event of his entire career in the service of the Mongol Empire.

With every mile he traveled on the Silk Road and beyond, Marco composed his own epitaph, combining the fragments of experience to form a great, if erratic, epic, romantic yet existential, purposeful yet impulsive. Marco never set out to discover a particular place, and never thought of himself as an explorer—"wayfarer" was the term he used to describe himself. His adventures occurred, and would continue to occur, by accident rather than design. He did not, and could not, plan; he lived by his wits and his talent for improvisation. A wanderer by temperament, he knew how to blend in rather than stand out.

Although Marco never stopped seeing himself as a merchant, he evinced little interest in becoming wealthy himself even as he constantly tallied the wealth of others. He believed in commerce as he did in little else. For Marco, commerce and travel were synonymous, and beyond that, they were the essence of life. They were, it seemed to him, more comprehensive undertakings than politics or war; in fact, he implicitly viewed war as an ill-considered obstacle to the essentially commercial nature of human endeavor. Kublai Khan's charisma (and concubines) held more fascination for Marco than gold or gems. Surely there were easier ways to grow rich than traveling across a continent, exposing himself to danger every step of the way. But it was the process—the negotiations, the observations, the conflict—that engaged Marco's attention, not the outcome. By the time he began his trip home, he counted himself wealthy in knowledge and experience rather than in tangible assets.

JUST BEFORE the Polo company left the Mongol court, Kublai Khan, exuding a melancholy dignity, gave new, even more elaborate *paizas* to the travelers to guarantee their safety and well-being. The *paizas* were things of beauty, "two tablets of gold sealed with the royal seal with orders written thereon that they should be free and exempt from every burden and secure through all his lands." The Polos' manner of travel promised to be equally luxurious. "Wherever they might go," Kublai ordered, "they must have all the expenses for themselves and for all their train, and an escort given them that they may be able to pass in safety."

In fact, Kublai Khan had elaborate plans for his favored merchant ambassadors, and he transformed their passage into an international mission of considerable significance. "He entrusted them with many things on his own behalf"—presumably letters and other personal items—"and with an embassy to the pope and to the king of France, and to the king of England, and to the king of Spain and to the other crowned kings of Christendom."

Fully assembled, the expedition was magnificent: fourteen large ships, each equipped with four masts and twelve sails. Marco's enthusiasm at the adventure before him in 1292 fairly bursts from the account. His yearning for blue water and the tang of the open sea is palpable. The prospect engaged his nautical expertise. "I could tell you how they [the ships] were made," he says, "but because it would be too long a matter I will not mention it to you at this point"—although he does remark that four or five of the ships held 250 men each. A mighty fleet would be making its way to King Argon, bearing him a longed-for princess.

The actual departure occasioned still more generosity from Kublai Khan and the seemingly inexhaustible Mongol treasury. "When the ships were fitted out and furnished with food and with all things necessary, and the three barons and the lady and these three Latins, the two brothers Master Niccolò and Master Maffeo, and Master Marco, were ready to go to King Argon, they presented themselves to their lord, and took leave of the Great Khan and with great joy came to the ships that were prepared and assemble themselves on the ships with a very great company of ladies and gentlemen. And the Great Khan made men give them many rubies and other very fine jewels of great value, and also expenses for ten years."

The ceremony marked the last time they would see Kublai Khan. After twenty years abroad, their long voyage home commenced, and the adventure of a lifetime began to draw to a close.

THE POLO COMPANY'S mission to deliver Princess Kokachin to her rightful king and kingdom has attained special significance in recent years because it is the only event described by Marco that is confirmed in detail by Chinese and Mongol sources. In 1941 and again in 1945, Yang Chih-chiu, a Chinese scholar, compared Yüan dynasty sources with Marco's detailed rendition of the circumstances of his departure from China and discovered that they matched almost perfectly, with the significant omission of the names of the three emissaries from Kublai Khan.

An account written in about 1307 by Rashid al-Din, the authoritative chronicler of the era, told very much the same story, mentioning Princess Kokachin and the three ambassadors who accompanied her, corresponding closely with the details Marco set forth. Like his Chinese counterparts, Rashid al-Din did not mention the three Polos by name, but the existence of an independent informant confirming precise features of Marco's description amounts to more than coincidence. Taken together, these sources confirm that Marco escorted the princess to King Argon and was in service to Kublai Khan, just as he claimed.

. . .

"THEY SET OUT from that island, and I tell you that they sailed through the great sea of India for eighteen months before they came to the land of King Argon," Marco reports, "and in this journey they saw strange and different things and they found many great marvels." In his haste, he never did tell his collaborator, Rustichello, what those things were, but to judge from the scant information about the voyage that he did provide, the 1293 ocean voyage was violent and traumatic.

"When they entered into the ships in the land of the Great Khan," Marco reports, "there were between ladies and men six hundred people, without [counting] sailors. And when they reached the land where they were going, they made a count that all had died on the way except only eighteen. And of those three ambassadors there remained but one, who was named Coja; and of all the women and girls none died but one." Disease, shipwreck, and pirates were the likely culprits, but Marco does not offer an explanation, despite his penchant for depicting dramatic events and circumstances that would show him in a heroic light. Given his fascination with ships, it seems likely that an important and dramatic segment of his account devoted to these matters has been lost. All that remains of the traumatic episode is a collection of tantalizing fragments hinting at extreme suffering and sorrow. Despite all, the Polos and the young Mongol princess survived.

Marco had endured an ordeal surpassing anything he had previously faced, even as a young man making his way across the Steppe for the first time. In his descriptions, he was now more subdued, less inclined to boasting, not so much disillusioned as disoriented. Marco recovered his former vitality when reliving previous episodes for the sake of entertaining his readers, but as he narrates the latter part of his tale, he no longer gives the impression of leading a charmed existence. Instead, his more reverent tone suggests that he felt fortunate simply to count himself among the living.

THE SURVIVORS' unanticipated arrival in Argon's kingdom generated shock rather than relief. Matters in this distant land had changed drastically since those three ambassadors had left for Kublai Khan's court several years earlier. Argon was dead—poisoned, perhaps, by his enemies.

Marco was dismayed. In Argon's place, the Polos found that "one named Quiacatu held the lordship of Argon, for the boy who was not yet fit to rule, for he was young." Not knowing what to do with the princess whom they had risked their lives to escort, they eventually decided to present her to "Caçan, the son of Argon, to wife," and despite his youth, the two were joined in matrimony.

If Marco and his father and uncle believed that they had discharged their responsibilities and could at last leave the service of Kublai Khan, they were disappointed. Once again, they were nearly undone by their loyalty and their ability to accomplish seemingly impossible long-distance assignments in the service of the Great Khan. The young princess did not wish them to leave her alone in this strange and threatening land, and because she was a princess, her wish was law. They tried to comply with her every request, but in the end, Marco reports, "when Master Niccolò and Master Maffeo and Master Marco had done all the duties about the lady and the missions, with which the Great Khan had charged them, they returned to Quiacatu, because their road must be that way, and there they stayed nine months."

Nine months! They could only have wondered, with good reason, if they would ever see the great domes of San Marco, greet their wives, and resume their comfortable lives in Venice. During the endless lay-over, the Polo company endured a suffocating excess of hospitality and affection from their grateful hosts. Even when the weather cooperated, and political conditions permitted them to leave, the young woman whom they had escorted across China did not wish to see her guardians depart. Once more, the Polos found themselves pleading and making far-fetched promises to return in exchange for permission to leave. At last their wish was granted, but even then, "when these three messengers left her to return to their country, she wept for grief at their departure." Perhaps she finally came to the realization that she had been the vehicle of their escape from the Mongol Empire. The unfortunate Kokachin, who had risked all to journey to this distant kingdom, died a short time later, in June 1296. Poisoning by a faction opposed to Kublai Khan is the most likely explanation for her untimely death.

As the Polo company prepared to depart, Quiacatu, in the spirit of Kublai Khan, bestowed a series of gifts, blessings, and burdens in the form of elaborate *paizas*: "four tablets of gold . . . two with gerfalcons and one with a lion and the other was plain, each of which was one cubit long and five fingers wide." The tablets declared "that these three messengers should be honored and served through all his land as his own person, and that horses and all expenses and all escort should be given them in full through any dangerous places for themselves and the whole company."

The beneficence of Kublai Khan was endless, even now. "Many times there were given them two hundred horsemen, and more or less according as was necessary for their escort and to go safely from one land to another. And this was very necessary many times, for they found many dangerous places, because Quiacatu had no authority and was not natural nor liege lord and therefore the people did not refrain from doing evil as they would have done if they had a true and liege lord." The farther the Polos strayed from Argon's kingdom, the less they could count on their *paiza*s to protect them against brigands with no allegiance to Kublai Khan.

From this point on, they would have to fend for themselves if they were to survive the long voyage home.

IT WAS NOW 1294, with the Mongol New Year beginning in February. Kublai Khan was so weary and depressed that he shunned those who had traveled to the court to offer their greetings and good wishes for the coming year. His favorite general, Bayan, attempted to remind him of the great military victories they shared, but even he failed to revive the khan.

On February 18, Kublai Khan died at the age of eighty in the safety and comfort of his palace.

Two days later, a funeral caravan bearing Kublai Khan's mortal remains slowly made its way from the palace north toward the Khenti Mountains. In keeping with Mongol custom, his burial place, believed to be near that of his grandfather, Genghis, was concealed amid the setting's brooding majesty. No records describing it survive, nor has the site itself been located. It was a singularly subdued conclusion for an emperor noted in his lifetime for daring and excess.

Kublai's chosen successor, Chinkim, had died years before. In his place, Kublai's grandson Temür became the next Mongol emperor, inheriting a kingdom in disarray. He commanded that an altar be built in Kublai Khan's memory, and conferred on him a posthumous Chinese name: Shih-tsu, "Founder of a Dynasty."

Early chroniclers of the Yüan dynasty spread Kublai Khan's fame far and wide. Muslims came to know of this extraordinary man through the writings of Rashid al-Din. Chinese and Korean chroniclers celebrated Kublai Khan's accomplishments, and Bar Hebraeus wrote warmly of Kublai's long and momentous reign. For all their scope, none of these accounts compares with the vivid account left by Kublai's best-known European chronicler, Marco Polo. He alone had extensive personal experience with his subject, and he still held the *paiza*, or passport, that the emperor had given him years before, when Marco first left Cambulac. He wrote about the Mongol leader with such passion, tinged with awe, that he single-handedly enlightened the West about one of the most powerful rulers who had ever lived.

MARCO POLO learned of Kublai Khan's death during his passage home to Venice with his father and uncle. If he always remembered where he was or what he was doing when he heard the momentous news, he did not confide the details to Rustichello. He simply recalled, "While Masters Niccolò, Maffeo, and Marco were making this journey, they learned how the Great Khan was cut off from this life, and this took away from them all hope of being able to return any more to those parts."

Instead of conferring the liberation that Marco anticipated, Kublai Khan's demise tolled the death of adventure, and even of hope itself. At the time of their leave-taking, the Polos had employed their negotiating skills to free themselves from privileged servitude. Now that they were beyond the reach of this beneficent tyrant who had controlled their destiny, they could only reflect that they would never see Cambulac again. The splendor and immensity of Asia were lost to them forever. The end of Kublai Khan's long reign terminated a unique partnership between East and West, a powerful ruler and a small merchant family. The Mongol leader had given the Polo company standing, but more than that, he had imparted to his protégé a sense of purpose. He was the personification of magic and might.

IN THE FINAL CHAPTERS of his chronicle, Marco's boundless curiosity alights on the largely unexplored land of Russia. In reality, his route home did not take him anywhere near Russia, or any of the other northern lands that suddenly piqued his interest, but his account, a

careful summary based on admittedly secondhand information, is
memorable for its eloquence and its evocation of a landscape and way
of life that other Europeans could scarcely imagine.

The approach to Russia from the east, to hear Marco tell it, could
deter even the hardiest merchant. "No horse can go there," he advises,
"because it is a land where there are many lakes and many springs and
streams that make that region very marshy, and because of the exceeding cold of that province there is almost always ice so thick that boats
cannot pass by there, and yet there is not so much strength in the ice
that it can bear heavy carts or heavy animals." Nevertheless, merchants
or trappers trading in fur managed to traverse this wasteland, turning a
"great profit" for their trouble, and these hardy souls were his likely
source of information for the region.

Marco had heard that travel across this difficult territory could be
accomplished in stages lasting thirteen days, known as a "journey," at
the end of which the weary, frozen traveler could count on finding a
hamlet consisting of "several houses of timber raised above the ground
in which can comfortably live men who bring and receive merchandise." Commerce again surmounted nearly every obstacle; to Marco,
this was more a fact of life than a source of wonder.

"In each of these hamlets," he continues, "is a house which they call
a post where all the messengers of the lord who go through the country lodge." A cold-weather version of the caravans that served as
Marco's primary means of travel over the years, they struck familiar
notes in the way they were organized. "At each of these posts are keepers with forty very large dogs, little smaller than an ass, and these dogs
are all accustomed and taught to draw just as oxen do in our country,
and they draw sledges, which are called *sliozola*, . . . to carry the messengers from the one post to the other, that is, from one journey to the
next."

The sleds, in particular, intrigued Marco, who may have heard
about them in detail from a fellow merchant. "A sled," he explains for
an audience unfamiliar with the idea of travel across frozen wastes, "is
a vehicle that has no wheels, but they are made of very light wood and
flat and smoothed underneath, and they are raised at the ends in the
way of a semicircle, in such a way that they go up over the ice and over
the mud and over the mire."

Marco familiarized himself with the details of dog handling to an
uncanny degree. His account reads as if written by one who held the

reins himself: "Those who conduct the sledges harness six dogs of those large ones . . . with yokes, two and two in proper order, to take those sledges. And these dogs, no one leads them but they go straight to the next post and draw the sledge very well both through the ice and through the mire. And so they go from one post to the other. . . . He who guards the post mounts on a sledge also, and has himself taken by the dogs, and he takes them by the straightest way and by the best. And when they are come to the next post that is at the end of the journey, they find there are also the dogs and the sledges and another guide ready to carry them forward for the second journey; and this is done because the dogs could not bear such labor as that for all the thirteen days' journey; and so those that have brought them turn back. And so it goes through all these journeys, changing dogs, sledge, and guide at every stage . . . till the messengers of the lord are carried . . . to the mountains, and buy the skins, and return to their own land through the plain."

Marco radiates enthusiasm for the trade, especially when he enumerates the skins in which the messengers deal—"little animals of great value," he marvels, "from which they have great profit and great benefit; these are sables and ermines and squirrels and ercolins and black foxes and many other precious animals from which are made the dear skins." Nevertheless, when he considers the conditions endured by merchant trappers in this harsh climate, Marco, the restless traveler and sensualist, turns away. "They have all their houses underground because of the great cold that is there, and they always live underground." Equally damning is the Venetian's last word on the subject: "They are not a beautiful people." The prospect of being confined for months in a subterranean dwelling with them ended Marco's daydreams about growing rich in the skin trade.

It was time for the lover of open spaces, sunlight, and intrigue to move on.

NEXT TO THE fur-trapping wastes, Marco located an even grimmer region, the Valley of Darkness, so called because of the dense mists obscuring the area, which he occasionally calls "the land of shadows." Although he seems to be describing an allegorical domain, he believed he was depicting an actual place just beyond the Mongol sphere of influence—far indeed from the centers of power to which he has become accustomed during the previous two decades. Men here, he relates, "live like animals."

Despite the inhospitable climate, a handful of Mongols ventured into the area, taking unusual precautions to guard their safety. They "come in on mares that have foals, and they leave the foals outside, and have them watched by keepers whom they set at the entry of that region, because the mares when they have made their journey go back to their children and by the perception and scent of the foals know the way better than the men know." The only reason Marco finds for risking travel to the area is, inevitably, the prospect of trade in sable, ermine, "and many other dear skins."

Surprisingly, Marco has kind words for the inhabitants of the land of shadows. "These people are handsome, very large, and well made in all their parts," he notes with relief, "but they are very pale, and have no color, and this happens because of the want of sunlight."

Marco had endured his share of frigid Mongolian weather, but he describes the Russian winters as more brutal than anything he had experienced—"the greatest cold that is in the world, so that with great difficulty one escapes it"—and he evokes the sting of the cold so vividly that it seems as if he had suffered it himself. "If it were not for the many stoves that are there," he advises, "the people could not escape from perishing by the too great cold. But there are very frequent stoves, which the noble and powerful piously cause to be built just as hospitals are built with us. And to these stoves all the people can always run when there is need. For cold so intense prevails at times that while men go through the land toward home or from one place to another for their business, when they go from one stove they are almost frozen before they reach another, though the stoves are so frequent that one is separated from another by sixty paces."

Seeing no reason to doubt this arrangement, Marco reports: "It very often happens that if a man who is not well-clothed, or cannot travel so fast because he is old, or is of weaker constitution and nature than others, or because his house is too far off, falls to the ground frozen by the too great cold before from one stove he can reach another, and would die there. But others passing by take him immediately and lead him to a stove and strip him, and when he is being warmed there his nature is restored, and he comes back to life."

Marco is on surer ground when he describes the peculiar stoves, which resembled saunas. He speaks of "thick beams placed in a square one above the other," and says, "they are so closed up together that nothing could be seen between one and another, and between the joints they are very well caulked with lime and other things so that wind nor rain can come in anywhere. Above at the roof they have a window by which the smoke goes out when fire is lighted in them to warm them. Logs are kept there in abundance, of which the people put many on the fire and make a great pile, and while the logs burn and give out smoke, the upper window is opened and the smoke goes out of it." These contraptions were so numerous throughout Russia that "every noble or rich man" talked of having one.

MARCO'S LOCAL sources—traders and merchants who had actually ventured into this curious land—confirmed that the Russians were inordinately fond of their liquor. They told how nobles and "magnates," men and women, as well as "husbands, wives, and children," gathered in companies as large as fifty solely to drink a "perfect wine, which is called *cerbesia*," flavored with honey. "There are men who might be called innkeepers," Marco goes on, "who keep this *cerbesia* for sale. These companies go to these taverns and continue the whole day in drinking. They call that drinking *straviza*. In the evening, the innkeepers make reckoning of the *cerbesia* they have consumed, and each pays the share belonging to himself and wife and children, if they are there."

Special times were reserved for women only to drink their fill of *cerbesia*, with customs unique to their sex. "When the ladies stay all day," Marco reports, "they do not leave them because they wish to pass water, but their maids bring great sponges and put them under them so stealthily that the other people do not notice. For one seems to be talking with the mistress and another puts the sponge under, and so the mistress passes water in the sponge as she sits, and afterward the maid takes away the sponge quite full, and so they pass water whenever they wish to do so."

Marco's final vision of the Russian people, based on an anecdote he had heard, is comic and grotesque. He begins: "While a man was leaving the drinking with his wife to go home in the evening, his wife set herself down to pass water, the hair of her thigh being frozen by the exceeding cold was caught up with the grass, so that the woman being unable to move herself for pain cried out."

Marco concludes his tale with a bawdy turn: "And then her husband, who was very drunk, being sorry for his wife, stooped down there and began to blow, wishing to melt that ice with warm breath. And while he blew, the moisture of the breath was frozen and so the hairs of the beard were caught together with the hair of the woman's thigh. Therefore in the same way he could not move because of the exceeding pain; and there he was bending down like this." At this point, Marco, if he was telling the tale in company, may have demonstrated just what he meant for the amusement of his audience.

"Thus, if they wished to leave that spot, it was necessary for some[one] to come by who should break up that ice." Given enough drunken laughter, it is possible that no one would have been able to hear Marco utter the last words of his crude joke.

MARCO CONVEYS the impression that he could go on forever with his histories, tales, miracles, myths, jokes, and unique experiences. "Now you have heard all the facts that were possible to tell of Tartars and Saracens and of their life and customs," he advises, "and of as many other countries in the world as was possible to search and know"— with one significant exception.

By way of an encore, Marco wished to narrate a journey by water; he had been landlocked for too many years, and he craved a fresh wind and a billowing sail. "We have said or spoken nothing of the Greater Sea nor of the provinces that are around it, though we have well explored it all." He briefly flirted with the temptation to embark on the sequel, but he ultimately rejected the idea, since, he explains, "it seems to me to be wearisome to speak that which may be unnecessary and useless, since they are so many who explore it and sail it every day. As is well known, such as are Venetians and Genoese and Pisans and many other people who make that journey so often that everyone knows what is there." In fact, not everyone in the last decade of the thirteenth century, when most people never wandered more than a few miles from their place of birth, knew what was there, but perhaps those whom Marco knew and respected did.

"Therefore, I am silent and say nothing to you of that." Another time, perhaps.

In the end, Marco acknowledges there was little he could have done to alter the trajectory of his life. "I believe our return was the pleasure of God," he concludes, "that the things that are in the world might be known. For, according as we have told at the beginning of the book, . . . there was never any man, neither Christian nor Saracen nor Tartar nor pagan, who has ever explored as much of the world as did Master Marco, the son of Master Niccolò Polo, noble and great citizen of Venice."

The result was an epic that overflows its limits, one that is inexhaustible and self-replenishing. In it, Marco traveled through time as well as space. Along the remote westernmost stretches of the Silk Road in the Pamir highlands, he visited a more primitive world, and encountered people and societies unchanged since prehistoric times. In China, he moved forward hundreds of years into a technological and cultural utopia. Yet his vision of the future, as embodied in the highly civilized city of Quinsai, was troubled by new manifestations of ancient struggles. Undone by their success in commerce, and subverted by superstition and sensuality, the Chinese of Quinsai, as depicted by Marco, were not masters of their national destiny; they were vulnerable to aggressive warriors like the Mongols, preferring to deter threats at home, such as fire, to those coming from afar, such as warriors on horseback, bent on conquest. In China, Marco saw the future, but it was hardly less chaotic than the present.

Sealed off from one another by brigands, warring kingdoms, and the rise of Islam until the coming of the Pax Mongolica, East and West had their Silk Road for conveying goods—as well as religious figures—back and forth. Perhaps the most influential aspect of that Sericulture Superhighway was not silk itself, or any other tangible item, but intelligence about distant places whose nature was seriously misunderstood, or whose existence had been unknown. Marco visited many of those places; he considered himself a trader in fabrics, gems, and spices. But ultimately he traded in knowledge of the world and its people, thereby anticipating the Renaissance, and beyond. Through his account, he led both East and West into the future.

It was not a peaceful prospect, as experienced and presented by Marco. It was as pagan as it was pious, but it was recognizably human; it was a world in which people reached across geographic, religious, and political boundaries to connect. Unlike the isolation imposed by the harsh conditions of the Middle Ages, Marco's vision of the future required constant travel, endless trading, and ceaseless communication in many languages. It was a world in which Christians traded with

Muslims, with "idolaters," with anyone who grasped the rudiments of trade—and in which an entire regime, such as the Yüan dynasty, incorporated individuals from an astonishing variety of cultures, all in the service of an ideal. It was blended and heterodox, ultimately unified not by a government, or a system of belief, but by a force Marco believed to be even more universal, and thus more powerful: the impulse to trade.

WHEN THE POLO COMPANY reached Trebizond, a compact and corrupt little kingdom in the Byzantine Empire located on the Black Sea, disaster struck—though not in the form of a storm, or disease, or even violence. Rather, the Polos became victims of thievery, despite all their precautions and connections. In Trebizond, they finally exceeded the limits of the *paiza*'s influence. The local government confiscated four thousand hyperpyra (a widely circulated gold Byzantine coin) from the company. While it is difficult to affix a modern value to the hyperpyra, that amount could have purchased a thousand pounds of silk. In other words, they were robbed of a significant part of the fortune they had risked their lives to acquire during their decades abroad.

Marco omitted the painful and embarrassing Trebizond episode from his account. No mention of it would be made until years later, in his uncle Maffeo's will, which addressed the sensitive subject of family debts. In omitting it, Marco avoided reopening old wounds. Equally important, the setback did not square with the successful image of the enterprising Polo company that he wished to project throughout his *Travels*.

Instead of dwelling on the loss, Marco lists the stops along the way to suggest their brisk progress home: "From Trebizond they came away to Constantinople, and from Constantinople they came away to Negrepont, and from Negrepont with many riches and a great company, thanking God who had delivered them from so great labors and infinite perils, they went into a ship and came safe at last to Venice; and this was in the year 1295 from the Incarnation of the Lord Christ."

AFTER TWENTY-FOUR years of adventures, narrow escapes, trading in exotic lands, and high-level diplomatic missions, the Polo company's expedition through Asia, India, and Africa had come to an end. The

Polos had changed beyond recognition during their years abroad. In their dress and manner they resembled Mongols, and they had almost forgotten their native tongue.

In the late thirteenth century, Venetians wore plain garb. Women dressed in long, flowing skirts cinched at the waist with a broad embroidered belt, and they covered their heads with hoods or veils for the sake of modesty. Beige and heather fabrics predominated, occasionally enlivened with an orange or reddish hue. Men wore sleeveless tunics, buttoned in front over a long-sleeved, collarless white chemise, and loose-fitting breeches and a soft cap with a narrow brim.

The three Polos, in contrast, wore the Mongol clothing to which they had become accustomed over two decades. Mongol dress, resplendent in scarlet and yellow and sky blue silks, was far more flamboyant than the Venetian fashion. Mongol men and women alike wore the *del,* or caftan, a long garment like a coat, with a flap in front and full sleeves long enough to be pulled over the hands in cold weather. It was often made of silk. Mongol men and women also wore loose trousers underneath their caftans, and the women had underskirts, too.

As they walked along the canals and piazzas of Venice attired in their brightly colored caftans, the Polos turned heads and excited comment. And if they wore their hair in the Mongol style, they would have been even more conspicuous. Whereas Venetian men concealed their hair under caps, Mongol men had long braided hair looped up behind the ears, and they shaved the tops of their heads, leaving just a forelock.

Marco Polo had learned to overcome being a stranger in the Mongol Empire, only to find that he had become a stranger once more, now that he was home.

CHAPTER FIFTEEN

The Prodigal Son

Weave a circle round him thrice,
And close your eyes with holy dread,
For he on honey-dew hath fed,
And drunk the milk of Paradise.

T HE THREE POLOS arrived at the Ca' Polo after their quarter-century absence and rapped on the door, only to be ignored by the stranger who opened it. So ran a popular account published in 1559 by a Venetian official and scholar named Giambattista Ramusio; he compared their plight to that of Odysseus, who returned home to Ithaca disguised as an old man after a lengthy absence and found that no one recognized him. Similarly, the Polos learned to their dismay that relatives had taken up residence in their home in the mistaken belief that Marco and his father and uncle were long dead or had vanished permanently to another land.

To add to the inhabitants' skepticism, the three strangers claiming to be Polos did not resemble genuine Venetians in the least. "They had an indescribable something of the Tartar in their aspect and in their way of speech, having forgotten most of the Venetian tongue. Those garments of theirs were much the worse for wear, and were made of coarse cloth, and cut after the fashion of the Tartars," Ramusio reported.

Chief among those who speculated about the new arrivals' identity was Maffeo Polo, Marco's half brother. The two had never before met; Marco probably was unaware of Maffeo's existence until that moment. But Maffeo had heard of Marco; moreover, legal provisions, however skimpy, had been made concerning the eventual return to Venice of his father and uncle. Fifteen years earlier, on August 27, 1280, Marco's uncle, also named Marco, had drawn up his will, appointing as his trustees his sister-in-law Fiordilige and her husband, Giordano Trevisan, "until my brothers Niccolò and Maffeo should be in Venice. And then they alone are to be my executors." When he dictated these words, the elder Marco had no way of knowing if they would ever apply, but with the unexpected appearance of Niccolò, Maffeo, and the younger Marco, they suddenly did.

The terms of the will gave the brothers, if not Marco, much-needed legal standing in the Polo family and in the Venetian merchant community.

ANOTHER OFT-REPEATED tale involved the misadventures of Marco's uncle Maffeo on returning home. Although his wife recognized him, she could not abide the Mongol *del* that he insisted on wearing. To break her husband of the habit, she took it upon herself to donate his exotic clothing to a passing vagabond. That night, when Maffeo arrived home, he naturally asked what had become of his Mongol outfit; he was particularly concerned because, according to his longstanding custom, he had sewn all of his gems into the lining for safekeeping.

When his wife reluctantly admitted what she had done with his clothes, the story goes that he tore his hair and thumped his chest, as he tried to think of a way to find the anonymous beggar who had come into possession of his fortune. Fortunately, Venice is a small place. The next morning, he went to the Rialto, the center of Venetian commerce, and awaited the appearance of the man in question. It was said that Maffeo carried a spinning wheel without wool, and turned it, as if he were deranged. A crowd gathered around the spectacle, and onlookers shouted questions at him, to which he replied, "He will come, God willing."

Word spread through Venice about the appearance of the elderly madman Maffeo Polo on the Rialto, generating curiosity. The vagabond who held Maffeo's fortune failed to appear. The next day, Maffeo repeated his performance, and the day after that. This time, someone did appear—the vagabond, wearing Maffeo's discarded Mongol attire. On seeing the strange man, Maffeo fell on him, took back the clothing, and felt for the concealed gems. All were there, just as they had been before the beggar came into possession of the discarded garments. Maffeo rescued his fortune and sent the hapless beggar on his way.

RAMUSIO PASSED on another Polo legend. He had learned it, so he said, from the "magnificent Messer Gasparo Malpiero, a very old gentleman, and of singular goodness and integrity, who had his house . . . exactly at the middle point of the . . . Corte del Milion"— the location of the Polo ancestral home. "He stated that he had heard it in turn from his own father and grandfather, and from some other old men, his neighbors."

The old gentleman's story began with the Polos of Venice evincing skepticism about the identity of their long-absent relatives. Instead of showing pride and relief at their return, they seemed embarrassed. To establish their credibility, Marco and his father and uncle decided to invite all their relatives to a lavish feast. They prepared for the event in "honorable fashion, and with much magnificence in that aforesaid house of theirs." As the feast began, gondolas jammed the canals; the guests disembarked and awaited the travelers, hoping to receive gifts from afar, or some proof that the three had traveled the length and breadth of the Silk Road, as they claimed. Instead, the guests found themselves attending a most unusual costume party.

Once the guests were seated, the reassembled Polo company appeared. The three travelers were dressed in long, flowing robes made from costly fabric, in the Venetian style. Later in the evening, they removed the robes and tore them apart, distributing the pieces to the servants in attendance. Puzzled, the guests fell to eating, while the Polos once again changed clothing, reappearing in red velvet robes; as before, they tore these garments apart, and distributed the scraps to the servants. If Marco and his father and uncle wished to create the impression that they were so wealthy after their trip to Asia that they could give away valuable fabrics without blinking an eye, they succeeded completely.

Their demonstration was not yet over. Near the feast's conclusion, the Polos changed their attire once more, and once more gave away the pieces, as their guests marveled at this display of wealth. At that moment, they disappeared, and then returned clad in the Mongol clothing all three had been wearing on the day of their return to Venice, only to have their identity doubted.

According to Ramusio, who was probably embellishing but not inventing, the three took up knives and tore at the seams of their Mongol robes, "to bring forth from them enormous quantities of most precious gems such as rubies, sapphires, carbuncles [a deep red garnet], diamonds, and emeralds which had been sewn up in each of the said garments with much cunning and in such fashion that no one would have been able to imagine they were there. For when they took their departure from the Great Khan, they changed all the riches which he had given them into so many rubies, emeralds, and other precious stones, knowing well that had they done otherwise, it would never have been possible for them to carry so much gold with them over such a long, difficult, and far-reaching road."

This demonstration left their guests astounded and, most important to the Polos, impressed. "Those whom they had formerly doubted," wrote Ramusio, "were indeed those honored and valorous gentlemen of the House of Polo, and they did them great honor and reverence. And when this thing became known throughout Venice, straightway did the whole city, the gentry as well as the common folk, flock to their house, to embrace them and to shower them with caresses and show demonstrations of affection and reverence, as great as you can possibly imagine."

Although Ramusio's tale concluded happily, it stands as a sardonic commentary on the superficiality and materialism of Venetians. They were unwilling—indeed, unable—to recognize Marco, Maffeo, and Niccolò until the three staged a theatrical display of their wealth.

The startling dinner marked the beginning of the rehabilitation of the newly returned Polos. Thereafter, the three received the respect they felt they deserved from their fellow citizens, with Marco singled out for special attention. "All the young men went every day continuously to visit and converse with Messer Marco," Ramusio claimed, "who was most charming and gracious, and to ask of him matters concerning Cathay and the Great Khan, and he responded with so much kindness that all felt themselves to be in a certain manner indebted to him."

IT IS EASY to understand why Marco attracted notice. The significance of the inventions that he brought back from China, or which he later described in his *Travels*, cannot be overstated. At first, Europeans regarded these technological marvels with disbelief, but eventually they adopted them.

Paper money, virtually unknown in the West until Marco's return, revolutionized finance and commerce throughout the West.

Coal, another item that had caught Marco's attention in China, provided a new and relatively efficient source of heat to an energy-starved Europe.

Eyeglasses (in the form of ground lenses), which some accounts say he brought back with him, became accepted as a remedy for failing eyesight. In addition, lenses gave rise to the telescope—which in turn revolutionized naval battles, since it allowed combatants to view ships at a great distance—and the microscope. Two hundred years later, Galileo used the telescope—based on the same technology—to revolutionize science and cosmology by supporting and disseminating the Copernican theory that Earth and other planets revolved around the Sun.

Gunpowder, which the Chinese had employed for at least three centuries, revolutionized European warfare as armies exchanged their lances, swords, and crossbows for cannon, portable harquebuses, and pistols.

Marco brought back gifts of a more personal nature as well. The golden *paiza*, or passport, given to him by Kublai Khan had seen him through years of travel, war, and hardship. Marco kept it still, and would to the end of his days. He also brought back a Mongol servant, whom he named Peter, a living reminder of the status he had once enjoyed in a far-off land.

In all, it is difficult to imagine the Renaissance—or, for that matter, the modern world—without the benefit of Marco Polo's example of cultural transmission between East and West.

BENEATH ITS PLACID SURFACE, the Republic of Venice was ailing at the time of Marco's return. The reign of Lorenzo Tiepolo, the doge when the Polo company departed, had been marked by one setback after another—first famine, then unnecessary squabbles with neighbors whom Venice alienated by imposing tariffs on foreign shipping, a gesture that served only to lessen trade. At about this time, the Republic embarked on three years of military skirmishes with Bologna. Not surprisingly, relations with northern Italy deteriorated badly.

Matters worsened when Venice refused to aid the Church in the War of the Sicilian Vespers, a protracted conflict (1282–1302) pitting King Peter III of Aragon against Pope Martin IV. In retaliation, the Church put an ironclad ban in place, beginning in 1284. Mass could not be said in San Marco; the bells high in the campanile remained eerily silent. The religious pageantry that marked Venetian life—weddings, funerals, even baptisms—was strictly forbidden. The ban extended to the last rites; those denied them might suffer even worse torments in the afterlife. Winter arrived and departed without the celebration of Christmas. As Venice fell silent and penitent before the Absolute, it seemed that God had banished it to a mournful purgatory. "For the past twenty years nothing seemed to have gone right for them," writes the historian John Julius Norwich of the Republic's plight. "Militarily they had suffered defeats on land and sea, with serious losses, both in ships and human lives. They had been forced to watch, powerless, while the enemy penetrated to the very confines of the lagoon. Their neighbors, on many of whom they depended for trade, were in a greater or lesser degree unfriendly. Their chief colony, Crete, was once again in revolt."

As if to confirm the impression of divine disfavor, an earthquake shook the fragile city to its foundations that winter. When the earth's crust trembled, floods wrought havoc in Venice, claiming homes, destroying lives, leaving some citizens to starve amid ruined splendor. Its civic infrastructure still intact, Venice rallied and managed to maintain a veneer of prosperity and might despite disaster. But behind the scenes, the Republic had fallen on hard times, with no prospect of relief.

VENETIANS BLAMED their decline on a coterie of elite families that had amassed wealth during these difficult years, rather than on natural disasters such as earthquakes and floods, the Republic's disastrously confused foreign policies, the Church, or jealous rivals—all of which had done actual harm to Venice. In particular, the tightly knit Dandolo clan was held responsible; during the worst of the Republic's recent troubles, two doges had happened to be Dandolos, including Giovanni Dandolo, who held the office during the trying period from 1280 to 1289.

During his tenure, the Piazza San Marco reverberated with public demonstrations in favor of a rival family, the Tiepolos, who harked back to the Republic's traditional democratic character. Giacomo Tiepolo, the son of a doge, found himself poised to lead the Republic in these troubled times. Marco may have reflected that Tiepolo faced some of the same pressures as the Great Khan. On the one hand, Tiepolo had to satisfy a core group of like-minded supporters, and on the other, he had to cultivate his popular base. Insiders warned that Venice was becoming too democratic and was teetering on the verge of mob rule, while populists believed that Tiepolo planned to establish a hereditary monarchy in Venice.

Under pressure from all sides, Tiepolo went into exile on the mainland. At the same time, 1289, Pietro Gradenigo, the thirty-eight-year-old scion of a newly rich merchant family, was grudgingly elected the next doge, acquiring in the process a condescending nickname, Pierazzo. No matter who occupied the Doge's Palace, whether autocrat or populist, Venice's deterioration accelerated.

In 1291, the sultan of Egypt, Al-Ashraf Khalil, fulfilling a long-held vow, had overrun Acre and killed most of its residents. The shock was felt thousands of miles away in Venice, since Acre had served as a staging area for merchants and their goods, just as it had for the Polos.

With the fall of Acre and other Christian outposts in the Middle East, Venetians turned their attention toward Europe. Ships sailed to destinations as varied as Amsterdam, London, and Marseilles. Venetian merchants learned to distract and entertain neglected feudal barons with a traveling menagerie of animals, clowns, musicians, and acrobats before transacting business. The doge encouraged trade with the West, exempting himself alone from the necessity of paying duty on the items he acquired.

In time, the Republic's struggles against commercial and military rivals drew Marco Polo into the fray. On this occasion, the main irritant was Genoa. That city-state, every bit as avaricious as Venice, jealously guarded its trade in spices from India and grain from the Crimea, as well as fish, salt, furs, and even slaves. Anything that could be bought and sold became fuel for Genoa's economic engine.

To prevent outright conflict, Venice and Genoa had established a flimsy treaty, but the fall of Acre upset the balance, for both parties wanted control over that city. In preparation for war against its rival, Venice joined forces with a lesser power, Pisa. This time, the allies meant business: all those of sound mind and body between the ages of seventeen and sixty were eligible to be drafted at any moment. Furthermore, the wealthiest families were each expected to finance and equip one or more galleys. The Polos were not of their exalted rank; nevertheless, Marco became caught up in war fever. He was responding, in part, to a dramatic change in the Venetian mood. After years of decline, the Republic was suddenly ready to fight to defend its reputation and interests.

Marco may have thrown himself recklessly into the conflict out of boredom with his life. In Venice, he was hemmed in by gray, brown, and ocher buildings looming over cramped, sometimes fetid canals. Instead of roaming the Steppe on horseback, or trekking across deserts in a camel caravan, Marco was negotiating the streets of Venice, some of them so narrow that he had to turn sideways to thread his way along them. Instead of seeing all the way to the horizon, he looked no farther than the windows of his neighbors as they went about their domestic routines. The grandeur and sense of adventure had been drained from his life, replaced by the routines of the merchants of Venice, their accounts and debts, their tiresome lawsuits and contentious families. For the man who had ridden with the Mongols and worshipped with the Buddhists, these restraints may have become unbearable.

In 1298, Marco was only forty-three, still capable of responding to any hint of adventure that came his way. The Battle of Curzola, in which he was taken prisoner, was not the glorious occasion for which Venice had hoped. But it may have offered the escape that he needed.

It is possible that Marco's capture by the Genoese and privileged confinement came as a relief, allowing him to keep his distance from Venice and its restraints for a while. Paradoxically, he was freer in jail, where his daily needs were met and his mind could roam across the face of the world—the Pamir highlands, the Gobi Desert and the emerald Steppe, the *ger*s of Mongolia, all the way to the fantastic palaces of Cambulac and Xanadu. It took the ordeal of confinement in prison to get the world traveler to sit still long enough to tell his story, and it is easy to imagine him talking night and day about his adventures to Rustichello, who enthusiastically assembled Marco's feverish outpourings for European consumption. It had been an open question as to whether Marco could persuade his contentious Venetian neighbors, let alone all of Europe, of his fabulous exploits, but his collaboration with Rustichello promised to do just that.

As a popular writer accustomed to filling out his tales with courtly Arthurian romances and stirring battle scenes, Rustichello had distinct ideas about how to embellish Marco's factual account with stock elements. But the veteran merchant preferred to emphasize events he had witnessed. Yet Marco's perspective differed from that of his audience; his assumptions about the world, and Christendom's place in it, were not their assumptions. After decades abroad, he was steeped in Mongol customs, Mongol languages, and the Mongol worldview, and he looked at life through Mongol eyes—vital, barbaric, and reverent.

RUSTICHELLO OF PISA was not merely a romance writer. He belonged to a family of notaries, and was qualified in the profession. In Italy, notaries have long enjoyed high status. In Roman antiquity, they were august public officials who drew up contracts and financial arrangements, and recorded and approved transfers of property, deeds, and wills; they left the tedious work of copying to their slaves. Their name derived from a widely employed system of shorthand writing, known in Latin as *notae Tironinae*, after Cicero's secretary, M. Tullius Tiro, said to have invented the system while taking down Cicero's prolix speeches. A scribe employing the system was called a *notarius*, and he traveled in the highest circles of the Roman government bureaucracy; his Christian successors, *notarii*, dutifully recorded the sermons of preachers as well as legal proceedings against Christian martyrs. After the collapse of the Roman Empire, notaries became papal appointees whose authority extended throughout Christendom. They were an integral part of the legal system. In his capacity as a notary, Rustichello could certify the veracity of Marco's adventures.

Rustichello's literary imagination tended toward battles and knights errant and virtuous maidens, but his legal training prompted him to require verification from Marco. How could he document his travels, to say nothing of the fantastic episodes he claimed to have witnessed? In answer to this question, Rustichello offers a glimpse into Marco's working method. Marco, Rustichello writes, "noted down only a few things which he still kept in his mind; and they are little compared to the many and almost infinite things which he would have been able to write if he had believed it possible to return to these our parts; but thinking it almost impossible ever to leave the service of the Great Khan, king of the Tartars, he wrote only a few small things in his notebooks."

Fortunately for posterity—and for Rustichello—all was not lost, because Marco sent for and received his notebooks while in prison, and with these in hand to prompt his memory, he "caused all these things to be recounted in order by Master Rustichello, citizen of Pisa, who was with him in the same prison in Genoa, at the time when it was 1298 years since the birth of our Lord Master Jesus Christ."

MARCO WAS FAMILIAR with Persian and with Mongol tongues unknown in the West, not to mention the Venetian dialect, but none suited the epic that Rustichello and he contemplated. Only French, the language of romances—that is, adventure tales—would do, but there is no evidence that Marco was familiar with it. Rustichello, however, did know French, or at least an idiosyncratic, nongrammatical version of the language (the thought of his attempting to speak French is painful to contemplate); so the two Italians composed their Asian epic in that tongue. The rigors of language posed a serious problem for Marco's amanuensis. Rustichello mangled French syntax. At times he refers to Marco Polo in the first person, at other times, in the third, without any apparent reason for the change. The book itself is sometimes described as "my book," meaning Polo's, and sometimes as "our book," the fruit of a collaboration. Rustichello frequently spells the same word various ways, even on the same page. Tenses, which can be especially complex in French, proved difficult for him to master, and so the narrative fluctuates between the present tense and various past tenses, often in the same sentence. His nongrammatical French would become the despair of centuries of translators trying to divine his precise meaning.

MARCO'S EXPERIENCE of the world, his imagination, and his ego far exceeded Rustichello's capacities, and the two collaborators often failed to achieve a harmoniously blended voice. Rustichello tried to impose his idea of proper literary form and Christian ideals on the unruly Marco, but as their account took wing, Rustichello apparently let the hyperactive traveler have his blasphemous way. With his con-

ventional narrative formulas and mannerisms, and his constant straining for effect, Rustichello lacked the gift of *sprezzatura*, the art that
conceals art. But Marco, having honed his stories by telling and
retelling them, and fired by his shrewd and contagious enthusiasm,
overflowed with *sprezzatura*. As a result, the amateur storyteller outdid
the professional. Given the stark differences between the collaborators, one can practically hear them quarreling over the narrative, with
all its awkward compromises, abrupt shifts in tone, and glaring inconsistencies. Like a medieval cathedral fashioned by anonymous artisans,
the result is a spectacular but disorderly accretion of ideas, and of first,
second, and third thoughts—an accidental monument to vanished
civilizations.

Despite his limitations, Rustichello ultimately succeeded in his
task. Without the stubborn Pisan to force the Venetian wayfarer to sit
still long enough to dictate his overflowing reminiscences, the story
of Marco's travels would never have been written. It would have
remained nothing more than outlandish scuttlebutt among the fraternity of merchants traveling the Silk Road, and the stories that Marco
told would have died with him.

SEASONED ROMANCE WRITER that he was, Rustichello of Pisa did
not hesitate to include a colorful, entertaining battle scene lifted nearly
word for word from one of his earlier works. He borrowed the opening
of his earlier success, *Méliadus*, a compilation of traditional Arthurian
romances, employing nearly the same words for the introduction to
Marco Polo's account.

"Lords, Emperors, Kings, Dukes and Marquesses, Counts, Knights,
and Burgesses, and all people who are pleased and wish to know the
different generations of men and the diversities of the different regions
and lands of the world," Rustichello begins, "take then this book and
have it read, and here you will find all the greatest marvels and the
great diversities of the Greater and Lesser Armenia, and of Persia,
Media, Turkey, and of the Tartars and India and of many other
provinces about Asia Media and part of Europe, going toward the
Greek wind, levant, and tramontaine, just as our book will tell you
clearly in order, as Master Marco Polo, wise and noble citizen of
Venice, relates because he saw them with his own eyes."

From that point forward, Marco's account departs from traditional romances, and he emerges as the beguiling and boisterous traveler of renown, a man who became the intimate of Kublai Khan, and even something of a Mongol himself. Caught up in their mutual excitement, the collaborators remark that no one, neither "Christian, Saracen, nor pagan nor Tartar nor Indian nor any man of any kind . . . saw and knew or inquired so much of the different parts of the world and of the great wonders so much as this Master Marco Polo searched out and knows." With that, his tale takes on an unpredictable life of its own.

Marco's voice, even when adulterated by Rustichello's conventional derring-do, is like no other, one moment as dry and precise as the tax assessor and merchant he had been, the next as florid as a fabulist, his sense of conviction lightened with a conspiratorial wink. If this narrative voice, as rendered by Rustichello, captures the energy and intensity of the Marco Polo who appeared before his Genoese captors, it is easy to understand why he transfixed them. Only Marco had had the luck, for good or ill, to be imprisoned within the Mongol Empire for decades, and only Marco possessed the sympathetic imagination to identify completely with it, and to portray it with passion and authenticity.

No original manuscript survives from the months that Polo and Rustichello spent together in prison. Produced before the invention of movable type in the West, the account was circulated throughout Europe in handmade copies in different languages, transcribed by monks, and collected by nobles for their libraries. In the process, it was often altered—sometimes intentionally and sometimes through sheer carelessness or accident. As a result, many sections are plainly out of order; often, chapters, paragraphs, and even sentences appear in the wrong place, breaking the narrative flow.

On the basis of internal evidence—episodes that Marco promises to narrate, but that never turn up in the narrative—it is incomplete, particularly the latter chapters. It is not that Marco's energy is flagging; whole sections seem to be missing or truncated. In the absence of a definitive manuscript, scholars and translators have relied on the incomplete versions that have turned up in libraries and archives, both secular and religious, over the centuries, although the versions vary greatly, with some containing many more chapters than others. None of them feels complete in all respects. They resemble scripts without stage directions; the audience must supply its own, and make its best guess about where Marco might be when he describes an encounter, and even about his attitude—is he being reverent or ironic, amused or outraged? He was capable of registering all these emotions, and more, but they have to be coaxed from Rustichello's fractured French. Despite his limitations, Rustichello manages to convey Marco's narrative voice, by turns histrionic, reverent, and bawdy, constantly shifting in tone and tempo. Marco bubbles over with stories of his travels in Asia, and embellishes his years in the service of Kublai Khan with bawdy jokes, double entendres, and asides. The result is a compendium of his personal experiences along with the impersonal forces of history, like graffiti on granite.

Rustichello reveals Marco as volatile, high-strung, self-dramatizing, and subject to endless mood swings. He captures Marco's nonstop rush of memory and language, as well as his addiction to overstatement. Marco's naïveté shines through undiminished, especially the sense that he never met a ruler he did not admire wholeheartedly. The Marco of the manuscript talks too loudly and quickly; he likes to throw his voice, and to mimic whenever he can. Unlike many compulsive talkers, he rarely repeats himself, and he is fully aware that he is spinning one of the greatest stories ever told. Beneath the lively surface of the narrative a different Marco can be glimpsed: a person of lucid intelligence, phenomenal memory, and, if he relied on records kept in China as he tells his story, attention to detail. Although he gives in to the passions of the moment—hero worship of Kublai Khan, fascination with the countless women who cross his path—he is rarely fooled in the long run, but remains skeptical. The impulsive sensualist grows into a seeker after truth and spiritual fulfillment, goals that prove to be far more elusive than the profitable trading that is the basis of his livelihood. With his quicksilver intelligence, Marco constantly evaluates the sights and people he encounters, and he tries to make them comprehensible to his readers. Like any diligent reporter, he takes care to furnish the who's, what's, and where's of his story, but he is much weaker on the when's, for he does not provide a true chronology of his decades in China, with the exception of his voyage into and out of Asia. Rather, he assembles thematic descriptions of places he visited or heard about, studded with anecdotes and bits of history that he picked up along the way.

The impassioned storyteller is never less than chatty, and often rises to great heights of eloquence as the recording angel of vanished civilizations. If this narrative as rendered by Rustichello is anything like the tales Marco spontaneously told his Genoese captors, it is easy to understand why they were transfixed. Marco's hybrid persona, part Venetian, part Mongol, imparts a distinctive flavor to his account; no other record of a pilgrim's progress through China matches his zest, his profusion of data, and his imaginative sweep.

No storyteller ever had a surer sense that an audience would materialize, prepared to hang on every word. Marco exudes confidence that he is writing for the present, and for history; his chronicle seems, among other things, an obvious bid for fame, a stratagem to perpetuate his name. If that indeed was his goal, he succeeded perhaps more than he imagined, for "Marco Polo" has become synonymous with travel both real and metaphorical, and the peaceful exploration of the unknown.

Throughout the brief chapters of his account, Marco displays an exaggerated sense of self. He places himself center stage during the great events of his day—battles, court intrigues, scandals—when the historical record often shows that his role was minor or nonexistent: that he was more onlooker than actor. Nevertheless, his penchant for self-aggrandizement, which is startlingly apparent compared with the self-effacing tone of accounts left by other travelers and pilgrims of that era, imparts urgency, meaning, and emotion to his chronicle. It is memorable in large part because it overflows with amour propre. Everything that Marco encounters or hears about matters greatly to him, and he makes it matter to his audience as well. He jealously guards his privileged seat at the pageant of history; in an astonishing act of daring, he appoints himself chronicler of the East and the West.

EVENTUALLY, copyists created more than a hundred versions of Marco's account, and no two versions were alike. To simplify the enormous textual puzzle these versions presented, scholars adopted the convention of assigning them to either of two groups, labeled simply A and B. Many A manuscripts contain obvious interpolations—that is, additions made by overzealous translators—and errors abound. For example, a sixteenth-century Tuscan translation derives from a Latin translation of an earlier Tuscan version, thought to be based on a very early version of Rustichello's French. Marco's nuances, flashes of humor, and irony often did not survive the translating and retranslating. To complicate matters even more, the B manuscripts often contain material not found in the A group. Some scholars believe that Marco may have overseen the B versions on his return to Venice, to satisfy the curiosity of readers seeking a fuller account than the one he had composed while in jail. Like a series of studies of the same subject by an artist, each of the manuscripts has some claim to authenticity, but none contains the last word on the subject of his travels.

WHILE MARCO REMAINED in captivity in Genoa, his father, Niccolò, and his uncle Maffeo stayed behind in Venice, concerned for his safety. They repeatedly attempted to ransom him. They had no idea that he actually enjoyed a certain amount of comfort and status in captivity, and was engaged in a collaboration about his fantastic travels.

They also had plans for Marco's future, even if he had none. Since their return to Venice, they had been trying to arrange a respectable marriage for him, if only to retain wealth on their side of the family in future generations. Marco had resisted the idea, but while he was in captivity they were trying to find him a suitable match in expectation of his safe return.

It seems they eventually despaired of doing so. "Seeing that they could not ransom him under any condition," Ramusio later wrote, "and having consulted together, they decided that Messer Niccolò, who though he was very old was nonetheless of robust constitution, should take a wife unto himself." Marco might have been troubled by this development, had he known of it, or, indeed, if it actually occurred. Documents from the era tell a contradictory tale. If Niccolò proceeded with his nuptials, he immediately started his new family, which would eventually consist of three sons.

In Genoa, Marco Polo and Rustichello continued to compose their epic, with no idea of their own fate, or that of their remarkable literary collaboration.

ON MAY 25, 1299, Genoa and Venice ended hostilities by agreeing to a "perpetual peace." After years of conflict, the two city-states had fought to a draw, much to everyone's relief. Neither side had to pay reparations, and few recalled what had sparked the battles in the first place—pride, perhaps.

Three months later, on August 28, Marco Polo and his collaborator, Rustichello of Pisa, won their freedom from the Genoese prison in which they had languished. Marco promptly returned to Venice; Rustichello, his task completed, dropped from view. The Venetian was forty-five years old, and he was ready at last to take his place in the Polo family hierarchy. After the dreary months of confinement, Venice appeared as a seductive haven, not as enticing as the glories and excesses of the Mongols, perhaps, but safer than any place he had known since embarking on his travels as a very young man.

In his absence, family members had improved their standard of living and social status. They had bought a tidy, elegant palazzo, complete with courtyard and tower, in the fashionable San Giovanni Crisostomo neighborhood. It was here that Marco would live out the rest of his years. Exactly how the Polo family financed their impressive new home is a matter of speculation; it is possible they invested the profits from their trading business, but the suspicion lingers that they paid for it with the rubies and sapphires that they had brought back to Venice.

Marco's place in Venetian society was secure, his fortune intact. And once again his elders raised the question of an advantageous marriage—not to the exotic Indian or Mongol princess of his daydreams, but to a woman of a Venetian family equivalent to the Polos in status. After all the mating customs and behaviors he had witnessed in Asia, the thought of marital monogamy may not have been entirely welcome. Nevertheless, a match was arranged in 1300.

MARCO'S PROSPECTIVE BRIDE was named Donata, the daughter of a merchant named Vitale Badoèr. Venetian weddings were elaborate affairs, notable for feasting and business arrangements between the two parties. Representatives of the bride and groom formally contracted on the *dies desponsationis*. On this occasion, the groom made a formal visit to the bride, and, reenacting a ritual handed down from their Roman ancestors, anointed her head. The wedding ceremony itself occurred on the *dies nuptiarum*, and it was marked by additional rites. In the *transductio ad domum*, the groom escorted the bride to his home for the first time, to the accompaniment of celebrating relatives. Afterward, the couple performed the *visitatio* to the church where the service would occur, highlighted by the *benedictio*, devoted to the presentation and blessing of the wedding ring. Immediately afterward, the bride produced her *repromissa*, or dowry, in this case coffers filled with jewelry, linens, damasks, silk, and jewels. Donata's dowry also included a considerable amount of property, including real estate. (According to a legal document dated March 17, 1312, Donata's uncle liquidated her dowry for her husband's benefit.)

Venetian wedding tradition prescribed that eight days after the ceremony the bride pay a visit to her father's house; known as the *reverentalia*, the visit was marked by another feast, and presents were distributed to the guests. With this observance, Marco and Donata's formal wedding rites concluded.

AFTER MARRYING so late in life, Marco Polo behaved in accordance with traditional Venetian life. In rapid succession, he and his wife welcomed three daughters into the world: Fantina, Bellela, and Moreta (the names, common in Venice, frequently appeared in legal documents with variant spellings). His father had died at some point before 1300, when a record referred to him as "the late" Niccolò Polo, but the precise date of death is unknown. Although Marco alone is remembered for his travels, the elder Polo's career in exploration was perhaps even more extraordinary than his son's, for Niccolò completed not just one but two round-trip expeditions to the court of Kublai Khan.

Although Marco gave his father and his equally adventurous uncle Maffeo scant attention in the *Travels*, and often seemed eager to take all the credit for their joint endeavors, he did pay respect to his father in Venice. "His father being dead," according to Ramusio, "he, as befits a good and pious son, caused to be made for him a tomb that was very much honored for the conditions of those times, which was a sarcophagus of living stone that may be seen to this day"—Ramusio was writing 250 years later—"placed under the portico that is before the Church of San Lorenzo of this city, on the right-hand side as one enters, with such inscription as indicates that it is the tomb of Messer Niccolò Polo."

AFTER NICCOLÒ'S DEATH, Marco and his uncle Maffeo continued to trade profitably, but their travels had come to an end. It is likely they never went farther than the Venetian province of Dalmatia. As for Marco, he never again set foot on the Silk Road, nor did he return to Asia and its sense of promise, magic, and danger. It seems that prosperity instilled caution to the point of respectability. He remained tethered to Venice, domiciled with his wife and daughters, his uncle

Maffeo, and other family members in a large, crowded household, where they weathered the political storms assailing the Republic.

IN 1300, irate citizens greeted the new century by mounting a rebellion against the doge, Pietro Gradenigo. Venetian forces subdued it, and the bodies of the upstart leader, Marin Bocconio, and ten of his followers swung from gibbets erected in Piazza San Marco, as a stark warning to others who might have entertained similar notions.

In time, Venice recovered a measure of economic stability and capitalized on the misfortune of its rivals. Talented weavers from Lucca exchanged the conflicts of their home for the promise of Venice, quickly finding a place for their looms near the Rialto. As a result of this migration, Venetian silks and velvets became celebrated for their rich texture and vibrant color; guilds enforced high standards, and substandard goods were publicly burned.

Venetian business practices, long the most aggressive and innovative in Europe, continued to evolve. For centuries, merchants such as the Polos had relied on barter for their transactions, usually trading gems and fabric for goods. But during his troubled reign as doge (1280–1289), Giovanni Dandolo had urged Venice to adopt the financial symbol for which she eventually became known throughout the world: the gold ducat. Ducats had been around for some time, but Dandolo raised the monetary unit to a new standard of quality, declaring, "It must be made to the greatest possible fineness, like to the florin, only better." The florin was the commercial symbol of rival Florence, but it was soon eclipsed by the Venetian ducat. The name of the Venetian mint, the Zecca, that produced these valuable ducats was derived from the Arabic *sikkah*, denoting a stamp or seal, and ducats were often called *zecchini* (the basis of the word "sequin"). The ducat was beautiful to behold, heavy and gleaming. The obverse was adorned with an image of the doge kneeling before Saint Mark, and the reverse with one of Jesus. Henceforth, merchants such as the Polos tallied their fortunes in ducats rather than gems.

DESPITE MARCO'S eventual embrace of Venetian life and customs, there remain tantalizing suggestions that he never gave up his Asian obsessions.

Wherever he went, Marco carried manuscript copies of his travel narrative. He talked constantly of his adventures, and on occasion gave a copy of the narrative to an important noble, who would, Marco hoped, preserve it in his library for safekeeping. The interest or indulgence of a wealthy patron was the only way—aside from storing a copy in a monastery—Marco could be assured that his stories would outlive him. The inscription on one very early manuscript indicates that he presented it to a "Monseigneur Thiebault, chevalier, seigneur de Cepoy" in August 1307. According to the inscription, the knight, in Venice on behalf of Charles of Valois, the king of Aragon, requested a manuscript from its author, and one can imagine that Marco was only too glad to comply.

All the while, the Republic's long-standing feud with the Church was fraying the delicate fabric of economic life. On March 27, 1309, the Church issued another punitive papal bull, this one far more serious than the earlier one. Trying to teach the unruly city a lesson for all time, the Church excommunicated the Republic and its citizens. All of Venice's treaties were declared void—a potentially disastrous blow to its trade relationships. Venetian properties beyond the lagoon were subject to seizure by the Church. Christians everywhere were forbidden to trade with Venice. Banks, ships, factories, storehouses, and trading posts with Venetian interests in foreign lands reportedly were burned.

At first, Venetians, toughened in conflict, took the latest uproar in stride, but when their soldiers fell prey to disease, the Republic's enemies decimated its fleet. La Serenissima seemed to face the end of her long reign. Even the self-confidence of the Venetian merchant aristocracy crumbled, and the doge, Pietro Gradenigo, humbly dispatched a mission to Pope Clement V, now in Avignon, to seek forgiveness. The gesture succeeded, and the excommunication of Venice ended. Nevertheless, the doge fell into disrepute with the citizens of the Republic.

THERE WAS ANOTHER whiff of rebellion in the air, as a conspiracy of nobles sought to remove Gradenigo from power. Their plan was bold: on the morning of June 15, 1310, they would storm the Piazza San Marco, kill the doge, and then slaughter his closest aides. Fortunately for the stability of the Republic, the weather refused to cooperate. A violent storm blew up, lashing the lagoon with rain and thunder, as if to warn of the awful deed to come. Street thugs chanting *"Morte al doge Gradenigo!"* could barely hear themselves and scattered under the onslaught of foul weather. Amid the ensuing chaos, the doge's guard learned of the uprising and attacked at least one hostile group, driving them off.

The rebels suffered another disaster from a most unlikely source. As Bajamonte Tiepolo, one of the leaders, led a vicious mob near the Rialto, the racket infuriated one of the residents, a woman named Giustina Rosso, who opened her window, seized a heavy pot planted with carnations, and hurled it straight at Tiepolo. The missile almost found its target; Tiepolo was spared, but his standard bearer fell to the wet pavement, lifeless, his skull shattered by the flower pot. Tiepolo's rabble suddenly panicked, as enraged residents hurled one object after another at their exposed heads. The rebels scattered, leaving Tiepolo with no choice but to surrender and bargain for his life. Luckily for him, he managed to negotiate banishment to Dalmatia for four years, while others paid for their rebellion with their lives.

Giustina Rosso, who had thrown the fatal flower pot, received heartfelt thanks from the doge. Asked what reward she desired for her valiant deed, she modestly declared that she wished to display a banner of Saint Mark, patron saint of Venice, every June 15 to commemorate the event. She had only one other request—that her annual rent never exceed fifteen ducats.

On such whimsical deeds turned the fate of Venice.

MARCO AVOIDED the political disputes of his day, preferring to watch over his holdings. He challenged the established order only once, in 1305, when he appeared in court on behalf of a disreputable smuggler, Bonocio of Mestre, to indemnify him. The scenario suggests that the troublemaker may have been operating at Marco's behest.

ON FEBRUARY 6, 1310, Marco's uncle Maffeo felt his days coming to an end. He drew up his will, and died soon thereafter. Though married, Maffeo had no children, and therefore he left most of his substantial estate to his nephews, including Marco. Soon after, Marco's half brother died without a male heir, and left most of his estate to Marco as well. These bequests, combined with his father's estate, meant that Marco controlled the lion's share of the Polo enterprise.

The newfound wealth failed to make him comfortable or generous. Accounts of Marco's animated storytelling yield to records of his litigiousness and pettiness in the latter years of his life. He became increasingly preoccupied with the pursuit of wealth for wealth's sake, and known for his combativeness and irritability. This sort of behavior, so unlike the engaging attributes of his youth, suggests a tendency to depression. The world's greatest traveler journeyed no more. He ceased to add to his storehouse of experiences, preferring to strengthen his financial status in the years remaining to him. Documents attest that Marco could be greedy when it suited him, as if he believed having great wealth entitled him to still more. On occasion he lent money to needy relatives, but he always charged them interest; when they were unable to pay, he did not extend or forgive the debt, he took them to court, heedless of the spectacle of one Polo suing another.

In 1319, Marco brought suit against his cousin Marcolino to recover a debt incurred by Marcolino's father in 1306. The Venetian court ruled that the plaintiff was entitled to seize goods equal to the debt, in addition to twice that amount in the form of a fine, as well as 20 percent interest accumulated over a period of thirteen years. The total exceeded poor Marcolino's liquid assets, and on September 10 he was forced to transfer ownership of two properties in the San Giovanni Crisostomo neighborhood to Marco Polo—now wealthier than ever.

Marco did not hesitate to take others to court for small matters as well as large. He called a fellow Venetian, Paolo Girardo, to account for a modest unpaid commission for the sale of a pound and a half of musk. To complicate matters slightly, Girardo had surreptitiously sold a small portion, and then returned the remainder to Marco, who, on weighing it, discovered that one-sixth ounce was missing. Outraged, he sued. Described in legal documents as a "noble man," Marco won a resounding victory and had the paltry satisfaction of being repaid by Girardo, who faced jail if he failed to make Marco whole within a reasonable amount of time.

MARCO POLO'S reputation survived this petty episode and others like it.

At one point Marco drew the attention of Pietro d'Abano, a professor of medicine and philosophy. The two met several times to discuss Marco's voyage beyond Venice, and each time d'Abano came away impressed by his wide-ranging knowledge, his retentive memory, and, as is obvious on every page of the *Travels*, his outstanding powers of observation. Returning to Padua, d'Abano composed a treatise in which he complimented "Marco the Venetian" as "the man who has encompassed more of the world in his travels than any I have ever known, and a most diligent investigator," and proceeded to recount their conversations concerning astronomy, of all things, and, in particular, a certain "star" visible in Zanzibar, the island Marco claimed to have visited near the end of his journey. "He saw this same star under the Antarctic Pole, and it has a great tail, of which he drew the figure, thus."

Thereafter, Marco spoke as the endlessly curious traveler he once had been, gushing forth details in wild profusion, as if he had found a new Rustichello ready to immortalize his experiences. "He informs me furthermore," d'Abano wrote, "that thence camphor, lignum aloes, and brazilwood are exported to us. He informs me that the heat there is intense, and the habitations few in number. These things indeed he saw on a certain island at which he arrived by sea. He says, moreover, that the men there are very large, and that there are also very great rams that have wool coarse and stiff as are the bristles of our pigs."

D'Abano asked Marco whether it was true that people who live "in hot places are timid, and those who are, on the other hand, in cold places, virile," as Aristotle claimed. Marco attempted to reconcile Aristotle with his own experience as best he could. "I heard from Marco the Venetian, who traveled across the Equator, that he had found there men larger in body than here, and he had found this because in such places one does not meet with the cold that is exhausting and consequently tends to make them smaller." According to d'Abano's account, Marco was debunking classical theories in a free-flowing, nonsystematic way drawn from personal observation, yet the professor continued to hold him in the highest esteem. If no longer a traveler, Marco could at least enjoy a burgeoning reputation as the sage of Venice.

By 1318, when Marco was sixty-four, he could look with some satisfaction on his growing family. Fantina, the oldest of the three daughters, married Marco Bragadin, with a splendid dowry provided by her wealthy father. Her younger sister, Bellela, followed the same pattern when she married Bertuccio Querini, from an old Venetian family; the union produced two children. Less is known of Moreta, Marco's third daughter, who left no recorded issue, and probably did not marry while her father was alive.

Marco's new sons-in-law became his allies in his continuing quarrels with other Polos. Ignoring blood relatives who perhaps had more claim on his loyalties, he chose instead to work with Fantina's husband, Marco Bragadin; they were so close that the young couple and their four boys and two girls all lived with the patriarch in the Ca' Polo.

APPROACHING his seventieth winter, the sage of the Ca' Polo fell out of favor with Venetians. With the Mongol Empire in decline, and the Silk Road no longer passable, the moment in history to which Marco belonged receded in time, even though the implications of his travels had yet to be understood, or his *Travels* fully appreciated.

When he ambled through the streets of Venice, children followed after, calling out, "Messer Marco, tell us another lie!" Or so one legend has it. Another tradition holds that a Venetian masque witnessed the appearance of a reveler disguised as Marco Polo, who amused the guests by telling the most outrageous stories imaginable as though he believed them to be completely true.

By 1323, Marco had become sickly and bedridden. By this time, his *Travels* had come to the attention of a Dominican friar named Jacopo d'Acqui, who, as was common, reproduced parts of the narrative in his own work, *Imago mundi*, in which he related a tantalizing story: "Because there were to be found great things, things of mighty import, and indeed almost unbelievable things, he"—that is, Marco—"was entreated by his friends when he was at the point of death to correct his book and to retract those thing that he had written over and above the truth. To which he replied, 'Friends, I have not written down the half of those things that I saw.' "

What did Marco omit from his travels? Perhaps gossip from the Mongol court, or his own peccadilloes as a young man far from home. Yet that is not exactly the sense Marco's statement conveys. Rather than referring to a specific idea, his admission suggests that although he was done with his book, it was not done with him. The experiences contained within its pages would not leave him alone. He had been reliving them since his return, but had found no relief in committing them to paper; describing them only reinforced his obsession. If the accuracy of d'Acqui's report is to be trusted, Marco's startling comment tells us that his propensity to relive endlessly his travels along the Silk Road was both a gift and a burden; he could never put those experiences behind him. Although his account draws to a conclusion with his release from Kublai Khan's empire and return to Venice, his story is amorphous, an odyssey without limits. Asia was so large and varied, so rich in natural resources, customs, politics, in wars and wisdom, and so far advanced over Europe, that no one could manage to include it all in one book.

As MARCO'S health deteriorated, a physician was summoned—a measure tantamount to calling a priest to administer the last rites. Venetian physicians occupied a respected role in society, but their professional skills were severely limited. By law, they were required to advise a patient suffering from a serious illness to allow for time to draw up or revise a will, and to seek absolution.

On January 8, 1324, Marco lay at home dying, despite the ministrations of the exalted physicians. The day was short; the pale sun cast somber, drawn-out shadows. His family called for the priest of San Procolo, Giovanni Giustiniani, who conveniently doubled as a notary, which meant that he could draw up the dying man's will and certify it. For Marco, this was his last transaction, his contract with eternity, and he approached it with the skill of an experienced merchant. Working from Marco's precise notes, Father Giustiniani, writing in the vulgate Latin of the late Middle Ages, drew up the document, long on specificity but short on consistency.

Marco appointed his wife, Donata, and three daughters as co-executrices, and much of the will's language was formulaic, in accordance with Venetian customs. He directed that the Church was entitled to tithe his estate, as provided by law, and further directed that additional sums were to be paid to the monastery of San Lorenzo, "where I wish to be buried." In addition, he listed a number of bequests to people, to religious institutions, and to "every guild and fraternity to which I belong."

On his deathbed, Marco declared, "I cancel the debt of three hundred lire that my sister-in-law owes me," and proceeded to cancel other debts owed to him by the convent of San Giovanni, San Paolo of the Order of Preachers, and a cleric named Friar Benvenuto. At the same time, he specified that a fee of 220 soldi be paid to the notary, "for his labor on this my testament and that he may offer prayers to the Lord for me."

When he came to his servant Peter, the Mongol who had served him in Venice, Marco suddenly turned magnanimous: "I release Peter my servant, of the Tartar race, from all bonds of servitude as [I pray] God may absolve my soul from all guilt and sin, and I likewise release to him all that he may have earned by his labors in his own house, and over and above this I bequeath to him one hundred lire of Venetian denari."

Only then did Marco consider bequests to his family. Donata would receive an annuity, a prearranged settlement, and the household furnishings, including three beds and all that went with them. The daughters were instructed to divide whatever was left among themselves in equal measure, with a significant exception. Moreta, still unmarried, was to receive "a sum equal to that given to each of my other daughters as dowry and outfit."

Marco's will ended with a strict admonition: "If anyone should presume to break or violate this will, may he bring upon himself the curse of almighty God and may he remain bound under the anathema of three hundred and eighteen Fathers, and over and above this he shall pay over to my abovementioned executrices five pounds of gold and may this document, my will, remain in force." The document ended: "The signature of the above written Messer Marco Polo, who requested that this be drawn up."

He did not actually sign his will, now on deposit at the Biblioteca Nazionale Marciana in Venice—an omission that has led to the suspicion that he was so infirm he could no longer perform even this simple act. In any case, his signature was not necessary. Giovanni Giustiniani, the priest and notary, signed and authenticated Marco's last will and testament under Venetian law. To forestall the possibility of forgery, he affixed his *tabellionato*, a distinctive flourish.

Marco's will reveals that he had amassed a considerable estate, including items in which he traded, such as fabric, and valuable real estate, including the Ca' Polo, all of which might have belonged to any prosperous Venetian merchant, with the exception of a few exotic items that bore witness to his exceptional past. Each of the items told a story to those able to understand it.

The first was a "golden tablet of command" conferred on him by

Kublai Khan when Marco left Cambulac, and which appointed him to high rank in the Mongol court—a court that barely existed by the time of Marco's death. The tablet spoke to the depth of the relationship between the Great Khan and the Venetian who had served him for so many years.

The second was a "Buddhist rosary," made, according to an inventory of Marco's possessions, from boxwood "in the manner of a paternoster"—a carefully wrought turn of phrase designed to distinguish it from its Christian counterpart. This object spoke to Marco's once-fervent search for spiritual enlightenment in Asia and India.

The third was a *bochta*, or Mongol helmet or headdress, decorated with gems and pearls. This unusual item may have been the same headdress worn by the young princess Kokachin, whom Marco had escorted across China. The bestowing of a royal garment on a favorite servant was common practice, and it would have been natural, perhaps even expected, for her to thank the Venetian who had helped to guide her safely across Asia to her new home. Marco wrote that she had shed tears when she and the Polos parted company, and perhaps she had offered the prize at that emotional moment.

By itself, Marco's documented wealth did not qualify him as a member of the Venetian financial elite, but it may not tell the entire story. A significant part, or even most, of his assets may have been in the gems he carried back with him from Asia. Rubies and sapphires lent themselves to concealment from commercial rivals, tax collectors, and even family members. Marco and his father and uncle had lived for years among the Mongols while concealing gems in the lining of their robes, and the story of Maffeo's despair on learning that his wife had inadvertently given his apparently ordinary robe to a beggar suggests the critical importance of those hidden assets. It would have been natural for Marco to continue the custom of hiding his gems after he returned to Venice, even until his death. If this is the case, then the true dimensions of his wealth escaped the notice of the local authorities and will likely never be known.

AS THE HOURS DRAGGED BY, Marco approached death. According to Venetian law, the day commenced at sunset, and it was soon January 9. The all-important notary dated Marco's will January 8, which meant that his life's journey ended between sunsets on January 8 and 9, 1324.

The world's most famous traveler was a prisoner for long periods of his life. He endured decades in two separate forms of confinement, the first when Kublai Khan held him in luxurious captivity in China, the second when he became a prisoner of war in Genoa. Paradoxically, it was during those periods that he was at his best. He had possessed immense patience in the face of trying conditions. That resolve made it possible for him to return safely home from his wayfaring, and later to complete his account in the unlikeliest of circumstances, an enemy prison. Infused with his restless spirit, the *Travels* survives as both a historical chronicle and a work of art, a depiction of vanished worlds in the form of a timeless adventure.

VENETIAN FUNERALS of the era were public ceremonies redolent of Byzantine influences. The deceased was taken from his deathbed and placed on a floor or pallet strewn with ashes. Then a mournful bell tolled, and priests chanted prayers in Latin. The widow was expected to display tremendous public grief, crying, howling, and pulling her hair out by the roots. When funeral assistants wrapped the body in a sheet and tried to carry it out the door to its final resting place, she was expected to block their path and carry on with renewed force. As the mourners took the body to the church, family members followed close behind, bewailing their loss in as public a manner as they could muster; the histrionics were repeated at the grave site. The poor of Venice displayed the corpses of family members on the street for days as a way to collect alms from passersby, but the wealthy Polo family arranged for Marco's prompt burial in the cemetery of the church of San Lorenzo, close to his father, Niccolò, with whom he had traveled the world. Some years later, in 1348, the will of his youngest daughter, Moreta, indicated her desire to be buried in the same location, "in the tomb of my parents."

Tradition holds that Marco's final resting place was marked by his father's sarcophagus, and it appears that the most famous Venetian citizen of all had no monument of his own, except, of course, his *Travels*.

Most of Marco Polo's contemporaries scorned or simply ignored his feats, but eventually history remembered.

The Storyteller

DESPITE THE ESSENTIAL ACCURACY of the *Travels*, the name Il Milione clung to Marco Polo after his death. He was seen, initially, more as an entertainer and fabricator than as a historian. For instance, Amalio Bonaguisi, a Florentine translator of Marco's account, wrote in 1392 that the Venetian had undertaken his labors purely "to pass the time and [avoid] melancholy." He warned those who read his version of the *Travels*, "the contents appear to me to be incredible things and his statements appear to me to be not lies but more likely miracles."

Bonaguisi's reaction was understandable. Marco's collaborator, Rustichello, freely interpolated several Christian miracles in the belief that the story needed more excitement than it already had; in the process, the outright literary fabrications, though few in number, cast doubt on Marco's actual experiences. "It may well be true that about which he tells," Bonaguisi concluded, "but I do not believe it, though nonetheless there are found throughout the world many different things in one country and another. . . . I copied it for my pleasure . . . , not to be believed or credited."

This state of affairs was not as unlikely as it sounds because the only other account even roughly comparable to Marco Polo's *was* a collection of tall tales and beguiling myths passed off as fact. Sir John Mandeville, whose *Travels* first appeared in a French edition in 1356, might be called the English Marco Polo, except that Sir John in all likelihood never traveled farther than a well-stocked nobleman's library. Identified only as an English knight from Hertfordshire, the mysterious Mandeville said that he left home in 1322—or, in some versions, 1332—and traveled to the Holy Land, and later on to India, Persia, and even China, and returned home in 1356 (or 1366). He claimed to have shown his report to the pope, who proclaimed it true. But the account was actually an artful compilation of stories gleaned from historians and others—including Pliny, Herodotus, and the mythical Prester John, to whom Marco was also susceptible—as well as from various Alexander romances, legends about Alexander the Great. He also incorporated works of lesser-known writers such as Albert of Aix, William of Tripoli, Odoric of Pordenone, and Vincent of Beauvais, who in turn had borrowed heavily from authors of antiquity. Fittingly, Mandeville's opus was later pillaged by others bent on compiling their own fabulous histories.

Mandeville's imaginary *Travels* became a popular work in late medieval and Renaissance England. In the fifteenth century, more than five times as many editions of Mandeville's book were published as of Polo's. For at least two centuries, the two books were often bracketed together as fanciful, entertaining accounts of voyages that might have been. By the early eighteenth century, Mandeville's work underwent a reevaluation and was finally debunked as "enchanted ground and Fairyland."

Unlike Mandeville, who set out to fabricate, Marco believed every word he dictated; however, his notion of the truth was not merely literal but incorporated subjective, imaginative, and even mythological elements in an attempt to fashion a larger, more persuasive reality. Had Marco relied on facts alone, his account would have been as dry as those left by his clerical predecessors. Although it contained puffery, it was not a fabrication, and he expected—in fact, demanded—that his audience believe every word. While this approach may appear to have placed a huge burden on him, since he was obliged to attest to the veracity of all he described, the burden was transferred to his readers, whom he repeatedly challenged to accept whatever he had to say.

Two decades of travel had taught Marco that fact was stranger than fiction, but he strained to persuade others of that paradox. Did any writer equipped with Marco's experience ever feel the need to boast as much as he did, or to plead with his audience to accept what he was saying as the truth? Yet he possessed a unique asset to convince the doubters: personal reflections as well as historical commentary about the most powerful ruler in the world, Kublai Khan. Without his portrayal of this larger-than-life figure, Marco's account would have been just another colorful report of life on the Silk Road. His long service to the Mongol leader lifted his book onto another plane entirely; more than being a mere traveler, he led a charmed existence at the juncture of two civilizations, acting as an intermediary and, best of all, living to tell the tale.

Yet Marco has his blind spots. Once Kublai Khan enters his decline, the Venetian lacks a vocabulary to describe the deterioration of his former hero. Elsewhere, he is prone to sudden enthusiasms—for women, or art, or even religions—which he discards as quickly as he takes them up, as if he were a merchant in a bazaar, handling, considering, and finally rejecting the merchandise placed before him. His grasp of history is unreliable, in spite of his efforts to appear learned. He knows a little bit about many things, but he remains a dazzling dilettante.

THREE CENTURIES after Marco's death, Francesco Sansovino's guidebook to Venice, considering the Church of San Lorenzo, mentioned the Venetian traveler in conjunction with Columbus, the Genoese navigator and explorer: "Under the portico is buried Marco Polo, surnamed Milione, who wrote the travels of the new world, and who was the first before Christopher Columbus who discovered new countries." Had Marco been alive to receive these accolades, he would have accepted them readily, although he might have pointed out that he did not think of himself as an explorer of unknown lands but as an exceptionally well-traveled merchant following traditional routes, making observations of ancient worlds in Asia and in India. The lands and peoples he investigated were new only to Europe.

It appears that by 1685 Marco's reputation in Venice was secure at last. In his encyclopedic ecclesiastical history, Tomaso Fugazzoni, describing repairs to the Church of San Lorenzo, remarked, "In the center of the portico was the burial place of the most famous Marco Polo, noble Venetian"—a description grand enough to satisfy even its subject's vanity.

But the site did not survive. By 1827, Emmanuele Antonio Cicogna, writing in his comprehensive catalog of Venetian inscriptions, mentioned the lost memorials of the Polo family. In fact, the entire church of San Lorenzo had fallen into decrepitude. It was later rebuilt, and more recent investigations suggest that the bones of the Polos and others buried within its walls were collected in a common grave, and perhaps later used as filling to support the new floor of the remodeled church. In any event, the sarcophagus and other items marking the final resting place of Marco, his parents and uncle, and his wife and children were all lost.

If any surviving member of the Polo family could be said to have carried on the family legacy, it was Fantina, the oldest of the three daughters, and she did so not as an explorer but as a persistent litigant. Records show that she was in and out of court defending the inheritance she received from her father; on August 4, 1362, she claimed that her late husband had fraudulently appropriated her legacy before he died in the Venetian colony of Crete. For decades thereafter, Polos squabbled among themselves as they competed for the assets of the family—its gold, spices, fabrics, and real estate. None of them appears to have taken an interest in or furthered the cause of Marco's greatest asset, the chronicle of his travels. That mission was left to others, as manuscripts proliferated across Europe, and the *Travels* took on a life of its own, far removed from the provincial circles of Venice.

MARCO POLO'S collaboration with Rustichello of Pisa gave rise to a cottage industry of reproduction, all of it spontaneous and independent. The earliest patrons and readers of the *Travels* were scholars, monks, and interested noblemen. Less-educated and less-privileged people in Venice and elsewhere, if they knew of the book at all, relied on hearsay concerning Marco Polo's fantastic account.

One hundred and nineteen early manuscript versions of Marco's book survive. All are different. An early version, in the Tuscan dialect, may have been composed while Marco was alive. The *Travels* soon appeared in other European tongues, including Venetian, German, English, Catalan, Aragonese, Gaelic, and of course Latin. In an era before movable type, the *Travels* received wide distribution, but others outdid it for popularity. At least 275 manuscripts of John Mandeville's fictional account circulated, and in the fourteenth and fifteenth centuries, no fewer than 500 manuscripts of the *Divine Comedy* placed Dante's vision before the reading public.

In contrast, Venetian skepticism rendered Marco a prophet without honor in his own land. Dante, his contemporary, never mentioned him (although some scholars believe they have discerned a cryptic reference to the traveler). Of all the early manuscripts, just two circulated in Marco's native city, and they were dated 1445 and 1446, nearly 150 years after Marco served time in Genoa with Rustichello. A fortunate few may have been able to consult a public copy of the book—version unknown—said to be chained to the Rialto Bridge, in the heart of Venice's commercial district. Jostled by bickering merchants and tradesmen, dedicated readers would have gathered to be transported to another world, one inhabited by Kublai Khan, his alluring concubines, and his limitless armies—the fruit of Marco Polo's travels no less than of his imagination.

Marco's sensational manuscript eventually became general knowledge. Ramusio's claim that "all Italy in [a] few months was full of it" was something of a well-intended exaggeration. In reality, the work was disseminated slowly, one handwritten copy at a time, and required more than a century to win a permanent place in the European historical and literary consciousness. Marco Polo eventually attained the status of a culture carrier, one of the rare individuals of wide experience who embody and transmit an entire ethos to succeeding generations. The culture was that of the global traveler and trader, comprising numerous subcultures—those of the Mongols, the Chinese, the inhabitants of the Indian subcontinent, and Asian tribes. His reach extended from Armenia to Zanzibar. His portrayals of these cultures, and especially of China, became Europe's primary source of information about them until the nineteenth century. Marco provided Europe with a description not of the world, as his original title promised, but of its missing half. In the process, he rescued crucial people and events from utter obscurity.

EDITORS AND SCHOLARS attempted to reconcile the disorderly manuscripts, to verify or express skepticism about various details, and to guide readers through the distant and occasionally unfathomable Asia and the Indian subcontinent. Among the most prominent was a monk who was none too happy about the task of translating the immense manuscript into Latin. "I, Brother Francesco Pipino of Bologna of the Order of the Brothers Preachers," he began, "am forced by many of my fathers and masters to reduce the true and faithful translation from the common tongue"—probably Tuscan or a Venetian dialect—"to Latin." He completed his work between 1310 and 1314, during the last years of Marco's life. The manuscript that Pipino used was close to the original, but it seems that Marco kept adding to his account until his death. For this reason, Pipino feared that his scholarly translation might not be the last word, and furthermore, it would lack the raw excitement of the "common tongue."

Whatever his misgivings, Pipino brought distinct religious ideas to bear on his labors. The Latin translation was intended to brief the monks of his religious order about the East in preparation for establishing distant missions. He edited with an eye toward propriety and religious doctrine, and omitted sexually explicit references as well as many of Marco's sly double entendres. When he felt it necessary, Pipino interpolated words of his own. He expressed the hope that his pious readers "seeing the gentile peoples wrapped in such darkness and blindness and in such uncleanness may give thanks to God who lighting his faithful with the light of truth has deigned to call them from so dangerous darkness into his wonderful light."

Marco's spiritual perceptions throughout his account are, of course, far more nuanced and paradoxical than Fra Pipino's. Although Marco, for example, never gained an appreciation of the subtlety, power, and sophistication of Islamic culture, Pipino outdid him by inserting the world "hated" or similar adjectives each time the Venetian referred to Muslims or infidels; the result exaggerated Marco's indifference toward Islam to the point of outright hostility—but the rancor existed in Pipino's mind, not Marco's. Nevertheless, Pipino's distortions survive even in some modern versions of the *Travels*.

THE FIRST PRINTED VERSION of the *Travels* appeared in Nuremburg in 1477, about 175 years after Rustichello set the account down in manuscript form. The book featured a full-page idealized representation of the young traveler on the frontispiece. Demand for Marco's work led to a second German printed version, this one produced in Augsburg, four years later. Printers in other countries followed suit. Pipino's rendition of Marco's account served as the basis of a popular French translation (not to be confused with the French dialect in which Rustichello likely wrote), issued in book form in 1556.

For many years, the leading Italian version was Ramusio's. It was published in several editions, with the definitive impression appearing in 1557, two years after Ramusio's death in Padua (and more than two centuries after Marco's death). The endlessly enthusiastic Ramusio, who was privy to the gossip surrounding Marco, breathed new life into the Venetian traveler's legend and fully realized his contribution to understanding the world in which they lived. "Seeing that so many details of that part of the world of which . . . Marco has written are being discovered in our time," Ramusio wrote, "I have judged it a reasonable thing to make his book come to light with the help of different copies written more than two hundred years ago (in my judgment) perfectly correct and by a great length much more faithful than that which is read hitherto; so that the world should not lose that fruit which can be gathered from so great diligence and industry about so honorable a science."

Of all the explorers, ancient and modern, Marco Polo impressed Ramusio as the greatest—greater, even, than Columbus. Ramusio admitted his judgment was biased, for Columbus hailed from Venice's archrival, Genoa, and sailed under the flag of rival Spain. Still, he opined, "it seems like to me that a [voyage] by land should take precedence over one by sea," considering the "enormous greatness of soul with which so difficult an enterprise was carried out and brought to conclusion along such an extraordinarily long and harsh route," not to mention the "lack of food—not for days, but for months."

Columbus carefully annotated a copy of Marco's account during the four voyages he made to the New World, as the Genoese navigator tried in vain to find Marco Polo's China. (It could be said that Marco misled rather than inspired Columbus into thinking that China lay in proximity to the Caribbean.) In his personal copy of the Italian translation of the *Travels*, Columbus made copious marginal notes indicating that he paid particular attention to potential cash crops that Marco mentioned—pepper, cinnamon, and cloves—all of which Columbus dreamed of importing to Europe at great profit. And, hoping to take up where the Polo company left off, he planned to meet the "Grand Khan" and present him with official letters from King Ferdinand and Queen Isabella of Spain, his royal sponsors, and instruct him in the ways of the West, especially Christianity—all without realizing that the Mongol Empire was a thing of the past.

The *Travels* inspired another impressionable voyager, a young diplomat named Antonio Pigafetta, who served as the official chronicler of Ferdinand Magellan's circumnavigation of the globe, beginning in 1519. One of only eighteen survivors of that disastrous expedition, Pigafetta wrote his account of the circumnavigation in emulation of his hero and fellow Venetian, Marco Polo.

. . .

INCOMPLETE AND INCONSISTENT, the *Travels* remained an unfinished masterpiece that spoke to succeeding generations of voyagers and visionaries alike.

On a summer's day in 1797, relates Samuel Taylor Coleridge, "the Author, then in ill health, had retired to a lonely farm-house between Porlock and Linton, on the Exmoor confines of Somerset and Devonshire." Coleridge was twenty-five years old, the youngest of fourteen children of a country vicar. He had recently left Jesus College, Cambridge, without a degree, and set his heart on becoming a poet and utopian radical. Plagued by an unstable constitution and extreme melancholy, he sought relief in laudanum, a tincture of opium.

"In consequence of a slight indisposition," he continues, "an anodyne had been prescribed, from the effects of which he fell asleep in his chair at the moment that he was reading the following sentence . . . in 'Purchas His Pilgrimage' "—the chronicle published in 1613 by Samuel Purchas, which incorporated broad swaths of Marco's book. "In Xanadu did Cublai Can build a stately palace," wrote Purchas, never imagining he would inspire some of the most famous words in English poetry, words that would be attributed to someone else, "encompassing sixteen miles of plain grounde with a wall, wherein are fertile Meadows, pleasant Springs, delightful Streames, and all sort of beasts of chase and game, and in the middest thereof a sumptuous house of pleasure, which may be removed from place to place . . . Here the Kubla Khan commanded a palace to be built, and stately garden thereunto. And thus ten miles of fertile ground were inclosed within a wall."

After reading those words, Coleridge passed three hours "in a profound sleep, at least of the external senses." It seemed to him that while he drowsed, his unconscious mind composed "two to three hundred lines" of verse "without any sensation or consciousness of effort." When he roused himself from his drug-induced stupor, he "instantly and eagerly" tried to set down as many of these dream verses as he could remember. The phantom verses presumably concerned Kublai Khan, given the material that Coleridge had been reading when he nodded off.

Just then, the infamous "person on business from Porlock" arrived to distract the young poet from his labors. Afterward, the poet, "on his return to his room, found, to his no small surprise and mortification, that though he still retained some vague and dim recollection of the general purport of the vision, yet, with the exception of some eight or ten scattered lines and images, all the rest had passed away like the images on the surface of a stream into which a stone has been cast, but, alas! without the after restoration of the latter!"

After struggling with his half-forgotten material, stolen as if from a dream, Coleridge commenced writing the first lines of "Kubla Khan":

> *In Xanadu did Kubla Khan*
> *A stately pleasure dome decree:*
> *Where Alph, the sacred river, ran*
> *Through caverns measureless to man*
> *Down to a sunless sea.*

The euphoric mood builds until Coleridge concludes with a warning about the dangers of unrestrained rapture. He imagines others observing him, or a kindred spirit, and crying out:

> *Beware! Beware!*
> *His flashing eyes, his floating hair!*
> *Weave a circle round him thrice,*
> *And close your eyes with holy dread,*
> *For he on honey-dew hath fed,*
> *And drunk the milk of Paradise.*

Coleridge's harmonious vision of power and space extended so far ahead of its time that almost twenty years passed before he felt ready to publish his poem about "Kubla Khan," the work that gave the Mongol leader a permanent place in the Western imagination.

Despite the difference in temperament between Marco, the peripatetic merchant, and Coleridge, the neurasthenic poet, the grandeur of the Mongol Empire spoke to them both. Coleridge was no stranger to hallucinations; they served as the source of his poetic visions. Without realizing the true source of his inspiration, he fell under the spell of the Venetian's hypnotic descriptions, as paraphrased by Samuel Purchas. Marco, for his part, may have become familiar with opium while in Afghanistan, and the drug might have been connected with his illness there. Perhaps both men employed drugs, which would have heightened their perceptions and imparted unnatural vividness to their literary works. As Marco learned to tolerate opium, it may well have altered and sharpened his perceptions—and the *Travels*. In this case, it would be more accurate to say that he was an amplifier rather than exaggerator, that he was unnaturally prone to suggestion. That would explain why extensive parts of his account display a high degree of acuity and detail, while other parts are so fanciful. If Marco stopped using drugs such as opium when he returned to Venice, his withdrawal could have contributed to his transformation from the exuberant emissary who traveled from one kingdom to another to the vindictive merchant who pursued one lawsuit after another.

ALTHOUGH MARCO POLO was nearly forgotten, his book—considered an unclassifiable amalgam of fact and fiction, a gazetteer gone wild—lived on. That state of affairs began to change in the nineteenth century, when researchers tried to bring order to the chaotic state of Polo scholarship and to produce an authoritative version of his account. Drawn to Marco's book as an expression of *orientalisme*, the vogue for Asian art and thought, the French were in the vanguard. In 1824, the Société de Géographie, based in Paris, issued a carefully annotated edition of the *Travels*. No longer did scholarship dwell on what was false; it was now concerned with documenting how much of Marco's account was true. Despite his rhetorical excess, most of what he described withstood scrutiny. The *Travels* came to be seen as a storehouse of generally reliable information about an inaccessible continent, and it attracted cadres of new admirers. What once sounded like fantasy came to be seen increasingly as history.

Four decades later, M. G. Pauthier, a French linguist, compared Polo's account, as expressed in the 1824 edition, against Mongol and Chinese annals and realized that it was not some fable, drug-induced or otherwise, but a strikingly accurate report. The annals confirmed that Marco diligently recorded commercial activity, court rituals, and exotic religious and burial and marital customs.

Pauthier's scholarly labors were enhanced and embellished by two subsequent commentators, Henry Yule and Henri Cordier, who burnished Marco's reputation for English-speaking audiences everywhere. For these two scholars, the chief "fascination" of Polo's account resided not in its content, or the unique way it came into being, but in its "difficult questions." In ringing tones, Yule and Cordier declared, "It is a great book of puzzles, whilst our confidence in the man's veracity is such that we feel certain every puzzle has a solution." With the vigor and certainty of the era to which they belonged, they proposed to find the answers. Drawing on a global network of correspondents, they tirelessly pinned down Marco's references to people and places across Asia, and demonstrated that he could have written his account only from direct observation. Yule and Cordier considered this evidence sufficient vindication for their peripatetic hero, but their prodigious fact-checking partly obscured Marco's imaginative essence. If he had simply written an encyclopedia of Asia, it is unlikely that his work would have been as popular and influential as it became.

Yule and Cordier's heavily annotated edition, four times longer than Marco's original, portrayed him as a harbinger of the Age of Discovery and the most ambitious and accomplished of all explorers— more successful even than Ferdinand Magellan and Christopher Columbus, who were inspired in part by Marco's travels. Unlike them, Marco did not wield a sword; he launched no wars, took no slaves, killed no enemies. Alone among the journeys of European explorers, his served as the basis for works of literature whose impact continues to be felt. "He was the first traveller to trace a route across the whole longitude of Asia," Yule and Cordier observed with a flourish,

> naming and describing kingdom and after kingdom which he had seen with his own eyes: the Deserts of Persia, the flowering plateaux and wild gorges of Badakhshan, the jade-bearing rivers of Khotan, the Mongolian Steppes, cradle of the power which had so lately threatened to swallow up Christendom, the new and brilliant court that had been established at Cambulac. The first traveller to reveal China in all its wealth and vastness, its mighty rivers, its huge cities, its rich manufactures, its swarming population; the inconceivably vast fleets that quickened its seas and its inland waters; to tell us of the nations on its borders, with all their eccentricities of manners and worship; of Tibet with its sordid devotees; of Burma with its golden pagodas and their tinkling crowns. . . .

Even with its excessive eloquence, this was an accurate assessment of Marco's accomplishment. Like Alexis de Tocqueville, Marco Polo was one of those rare strangers who saw a land for what it was more clearly than those who lived there.

ITALIAN SCHOLARSHIP concerning the *Travels* reached its zenith with the appearance of an ambitious edition compiled by Luigi Foscolo Benedetto. Published in Florence in 1928, this work attempted to collate all the various manuscript versions. Benedetto appeared to have the last word in Marco Polo studies, but in 1932, a remarkable manuscript surfaced, containing both more detailed episodes and new material. Sir Percival David, who was responsible for the discovery, was a collector and scholar based in London, and an expert in Chinese ceramics. His interest in Marco Polo's travels in China led him to Toledo, Spain, and the library of Cardinal Francisco Xavier de Zelada (1717–1801), whose holdings included a Latin translation of Marco Polo's manuscript, 50 percent longer than other versions. Scholars concluded that it was written, or translated, in Italy sometime during the fifteenth century, at a time when other Marco Polo accounts were making the transition from handwritten manuscripts to printed books. It became known as the Zelada text, or sometimes the Toledo manuscript.

To bring the most complete version of Polo's book to a wider audience, two scholars, Professor A. C. Moule, of Cambridge, and Paul Pelliot, based in France, compiled an ambitious "composite translation" that would "attempt to weave together all, or nearly all, the extant words which have ever claimed to be Marco Polo's and to indicate the source from which each word comes." The result, incorporating the Zelada text, was published, in English and in French, in 1938, and two volumes of notes followed. The result was not just the most complete manuscript, it was also the freshest, for Moule and Pelliot's rendering captured some of the fire and spontaneity of Marco's original voice. Mixing colloquial speech and scholarship, it evoked Marco's volatile spirit with more clarity than its reserved and stately predecessors.

MARCO POLO was not merely a traveler; he was a participant in the history of his times. He had grown from a naïve seventeen-year-old in the shadow of his father and uncle into a skillful and assured minister of the most powerful ruler in the world. His book is an account of, among other things, history that he witnessed, and, to a limited extent, helped to fashion. Perhaps no single individual would have been able to fulfill all the literary and historical tasks that he set for himself; the range of knowledge and the distances he covered were just too immense for one gentleman of the late thirteenth century and early fourteenth to discuss with complete accuracy. But in his ambitious attempt, he extended the bounds of human knowledge and experience and imagination.

The ultimate meaning of the *Travels* continues to elude, tantalize, and exasperate those who read it closely. Does it offer a guide to the natural world, as when Marco relayed his observations to Kublai Khan after various missions, or something more internalized and provocative? Is it a dreamscape, or perhaps the residue of an opium-fueled fantasy?

Marco's peculiar sensibility stemmed from the decades he spent among the Mongols. Having come of age among them, he thought of himself as one of them; he could think like a Mongol, and see the world as they saw it. As a result, his account offers a view of Asia that is part Western, descriptive and factual, and part Mongol, with a sweeping vision of an animistic universe, and a sense of supernatural forces guiding human endeavors. Although Marco takes pains to present himself as a good Christian, that impression was an overlay created by the conventionally pious Rustichello and enhanced by translators such as Pipino and Ramusio, all of whom sought to bring him back into the embrace of the Church, when, in fact, he was as eclectic as his mentor Kublai Khan in matters of faith, and his belief system was as inclusive and porous as that of the Mongols.

With his habit of incorporating Mongol ways of thought to the point where they were second nature to him, Marco seems, to Western skeptics, to blend fantasy and reality with abandon. This odd mixture, extending beyond the limits of history, both intrigued Europeans and aroused their suspicions. For those willing to accept his vision, Marco's account offers a kaleidoscopic rendering of Eastern and Western cultures, revealing hidden facets to the reader willing to indulge his occasional foibles.

Yet Marco was a not an explorer in the modern, goal-oriented, scientific sense. He went wherever the winds of fortune carried him. He remained open to the vagaries of experience, constantly adjusting his attitudes to the people, places, and events before him. His lack of a mission made him the most amiable and peaceful of travelers.

Although he identified himself as a Christian at the beginning and end of his life, he moved among Muslims, Buddhists, and other religious groups. By example he taught that there is no limit to the possibility of self-invention. In his worldview, the real and the marvelous mingle freely—sometimes harmonizing, sometimes colliding.

With his malleable beliefs and lack of fixed purpose, he was utterly unlike later explorers. His world is enchanted, a place where lands teem with amazons and dragons, spirits and demons. It is a world in which the forces of Christianity have strangely circumscribed powers and merely to survive must constantly do battle against ubiquitous darkness in the form of other gods and other peoples. And it is a world in which magic and logic coexist, although they rarely coincide.

The world Marco Polo explored is in many ways lost to history, but important aspects of his portrayal are strikingly contemporary. As a merchant, he understood that commerce was the essence of international relations, and that it transcended political systems and religious beliefs, all of which, in Marco's descriptions, are self-limiting. Throughout Marco's world, people lived according to absolutes, both political and spiritual, but he recognized that in a tumultuous, ever-changing time the only absolute was the power of belief itself.

MARCO'S BOOK found a surprising application: in cartography. There is no evidence that he intended his *Travels* to serve as a practical field guide to Asia; it was a compendium of information and anecdote, history and myth. In any case, no map of his has survived, if any ever existed. Even if he had drawn maps, or incorporated those made by others, his view of the world was too conventional—Jerusalem at the top, three continents, no knowledge of what later became known as the New World—to be useful to those trying to follow in his footsteps. His basic unit of distance was the rather elastic "day's journey," and his concept of direction was subjective rather than scientific. Nevertheless, the Catalonian Jews who worked in Majorca and produced the influential portolan charts and atlases for navigators in the latter part of the fourteenth century scrutinized Marco's book for features of the world not referred to by other writers and historians, and they incorporated them into their maps. Other European mapmakers followed suit, and considered his references completely reliable—and they were, compared with the often fantastic references in the works of Greek and Roman authors. Perhaps the highest accolade accorded to

Marco's skills in geography came from Fra Mauro, whose celebrated map of the world, dating from 1459 and still displayed in the Biblioteca Nazionale Marciana in Venice, includes features gleaned from Marco's *Travels.*

Two other maps dating from roughly the same era, those of Giovanni Contarini, published in Venice, and Johann Ruysch, issued in Rome, also incorporated data gleaned from the pages of the *Travels.* Ruysch remarked that his map contained the features of the interior of East Asia "no longer based on . . . Marinus of Tyre and Ptolemy . . . but on more modern reports, especially those of Marco Polo."

THE MAPMAKERS of the Renaissance expected that legions of other merchants would use their maps to follow in Marco's footsteps along the Silk Road to Cambulac, but after the death of Kublai Khan, the Mongol Empire rapidly disintegrated. The lesser khans of the domains west of China no longer proclaimed their fealty to the Yüan dynasty and instead embraced Islam. By 1368, Kublai Khan's descendants were forced to abandon their capital, Cambulac. The end of the Mongol dynasty, and with it the Pax Mongolica, meant that the Silk Road was no longer safe, as it had been in the days when the Polo company had traveled it. The nascent Ming dynasty in China did not share Kublai Khan's interest in promoting trade with European merchants, nor did the Islamic khans. Trade with the West diminished, and once more China sealed itself off from the rest of the world. The Mongol Empire described by Marco no longer existed; Kublai Khan was gone, and with him the merchants, scientists, and intellectuals he had attracted.

The Mongol population, always sparse, retreated to their original homeland on the arid northern Steppe. Their violent, glorious empire was only a memory set down in Chinese and Mongol annals, and celebrated in *The Secret History of the Mongols.* Marco had been there at its zenith, and in his *Travels* he had preserved its fierce leaders, alluring women, military campaigns, and exotic customs like flies in amber.

KUBLAI'S CHOSEN SUCCESSOR, his grandson Temür, died young, in 1307. After his death the Yüan dynasty stumbled to a chaotic conclusion.

Over the next five decades, the Chinese rose, as they always believed they would. Beginning in 1368, the first Ming emperor, Chu Yüan-chang, pushed the Mongol presence back to its original borders in the north. At the same time, the loose federation of Mongol-controlled states stretching across Asia disintegrated, allowing Islam to spread throughout Persia. Without Mongol forces to guarantee safety, the northern branch of the Silk Road fell into disuse. Had Marco returned to Asia in his later years, he would have been bewildered to learn that the protective *paiza* given to him by Kublai Khan had become an artifact of a bygone era. And he would have been amazed that his *Travels* outlasted the seemingly invincible Mongol Empire by centuries. Even today, the world is still catching up to Marco Polo.

LONG AFTER the authenticity of Marco Polo's account seemed settled, questions—some of them quite understandable, others stubbornly perverse—arose to bedevil his reputation. In 1995, Frances Wood teasingly insisted in *Did Marco Polo Go to China?* that Marco never went farther than Constantinople and that he compiled his *Travels* from the accounts of more adventurous travelers. Or perhaps he relied on Persian guidebooks for his information.

That hypothesis had been considered years earlier by Herbert Franke, a German scholar, more as a jest than as a statement of fact. By the time Wood, affiliated with the British Library, revived the issue of Marco's veracity, indignant scholars were ready for the challenge. They pointed out that no "Persian guidebooks" existed. And when Wood wondered why no Chinese sources mention Marco Polo, they recalled that the modern Chinese scholar Yang Chih-chiu had located a reference to the Polos' mission to Persia to escort the Mongol princess Kokachin.

Still more provocatively, Wood argued that if Marco had reached China, he surely would have discussed the Great Wall, yet the *Travels* fails to mention it. So, for that matter, do other written accounts of Marco's time. There is a very good reason for the omission: the Great Wall had yet to be built.

Arthur N. Waldron, writing in the *Harvard Journal of Asiatic Studies*, demonstrated that the Great Wall was constructed during the Ming dynasty (1368–1644), long after Marco Polo's day. "Let us beware the myth of the Great Wall," he concluded. "That myth . . .

blossomed in the West almost four centuries ago. While it is a promising subject for students of folklore and myth, it can only mislead the historian." And Igor de Rachewiltz of the Australian National University noted that Chinese cartographers made no mention of the Great Wall until 1579. "This means that *until 1579* the Chinese geographers themselves had ignored the existence of the Wall. No wonder that Marco Polo failed to notice it!"

De Rachewiltz painstakingly showed that nearly all the misunderstanding about the *Travels* arose not from fabrications but from corruptions of the text and mistranslations. Nor did Marco borrow from other sources to piece together his account. De Rachewiltz wrote: "The sheer fact of having been able to gather so much varied and detailed intelligence about most of thirteenth-century Asia without actually going there is, in my view, an even greater feat than that of compiling a genuine eyewitness account of the magnitude of the *Description of the World*."

Even Herbert Franke, who had raised the idea that Marco may have stayed home, rejected it after seeing what Wood tried to make of it. Although Marco—and his collaborator Rustichello—occasionally distorted or omitted elements that some wished had been included, the Venetian delivered a generally truthful account, especially according to the elastic standards of his day.

The most interesting question raised by the global controversy is not whether Marco Polo actually went to China—the evidence overwhelmingly shows that he did—but why the suspicion persists that he did not. The reason could have to do with his particular way of looking at the world. He went east at the age of seventeen, and he came of age in the Mongol Empire, speaking languages he acquired en route, and living in a vibrant ethos combining Mongol, Chinese, Buddhist, Nestorian Christian, and Indian influences—all of which amplified his vocabulary and his thinking. His account reflects his Mongolian coming of age and sensibility, and that may be why it seems so strange and wonderful to many, and so suspect to a few.

THE MODERN TRAVELER seeking to retrace Marco Polo's route will find much that stubbornly survives from the thirteenth century. In Venice, landmarks such as the Basilica di San Marco and its campanile have hardly changed at all. Visitors seeking further evidence of Marco's era will find the Corte seconda del Milion, a compact piazza. A new edifice occupies the lot where generations of the Polo family once lived, traded, and litigated, but a few structural elements of the Ca' Polo and Marco's old neighborhood exist today. Decorative Byzantine archways, under which Marco once walked, survive intact, artifacts of a bygone era when Venice ruled the seas and traded with the world.

Afghanistan remains as wild and beautiful and dangerous, and as opium-ridden, as it was in the days when the Polo company traversed its mountains on the way to Balkh, and the beginning of the Silk Road. The Pamir highlands are even now as remote and isolated as they were in the thirteenth century, the silence barely disturbed by trucks and cars, with donkeys the preferred method of travel. The Gobi Desert remains inaccessible to all but the most determined traveler, and the Singing Sands still tempt the unwary visitor into oblivion—although these days, the Global Positioning System can help explorers track a precise route through the remotest regions of the planet. Today's Mongols are as open to foreign influences as they were when Marco first encountered them: they are nomads still, masters of the Steppe, living in *ger*s and surrounded by their livestock as they were during the reign of Kublai Khan, but now satellite dishes stand beside their dwellings. With the departure of the Soviets in 1989, Mongolia became an independent nation, struggling to adapt its nomadic past to the demands of the present.

The ancient Mongolian capital of Karakorum, founded by Genghis Khan as a symbol of national unity, is now a ruin, a faint reminder of the splendor that once animated his rule. One of the few surviving objects from the height of the Mongol Empire is a large granite tortoise, for which a distant mountain is named. It stands alone on a field, awaiting a more fitting resting place. Of Kublai Khan's magnificent Xanadu, little survives beyond a few evocative mounds rising from a grassy plain, and whispers of lost grandeur carried on the wind.

ACKNOWLEDGMENTS

THROUGHOUT MY TRAVELS in search of Marco Polo, many people helped to make this book a reality.

At Alfred A. Knopf, I have been privileged to enjoy the support of Sonny Mehta, Ashbel Green, and Carol Janeway, all of whom brought constant enthusiasm and generous editorial wisdom to my labors; I am grateful for the inspiration of these legendary individuals. In addition, I wish to extend my appreciation to Sara Sherbill and Katherine Hourigan.

Suzanne Gluck, my literary agent at William Morris, has been a source of steadfast belief and refreshing candor from the moment of this project's inception; it is always a pleasure to learn from her keen insights. I am also indebted to her able assistants, including Christine Price, Erin Malone, and Georgia Cool.

At the New York Society Library, I wish to thank Mark Piel for his help with this and my previous books, and Arevig Caprielian, Rare Books Librarian. I also wish to thank the John Carter Brown Library in Providence, Rhode Island, and especially librarian Richard Ring for his help; and the Thomas J. Watson Library of the Metropolitan Museum of Art in New York. I wish to extend particular appreciation to the Columbia University Libraries, including Butler Library, the Barnard College Library, and the C. V. Starr East Asian Library, whose collections I often consulted while researching this book. My friend of more than thirty years, Patrick Ryan, S. J., generously agreed to review the manuscript, especially concerning matters relating to Church history, and I am grateful for his scholarly clarification.

In addition, I wish to express my appreciation to Ludwig W. Adamec, for his expertise on Afghanistan; Caroline Alexander; Susan Beningson; Sheila Callahan; Kimball Chen; Kristina Cordero, who assisted with translations; Daniel Dolgin, whom I can never thank enough yet must go on thanking because there is no alternative in light of his generosity of spirit and intellect; Dr. James B. Garvin, NASA's chief scientist, who advised me on the geologic highlights of Marco Polo's route through the Pamir; Toby Greenberg, whose knowledge of art history and perceptive eye made her an ideal researcher for the images reproduced in this book; Lila Haber, for her assistance in the early phases of this work; Jack Hidary; Fritz Jacobi; Ted Kaplan, for his Silk Road expertise; Laura Kopp, for her elegant translations; the distinguished medievalist James Muldoon of Brown University; Robert B. Oxnam, President Emeritus, the Asia Society, USA, and President, The Needham Research Institute, USA; Alice Petillot, my researcher and translator in Paris; the always inspiring Peter Pouncey of Columbia University; Igor de Rachewiltz of the Australian National University; Morris Rossabi of Columbia University, the author of an outstanding biography of Kublai Khan, and a generous source of wisdom on the Mongols; James D. Ryan of the City University of New York; Denise Sinclair, a board member of The Needham Research Institute, USA, for her insights on Chinese science and Joseph Needham; Jonathan Spence of Yale University; and Joseph Thanhauser III, who, along with the gang at Byrnam Wood, cheerfully distracted me.

My daughter Sara graciously became an informal Buddhism consultant as I worked on this book, and my son Nick contributed enlightening historical perspectives.

In England, I owe a considerable debt to the following individuals and institutions who generously assisted me during my research visits: the late David Patterson, Emeritus President of the Oxford Center for Hebrew and Jewish Studies; Christopher Cullen; and Susan J. Bennett and John P. C. Moffett of The Needham Research Institute at Cambridge University. During my time at the library of the Ancient India and Iran Trust in Cambridge, I received guidance from Wieslaw Mikal and James Cormick. And in London, I consulted the British Library's comprehensive collection concerning Marco Polo, perhaps the largest of its kind.

In France, the Bibliothèque Nationale provided additional useful material about Marco Polo and China.

Finally, in Washington, D.C., my research at the Library of Congress afforded me a window on the holdings of libraries around the globe.

I was fortunate to have admirable support in researching Marco Polo from an Eastern and Middle Eastern perspective. Anna Basoli, my resourceful Italian translator, while spending months in Afghanistan to pursue her journalistic goals and without even being asked, tracked down documents relating to Marco Polo's yearlong sojourn in that part of the world. In addition, her husband, Shoaib Harris, brought to my attention documents and histories about the Silk Road, some unknown in the West, and ably translated them for this book, especially commentary by the Persian historian Vassaf, a contemporary of Marco Polo. My thanks also to Professor Mir Ahmad Joyenda, the head of Afghanistan's Research and Evaluation Unit, for his assistance.

In Venice, I conducted research at the Biblioteca Nazionale Marciana, where the archivists proved most helpful in guiding me through a maze of records to the relevant documents; the Archivio di Stato, the Istituto Veneto di Scienze, Lettere e Arti; and the Archivio Veneto.

Thanks also to the Società Ligure di Storia Patria in Genoa for information relating to Marco Polo's incarceration in that city.

During my visit to China in 2005, the dedicated Marco Polo scholar Bohai Dang of Peking University brought me up to date on the state of Chinese scholarly inquiry into Marco Polo, and made many Chinese sources, both his own and others', available to me.

During my travels in Mongolia in 2006, I was fortunate to make the acquaintance of Nomin Lkhagvasuren, my seemingly omniscient guide and interpreter during my travels around the country. At times her sister Kuka capably stood in, aided by our interpreter Batchuluun Baldandorj, and our driver and mechanic, Dugeree, who performed vital repairs late one night to the malfunctioning stove in my smoke-filled *ger*. My thanks to them all, and especially to Dan Dolgin and Loraine Gardner, who came along on the adventure, and added so much, including some spirited throat-singing.

My thanks also to the Mongolian Natural History Museum in Ulaanbaatar, where I was able to handle Yüan dynasty armor and weapons dating from the failed invasions of Japan in the thirteenth century. The lamas of Gandan, Erdene Zuu, and Chojin Lama monasteries of Mongolia graciously welcomed me during my visits. In addition, I wish to express my appreciation to the Mongolian Fine Arts Museum, with its exceptional collection of period artifacts.

I also wish to record my gratitude to the Mongolian scholars who generously gave of their time and scholarship during my face-to-face interviews with them in Ulaanbaatar: Dr. Kh. Lkhagvasuren, President of the Mongolian Archeological Federation; Professor Shagdaryn Bira, Secretary General of the International Association for

Mongol Studies; Professor O. Sukhbaatar, Vice Director of Chinggis Khan University; and Professor S. Tsolmon of the Mongolian Academy of Sciences.

Finally, during my stay in Taiwan, I benefited from the encouragement of Harvey Chang, from the collection of the National Palace Museum, and from the scholarly companionship of Professor Hsiao Ch' i-ch'ing of National Tsing Hua University.

NOTES ON SOURCES

FOR ALL ITS RICHES, Marco Polo's *Travels* presents several challenges for modern readers. The first concerns the absence of an authoritative version of his account. There are scores of early Polo manuscripts, many of them drastically different from one another. Some versions rely on a single text, while others blend several; some contain abridgments, both subtle and obvious. Some, such as those rendered into French by Pauthier, and into English by Yule and Cordier, contain valuable annotations. Yet these versions tend to obscure the energy and quirky charm of the original by imposing a uniform tone on the entire work. The result can resemble a master painting dimmed by centuries of accumulated grime. But a relatively recent English translation by A. C. Moule and Paul Pelliot of the Latin manuscript discovered in the library of the cathedral of Toledo, Spain, in 1932 manages to evoke the spirit and substance of the original, or so it seemed to me after studying a number of other versions. Published in 1938 and based on the longest manuscript of Marco's account known, it is 50 percent longer than other versions. In quoting this version, as well as others, I have made a number of changes for the sake of clarity and syntax. Where Moule and Pelliott stumbled or repeated patches of garbled text without clarification, I had recourse to the venerable 1818 translation by William Marsden, who based his version on the Italian translation by Giovanni-Battista Ramusio, as well as to various early manuscripts in Middle French, and to other translations that better conveyed the sense of a particular passage.

Another significant problem with Marco's book that translators often overlook concerns the order of events, no small matter in a chronicle of this scope. In his prologue, Marco promises accounts of happenings that he never gets around to describing in the body of his text. And on occasion he describes events at the beginning of his account even though they occurred near the end of his travels. Some of this confusion, I suspect, arises from the circumstances under which the work was composed (Marco Polo in prison, telling his story to a collaborator who was a stranger to him), and some from errors that crept into the narrative as it passed from one set of scribes to the next, in the pre-Gutenberg era. Yet even various paragraphs or sentences within the *Travels* seem out of order. The disarray often reminded me of a manuscript dropped on a flight of stairs, then gathered up, with many of the pages out of order. To minimize confusion, I have related all the major events chronologically, which has meant departing from the order in which certain episodes appear in the original text.

I am indebted to the labors of several French scholars, including Jacques Gernet, A. C. Moule, M. G. Pauthier, and Paul Pelliot, for their elucidation of aspects of the text. In addition, Leonardo Olschki's erudite *Marco Polo's Asia* is valuable for its breadth and precision, despite Olschki's tendency occasionally to overstate what Marco or the Mongols "always" or "never" did. In reality, the *Travels* is one of those multidimensional records in which most everything and its opposite are true, at different times and in different contexts.

A second group of challenges concerns the many languages involved in trying to understand the Mongols who dominate Marco Polo's account. In his 1990 book *The Mongols*, David Morgan writes: "The sources available to the historian are in Mongolian, Chinese, Persian, Arabic, Turkish, Japanese, Russian, Armenian, Georgian, Latin, and other languages. No one can hope to be able to read more than a fraction of them in the original." Fortunately, I was able to turn repeatedly to the sound advice of Professor Morris Rossabi of Columbia University, the author of a distinguished biography of Kublai Khan and a scholar of Mongolia and Mongol history, to guide me through these linguistic thickets. I have also consulted the works of three thirteenth-century Persian chroniclers—Vassaf al-Hazrat, Juvaini, and Rashid al-Din—who discussed the exploits of the Mongols as a more-or-less contemporary phenomenon. All were court historians, and Rashid al-Din served as grand vizier in the Ilkhanate. True, they expressed their patrons' convictions, but as a result of their privileged positions they had access to many sources that might otherwise have been lost. Wherever possible, I have let their words speak for themselves.

THE EPIGRAPHS to the chapters of this book are taken from Samuel Taylor Coleridge's poem *Kubla Khan*.

PROLOGUE / The Commander

Concerning Marco Polo's involvement in the Battle of Curzola, some commentators have suggested that Marco blundered into combat while leading a merchant vessel rather than a warship. Still others insist that he did not participate in the battle at all and was instead captured in a subsequent military skirmish at sea. Henry H. Hart's brief, pithy *Marco Polo, Venetian Adventurer*, page 207, has Dandolo's speech at the height of the Battle of Curzola, but Hart is among those who place Marco Polo's capture in a different engagement between the Venetians and the Genoese.

Although Venice and Genoa were both city-states famed for their aggressive maritime trade, they were very different from each other. The Genoese were stubborn individualists. Their trading ventures were privately financed, and their sense of civic duty was minimal. Venetians, in contrast, were known for their collective behavior, and for their exclusiveness. Their ships were communal property, their sailors not permitted to serve other governments.

Henry Yule and Henri Cordier, volume 1, page 55, of their version of *The Description of the World*, provide a variant account of Marco Polo's capture and imprisonment, quoting the Dominican friar Jacopo d'Acqui's *Imago mundi*. Many details are familiar, but d'Acqui says that Polo was captured in a different military engagement. There is no reason to assume that d'Acqui has more claim to accuracy than other sources, but he was a contemporary of Marco Polo, and therefore wrote shortly after the events. But even d'Acqui commits obvious errors. Maria Bussagli's essay in *Marco Polo: Venezia e l'Oriente*, edited by Alvise Zorzi, contains another variant. In this version, Marco Polo was on his way back to Trebizond to recover valuable possessions that had been confiscated several years earlier. I have also consulted *Annali genovesi dopo Caffaro e suoi continuatori*.

Few accounts of the naval actions off Curzola in 1298 fully agree on dates. For a variant, see W. Carew Hazlitt, *The Venetian Republic*, volume 1, pages 454–472. Conditions in a Genoese jail are described at length in Leondia Balestrieri's "Le Prigioni della Malapaga."

CHAPTER ONE / *The Merchants of Venice*

For a lucid exploration of the medieval ethos of Marco Polo's era, see Janet Abu-Lughod's eye-opening work, *Before European Hegemony: The World System A.D. 1250–1350*, and Barbara Tuchman's *A Distant Mirror: The Calamitous Fourteenth Century*, especially pages 55–56. The best modern history of Venice is John Julius Norwich's *A History of Venice*. Mrs. Oliphant's *The Makers of Venice: Doges, Conquerers, and Men of Letters* also has its charms.

The surprisingly sophisticated world of medieval Venetian and Italian contracts and commercial practices has been described in detail in Robert S. Lopez and Irving W. Raymond's *Medieval Trade in the Mediterranean World*; pages 14–15 and 168–178 are especially illuminating. See Benjamin Z. Kedar's *Merchants in Crisis: Genoese and Venetian Men of Affairs and the Fourteenth-century Depression* for additional context. Lore about *veneto* comes from Jan Morris's effervescent account, *The World of Venice*, page 31 in the 1993 Harcourt Brace edition.

Some of what is known about Marco Polo's early years can be found in Hart's *Marco Polo*, which has more context than biography, but see especially pages xvii, 55–56, and 63–64.

Rodolfo Gallo discusses the Ca' Polo in "Nuovi documenti riguardanti Marco Polo e la sua famiglia," note 3.

In *Venice: Lion City*, pages 30 and following, Garry Wills analyzes the basis of power in the Republic. Michael Yamashita describes the ceremony of marriage to the sea in *Marco Polo: A Photographer's Journey*, page 41. Alvise Zorzi's *Vita di Marco Polo veneziano* is a useful introduction to Marco in a Venetian context.

CHAPTER TWO / *The Golden Passport*

In their consideration of foreigners who found employment in the Mongol regime, Yule and Cordier mention an oral tradition placing Jews in China since the first century. Accounts of synagogues and Jewish travelers crop up occasionally in Chinese annals as early as the twelfth century, although the terminology thought to refer to Jews may indicate another group. For more on the long but tentatively understood history of Jews in China, see Yule and Cordier, volume 1, page 347. (All citations to Yule and Cordier refer to their version of *The Description of the World*.)

In his incisive *The History of the Mongol Conquests*, J. J. Saunders describes Mongol-Chinese segregation; see page 124. See also Hart, *Marco Polo*, page 16.

Igor de Rachewiltz, in "Marco Polo Went to China," page 66, suggests that by "Latin," Marco (or his translator) actually meant "Italian," and thus the Polo brothers were the first *Venetians* that Kublai had met. If so, Marco was not, in this instance, exaggerating. Hart's *Marco Polo*, page 38, note, traces the Polo company's uncertain progress, and includes Ludolph von Suchem's description of Acre. See also Richard Humble's illustrated *Marco Polo* for another retelling.

CHAPTER THREE / *The Apprentice*

Just what Marco meant by "muslin" is open to question. The term generally refers to white or unbleached cloth woven from cotton, but his was made of silver and gold, in which case he may have had another fabric in mind; or perhaps he meant that the muslin fabric was trimmed with silver and gold threads.

Gibbon's remark comes from *The Decline and Fall of the Roman Empire*, volume 2, page 818. More about the caliph and Hülegü can be found in Zorzi's *Vita di Marco Polo*. Yule and Cordier (volume 1, page 344, note 1) consider the Mongol taboo against spilling blood. For a diverting introduction to Mongol culture, see Ian Frazier's "Invaders," *New Yorker*, April 25, 2005. Kuo P'u's remark appears in Irene M. Franck and David Brownstone, *The Silk Road: A History*, page 48. For extended analysis of the Dry Tree's potential significance, see Yule and Cordier, volume 1, pages 128–139. The validity of Marco's account of the Assassins has generated debate; some commentators believe that the hashish connection may be spurious, and that the Old Man did not drug his followers. For more, consult Leonardo Olschki, *Marco Polo's Asia*, pages 369–370, and for recent observations on the Assassins, see Bernard Lewis, *The Assassins: A Radical Sect in Islam*, and Farhad Daftary, *The Assassin Legends: Myths of the Isma'ilis*.

The description of Balkh by Nancy Hatch Dupree can be found in *The Road to Balkh*, page 1. Juvaini's comments appear in the same work on page 75 and following. Hart, *Marco Polo*, page 97, adds background. See also Dupree's *An Historical Guide to Afghanistan*, page 42, for the destruction of Balkh by the Mongol invaders.

CHAPTER FOUR / *The Opium Eater*

Manuel Komroff includes an account by Benjamin of Tudela in *Contemporaries of Marco Polo*, pages 268–269. John Larner's *Marco Polo and the Discovery of the World*, pages 12–13, has additional context; William of Rubruck's comments on what he took to be Mongol squalor are on page 25. Carpini's account is quoted in Christopher Dawson's *The Mongol Mission*, pages 6–7, and in Margaret T. Hodgen's valuable *Early Anthropology in the Sixteenth and Seventeenth Centuries*, pages 90–92.

James D. Ryan's "Preaching Christianity Along the Silk Route: Missionary Outposts in the Tartar 'Middle Kingdom' in the Fourteenth Century" contains a trove of useful data concerning the issues confronting early missionaries to Asia.

The story of Genghis Khan's horse is told by Mike Edwards in "Genghis: Lord of the Mongols," *National Geographic*, December 1996. Juvaini's observation about perdition is drawn from Morris Rossabi's *Khubilai Khan: His Life and Times*, page 2.

For an interesting if technical discussion of the origins and evolution of the Silk Road, see Joseph Needham's *Science and Civilisation in China*, volume 1, pages 181–204. This is but a brief sample of an extraordinary, multivolume survey of Chinese knowledge compiled by a scholar of China of exceptional gifts and vision.

Dr. Sarah Schlesinger of Rockefeller University generously outlined the prevalence of tuberculosis in Marco's time, and the ramifications of the illness as he may have experienced it in Afghanistan.

CHAPTER FIVE / *High Plains Drifters*

Concerning asbestos, see Joseph Needham's *Science and Civilisation in China*, volume 3, page 660. As Needham demonstrates, the Chinese were aware of asbestos for centuries, calling the material, not inaccurately, "stone veins."

Of the Pamir, Dr. James B. Garvin, NASA's chief scientist, and a geologist by training, notes, "Because of the arid environment, lack of human degradation of the landscape, [and] spectacular exposures of the effects of recent earthquakes and of the uplift of the mountain, this area is a premier natural laboratory for the investigation of . . . significant [geological] problems."

CHAPTER SIX / *The Secret History of the Mongols*

Carpini's account of life among the Mongols is drawn from Christopher Dawson's *The Mongol Mission*, page 37. Vassaf's observation can be found in the *History of Vassaf*, volume 1. The work dates from 1302. Shoaib Harris translated.

The various English translations of *The Secret History of the Mongols* differ dramatically from one another. Those wishing to learn more about this remarkable document would do well to compare them all. Among the more significant are the translation by Francis Woodman Cleaves; a verse adaptation by Paul Kahn; and the extraordinarily detailed rendering by Igor de Rachewiltz. I have relied on the English-language version by Urgunge Onon, published in Mongolia in 2005, which appears faithful to the letter and spirit of the original saga. My thanks to Nomin Lkhagvasuren for bringing it to my attention. The stanza quoted can be found on page 110.

Nicholas Wade in *The New York Times* quoted Juvaini on Genghis Khan; see "A Prolific Genghis Khan, It Seems, Helped People the World," February 11, 2003. Chris Tyler-Smith's "The Genetic Legacy of the Mongols" sheds light on Genghis Khan's many descendants.

The evocative description of the Mongol conception of the soul comes from A. C. Moule and Paul Pelliot's edition of Marco Polo, *The Description of the World*, volume 1 (reprinted 1976), pages 257–258. The quotations from David Morgan and from Juvaini are drawn from Morgan's *The Mongols*, page 55. For a detailed analysis of the Chinese and Mongol military systems, see Chi'-Ch'ing Hsiao, *The Military Establishment of the Yüan Dynasty*.

The Mongol recipes offered here can be found (along with other dishes) in Paul Buell's "Pleasing the Palate of the Qan." But there is more to say about the Mongol diet and its effect on Mongol dynastic history. In "Dietary Decadence and Dynastic Decline in the Mongol Empire," John Masson Smith Jr. offers a drastically different assessment of the healthiness of the Mongol diet. "Most Mongol rulers lived short lives," he states. "Those in the Middle East died, on average, at about age 38, and the successors of Qubilai raised the ages, since he lived, atypically, for 78 years [sic]; Chinggis lived into his 60s; for the rest, few passed 50." Smith blames the Mongols' lack of longevity on "dietary inadequacies and improprieties," by which he means too much mutton, mare's milk, and alcohol, and not enough of other foods. He cites Marco Polo's statistics as evidence, in part, of the Mongols' tendency toward excess. They were, in short, eating and drinking themselves to death.

CHAPTER SEVEN / *The Universal Emperor*

Bar Hebraeus's praise of Sorghaghtani can be found in *The Cambridge History of China*, volume 6, page 414. My thanks to Professor S. Tsolmon of the Mongolian Academy of Sciences for outlining the four major population segments.

Morris Rossabi's *Khubilai Khan* offers the best modern assessment of Kublai's ascent to power. I have drawn especially from page 8 and from pages 46 and following. Arigh Böke's machinations are recounted in M. G. Pauthier's notes for *Le Livre de Marco Polo*, beginning on page 237.

For a technical comparison of Chinese and Mongol currency, see Yule and Cordier, volume 1, pages 426–430. In *Marco Polo's Asia*, pages 234–240, Olschki dissects the tensions animating relationships among Mongols and Muslims and considers reasons why Islam did not gain a firm grip on the Mongol Empire.

In *Khubilai Khan*, pages 40–41 and 155–160, Rossabi ably tells the story of

'Phags-pa and his script. See also Jack Weatherford's *Genghis Khan and the Making of the Modern World*, pages 205–206. And Zhijiu Yang's *Yuan shi san lun* has an interesting discussion of the languages Marco Polo may have known or used, with reference to M. G. Pauthier's thoughts on the subject. *Marco Polo's Asia*, by Olschki, also discusses 'Phags-pa script and contains interesting assessments, pro and con, of the Mongol impact on Chinese culture (pages 124–128). Some early accounts ascribe five or seven wives to Kublai Khan rather than four; see Yule and Cordier, volume 1, page 358, note 2. For an explanation of Mongol succession issues, see the same work, pages 360–361, note 1.

CHAPTER EIGHT / *In the Service of the Khan*

Marco Polo's accuracy in describing Cambulac can be gauged by the fact that the historian Rashid al-Din, his learned contemporary, described the city in very similar terms:

> The surrounding wall of the city of Khanbaligh is flanked by 17 towers; between each [two] of these towers there is the distance of a *farsang* (or *parasange*). *Daidou* [Ta-tu, or Cambulac] is so populous that even outside of these towers there are great streets and houses; in its gardens there are many kinds of fruit trees brought from everywhere. At the center of this city, Khoubilai-Khaan has established one of his *Ordou* (a Mongolian term which like the Chinese *Koung* means "imperial dwelling"), in a very large palace called *Karsi* (in Chinese, *tien*, a cluster of pavilions destined for the emperor's various uses).
>
> The columns and the floors of this palace are all in cut stone or marble, and of great beauty; it is surrounded and fortified by four walls. Between one of these walls and the next there is a space equal to the distance covered by an arrow flung with force. The external court is for the palace guards; the next one is for the princes (*omera*, emirs) who assemble there each morning; the third court is occupied by the great dignitaries of the army, and the fourth by those who are in the prince's intimate circle. The picture of this palace is based on one made on site.
>
> At Khanbaligh and at Daidou there are two large and important rivers. They come from the north, where lies the road leading to the Khan's summer encampment; at the frontier gorge of *Djemdjal* (the fortified gorge of *Kiu-young*) they join another river. Inside the town is a considerable lake which resembles a sea; there is a dam to bring the boats down. The water of the river further along forms a canal, and issues out into the bay which, from the ocean, extends into the vicinity of Khanbaligh. [From Pauthier's edition of Marco Polo's *Travels, Le Livre de Marco Polo*, page 266, note 5.]

For more on the complex subject of the Chinese calendar, see Yule and Cordier, volume 1, pages 388–389; Needham's *Science and Civilisation in China*, volume 3, pages 390 and following; and Robert Temple's *The Genius of China*, pages 36–38. Temple's illustrated book can be considered a simplified introduction to Needham's occasionally unwieldy magnum opus.

J. D. Langlois's notable *China Under Mongol Rule*, page 3 and following, has more on the conceptual and historical roots of the Yüan dynasty, and the emperor's role as personified by Kublai Khan.

The details of Kublai Khan's astonishing wardrobe are drawn from Pauthier's *Le Livre de Marco Polo*, page 285, note 4, and the General Ceremonial from the same work, page 290, note 4. The birthday rites were extremely intricate. Pauthier offers a record of an exhausting birthday worship service:

> The "first introducer" says in a cadenced voice: "Bow down!"—"Rise!" He goes toward the vermilion vestibule (that of the emperor), and makes his obeisances before the chair, or imperial throne. The "first orderer" announces that all is in order and well executed. Then "the usher in chief" cries in a loud and cadenced voice: "Bow profoundly!" The "perambulating ushers" cry: "Bow!"—"Bow profoundly!"—"Rise!"—"Bow profoundly again!"—"Rise!" When all this has been successively and punctually executed as a preliminary, the "chief of the ushers" then announces: "The emperor in person, who is accompanied by ten thousand felicities, is coming!" The "perambulating ushers" cry: "Resume your places!"—"Bow profoundly!"—"Rise!"—"Bow profoundly again!"—"Rise!"—"Bow!"—"Replace your ivory tablets in your belts!"—"Bow!"—"Tap the ground three times with your foot!"—"Bend your left knee!"—"Prostrate the head against the ground three times!"

Pauthier notes, "It is the famous form of salutation in the presence of the emperor, prescribed by Chinese ritual, consisting in three prostrations, with bended knees and head placed on the ground, to which many European ambassadors refused to submit. . . ." This was merely the introductory ceremony, which was followed by prolonged prayers to propitiate the heavens, also intricately choreographed, followed by more bowing, and concluded with processions. Only then did the formal birthday rites end.

Hart's *Marco Polo* discusses coal in China on page 121.

On the extent of Mongol charity, Pauthier observes on page 346: "One may see there that Marco Polo was far from exaggerating the acts of benevolence of this kind attributed by him to Kublai Khan. Thus in 1260, the food supply having fallen short, money was gathered for distribution to a certain number of the needy. In 1261, the government remitted the overdue duties or taxes to the inhabitants of the three sectors of the capital. . . . During the whole reign of Kublai Khan, there is not one year in which the Annals do not report remission of duties, of taxes, of charges, for one reason or another, to the inhabitants of the capital, of the imperial summer residence and to various provinces or departments of the Empire; and distributions of aid in times of famine or public calamities." He concludes, "We believe we can assert that the history of no sovereign and no dynasty in Europe could present a similar number of acts of generosity and benevolence."

CHAPTER NINE / *The Struggle for Survival*

For more on the Mongol *paiza*, see Yule and Cordier, volume 1, pages 352–353.

Marco Polo's account of the bridge has come under fire for its supposed inaccuracies. In some manuscripts he claims that the bridge had twenty-four arches, when other records maintain that it had thirteen, or eleven. Again, the discrepancy may be caused by descriptions of the bridge as it appeared at different times. For more on the history of this legendary bridge, see Yule and Cordier, volume 2, pages 4–8, note 1.

Dr. Sarah Schlesinger of Rockefeller University provided trenchant observations on the manufacture and molecular structure of silk.

Concerning the practice of making salt, Yule and Cordier (volume 2, pages 57–58, note 5) report that even in their day—that is, 1913—salt was being used for purchases in these markets.

The Penguin edition of the *Travels* includes remarks on the discrepancies concerning the date of Kublai's military offensive against the Song (page 187, note). Descriptions of Mongol armor and arrows are based on artifacts in the collection of the Mongolian Museum of Natural History in Ulaanbaatar.

CHAPTER TEN / *The General and the Queen*

The psychological dynamics of childbearing are discussed in "Why Do Some Expectant Fathers Experience Pregnancy Symptoms?" *Scientific American*, October 2004, page 116.

For more on Bayan's career, see Yule and Cordier, volume 2, pages 148–150. Details of Bayan's life have been drawn from *In the Service of the Khan: Eminent Personalities of the Early Mongol–Yüan Period (1200–1300)*, edited by Igor de Rachewiltz et al., pages 584–606.

CHAPTER ELEVEN / *The City of Heaven*

The chapter on Quinsai is the longest in Marco's account, and this signifies its importance. Nevertheless, intriguing uncertainties remain. In his book *Quinsai; with Other Notes on Marco Polo*, A. C. Moule notes that the term "City of Heaven," employed by Marco, does not appear in Chinese annals. Where Marco came by this term, or whether the residents of Quinsai used it, is open to question. Moule (page 11) attributes the precision with which Marco described Quinsai to "an official account which was sent to the Mongol general Baian [Bayan] when he approached the city." As a result, "the number and accuracy of the topographical and other details mentioned or implied exceeds those in the description of any other place in the book." Chief among the unanswered questions is Marco's exact role in Quinsai. For more on this issue, see the rigorous Olschki, *Marco Polo's Asia*, pages 174–175. It is possible that the notion that Marco was appointed governor of Quinsai by no less than Kublai Khan originated with Giambattista Ramusio long after the fact.

The controversy surrounding the number of bridges in Quinsai is taken up by Moule in *Quinsai*, pages 23–29. By coincidence, Marco also says there are twelve thousand houses in Quinsai, when there were, in fact, many times that number. "Twelve thousand" was a conventional term indicating *countless* houses. Despite Moule's statement to the contrary, it seems likely that Marco was simply employing the same figure of speech concerning the number of bridges.

Wu Tzu-mu, about whom little is known, left a poignant description of Quinsai at the peak of its prosperity, in a work known as the "Account of the Gruel Dream" (1274) wherein a peasant dreams of luxury while a modest innkeeper prepares a simple meal—in other words, the poor man dreams of the abundance that Quinsai symbolizes. "In no matter what district, in the streets, on the bridges, at the gates, and in every odd corner, there are everywhere to be found barrows, shops, and emporiums where business is done," he writes. "The reason for this is that people are in daily need of the necessities of life, such as firewood, rice, oil, salt, soya sauce, vinegar, and tea, and to a certain extent even of luxury articles, while rice and soup are absolute essentials, for even the poorest cannot do without them. To tell the truth, the inhabitants of Quinsai are spoiled and difficult to please."

He evoked the city's splendid teahouses catering to this demanding clientele:

"They make arrangements of the flowers of the four seasons, hang paintings by cele-brated artists, decorate the walls of the establishment, and all the year round sell unusual teas and curious soups. During the winter months, they sell in addition a very fine powdered tea, pancakes, onion tea, and sometimes soup of salted beans. During the hot season they add as extras plum-flower wine with a mousse of snow, a beverage for contracting the gall bladder, and herbs against the heat." And, like Marco, he rev-eled in the city's brothels: "Let us visit one of the chic establishments, with such promising signs as 'The Happy Meeting,' or 'The Seduction,' or 'The Pleasures of Novelty.' . . . A dozen prostitutes, luxuriously dressed and heavily made up, gather at the entrance to the main arcade to await the command of the customers, and have an airy gracefulness."

For reminiscences of the City of Heaven by Odoric of Pordenone and Ibn Battuta, see Pauthier's edition of Marco Polo's *Travels*, *Le Livre de Marco Polo*, page 502, note. Jacques Gernet's splendid *Daily Life in China on the Eve of the Mongol Invasion*, *1250–1276* discusses precautions against fire on pages 36–37 and 52.

Sexual mores in China receive extended treatment in R. H. van Gulick's *Sexual Life in Ancient China* (see especially pages 138–260). For another scholarly discussion of Chinese sexual attitudes and practices, see Needham's *Science and Civilisation in China*, volume 2, pages 146–150. Needham emphasizes the philosophical underpinnings of Chinese sexual customs, especially Taoism, and stresses the customs' social and psy-chological benefits.

T'ao Tsung-i, a scholar and writer of the late Yüan dynasty, wrote about eunuchs in a traditional dialogue between the Yellow Emperor and one of his subjects, known as Ch'i Po, a legendary figure credited with discovering the art of healing the body, as follows. "The Yellow Emperor said: 'There are men who because of injury to their genitalia have lost their sexual urge, their member will not rise and has become useless. Yet their beard and mustache do not disappear. Why is it that only eunuchs have no beard and mustache? I want to hear the reason for this.' Ch'i Po replied: 'In the case of eunuchs their genitalia are amputated, thereby their seminal duct is cut off and they can not emit semen. . . . Consequently their lips and mouth become arid, and no beard or mustache develop.' The Yellow Emperor asked: 'But there are some natural eunuchs who although they have not undergone that mutilation yet do not have beard or mustache. Why is this so?' Ch'i Po answered: 'That is because Heaven did not give them a sufficient sexual urge. Hence their seminal duct is not developed, and neither is their genitalia. They have ch'i [essence] but not semen.' "

Examples of Chinese public poetry can be found in Gernet, *Daily Life in China*, page 237, and the same work describes other customs in the City of Heaven on pages 184, 189–191, and 214–215.

Marco's "lost Christians" may have belonged to a little-known sect of Armenian Christians, who differed from the Nestorians. The Armenian Christians were mono-physites, asserting that Jesus had only one nature, which was divine, and incorporated his human nature. If they were Armenian Christians, they may have been reluctant to reveal their identity, fearing that the Nestorians outnumbered them.

CHAPTER TWELVE / *The Divine Wind*

In *Le Livre de Marco Polo*, his edition of Marco Polo's *Travels*, Pauthier offers details about the Mongol fleet (pages 540–543). See also Yule and Cordier, volume 2, page 263, note 3.

Marco generated centuries of controversy by giving the date of the treaty of surrender by the Mongols to the Japanese as 1269 (see Polo, *The Description of the World*, edited by Moule and Pelliott, page 362). This is another miscalculation on the part of Marco, or his translators, who did not accurately convert the Mongol or Chinese lunar calendar date to the Western equivalent. Yule and Cordier correct the date to 1279, but since Kublai Khan attacked Japan repeatedly between 1274 and 1283, it is difficult to know exactly when the treaty, or the siege preceding it, occurred. There is also a question as to whether the story of the thirty thousand castaways occupying the Japanese capital by resorting to disguise was based on fact, or was simply a yarn that Marco found irresistable. Unlike virtually all of the other facts he relates concerning Kublai Khan's failed siege of Japan, this element finds no corroboration in other sources. Yet Marco's account is so detailed and plausible, and fits so neatly with what is known of the failed effort, that it is likely based on historical fact, and lost sources, perhaps embellished with Marco's storytelling flare.

For Morris Rossabi's useful analysis of the exercise of Mongol power, see his *Khubilai Khan*, page 212. And for a thorough assessment of the role of Muslims in the Yüan dynasty, see the same author's "The Muslims in the Early Yüan Dynasty," in *China Under Mongol Rule*, edited by J. D. Langlois Jr., pages 256–295. Rossabi writes, "By serving as intermediaries between the Mongol rulers and their Chinese subjects, the Muslims performed valuable services but simultaneously provoked the wrath of the conquerors and the conquered." He also suggests that "the Mongols, consciously or not, used the Muslims as scapegoats, thereby diverting Chinese animosity from themselves."

The Ahmad affair occasioned oft-repeated misunderstandings in Marco Polo scholarship. Some accounts speak of a minister named Po-lo who became involved late in the scandal. For example, Yule and Cordier (volume 1, page 442, note 5) write, "It is a pleasant fact that Messer Marco's presence, and his upright conduct on this occasion, have not been forgotten in the Chinese Annals: 'The Emperor . . . desired Polo, Assessor of the Privy Council, to explain the reasons which had led Wangchu to commit this murder. Polo spoke with boldness of the crimes and oppressions of Ahmad, which rendered him an object of detestation throughout the Empire. The Emperor's eyes were opened, and he praised the courage of Wangchu.' " But Moule (*Quinsai*, page 84) has shown that the official in question, "Po-lo," was not our Marco, but rather a Chinese. It is not known by what name Marco Polo was called in the Mongol court, or in the Chinese or Mongol annals. There is no record that he warned Kublai Khan of Ahmad's treachery, or played an active part in the minister's downfall, even though he recorded events accurately.

In the Service of the Khan, edited by Igor de Rachewiltz et al., has the best account in English of Ahmad's rise and fall (pages 539–557); in this article, H. Franke draws heavily on Chinese sources as well as on Rashid al-Din, the Persian historian. And for another account of Ahmad's rise and fall, see R. P. Lister's *Marco Polo's Travels in Xanadu with Kublai Khan*, page 138. In *The Mongols*, said to be a favorite of Theodore Roosevelt, Jeremiah Curtin recounts the Ahmad and Sanga episode (pages 372–373).

Marco gives the year of Nayan and Kaidu's plot as 1286, but once again he seems to have become confused while converting a date from the Chinese or Mongol lunar calendar to the Julian calendar. Aspects of the rebellion appear in Pauthier's edition, *Le Livre de Marco Polo*, page 237, note 4. The fate of the Mongol invasion force is recounted by Rossabi, *Khubilai Khan*, on pages 220 and following.

CHAPTER THIRTEEN / *The Seeker*

For a discussion of what was meant by "India," see Yule and Cordier, volume 2, pages 426–427. Additional commentary on the final leg of Marco's journey can be found in Hart's *Marco Polo*, pages 145–167. And for a thorough and provocative discussion of Marco Polo's spiritual experiences and the evolution of his beliefs, see Mario Bussagli's "La Grande Asia di Marco Polo," in Zorzi's *Marco Polo, Venezia e l'Oriente*.

Marco associated Saint Thomas with a "race of men who are called gavi," who make a practice of sitting on carpets. "When one asked them why they do this," Marco reports, they replied, "because . . . we are sprung from the earth and to earth we must return." Despite the men's passivity, Marco insisted that ancestors of the gavi "killed Master Saint Thomas the Apostle long ago." As a result of this deed, "none could go into the place where the body of Master Saint Thomas is, which is in the province of Maabar, in a little town." Marco comments: "Twenty or more [men] could not put one of these gavi into the place where the body of Master Saint Thomas is buried, because the place does not receive them by virtue of the holy body." Realizing that this requires elucidation, Marco explains, "They say they tried the experiment, and that one of the said gavi, dragged by force by many men to make him enter where the body of Saint Thomas is buried, could by no amount of force be moved. . . . And this very special miracle our Lord God showed for reverence of the most holy apostle."

Those wishing to learn about differing interpretations of Thomas from a modern perspective would do well to consult Elaine Pagels's *Beyond Belief: The Secret Gospel of Thomas* (New York: Random House, 2003). The Buddhist influence on the Mongols is explained in Gianroberto Scarcia's "I Mongoli e l'Iran: la situazione religiosa," in Zorzi, *Venezia e l'Oriente*. And commentary on Marco's distinctive name for the Buddha can be found in Pauthier's edition of the *Travels*, *Le Livre de Marco Polo*, page 588, note, and in Olschki, *Marco Polo's Asia*, pages 254–255.

I wish to acknowledge the assistance of Patrick Ryan, S.J., for his enlightening comments about Zanzibar's religious history and traditions.

CHAPTER FOURTEEN / *The Mongol Princess*

Hart's *Marco Polo*, page 142, note, offers the conventional account of the meaning of Kokachin's name. My version relies on the convincing analysis of Professor S. Tsolmon in Ulaanbaatar on June 15, 2005, as it is better grounded in Mongol custom and language.

Francis Woodman Cleaves offers an exhaustive record of the sources of Kokachin's travels in "A Chinese Source Bearing on Marco Polo's Departure from China and a Persian Source on His Arrival in Persia." The last leg of Marco's journey receives colorful treatment by Mike Edwards in *National Geographic*, July 2001.

CHAPTER FIFTEEN / *The Prodigal Son*

The best, if not entirely reliable, source of information about Marco Polo's life after his return from China can be found in the works of Giambattista Ramusio, a prominent Venetian official and an accomplished scholar of geography. Ramusio called his three-volume compilation of accounts by celebrated explorers *Navigazioni e viaggi*, and he led off with Marco's chronicle, thus canonizing it. The well-connected Ramusio wrote that he believed the very first copy of Marco's manuscript was in Latin; Ramusio based his translation on that manuscript and several others.

Although Ramusio sounds scholarly enough, he breathlessly reported and reinforced traditions concerning Marco Polo instead of relying on facts alone. Ramusio explained, "Because in the continual repetitions of the story that he gave more and more often when speaking of the magnificence of the Great Khan, he stated that his revenue was from ten to fifteen millions in gold, and in the way in speaking of many other riches of those countries, he spoke always in term of millions, they gave him as a nickname, Messer Marco Milioni, and thus I have seen it noted in public books of the Republic where mention is made of him, and the court of his house from that time to the present is commonly called the Corte del Milioni"—as it is to this day.

The story of the Polos' return has been recounted by Hart (*Marco Polo*, page 171), among others. Ramusio's comment about the "charming and gracious" Marco Polo can be found in Hart's book, pages 175–177.

The best English-language account of the Republic's travails is contained in John Julius Norwich's *A History of Venice*. "For the past twenty years nothing seemed to have gone right for them," he writes on page 173. "Militarily they had suffered defeats on land and sea, with serious losses, both in ships and human lives. They had been forced to watch, powerless, while the enemy penetrated to the very confines of the lagoon. Their neighbors, on many of whom they depended for trade, were in a greater or lesser degree unfriendly. Their chief colony, Crete, was once again in revolt. They had suffered the chilly joylessness—to say nothing of the spiritual dangers—of an interdict, the terrors of an earthquake, the misery of flood."

Giorgio del Guerra's *Rustichello da Pisa* has the fullest record of its subject's life. For more on Rustichello's efforts in the Arthurian romance genre, see Fabrizio Cigni's *Il romanzo arturiano di Rustichello da Pisa*. John Larner, in *Marco Polo and the Discovery of the World*, pages 47–49, presents a precise analysis of Rustichello's abilities and limitations.

It has long been assumed that Rustichello and Marco wrote their original manuscript in Latin, or perhaps an Italian dialect, but scholars have converged on French as the language in which they composed. As evidence, they cite a remark circulated by a Benedictine known as John the Long of Ypres; in 1350, he wrote that Marco's book was originally composed "in the French vernacular"—for better or worse. Yule and Cordier (*Travels*, volume 1, page 83) offer a pithy assessment of Rustichello's linguistic skills. "The author is at war with all the practices of French grammar; subject and object, numbers, moods, and tenses, are in consummate confusion," they complain. "Italian words are constantly introduced, either quite in the crude or rudely Gallicized." These grammatical and linguistic idiosyncrasies are consistent with the idea that the Venetian traveler dictated his account to the Tuscan romance writer, who wrote in French, "a language foreign to them both."

By way of illustrating the similarity to Marco's account, it is worth quoting the opening of Rustichello's earlier work, *Meliadus:* "Lords, emperors and princes, dukes and counts, barons and knights and vavasours [feudal tenants who ranked just below barons] and townsfolk and all the worldly men of this world who are accustomed to taking pleasure in romances, if you take this book and have it read from end to end, you will hear all the great adventures that befell the knight errants of the time of King Uther Pendragon. . . ."

For another summary of Marco's long and lively posthumous reputation, see Yule and Cordier, volume 1, page 116 and following. Harry Hart, in his *Marco Polo*, page 212, traces Ramusio's account of Marco's father's second family, but remains skeptical. Ramusio was prone to error, and may have mistaken other relatives for supposed offspring of Niccolò Polo. It is possible that Niccolò did not actually remarry.

Details of Marco's return come from Hart's *Marco Polo*, page 209, and Marco's new home is described by Larner in *Marco Polo and the Discovery of the World*, page 44.

Throughout his account, Marco evinces little curiosity about his father's earlier experiences among the Mongols, and loses track of him for years on end. Marco never appears to worry about his father's whereabouts or well-being, or, for that matter, his uncle's. Nor does he offer details about their trading activities. Marco concerns himself with his own experiences; it is as though his father and uncle exist for the sole purpose of transporting him to China and bringing him to Kublai Khan; thereafter, they cease to play an active role in his life.

Ramusio's remarks about Marco's reassuring gestures of filial piety are quoted in Hart, *Marco Polo*, page 215. Hart also discusses the Venetian mint (page 179).

Regarding the presentation copy given to Monseigneur Thiebault, Hart (page 219) suggests that the flattery of Charles of Valois contained in the inscription casts doubt on the document's authenticity. Nevertheless, the inscription demonstrates that Marco's work was held in high regard by important people.

Giuseppi Castellani notes that Marco's will referred to two kinds of coins, lire consisting of Venetian dinars and lire of Venetian dinar *grossi*. For further discussion of Venetian coins in the will, see "I valori delle monete espresse nel testamento di Marco Polo," *Rivista mensile della Città di Venezia* 3, no. 9 (September 1924): 257–258. It is generally considered to be futile to try to estimate the value of these coins in today's money.

The original Latin text of the will can be found in *The Travels of Marco Polo: The Complete Yule-Cordier Edition*, volume 1, beginning on page 70. Concerning the feminine headdress found among Marco's possessions, see Olschki, *Marco Polo's Asia*, pages 104–108. And Hart discusses Marco's death in *Marco Polo*, page 230, note.

For more on Marco's estate and the legal actions undertaken by his heirs, see Rolfo Gallo's "Nuovi documenti riguardanti Marco Polo e la sua familiglia." This is a useful survey, but details of these long-ago transactions may not be accurate, or accurately translated. Gallo surmises that on their return from China, Marco and his father and uncle devoted their riches to enlarging their home or buying a new one. Moneta's will is quoted by Hart in *Marco Polo*, page 61.

EPILOGUE / *The Storyteller*

Bonaguisi is quoted by Hart in *Marco Polo*, page 259; on page 248 Hart mentions Fantina's legal actions.

Moule and Pelliot discuss the dissemination of Marco Polo's account in *The Description of the World* on page 40 of volume 1. For an interesting analysis of its flaws and inconsistencies, see John Critchley, *Marco Polo's Book*, especially pages 1–11. Critchley can be rigorous to a fault, but he has a wonderful eye for contradictions and instances of illogic. For a comparison of various early Marco Polo texts, see Moule and Pelliot's version, *The Description of the World*, volume 1, beginning on page 499. And for a complete list of early Marco Polo books and manuscripts, see the same volume, beginning on page 509. Also see Yule and Cordier's edition, volume 2, beginning on page 523.

Il "Milione" veneto, edited by Alvaro Barbieri and Alvise Andreose, with an introduction by Lorenzo Renzi (who also refers to the possibility of manuscripts chained to the Rialto Bridge), contains a comprehensive, detailed account of the origins and relationships among various Marco Polo manuscripts. Renzi credits Luigi Foscolo Benedetto, who "untangled the dense mass of manuscripts . . . and devised the first systematic review of the multitude of witnesses" in 1928. Drawing on Benedetto's work, Renzi summarizes, in part: "The more than 130 codices that have handed down to us the different versions of Polo's work can be split into two main groups, labeled A and B, whose archetypes issue from a partially corrupted apocryphal version (01) of the lost original (0). Between the two derivative copies of 01, that differed one from the other for the degree of deterioration of the reading and reduction of content, the prototype of the B group was closer to the model. Group A is further divided into F, the only complete testimony in original linguistic form, and three conspicuous families that emanate from three lost Franco-Italian exemplars (F1, F2, F3), similar to F, but unrelated to it. F1 is the model of the rewriting in good French attributed to Grégoire (FG); from F2 issues the most ancient Tuscan abridgement (TA); from F3 the version of the Veneto region that we hereby publish. Group B comprises instead four editions that represent, to different degrees and levels, 'a phase before F,' meaning a more conservative stage in the transmission of Marco's book. It includes Z, a Latin version of rich content, V, a rather rough translation in Veneto dialect, L, a Latin abridgement and VB, a very free Venetian re-elaboration, full of interpolations and misunderstandings. These texts presume lost Franco-Italian influences that should have been very close to F in form and subject, but are generally more correct in interpretation and more complete through certain passages. . . ."

Some scholars insist that Columbus made his annotations in 1497 or 1498. For an extended discussion of the issue, see Larner's *Marco Polo and the Discovery of the World*, beginning on page 155, and *El libro de Marco Polo anotado por Cristóbal Colón*, edited by Juan Gil. Unlike Larner, Felipe Fernández-Armesto, in his *Columbus*, pages 36–37, states that the admiral consulted Marco's *Travels* in advance of the first voyage to the New World.

Hart (*Marco Polo*) presents the Samuel Purchas quotation on page 111. John Livingston Lowes, in *The Road to Xanadu: A Study in the Ways of the Imagination*, page 324 and following, opines that Coleridge's memory was faulty, and that the poet actually had his famous opium dream in 1796. Caroline Alexander's noteworthy study *The Way to Xanadu* contains a discussion of Coleridge and Marco Polo on pages xiv and xv.

In *The Medieval Expansion of Europe*, second edition, pages 194–195, J.R.S. Phillips discusses Mandeville and Polo. The enlightening introduction by C.W.R.D. Moseley to the Penguin edition of *The Travels of Sir John Mandeville*, pages 9–39, is also worth consulting.

Yule and Cordier's assessments of Marco Polo can be found in volume 1, pages 1 and 106–107, of their edition of the *Travels*. Despite its devotion to the minutiae of Marco's account, and its charming record of correspondence among Victorian gentleman travelers concerning their impressions of Polo, their massive edition has its idiosyncrasies, of which the modern reader should be cognizant. When they find a passage too explicit for their taste, they silently omit it. More seriously, they delete entire sections late in Marco's account, claiming that they are inferior, or, as they put it (volume 2, page 456), "are the merest verbiage and repetition of narrative formulae without the slightest value"—a highly questionable assessment, and not in keeping with their generally estimable scholarship.

The question of maps is one of the most vexed in all of Polo scholarship. It is possible that Marco intended to include some routes of use to merchants in his account, but they have been lost, or Rustichello, a romance writer rather than a geographer, failed to include them. Some contenders, or pretenders, to the status of Marco Polo maps have surfaced over time, but their authenticity is doubtful. For a review of these intriguing items, see Leo Bagrow's "The Maps from the Home Archives of the

Descendents of a Friend of Marco Polo." It should be noted that maps discussed by Bagrow are modern copies of older maps, or purported older maps. It is possible that the maps that have been attributed to Marco Polo are nothing more than an elaborate scholarly hoax. Johann Ruysch is quoted by Hart in *Marco Polo*, pages 260–261. Also refer to J. H. Parry, *The Discovery of the Sea*, first California edition (Berkeley: University of California Press, 1981), page 51.

The best discussion in English of the Great Wall, as it relates to Marco Polo's account, is Arthur N. Waldron's "The Problem of the Great Wall of China."

For a succinct discussion of the donnybrook kicked up by Frances Wood, see Luce Boulnois, *The Silk Road*, pages 353–355. Igor de Rachewiltz offers a persuasive and detailed critique of Frances Wood's book in his "F. Wood's *Did Marco Polo Go to China?*" For an even more detailed critique of Wood's book, see de Rachewiltz, "Marco Polo Went to China." My thanks to Professor de Rachewiltz for an appendix of additions and corrections to his work, which includes his observation about Chinese cartographers.

For a fine technical discussion about how Marco's account of escorting the Mongolian princess Kokachin to Persia amounts to proof that Marco Polo went to China and served Kublai Khan, see Francis Woodman Cleaves, "A Chinese Source Bearing on Marco Polo's Departure from China and a Persian Source on His Arrival in Persia."

SELECT BIBLIOGRAPHY

Abu-Lughod, Janet. *Before European Hegemony: The World System A.D. 1250–1350.* New York: Oxford University Press, 1989.

Adamec, Ludwig W., ed. *Historical and Political Gazetteer of Afghanistan.* Vol. 1, *Badakhshan Province and Northeastern Afghanistan.* Graz: Akademische Druck–u. Verlagsanstalt, 1972.

Alexander, Caroline. *The Way to Xanadu.* New York: Alfred A. Knopf, 1994.

Allen, Mark. *Falconry in Arabia.* London: Orbis, 1980.

Allulli, Ranieri. *Marco Polo.* Turin: Paravia, 1924.

Annali genovesi dopo Caffaro e suoi continuatori. Genoa: Municipio di Genova, 1941.

Ariz, Ghulum Jilani. *Shah Rahai Afghanistan* [King's Roads of Afghanistan]. Peshawar: Afghanistan Resource and Information Centre (ARIC), 2000.

Avon Caffi, Giuseppe. "L'Arte cinese a Venezia." *L'Italia che scrive,* anno 37, no. 10 (October 1954).

Bagrow, Leo. "The Maps from the Home Archives of the Descendants of a Friend of Marco Polo." *Imago Mundi* 5 (1948): 3–13.

Balazs, Etienne. *Chinese Civilization and Bureaucracy: Variations on a Theme.* Translated by H. M. Wright. Edited by Arthur F. Wright. New Haven: Yale University Press, 1964.

Balestrieri, Leonida. "Le Prigioni della Malapaga." In *Cassa di Risparmio di Genova.* Genoa: Marzo-Giugno, 1960.

Bar Hebraeus. *The Chronology of Gregory Abû'l Faraj.* Translated by E. A. Wallis Budge. London: Oxford University Press, 1932.

Barraclough, Geoffrey. *The Medieval Papacy.* London: Thames & Hudson, 1968.

Barrett, T. H. "Marco Polo Did Go to China, So There." *London Review of Books,* November 30, 1995, p. 28.

Bertúccioli, Umberto. "Il ritorno via mare di Marco Polo." *Giornale economico della Camera di Commercio di Venezia,* March 1954. Venice: Officine Grafiche F. Garzia, 1954.

———. "Marco Polo: Uomo di mare." *Ateneo Veneto,* anno 146, vol. 139, no. 1 (January–June 1955): 1–15.

Bira, Sh. *Studies in Mongolian History, Culture, and Historiography.* Edited by Ts. Ishdorj and Kh. Purevtogtokh. Ulaanbaatar: International Association for Mongol Studies, 2001.

Boorstin, Daniel. *The Discoverers.* New York: Random House, 1983.

Boulnois, Luce. *The Silk Road.* Translated by Helen Loveday. Hong Kong: Odyssey Books, 2004.

Boyle, John Andrew. "Marco Polo and His *Description of the World.*" *History Today* 21, no. 11 (London, 1971): 759–769.

Braunstein, P., and R. Delort. *Venise; portrait historique d'une cité.* Paris: Éditions du seuil, 1971.

Bratianu, G. I. *Recherches sur le commerce génois dans la mer Noire au XIIIe siècle.* Paris: P. Geuther, 1929.

Brice, Catherine. *Histoire de l'Italie.* Paris: Hatier, 1992.

Brown, Lloyd A. *The Story of Maps.* 1949. Reprint, New York: Dover, 1977.

Brunetti, Mario. "Venezia al tempo di Marco Polo." *L'Italia che scrive,* anno 37, no. 10 (October 1954).

Buell, Paul. "Pleasing the Palate of the Qan." *Mongolian Studies* 13 (1990): 57–81.

Cable, Mildred, with Francesca French. *The Gobi Desert.* New York: Macmillan, 1944.

Calvino, Italo. *Invisible Cities.* Translated by William Weaver. New York: Harcourt, 1974.

The Cambridge History of China. Vol. 6. *Alien Regimes and Border States.* Edited by Herbert Franke and Denis Twitchett. Cambridge: Cambridge University Press, 1966.

Capusso, M. G. *La lingua del "Devisament dou monde" di Marco Polo.* Pisa: Pacini, 1980.

Carter, Thomas Francis. *The Invention of Printing in China and Its Spread Westward.* New York: Columbia University Press, 1925.

Cary, George. *The Medieval Alexander.* Cambridge: Cambridge University Press, 1956.

Castellani, Giuseppi. "I valori delle monete espresse nel testamento di Marco Polo." *Rivista mensile della Città di Venezia* 3, no. 9 (September 1924): 257–258.

Chamerlat, Christian Antoine de. *La fauconnerie et l'art.* Courbevoie: ACR Éditeur, 1986.

Cigni, Fabrizio. *Il romanzo arturiano de Rustichello da Pisa.* Pisa: Edizioni Cassa di Risparmio di Pisa, 1994.

Cleaves, Francis Woodman. "A Chinese Source Bearing on Marco Polo's Departure from China and a Persian Source on His Arrival in Persia." *Harvard Journal of Asiatic Studies* 36 (1976): 181–203.

———. "An Early Mongolian Version of the Alexander Romance." *Harvard Journal of Asiatic Studies* 22 (December 1959): 1–99.

Collis, Maurice. *Marco Polo.* London: Faber & Faber, 1950.

Colón, Fernando. *The Life of the Admiral Christopher Columbus by His Son, Ferdinand.* Translated and annotated by Benjamin Keen. New Brunswick: Rutgers University Press, 1959.

Cordier, Henri. *Histoire Générale de la Chine.* Vol. 2. Paris: Librairie Paul Geuthner, 1920.

Crane, Nicholas. *Mercator.* London: Weidenfeld & Nicolson, 2002.

Crawford, F. Marion. *Venice, the Place and the People: Salve Venetia; Gleanings from Venetian History.* New York: Macmillan, 1909.

Critchley, John. *Marco Polo's Book.* Brookfield, Vermont: Variorum, 1992.

Crouzet-Pavan, Elisabeth. *Enfers et Paradis: L'Italie de Dante et de Giotto.* Paris: Albin Michel, 2001.

———. *"Sopra le acque salse": Espaces, pouvoir et société à Venise à la fin du Moyen Age.* Rome: École Française de Rome, 1992.

———. *Venise triomphante: Les horizons d'un mythe.* Paris: Albin Michel, 1999.

Curtin, Jeremiah. *The Mongols: A History.* New York: Da Capo, 2003. First published by Little, Brown in 1908.

Daftary, Farhad. *The Assassin Legends: Myths of the Isma'ilis.* London: Tauris, 1994.

Dalrymple, William. *In Xanadu: A Quest.* London: Collins, 1989.

Dang, Baohai. "Cheetah and Cheetah-Hunting in the Mongol Empire" [in Chinese]. *Nationalities Studies* 4 (2002).

Dawson, Christopher, ed. *The Mongol Mission.* New York: Sheed & Ward, 1955.

Del Guerra, Giorgio. *Rustichello da Pisa.* Pisa: Nistri-Lischi, 1955.

Delumeau, Jean-Pierre, and Isabelle Heullant-Donat. *L'Italie au Moyen Âge.* Paris: Hachette, 2000.

"Did Marco Polo Come to China?" [in Chinese] *Science World*, vol. 8, November 11, 2003.

Dizionario delle strade di Genova. 3rd ed. Vol. 1. Genoa: Edizioni Culturali Internazionali Genova, 1985.

Dotson, John E. "Foundations of Venetian Naval Strategy from Pietro II Orseolo to the Battle of Zonchio, 1000–1500." *Viator: Medieval and Renaissance Studies* 32 (2001).

Dunn, Ross E. *The Adventures of Ibn Battuta, a Muslim Traveler of the Fourteenth Century.* Berkeley: University of California Press, 1986.

Dupree, Nancy Hatch. *An Historical Guide to Afghanistan.* 2nd ed. Kabul: Afghan Air Authority, Afghan Tourist Organization, 1977.

———. *The Road to Balkh.* Kabul: Afghan Tourist Organization, 1967.

———. *The Valley of Bamyian.* 3rd ed. Peshawar: Abdul Hafiz Ashna, 2002.

Edwards, Mike. "The Adventures of Marco Polo: Part 1." *National Geographic Magazine*, May 2001.

———. "The Adventures of Marco Polo: Part 2." *National Geographic Magazine*, June 2001.

———. "The Adventures of Marco Polo: Part 3." *National Geographic Magazine*, July 2001.

———. "Genghis, Lord of the Mongols." *National Geographic Magazine*, December 1996.

———. "Sons of Genghis: The Great Khans." *National Geographic Magazine*, February 1997.

Fernández-Armesto, Felipe. *Columbus.* Oxford: Oxford University Press, 1991.

———. *Millennium: A History of the Last Thousand Years.* New York: Scribner, 1995.

Foglietta, Uberto. *Uberti Folietae clarorum Ligurum elogia.* Rome: Apud Josephum De Angelis, 1573.

Foltz, Richard C. *Religions of the Silk Road.* New York: St. Martin's Press, 1999.

Fong, Wen C., and James C. Y. Watt. *Possessing the Past: Treasures from the National Palace Museum, Taipei.* New York: Metropolitan Museum of Art, dist. by Abrams, 1996.

Forman, Werner, and Cottie A. Burland. *The Travels of Marco Polo.* New York: McGraw-Hill, 1970.

Franck, Irene M., and David Brownstone. *The Silk Road: A History.* New York: Facts on File, 1986.

Franke, H[erbert]. "Sino-Western Contacts Under the Mongol Empire." *Journal of the Hong Kong Branch of the Royal Asiatic Society* 6 (1966).

Frazier, Ian. "Invaders." *New Yorker*, April 25, 2005.

Frederick II, Holy Roman Emperor, 1194–1250. *The Art of Falconry: Being the "De arte venandi cum avibus" of Frederick II of Hohenstouffen.* Translated by Casey A. Wood and F. Marjorie Fyfe. Stanford: Stanford University Press, 1943.

———. *De arte venandi cum avibus.* Translated (into French) by Anne Paulus and Baudoin Van den Abeele. Nogent-le-Roi: J. Laget, 2000.

Friedman, John B., and Kristen Mossler Figg, eds. *Trade, Travel, and Exploration in the Middle Ages: An Encyclopedia.* New York: Garland Publishing, 2000.

Friedman, Thomas L. *The World Is Flat: A Brief History of the Twenty-first Century.* New York: Farrar, Straus & Giroux, 2005.

Frimmer, Steven. *Neverland: Fabled Places and Fabulous Voyages of History and Legend.* New York: Viking, 1976.

Gallo, Rodolfo. "Marco Polo; la sua famiglia e il suo libro." In *Nel settimo centenario della nascita di Marco Polo.* Venice: Archivio di Stato di Venezia, 1954.

———. "Nuovi documenti riguardanti Marco Polo e la sua famiglia." *Atti dell' Istituto Veneto di Scienze, Lettere ed Arti,* 1957–1958, tomo 116, 309–325.

Gaudio, Attilio. *Sur les traces de Marco Polo.* Paris: R. Julliard, 1955.

Gernet, Jacques. *Daily Life in China on the Eve of the Mongol Invasion, 1250–1276.* Translated by H. M. Wright. Stanford: Stanford University Press, 1962.

Gibbon, Edward. *The Decline and Fall of the Roman Empire.* Edited by J. B. Bury. 3 vols. New York: Modern Library, 1995.

Gil, Juan, comp. *En demanda del Gran Khan.* Madrid: Alianza, 1993.

Green, Peter. *Alexander of Macedon, 356–323 B.C.: A Historical Biography.* Berkeley: University of California Press, 1991.

Grossi Bianchi, Luciano, and Ennio Poleggi. *Una città portuale del Medioevo, Genova nei secoli X–XVI.* Genoa: Sagep, 1979.

Gulik, R. H. van. *Sexual Life in Ancient China.* Leiden: Brill, 2003.

Haeger, John W. "Marco Polo in China: Problems with Internal Evidence." *Bulletin of Sung and Yüan Studies* 14 (1978): 22–30.

Harley, J. B., and David Woodward, eds. *The History of Cartography.* Chicago: University of Chicago Press, 1987.

Hart, Henry H. *Marco Polo, Venetian Adventurer.* Norman: University of Oklahoma Press, 1967.

Hazlitt, W. Carew. *The Venetian Republic: Its Rise, Its Growth, and Its Fall.* Vol. 1. London: Adam & Charles Black, 1900.

———. *Marco Polo.* Paris: Fayard, 1983.

Hedin, Sven. *Across the Gobi Desert.* Translated by H. J. Cant. New York: Dutton, 1932.

———. *Overland to India.* London: Macmillan, 1910.

———. *Riddles of the Gobi Desert.* Translated by Elizabeth Sprigg and Claude Napier. New York: Dutton, 1933.

Heers, Jacques. "De Marco Polo à Christophe Colombe: Comment lire de *Devisement du monde?" Journal of Medieval History* 10 (1984): 125–143.

Heissig, Walther. *A Lost Civilization: The Mongols Rediscovered.* Translated by D.J.S. Thomson. New York: Basic Books, 1966.

Herodotus. *The Histories.* Translated by Robin Waterfield. Oxford: Oxford University Press, 1998.

Heyd, W. *Histoire du commerce du Levant au Moyen Âge,* 2 vols. Edited by Furcy Reynaud, 1885–1886. Reprint, Amsterdam: A. M. Hakkert, 1967.

Hildebrand, J. J. "The World's Greatest Overland Explorer." *National Geographic Magazine,* November 1928.

Hodgen, Margaret T. *Early Anthropology in the Sixteenth and Seventeenth Centuries.* Philadelphia: University of Pennsylvania Press, 1964.

Hourani, George Fadlo. *Arab Seafaring in the Indian Ocean in Ancient and Early Medieval Times.* Princeton: Princeton University Press, 1951.

Howard, Deborah. *Venice and the East: The Impact of the Islamic World on Venetian Architecture.* New Haven: Yale University Press, 2000.

Hsaio, Ch'i-ch'ing. *The Military Establishment of the Yüan Dynasty.* Cambridge, Massachusetts: Council on East Asian Studies, dist. by Harvard University Press, 1978.

Humble, Richard. *Marco Polo.* New York: Putnam, 1975.

Ibn Battuta. *Travels in Asia and Africa, 1325–1354.* Translated by H. A. R. Gibb. 1929. Reprint, New Delhi: Asian Educational Services, 1992.

Il romanzo arturiano di Rustichello da Pisa. Translated by Fabrizio Cigni. Pisa: Cassa di Risparmio di Pisa, 1994.

"I valori delle monete espresse nel testimento di Marco Polo." *Rivista mensile della Città di Venezia,* anno 3, no. 1 (January 1924): 257–258. Venice: Poligrafica Italiana, 1924.

Iwamura, Shinobu. *Manuscripts and Printed Editions of Marco Polo's "Travels."* Tokyo: National Diet Library, 1949.

Jennings, Gary. *The Journeyer.* New York: Atheneum, 1984.

Kahn, Paul. *The Secret History of the Mongols: The Origin of Chinghis Khan; An Adaptation of the "Yuan Ch'ao pi shih," Based Primarily on the English Translation by Francis Woodman Cleaves.* San Francisco: North Point Press, 1984.

Kedar, Benjamin Z. *Merchants in Crisis: Genoese and Venetian Men of Affairs and the Fourteenth-century Depression.* New Haven: Yale University Press, 1976.

Kimble, George H. T. *Geography in the Middle Ages.* London: Methuen, 1938.

Komroff, Manuel, ed. *Contemporaries of Marco Polo.* New York: Boni & Liveright, 1928.

Labande, Edmond-René. *L'Italie de la Renaissance: Duecento, Trecento, Quattrocento.* Paris: Payot, 1954.

Lach, Donald F. *Asia in the Making of Europe.* Vol. 1. Chicago: University of Chicago Press, 1965.

Lane Fox, Robin. *Alexander the Great.* New York: Penguin Books, 1986.

Langlois, J. D., Jr., ed. *China Under Mongol Rule.* Princeton: Princeton University Press, 1981.

Larner, John. *Marco Polo and the Discovery of the World.* New Haven: Yale University Press, 1999.

Lee, Sherman E., and Wai-Kam Ho. *Chinese Art Under the Mongols: The Yüan Dynasty, 1279–1368.* Cleveland: Cleveland Museum of Art, dist. by Press of Case Western Reserve University, 1968.

Lewis, Bernard. *The Assassins: A Radical Sect in Islam.* New York: Basic Books, 2003. First published 1968.

Li, Chih-ch'ang. *The Travels of an Alchemist.* Translated by Arthur Waley. London: Routledge, 1931.

Lister, R. P. *Marco Polo's Travels in Xanadu with Kublai Khan.* London: Gordon & Cremonesi, 1976.

Liu, Guojun, and Zheng Rusi. *L'histoire du livre en Chine.* Translated (into French) by Ann-Muriel Harvey and Olivier Pasteur. Beijing: Éditions en langues étrangères, 1989.

Liu, Xinru. *Silk and Religion: An Exploration of Material Life and the Thought of People, AD 600–1200.* Delhi: Oxford University Press, 1996.

Lopez, Donald S., Jr. *The Story of Buddhism: A Concise Guide to Its History and Teachings.* San Francisco: HarperSanFrancisco, 2001.

Lopez, Robert S. *The Commercial Revolution of the Middle Ages: 950–1350.* Cambridge: Cambridge University Press, 1976.

———, and Irving W. Raymond. *Medieval Trade in the Mediterranean World.* New York: Columbia University Press, 1955.

Lowes, John Livingston. *The Road to Xanadu: A Study in the Ways of the Imagination.* Princeton: Princeton University Press, 1986. First published in 1927 by Houghton Mifflin.

Man, John. *Kublai Khan: From Xanadu to Superpower.* London: Bantam Press, 2006.

Mandeville, John, Sir. *The Travels of Sir John Mandeville.* Translated by C.W.R.D. Moseley. Harmondsworth, Middlesex, England: Penguin Books, 1983.

Marshall, Robert. *Storm from the East: From Genghis Khan to Kublai Khan.* Berkeley: University of California Press, 1993.

Martin, Hervé. *Mentalités médiévales.* 2 vols. Paris: Presses universitaires de France, 1998.

McNeill, William H. *Plagues and Peoples.* Garden City, New York: Anchor Press, 1976.

Meibiao, Cai. "Marco Polo in China," translated by Wang Yintong, *Social Sciences in China* 14, no. 2 (1993): 171–179.

Ménard, Philippe. "Le problème de la version originale du *Devisement du Monde* de Marco Polo." In *De Marco Polo à Savinio; Écrivains italiens en langue française.* Paris: Presses de l'université de Paris-Sorbonne, 2003.

Miao, Wang, and Shi Baoxiu. *Tracing Marco Polo's Northern Route.* Beijing: China Intercontinental Press, 2004.

Miles, Keith, and David Butler. *Marco Polo.* New York: Dell, 1982.

Mingzhao, Cheng. *On the Shore of West Lake.* Translated by Tang Bowen. Beijing: Foreign Languages Press, 2001.

Mollat, Michel. *Les explorateurs du XIIIe au XVIe siècle.* Paris: Éditions J. C. Lattès, 1984.

The Monks of Kûblâi Khân, Emperor of China. Translated by E. A. Wallace Budge. London: Religious Tract Society, 1928.

Morgan, David. *The Mongols.* Cambridge, Massachusetts: Blackwell, 1990. First published in the United States in 1986.

Morgan, D. O. "Marco Polo in China—or Not." *Journal of the Royal Asiatic Society,* series 3, 6, 2 (1996): 221–225.

Morison, Samuel Eliot. *The European Discovery of America.* Vol. 2, *The Southern Voyages: A.D. 1492–1616.* New York: Oxford University Press, 1974.

Morris, Jan. *The World of Venice.* Rev. ed. San Diego: Harcourt Brace, 1993.

Moule, A. C. *Quinsai; with Other Notes on Marco Polo.* Cambridge: Cambridge University Press, 1957.

Mozai, Torao. "The Lost Fleet of Kublai Khan." *National Geographic Magazine,* November 1982.

Muldoon, James. *Popes, Lawyers, and Infidels: The Church of the Non-Christian World, 1250–1350.* Philadelphia: University of Pennsylvania Press, 1979.

———, ed. *Varieties of Religious Conversion in the Middle Ages.* Gainesville: University Press of Florida, 1997.

Needham, Joseph. *Heavenly Clockwork: The Great Astronomical Clocks of Medieval China.* Cambridge: Cambridge University Press, 1960.

———. *Science and Civilisation in China.* Vols. 1–3. Cambridge: Cambridge University Press, 1954–1959.

———, and Robin D. S. Yates. *Science and Civilisation in China.* Vol. 5, pt. 6. Cambridge: Cambridge University Press, 1994.

———, et al. *Science and Civilisation in China.* Vol. 5, pt. 7. Cambridge: Cambridge University Press, 1986.

Nel VII centenario della nascita di Marco Polo. Venice: Istituto Veneto di Scienze, Lettre ed Arti, 1955.

Norwich, John Julius. *A History of Venice.* New York: Alfred A. Knopf, 1982; Vintage Books, 1989.

Oliphant, Mrs. [Margaret]. *The Makers of Venice: Doges, Conquerors, and Men of Letters.* London: Macmillan, 1887.

Olschki, Leonardo. *Marco Polo's Asia.* Translated by John A. Scott. Revised by author. Berkeley: University of California Press, 1960.

Oriente poliano: Studi e conferenze tenute all'Is. M.E.O. in occasione del VII centenario della nascita di Marco Polo, 1254–1954. Rome: Istituto italiano per il Medio ed Estremo Oriente, 1957.

Parry, J. H. *The Discovery of the Sea.* Berkeley: University of California Press, 1981.

Pelliot, Paul. *Notes on Marco Polo.* Vols. 1 and 2. Paris: Imprimerie Nationale, Librarie Adrien-Maisonneuve, 1959–1963.

Phillips, E. D. *The Mongols.* New York: Praeger, 1969.

Phillips, J.R.S. *The Medieval Expansion of Europe.* 2nd ed. Oxford: Oxford University Press, 1998.

Pliny, the Elder. *Natural History: A Selection.* Translated by John F. Healy. New York: Penguin Books, 1991.

Plutarch. *The Age of Alexander: Nine Greek Lives.* Translated by Ian Scott-Kilvert. Harmondsworth, Middlesex, England: Penguin Books, 1973.

Polo, Marco. *La Description du monde.* Edited by Louis Hambis. Paris: Librarie C. Klincksieck, 1955.

———. *The Description of the World / Marco Polo.* Translated and annotated by A. C. Moule and Paul Pelliot. 2 vols. 1938. Reprint, New York: AMS Press, 1976.

———. *Le Devisement du monde.* Edited by Philippe Ménard et al. 2 vols. Geneva: Droz, 2001.

———. *El libro de Marco Polo / anotado por Cristóbal Colón.* Edited by Juan Gil. Madrid: Alianza, 1987.

———. *Le Livre de Marco Polo.* Translated into modern French and annotated by A.J.H. Charignon. 3 vols. Beijing: A. Nachbauer, 1924–1928.

———. *Le Livre de Marco Polo.* Edited by M. G. Pauthier. Geneva: Slatkine Reprints, 1978.

———. *Il Milione, prima edizione integrale, a cura di Luigi Foscolo Benedetto, sotto il patronato della città di Venezia.* Florence: Comitato Geografico Nazionale Italiano, 1928.

———. *Il "Milione" veneto.* Edited by Alvaro Barbieri and Alvise Andreose. Introduction by Lorenzo Renzi. Venice: Marsilio, 1999.

———. *The Travels of Marco Polo.* New York: Orion Press, 1958.

———. *The Travels of Marco Polo.* Translated by Ronald Latham. Harmondsworth, Middlesex, England: Penguin Books, 1958.

———. *The Travels of Marco Polo.* Translated by Aldo Ricci. New York: Viking Press, 1931.

———. *The Travels of Marco Polo.* Edited by Milton Rugoff. New York: New American Library, 1961.

———. *The Travels of Marco Polo: The Complete Yule-Cordier Edition.* 2 vols. New York: Dover, 1993.

———. *The Travels of Marco Polo, the Venetian.* Translated by William Marsden. Revised by Thomas Wright. Introduction by John Masefield. London: J. M. Dent, 1908.

Power, Eileen. *Medieval People.* Boston: Houghton Mifflin, 1924.

Prawdin, Michael [Michael Charol]. *The Mongol Empire, Its Rise and Legacy.* Translated by Eden and Cedar Paul. New York: Macmillan, 1940.

Prestwich, Michael. *Edward I.* London: Methuen, 1988.

Procacci, Giuliano. *Histoire d'Italie.* Paris: Fayard, 1968.

Rachewiltz, Igor de. "F. Wood's *Did Marco Polo Go to China?*" http://rspas.anu.edu.au/eah/Marcopolo.html.

————. "Marco Polo Went to China." *Zentralasiatische Studien* 27 (1997): 34–92.

————. *Papal Envoys to the Great Khans.* Stanford: Stanford University Press, 1971.

————, et al., eds. *In the Service of the Khan: Eminent Personalities of the Early Mongol–Yüan Period (1200–1300).* Wiesbaden: Harrassowitz, 1993.

Rashid al-Din. *The Successors of Genghis Khan.* Translated by John Andrew Boyle. New York: Columbia University Press, 1971.

Read, Bernard E. *Chinese Materia Medica: Insect Drugs.* Peiping, China: Peking Natural History Bulletin, 1941. Reprint, Taipei: Southern Materials Center, 1982.

Renouard, Yves. *Les Hommes d'affaires italiens du Moyen Âge.* Paris: A. Colin, 1968.

Rosengarten, Frederic, Jr. *The Book of Spices.* New York: Pyramid Books, 1973.

Rossabi, Morris. *Khubilai Khan: His Life and Times.* Berkeley: University of California Press, 1988.

————. *Voyager from Xanadu: Rabban Sauma and the First Journey from China to the West.* Tokyo: Kodansha, International, 1992.

Rossini, C. Conti. "Marco Polo e l'Etiopia." *Atti del Reale Istituto Veneto di Scienze, Lettere ed Arti,* 1939–1940, tomo 99, pt. 2, 1021–1039.

Runciman, Steven. *A History of the Crusades.* Vol. 3. Cambridge: Cambridge University Press, 1966.

Ryan, James D. "Christian Wives of Mongol Khans: Tartar Queens and Missionary Expectations in Asia." *Journal of the Royal Asiatic Society,* November 1998.

————. "Preaching Christianity Along the Silk Route: Missionary Outposts in the Tartar 'Middle Kingdom' in the Fourteenth Century." *Journal of Early Modern History,* November 1998.

Saunders, J. J. *The History of the Mongol Conquests.* London: Routledge & Kegan Paul, 1971.

The Secret History of the Mongols. Translated by Francis Woodman Cleaves. Vol. 1. Cambridge, Massachusetts: Harvard University Press, 1982.

The Secret History of the Mongols. Translated by Urgunge Onon. Ulaanbaatar: Bolor Sudar, 2005.

The Secret History of the Mongols: A Mongolian Epic Chronicle of the Thirteenth Century. Translated, with commentary, by Igor de Rachewiltz. 2 vols. Boston: Brill, 2004.

Severin, Timothy. *Tracking Marco Polo.* 1st American ed. New York: Peter Bedrick Books, 1986.

Shor, Jean Bowie. *After You, Marco Polo.* New York: McGraw-Hill, 1955.

Silverberg, Robert. *The Realm of Prester John.* 1st paperback ed. Garden City, New York: Doubleday, 1972. Athens: Ohio University Press, 1996.

Smith, John Masson, Jr. "Dietary Decadence and Dynastic Decline in the Mongol Empires." *Journal of Asian History* 34 (2000), 35–52.

Spence, Jonathan D. *The Chan's Great Continent: China in Western Minds.* New York: W. W. Norton, 1998.

————. "Marco Polo: Fact or Fiction?" *Far Eastern Economic Review,* August 22, 1996.

————. *The Memory Palace of Matteo Ricci.* New York: Viking Penguin, 1984.

Spuler, Bertold. *History of the Mongols, Based on Eastern and Western Accounts of the Thirteenth and Fourteenth Centuries.* Translated by Helga and Stuart Drummond. Berkeley: University of California Press, 1972.

Staley, Edgcumbe. *The Dogaressas of Venice.* New York: C. Scribner's Sons, 1910.

Stein, Aurel. *Innermost Asia: Detailed Report of Explorations in Central Asia, Kan-su, and Eastern Iran.* 4 vols. Oxford: Clarendon Press, 1928.

Sze, Mai-Mai. *The Way of Chinese Painting, Its Ideas and Technique.* New York: Vintage Books, 1959.

Temple, Robert G. K. *The Genius of China: 3,000 Years of Science, Discovery, and Invention*. Paperback ed. London: Prion Books, 1998.

Thiriet, Freddy. *La Romanie vénitienne au Moyen Âge*. Paris: Éditions E. de Boccard, 1975.

Tuchman, Barbara W. *A Distant Mirror: The Calamitous Fourteenth Century*. New York: Alfred A. Knopf, 1978.

Tyler-Smith, Chris. "The Genetic Legacy of the Mongols." *American Journal of Human Genetics* 72 (2003): 717–721.

Vassaf al-Hazrat. *History of Vassaf* [in Persian]. Vol. 1. Edited by Abdul Hameed Ayati. Tehran: Cultural Foundation of Iran, 1346 Hijri Shamsi (1959).

Waldron, Arthur N. "The Problem of the Great Wall of China." *Harvard Journal of Asiatic Studies* 43, no. 2 (December 1983): 643–663.

Waley, Arthur. *The Secret History of the Mongols: And Other Pieces*. London: Allen & Unwin, 1963.

Watanabe, Hiroshi. *Marco Polo Bibliography: 1477–1983*. Tokyo: Tokyo Bunko, 1986.

Weatherford, Jack. *Genghis Khan and the Making of the Modern World*. New York: Crown, 2004.

Whitfield, Susan, ed., with Ursula Sims-Williams. *The Silk Road: Trade, Travel, War, and Faith*. London: British Library, 2004.

"Why Do Some Expectant Fathers Experience Pregnancy Symptoms?" *Scientific American*, October 2004.

Wiet, Gaston. *Baghdad: Metropolis of the Abbasaid Caliphate*. Translated by Seymour Feiler. Norman: University of Oklahoma Press, 1971.

Wilford, John Noble. *The Mapmakers*. Rev. ed. New York: Alfred A. Knopf, 2000.

Wills, Garry. *Venice: Lion City; The Religion of Empire*. New York: Simon & Schuster, 2001.

Wood, Frances. *Did Marco Polo Go to China?* London: Secker & Warburg, 1995; Boulder, Colorado: Westview Press, 1996.

———. *The Silk Road: Two Thousand Years in the Heart of China*. Berkeley: University of California Press, 2002.

Wylie, A. *Chinese Researches*. 1897. Taipei: Ch'eng Wen Publishing Company, 1966.

Yang, Zhijiu. "The Great Kublai Khan in Marco Polo's Eyes." *Historical Monthly* (Taiwan), November 2000.

———. *Makeboluo zai Zhongguo* [Marco Polo in China]. Tianjin shi: Nan kai da xue chu ban she, 1999.

———. *Yüan shi san lun* [Three Articles Concerning the Yüan Dynasty]. Peking: Ren min chu ban she: Xin hua shu dian fa xing, 1985.

Yamashita, Michael. *Marco Polo: A Photographer's Journey*. New York: Barnes & Noble Books, 2002.

Yü, Chün-fang. *Encountering the Dharma*. New York: Global Scholarly Publications, 2003.

Yule, Henry, Sir, tr. and ed., and Henri Cordier, rev. *Cathay and the Way Thither: Being a Collection of Medieval Notices of China*. Reprint of 1913 ed. 4 vols. in 2. Taipei: Ch'eng-Wen Publishing Company, 1966.

Zorzi, Alvise, ed. *Marco Polo, Venezia e l'Oriente: Arte, commercio, civiltà al tempo di Marco Polo*. Milan: Electa, 1981.

———. *Vita di Marco Polo veneziano*. Milan: Rusconi, 1982.

INDEX

Page numbers in *italics* refer to illustrations and maps.